A MULTIPROCESSOR
OPERATING SYSTEM

A MULTIPROCESSOR OPERATING SYSTEM

Mathai Joseph
V. R. Prasad and
N. Natarajan
NCSDCT, Tata Institute of Fundamental Research, India

Prentice/Hall  **International**

Englewood Cliffs, NJ   London   New Delhi   Rio de Janeiro
Singapore   Sydney   Tokyo   Toronto   Wellington

Library of Congress Cataloging in Publication Data
Joseph, M.
 A multiprocessor operating system.
 Bibliography: p.
 Includes index.
 1. Operating systems (Computers) 2. Multiprocessors.
I. Prasad, V. R., 1950–   . II. Natarajan, N., 1950–   .
III. Title.
QA76.6.J68 1984   001.64   83 -11204
ISBN 0–13–605170–7

British Library Cataloguing in Publication Data
Joseph, M.
 A multiprocessor operating system.
 1. Multiprocessors
 I. Title II. Prasad, V. R. III. Natarajan, N.
 001.64   QA76.5
 ISBN 0–13–605170–7

0-13-605170 7

Prentice-Hall International, Inc., *London*
Prentice-Hall of Australia Pty, Ltd., *Sydney*
Prentice-Hall Canada, Inc., *Toronto*
Prentice-Hall of India Private Ltd., *New Delhi*
Prentice-Hall of Japan, Inc., *Tokyo*
Prentice-Hall of South-East Asia Pte., Ltd., *Singapore*
Prentice-Hall Inc., *Englewood Cliffs, New Jersey*
Prentice-Hall do Brasil Ltda., *Rio de Janeiro*
Whitehall Books Ltd., *Wellington, New Zealand*

Typeset in the UK by Alphabyte Ltd., Cheltenham
Printed in the United States of America

10 9 8 7 6 5 4 3 2 1

CONTENTS

FOREWORD

There are three reasons why I welcome the publication of this book in the Prentice-Hall International Series in Computer Science.

Firstly, it makes an exemplary contribution to the objectives of the series: it treats the design and implementation of major computing systems programs as a topic of national and professional study, of which a complete understanding can be obtained by reading well-crafted and elegant code.

Secondly, it brings wider recognition to the valuable and practically oriented research in Computer Science conducted at the Tata Institute of Fundamental Research in Bombay.

Thirdly, it appeals to my own long-standing personal interests, both in operating systems and in the programming of multiple processor networks. If all those engaged in systems programming were to study books like this, we should avoid perpetuating the long series of technical failures which have plagued us since the 1960s.

As I was personally responsible for one of the earliest of these failures, publication of a book describing a successful solution gives me special satisfaction.

C. A. R. Hoare

PREFACE

It is customary for a course on operating systems, as in many other fields, to teach principles and techniques. Such courses often end with exercises requiring students to construct parts of operating systems that illustrate the use of these techniques. But practical reasons force most courses to stop short of taking students through 'real world' operating systems and only a few particularly energetic participants pursue their interests through the inhospitable documentation of commercial operating systems. This reinforces the widespread belief that principles and theory are for courses, not for practical use, and that there is a welter of problems that are neither described in courses nor solvable by the techniques that are taught.

The purpose of this book is to present the design of what we hope will be seen as a 'real' operating system, in a manner that makes it possible to understand the problems that must be solved in the practice of constructing operating systems. The designs of major components of the operating system are described by developing programs and, finally, these programs are integrated to form the whole system. Thus, much of the book consists of program text written in an extended form of Pascal and, with some additional system-dependent code, these programs can actually be put together to form a working operating system. The material is presented in this form to illustrate the importance of studying well-structured programs in learning how to construct new programs in this area (and similar ones).

The first three chapters are purely introductory. Chapter 1 has a general introduction, Chapter 2 describes the CCNPascal language which is used for all the programs in the book, and Chapter 3 gives a summary of multiprocessor architectures. The design of the operating system starts in Chapter 4, where we take some simple requirements and develop the outlines for the components that must be constructed. The first such component is a basic memory allocator, whose design is described in Chapter 5, and this is then used for building a main memory allocator (Chapter 6) and a disk space allocator (Chapter 7). The next two chapters describe a complete file system; a relatively simple 'user' view of the file system appears in Chapter 8 and the details of the file system structure are presented in Chapter 9. The handling of input and output using physical devices (as opposed to virtual file 'devices') is described in Chapter 10. These components are brought together in Chapter 11, where they are used for the management of jobs; this chapter deals with scheduling and memory management and completes the design of the visible part of the operating system. Chapter 12 describes the kernel which underlies the operating system and provides abstract views of the physical hardware, in addition to supporting the implementation of CCNPascal programs. Chapter 13 reviews the techniques used in the book and the design of the operating system.

The book has not been designed for a particular teaching course, though we have envisaged its use in many different kinds of courses. Understanding the material in the book does require some background: familiarity with simple operating systems, and with the use of programming abstractions such as the *monitor*, the *class* and the *process*. With this in hand, the book could be used in several ways:

1. As *adjunct* material to a course, where parts of the book are used as case-studies,
2. As the basis of a one-semester second course on operating systems, using Chapters 1–8, Chapter 10 and the first part of Chapter 11, or
3. As a two-semester course on operating systems.

There are several sets of exercises, some to modify programs given in a chapter and others to write programs to meet different constraints. A few of the exercises are designated as group exercises, as they could profitably be attempted by small groups of students working together.

But the material in the book is not delimited by what can easily be taught. Chapter 9, on the structure of the file system, the second part of Chapter 11, which deals with fairly complex job management, and much of the description of the kernel in Chapter 12, are all undoubtedly difficult. Rather than simplify the design to eliminate this material, we have chosen to present it because of its use to another reader we have in mind: the professional programmer in industry. Moreover, having seen the tenacity and endurance with which some students plough through documentation on commercial operating systems, we feel that these parts of the book may even be of use to students.

Despite its size, there is much that is *not* described in the book. Consistency and crash-recovery in the file system, swapping policies and swapper programs, operator control of the system parameters, the use of virtual memory, and several other aspects that have bearing on the performance and usability of an operating system have only been outlined in text. Such areas are important in their own right, but a line must inevitably be drawn to separate what is presented from what is not. We have chosen to omit descriptions that would add considerably to the size of the book, and those where detail would appear to outweigh structure. This book will have served its purpose well if it encourages readers to write elegantly structured programs for these aspects of operating systems.

Historical Background

The operating system described in this book is based on a very similar one that was actually built for a multiprocessor system (a list of publications on this project is given in the References section). Since its development had some interesting aspects, a short account of the background is given here.

In the first few weeks of 1975, we had the opportunity of participating in a workshop organized at the National Centre for Software Development and Computing Techniques (NCSDCT) with the assistance of the United Nations Development Programme. Among other things at this workshop, two important new developments were described: P. Brinch Hansen gave a series of lectures on his language, Concurrent Pascal, and W. A. Wulf discussed the design of C.mmp, the multiprocessor then under construction at Carnegie-Mellon University, and Hydra, its operating system. At that time, some of us had already been talking of the possibility of building a multiprocessor system using Indian-made TDC 316 computers and the workshop served as a stimulus in crystallizing these ideas into the more definite proposal that was submitted a few months later to the Electronics Commission of the Government of India. This proposal was approved and, by the end of the year, the first TDC 316 machine had been delivered. In the meantime, we had been examining how Concurrent Pascal could be altered to meet the requirements we had in mind, and working on simple schemes for interconnecting several TDC 316 computers to form what we called the Close-Coupled Network (CCN).

By the end of 1976, we had an experimental compiler, modelled on the Pascal compiler and written in Pascal on the DEC System 10, for our version of Concurrent Pascal; by then, the changes we had made in the original language made it prudent to seek a new name and 'CCNPascal' suggested itself as a suitable alternative. Also, three TDC 316 computers had been linked together in equally experimental fashion. Having the well-known properties of experimental designs, neither the compiler nor the system worked with adequate reliability for sustained use and much of 1977 was spent in bringing them to a state where other kinds of experimentation, such as implementation of parts of the operating system, could begin. Various ambitious designs for the operating system were tried out and it was two years later that a final, and altogether simpler, operating system was completed and the first 'user' programs were executed.

In retrospect, it was risky to have attempted to use a new and relatively untested computer for a system of this nature, especially as the small project team (about 4–5 members at any time) was also involved in the design of the new features of the CCNPascal language, in the development of its first compiler, and in the use of this language for programming the operating system and its kernel, each of which went through several versions. Nevertheless, though we never quite solved the problems of hardware unreliability with our prototype system, much of the program development work went on without unmanageable difficulties. The lesson, that use of a good programming language and systematic design techniques are of irreplaceable value, is not one we are likely to forget.

Acknowledgements

The CCN project was financed by the Electronics Commission of the Government of India and we owe a great deal for this support. The National Centre for Software Development and Computing Techniques, to which all the authors are affiliated, provided support right through the project and, subsequently, during the writing of this book: our thanks go to its director, R. Narasimhan, and to many of our colleagues (past and present) who helped in the project. The Electronics Corporation of India Ltd. (ECIL) went far beyond the call of commercial duty to construct the special hardware needed to interconnect their TDC 316 computers and to help us to maintain the hardware.

At various times, and in various measures, several people at NCSDCT worked on the design and implementation of the CCN software: R. Viswanathan and K.V.S. Prasad were involved with the early designs for the Kernel, Satish Thatte designed the first version of the file system, Sandhya Desai wrote the system loader which linked together the modules of the operating system, and K.T. Narayana did a great deal of work on the first version of the CCNPascal compiler. The final form of the Kernel and the operating system, and their implementations, owe much to the work of Mukul Sinha, who also contributed to the system design of the hardware, and of I.V. Ramakrishnan. At ECIL, A. K. Kaul and P.V.S. Nayak worked on the design of the special hardware. During the course of the development, M.V. Wilkes was an annual visitor who commented on the design; another annual visitor, W.A. Wulf, spent considerable time and effort in studying our design and in providing details on the progress of the C.mmp project.

The suggestion that we write a book about the operating system came from C.A.R. Hoare, who is not only the editor of this series of books and the originator of many of the techniques we have used, but a long standing campaigner for the publication of programs; the fact that we accepted the offer is largely due to his persuasion that the effort was worth making. To him, to H. Hirschberg and R. Decent of Prentice-Hall International, and to R.M. McKeag and R. Gimson, who patiently and painstakingly reviewed the manuscript, considerable thanks are due.

Several other readers have helped us with comments on the manuscript: H.N. Mahabala, V.K. Joglekar, R. Chandrasekhar, and K. Lodaya, to name a few. To the others, and to the many people upon whose work this book has depended, we offer our special thanks.

Text for this book was typed, edited and formatted on the NCSDCT DECSystem10 using standard text editors and the NCSDCT text composition system DIP.

Mathai Joseph
V.R. Prasad
N.Natarajan

NCSDCT
November, 1982

1 INTRODUCTION

When good fortune, or a benevolent funding agency, presents us with a new computer system, one of the first tasks is to get hold of a manual for the operating system. A quick study of this manual leads us to a time-sharing terminal, to 'try things out'. A little later, those of us who have not retreated from the complexities of command formats, job control languages and inexplicable error messages, can be found going through the manual again to get a more complete idea of how the system can be used. And this goes on until each user has acquired the information needed to use the system for her or his problems. When a new problem arises, we return to the manual (or to a local wizard) to see if there is a simple solution; or, remembering that 'there's something about it in the manual', we look for the section that tells us how it can be done.

After some familiarity with the system, we begin to wonder *how* the operating system performs its functions. (The last course on operating systems taught us many useful principles but it did not prepare us for the way *this* operating system seems to work!). Discussions with the wizard prove to be tantalizingly incomplete, and there is no alternative but to see what documentation the 'system people' can produce. And there our problems begin. There are shelves full of manuals of internal documentation and each manual seems to expect us to know information present in other manuals. There are detailed flow charts, diagrams showing how bits are packed into table entries and, to confuse things further, amendment sheets that purport to alter what is in the manuals. Having been through the manufacturer's training course, the system programmers seem to navigate successfully through all this documentation. But, like other experts, they answer every request for general information with the question 'What exactly do you want to know?'

And that would be a reasonable question, were it not for the fact that before we know *exactly* what to look for in the detailed documentation, we need to know the *general structure* of the system!

This story is familiar to many of us, and it has different endings. There are those who, not surprisingly, decide that the gap between theory and practice in operating systems is too large for the field to be of any interest to them. Then there are those who are convinced that the theory is perfectly adequate, *as theory*, but that practical operating systems have so much more excitement to offer (at the other extreme, there are those who gratefully return to the theory to wait until the practice becomes more respectable). And, finally, there are the resolute few who find structure in the mass of documentation, and go on to examine this in the light of the available theory.

There is no particular moral to this story, or to its endings. But this book has been written to show that it *is* possible to understand both the structure and the detail of a reasonably large operating system. To do this, we shall go through the exercise of constructing such an operating system for a multiprocessor system. The program components for this operating system will be systematically developed and, towards the end, these components will be brought together to form the operating system.

Writing an Operating System

Like other large programs, the design of an operating system presents problems of specification and correctness, of testing and performance evaluation, and of documentation. This book will be concerned with many such issues because they must be resolved if a correct, efficient and useable program is to be constructed. But since we shall be looking particularly at the question of designing an *operating system*, we are also confronted with issues of concurrency—i.e., many actions taking place simultaneously— and we cannot take recourse to having some other program control the computer system and its peripherals, or handle the errors that arise in execution. These two factors play a large role in determining the kinds of design we can consider for an operating system.

Designing a new operating system, like studying or modifying an existing one, is an exciting exercise for many reasons. The simplest reason, though perhaps the most misleading one, is that an operating system is a program that has to execute 'close to the hardware'. (When people say 'software makes hardware happen', they usually have an operating system in mind!) It can be exhilarating to see an efficient operating system going through its steps of taking input from card readers and terminals and actually performing actions in what has been called the harmonious cooperation of various tasks. But we must go far beyond this to see the more basic issues behind the design of operating systems, and it is these that have made the study of operating systems a rewarding experience.

An operating system is not just a large program, but one in which different concurrent tasks must coordinate their actions so that the program will execute correctly under all conditions. Moreover, an operating system must provide a wide range of facilities to make it easy to use, efficient in execution, and reliable; its basic structure must be planned with care so that, as the system evolves with use, new features can be added to cater for new requirements. Every serious user of a computer system soon becomes aware of the possibilities and the limitations of its operating system but, to the operating system designer, these are the outcome of choices made as the program was developed.

Many of the essential properties of an operating system have been known for a long time (long, that is, for a new discipline like computer science!). Characteristic problems that arise in the design have been isolated and studied, solutions have been found, and many modern operating system designs demonstrate the fact that solutions to research problems can be of practical use. But to a programmer setting out to build a contemporary operating system, this fact may only be of limited consequence when the amount of practical detail to be faced appears so overwhelming that it is difficult to determine exactly where the problems exist.

We cannot really tell our programmer *how* his or her operating system should be constructed without studying the requirements to be met and the computer system to be used. In other words, many of the choices to be made in the design of a particular operating system will be unique. What we do attempt in this book is to offer a paradigm for the design of a fairly interesting class of operating systems. We shall take a set of real requirements, and realistic hardware, and develop the design of a complete operating system. Like other programmers, we will have to make choices at various points, and justify the path we decide to follow. There will be real problems, such as limitations of resources, and we must allow for the hardware to be less than perfect: there will be errors that must be securely handled. At each stage, we will produce program text for one component of the operating system, and use the features of this component to build other components. If we collect together all the program text, we will have a (virtually) complete operating system that can actually be executed on a computer.

How far will this take our programmer on the way to designing an operating system? If the requirements and the hardware are similar, the task is almost complete as the design can just be implemented (the alert programmer will, we hope, also want to make improvements in the design). For most programmers, those who have to build real operating systems and those who study the principles of operating system design, the exercise in this book should be treated as an example of how a design progresses from requirements to final program text. A particular programmer may find some components of this design to be directly useful, others that need to be modified, and still others that need to be completely replaced. Another programmer may find that the basic structure needs to be altered for the requirements. Yet another programmer may not want to do more than study this design, before starting to design a completely different operating system needed for some other requirements. One purpose of this book is to offer something to each of these programmers so that the task of designing an operating system can follow systematic procedures to produce expected results.

Design Problems

An operating system is a program that serves one primary function: to efficiently share the resources of a computer system among a set of competing user programs. This function has remained unchanged for twenty years. What really distinguishes the modern operating system from its forbears is that the resources of a system today include not only physical units (i.e., memory, processors and peripherals) but also abstract, or *logical*, resources produced by users (e.g., files). The complexity of a contemporary operating system arises largely from the need for these abstract resources to be shared among classes of users and, at the same time, to be protected from unauthorized and inconsistent access.

The methods by which resources are assigned to and then recovered from user programs have long been among the most important problems about operating systems to be studied. Several techniques have been developed for what is called *resource management*. The choice of suitable techniques for a particular operating system will depend on the type of computer system and on the kinds of user programs that will execute on the system. For example, a small computer system will usually have a simple and modest operating system as the resources of the system are few and there will be little flexibility in the way in which they can be allocated. A large computer system often has resources far in excess of those needed by any single user program and its operating system has the responsibility of efficiently allocating these resources among several users. An important reason for having large computer systems is that the unpredictable demands of many users can be averaged by a good operating system, giving each user program resources only when it needs them and dividing the rest among other users.

One view of an operating system is that of an *allocator of resources* and an *arbitrator* between the demands of user programs. To each user program, however, the operating system has a somewhat different appearance: it is the means by which the features of the system are made accessible. For example, a real-time operating system makes signals from an external process (e.g., a chemical plant, or a paper mill) available for an application program to perform calculations; this program can then send back controlling signals to alter the running of the process. A time-sharing operating system allows users at different terminals to execute independent programs and to share programs and data. Even a pocket calculator can be considered to have a (trivially!) simple operating system which reads commands and data from its keys and puts results on its display. An operating system is thus also an *interface* between the system and its users.

Like all interfaces, an operating system hides certain details of the operating environment from the user. For example, a programmer using a time-sharing system can run his programs without concern, say, to the number of processors in the system, or of what his colleagues may be doing at other terminals. Similarly, an operating system often hides the actual amount of memory in a system so that user programs can continue to execute (usually, though, rather more slowly) even if part of the memory is faulty. But an operating system may also make particular features of a computer system accessible to users. Instead of having to use a printer arbitrarily chosen from among those available, it may be possible for a user to specify that output should be printed only on those printers that have a special character set, or even that it should be printed on a particular printer.

These two aims, of hiding some features of a system and of making others explicitly available, are clearly going to be difficult to reconcile. While most users will not wish to be concerned about, say, where in the memory their programs will execute, there will always be some users who need to use special features of a system. How do we ensure that all users are able to see only those details that are essential to their needs? More generally, how do we choose between making some features of a system 'visible' and some hidden? Especially, how do we do this for the large and complex programs that operating systems tend to be?

There is no simple answer to such questions: many complex issues may be involved in the design of a large program, and new requirements may be discovered as the implementation progresses. What can be done is to follow systematic procedures in design and in implementation so that it is always possible to relate external requirements with the internal structure of the program. Then, when new requirements are to be met, it will be possible to know exactly how far the program structure will need to be modified.

* First, we must decide what it is that a system is to do: the external functions of the system must be accurately specified so that they serve as the goals for the design of the system.
* These external functions have to be performed by units of the operating system and it is to these that we now have to turn our attention. Often, for a program such as an operating system, there can be as many major units as there are major external functions to perform. This provides a correspondence between the external functions and the units of the program.
* Once we get the overall structure for the operating system, we may find that each major unit in this program is still too large to be easily programmed or understood. These units will then have to be broken down into their major functions so that each of these can be performed by some smaller unit of the program.
* This procedure may need to be repeated several times over so that what appears to be a coherent whole is actually composed of smaller pieces that are themselves made up of other smaller pieces, and so on. The last set of pieces, those that need not be broken up further, are the primitive units out of which the rest of the system is built.

The method of systematically decomposing a design in stages has been called 'stepwise refinement' and the units into which the design is broken are called 'abstractions'.

There are usually two kinds of abstractions that are used in the process of building a program: there are the abstractions of the *design*, which are the results of elaborating the initial, high-level design of the system, and the abstractions of the *language* in which the design is programmed. There is, naturally, great advantage in being able to use a single, consistent notation for both the design and its implementation.

The Language

In the not-so-distant past, system programs such as operating systems and compilers were *designed* using a higher-level notation, such as flow charts, and *implemented* in machine or assembly languages. There are two reasons why this is unsatisfactory. The first is that there is a large gap between the level of description of the design and the operations of the implementation. Correspondence between the design and the assembly language program is difficult to establish, and is severely affected by the ever-present need to alter or augment the design. If it is difficult to understand how a segment of assembly language code performs a function described in a flow chart, it is even more difficult to modify the code and ensure that it remains true to a description of the design. The problem is not solved by having a more detailed description because, for a large program, this will soon become so unmanageably voluminous that it serves its purpose still less satisfactorily.

The second reason is that solutions to many of the problems of programming an operating system require the consistent use of abstractions that ensure that the execution of the program always follows certain rules. In an assembly language program, such abstractions become mere segments of code that are not distinguishable from other segments. They cannot be taken just for granted, as they must be cautiously written and can be altered only at great risk (anyone who has looked at the text of an operating system coded in an assembly language will be familiar with comments such as 'The next 10 lines are required for consistency – *do not* modify them without consulting the system programmers', which raise the valid point of what is to be done when the original system programmers have moved on to other tasks). It is not that assembly language programs *cannot* be made to follow rules since, if nothing else, human ingenuity and industry have enormous capabilities. But if such attention must be lavished on this level of detail, the more substantial and important problems in the design will tend to be ignored.

The purpose of a high-level programming language is to incorporate the abstractions needed for programming as features of the language. For example, the string-processing language, SNOBOL, treats strings of text as primitive objects upon which well-defined operations can be performed. In the same way, it should be possible to identify the primitive structures needed for the particular problem of programming concurrent tasks in an operating system. Once these have been defined, we can leave it to the compiler to check (at least to a large degree) that operations are correctly used, and to the compiler writer that they are correctly implemented. Such problems need to be solved just once—when the language is defined—and each compiler then has a set of rules to follow in the compilation of programs.

In following this approach, we are asking the language designer to provide a set of mechanisms that we can use for our requirement. A good set of mechanisms will be capable of varied use and it should be possible to formally prove that they guarantee certain properties under all conditions. *No* set of mechanisms will be both flexible enough for *all* users and sufficiently well-defined for formal proofs of correctness to be easily made. There is an inevitable trade-off between flexibility and the formal properties of language mechanisms, and where the line should be drawn is strongly debated. However, these issues are a little off the course of this book. We shall be making a choice of a language with a particular set of features and we leave it to the reader to decide how well the features meet the need and, indeed, how far the design of the operating system is governed by these features.

In this book, we shall develop the design of the operating system using the notation of a programming language called CCNPascal. As we shall see in the next chapter, this language is based on Pascal, with many new features that are needed to program operating systems. Three of these features which play a large role in the development of the program are the **process**, the **monitor** and the **pure class**. The concurrent activities of the operating system will be represented by processes that can be simultaneously executed, and resources that can be shared between processes will be represented by monitors. Since the rules for access to one monitor can lead to delays or deadlocks when several monitors are used, pure classes are used to represent many of the more complex resources of the system. The discipline that these abstractions enforce allows us to program the operating system with little concern for interference between processes, as a compiler can automatically make many checks to ensure that processes interact only in well-defined ways through monitors. We can therefore concentrate on developing the *structure* of our operating system.

The Architecture

Languages can vary in their features but there are still far fewer (well known) languages than system architectures. Computer systems can differ in so many respects that there are few systems that can be said to be identical. Our operating system will be designed for a multiprocessor system consisting of several processors, memories and peripherals. There are many examples of multiprocessor systems, of one form or another. The commonest have two processors, often with one acting as the 'master', controlling the operation of the whole system, and the other as a 'slave'. Symmetric multiprocessors, of the kind we shall consider in this book, are less common: in such systems, both control and the execution of user jobs are shared between different processors and the system is, potentially at least, less vulnerable to the failure of a single processor.

We shall consider multiprocessor systems in which there is some memory that is private to each processor and some that is shared by them all. Chapter 3 will describe the kinds of architectures that can be used for building such systems. We shall not assume that our system is built of any particular brand of processor, or even that it has a particular configuration. In practice, most systems need to be expandable, so that more resources (i.e., processors, or memory, or peripherals) can be added when needed. At least for this reason, we would need to design the operating system so that it can be used with different configurations of hardware. But we shall be even less demanding in our choice of system, leaving the few parts of the operating system that are really dependent on the features of the hardware in skeleton form so that the necessary detail can easily be added for each particular system.

The Operating System

The fact that the system is a multiprocessor will, in many respects, not be visible to users of the system. We shall assume that our requirement is to design an operating system that can be used for batch processing and for access through terminals. User jobs should be able to generate and use files of data and programs. A user must be able to transfer rights to access a file to other users. The operating system must coordinate the execution of different jobs, use the resources of the system with some efficiency, and cater for errors in user programs or in the hardware. In other words, our design must produce a usable operating system, not just one that can be used to study some principles of operating system design.

We can ignore many hardware features and details of the configuration of the system if we can clothe them in abstractions that hide (or attempt to hide) their internal structure. To do so, we shall make extensive use of the features of CCNPascal that allow us to build abstractions. For example, the disk space allocator will be designed for a 'virtual' disk, rather than for any one of the many disks that are available in practice, and this abstraction will be programmed as a monitor. The set of disks in the system can then be represented by an array of monitors, but the visible part of this structure can be simplified by embedding this array in a pure class so that, to the rest of the system, there appears to be only one logical entity. This approach allows us some liberties, such as freedom from considering particular features of a disk, but the choice of such abstractions must be seen from two points of view: how much they simplify the structure of the operating system, and how well they perform in use. These two questions will recur right through the exercise of designing this operating system.

The Implementation

Using a high-level language like CCNPascal allows us to ignore details of the implementation and to concentrate on the design of the abstractions in the system. At some point, however, we are confronted with the fact that what we call a process in the language must be an entity that can be executed on a real processor and, similarly, that all the features of the language that we take for granted while programming must also be converted into features of the implementation of the language. The simpler features, such as arrays and records, and the basic statements of the language, can be implemented in well-known and straightforward ways so we shall not discuss them here. The implementation of the 'operating system' features of the language are very much the concern of this book as they play an important role in the design of the operating system and in its final efficiency.

We shall once again use abstraction in hiding a level of detail: in this case to hide particular features of the machine and the architecture from the operating system. This level is that of the system Kernel: from above, the Kernel makes the hardware system look like a rather sophisticated machine with many of the practical rough corners removed. In some senses, the Kernel *is* a CCNPascal machine as it provides the primitive operations to allow processes and monitors to be correctly implemented. But it goes beyond just this as it performs several common low-level operations required for an operating system. For example, the Kernel takes the responsibility of scheduling requests to the disk so that the access time is minimized, and of making different terminals look the same to the rest of the system. It also incorporates all the 'device driving' programs, to free the rest of the operating system from the routine duties of servicing device interrupts.

Summary

What we shall do in the rest of the book is an exercise, but one that is never far from practical consequences. Instead of a single operating system, we shall really be designing the structure of a family of operating systems. Particular members of this family can easily be constructed for specific machines or to meet special requirements. In fact, the entire design is derived from that of an operating system structure that was designed and implemented for a multiprocessor system called the Close-Coupled Network.

Practicality apart, this book is concerned with abstractions for program-ming operating systems. These abstractions, which come from features of the language and from design choices in the operating system, serve as nodes in the structure of the system. At one level, we can examine the structure of the system: at another, the techniques used for implementing the abstractions. Each abstraction encapsulates a set of decisions and it can be studied, altered or replaced with minimal structural effect on the rest of the system. We hope to convince the reader that this approach is not just advisable, but especially profitable when a real system is to be constructed.

2 THE CCNPASCAL LANGUAGE

As its name suggests, CCNPascal is a language based on Pascal (Wirth,1971). Its concurrent programming features are very similar to those of Concurrent Pascal (Brinch Hansen,1975). CCNPascal supports development of a program in small modules; these modules can be compiled separately and their interfaces checked at compile time. In this chapter, we introduce the distinctive features of CCNPascal, especially those that differ from Pascal and that are used in the programs in this book. We shall assume readers are familiar with Pascal—many of its features will be used here without explanation. We shall follow its rules of declaring all identifiers before use, and take advantage of its facilities for type definition. For example, we allow program abstractions to be created by declaring them either as variables, or as types which serve as 'templates' to be used in other variable or parameter declarations. The use of CCNPascal will be introduced informally through examples.

Note: At first reading, it is not necessary to get more than an overview of the material in this chapter. More detailed study of particular features can then follow the first use of each such feature in the text of the operating system.

SEQUENTIAL PROGRAMMING

Let us consider the exercise of designing an interface between user programs and a file system. A user program will call file system procedures to open a file, to read data from a file, to write data to a file, and to close a file. Data is transferred to and from the file in a buffer, with a buffer pointer indicating the last item. The file system will define a buffer type, FixedBuffer, and use it in the definition of its operations.

```
const
  FixedBufSize = 128;
type
  FixedBuffer =
    record
      BufPtr: 0 .. FixedBufSize;
      Buf: array [1 .. FixedBufSize] of char
    end FixedBuffer;

procedure Open(Fname:Name);
  {Assume that Name is a pre-defined string type}
  begin
    "Open the file Fname"
  end Open;

procedure Read(var UserBuf:FixedBuffer);
  begin
    "Read data from file into UserBuf";
    "Set UserBuf.BufPtr to point to the last character read"
  end Read;

procedure Write(UserBuf:FixedBuffer);
  begin
    "Write data from UserBuf to file"
  end Write;

procedure Close;
  begin
    "Close the file"
  end Close;
```

(At many places in the book we will use informal text to describe parts of program code— such text will be enclosed between a pair of double-quote (" ") characters. Comments will be enclosed in braces '{' and '}'. Note that the concluding **end** for a record or subprogram definition is immediately followed by the name of the record or subprogram.)

A user can declare a buffer of type FixedBuffer and pass it as a parameter to procedure Read or procedure Write. For example,

```
var
  UserBuf: FixedBuffer;
begin
  Read(UserBuf)
end;
```

A variable is declared as an *instance* of a type. Each instance of FixedBuffer is a record with a field, Buf, which can store up to FixedBufSize characters, and a field, BufPtr, which denotes the actual number of characters stored in Buf.

Generic Types

Using arrays of fixed size as buffers can often be very restrictive. For example, a text editor may need to read a whole page of text at a time while a compiler may choose to read characters, one at a time, from a source file. For general purpose or utility procedures, such as those in the file system, it would be a great advantage if different programs could pass buffers of different sizes as parameters. Notice that the need is for buffers of different sizes, and not for parameters of entirely different types.

Variability in parameter sizes, as in the example above, can be programmed in CCNPascal using *generic* types. Let us rewrite the type FixedBuffer (calling it Buffer) to accept an integer parameter (say, BufSize) and use the value of this parameter to determine the size of the buffer. This means that the definition of the type Buffer provides only structural information, without specifying its actual size. This is an example of a *generic type*.

```
type
   Buffer(BufSize: integer) =
      record
         BufPtr: 0 .. BufSize;
         Buf: array [1 .. BufSize] of char
      end Buffer;
```

For each variable of type Buffer, the required size of the buffer must be passed as an instantiation parameter. A type derived from the type Buffer by fixing the actual size (e.g. Buffer(100)) is called a *full type*.

```
var
   Buf1: Buffer(100);
   Buf2: Buffer(200);

type
   FixedBuffer = Buffer(FixedBufSize);
```

A full type is derived from a generic type by supplying actual values for all of its formal parameters. Every variable must be declared as an instance of a full type. (By definition, a type declared with no formal parameters is a full type.) Types can also be declared as derivatives of generic types (e.g. FixedBuffer).

An actual parameter passed to a generic type must either be a constant (as above) or a formal parameter of an enclosing generic type. As an example of the latter case, consider a generic type String defined as

```
type
    String(Size: integer) = packed array [1 .. Size] of char;
```

so that the generic type Buffer can be re-defined as

```
type
    Buffer(BufSize: integer) =
        record
            BufPtr: 0 .. BufSize;
            Buf: String(BufSize)
        end Buffer;
```

String is defined as a standard type in CCNPascal: we shall henceforth refer to it as **string**. As in Pascal, arrays and records in CCNPascal can be declared to be *packed* so that a good compiler can economize on the storage space required, but this will sometimes make access to such structures slow. We shall not make use of this feature in the programs in this book as it is only an implementation detail.

Note: Types are *not* allowed as parameters to generic types.

Subprograms

Procedures and functions are called *subprograms*: for example, the procedure Read described earlier is a subprogram. Using generic types, it is possible for the same Read procedure to operate on buffers of different sizes. For this, we require the notion of a *deferred type*.

The type of a formal parameter of a subprogram is said to be *deferred* if it is derived from a generic type and if values for some of its generic parameters are not known at compile time. Each unknown generic parameter must be preceded by a '?'. Such an identifier is then treated as an implicit formal parameter to the subprogram.

```
procedure Read(var UserBuf:Buffer(?BufSize));
    begin
        "Read a maximum of BufSize characters into UserBuf.Buf";
        "Set UserBuf.BufPtr to point to last character read"
    end Read;
```

The generic parameter passed to Buffer is written as ?BufSize because its actual value will be known only when the procedure is called. Different calls to procedure Read can pass parameters of type Buffer with different values for BufSize, i.e. they can pass buffers of different sizes.

```
var
   Buffer1: Buffer(100);
   Buffer2: Buffer(200);
begin
   Read(Buffer1);
   Read(Buffer2);
end
```

For each call, the actual size of the buffer is implicitly bound to BufSize and this is available within procedure Read as a value parameter.

A call to procedure Read should fail if there is no more data available in the file (a special case of this is when the file is initially empty). Such failures can be indicated to the caller by setting the buffer pointer (BufPtr) to zero. A better way, perhaps, is to provide a function subprogram to test if the file has any more data. We can do this and expect the user to test if the file has more data before calling the procedure Read. We assume that a global variable EndOfFile has the value **true** only when there is no more data to be read from the file.

```
var
   EndOfFile: Boolean; {false if there is data in file
                        true when the last item has been read}
function Empty return Boolean;
   begin
      return EndOfFile
   end Empty;
```

The type of the result of a function subprogram (sometimes called the 'result type') is specified by a **return** clause in its header. Any full type can be used as the result type of a function subprogram, but not a deferred type (i.e., a type using '?' parameters). A function subprogram returns a result by executing a **return** statement which supplies an expression of the result type; the value of this expression is returned as the function result. A return statement can also be used in a procedure to return control to the caller; in this case, the return statement does not supply an expression. *Note*: Types are *not* allowed as parameters to subprograms.

Repetitive Statements

The **while** and **repeat** statements of CCNPascal are identical to those of Pascal. The **for** statement has minor differences.

Consider the familiar problem of searching through a table for a particular item. Let the table be implemented as an array. In the search, we need to find the position (i.e., the index) of an item that is known to be present in the table. One way of implementing the search would be to use a **while** statement.

```
var
   Table: array [1 .. Size] of ItemType;
   Item: ItemType;
   I: integer; Found: Boolean;
begin
   Item := "Some Value";
   I := 1; Found := false;
   while (I ≤ Size) and not Found do
      if Table[I] = Item
         then Found := true
         else I := I + 1;
   {The required item is at index value I in the table}
end
```

The conditions under which the search is repeated through the table must be inferred from three separate statements: (a) the initial value of I is 1, (b) the value of I does not exceed Size (from the first part of the Boolean expression controlling the **while** statement), and (c) I is incremented by 1 at each iteration.

Another way to program this search in CCNPascal would be to use a **for** statement and an **exit** statement.

```
var
   Table: array [1 .. Size] of ItemType;
   Item: ItemType; Position: 1 .. Size;
begin
   Item := "Some Value";
   for I in 1 to Size do
      if Table[I] = Item then
      begin
         Position := I; exit
      end;
   {The required item in the table is at index value Position}
end
```

A **for** statement starts a new nested block in which the control variable (I, in the example) is implicitly declared. The bounds (starting and terminating values) for the control variable may be specified as run time evaluable expressions but their values are determined on entry to the **for** statement. The bound values must have a common type which must be a scalar type (other than type **real**); the control variable is treated to be of this type. The control variable cannot be modified within the **for** statement and is not available outside it (this is why the value of I had to be saved in Position). At the end of each iteration, the control variable is implicitly assigned a value which is the successor of its current value in the enumeration of the scalar type. The **exit** statement takes control out of the immediately enclosing **for** statement in which it appears. (What we have described here is a step-up **for** statement. CCNPascal also has a step-down **for** statement with similar syntax and semantics.)

A **loop** statement is also provided in CCNPascal. It executes indefinitely unless control is explicitly taken out of the loop by an **exit** statement. For an example, consider a program that reads characters and writes them out until a special character (SplChar) is read: it uses two procedures ReadChar and WriteChar to read and write a character.

```
var
  Ch: char;
begin
  loop
    ReadChar(Ch);
    if Ch = SplChar
      then exit
      else WriteChar(Ch)
  end
end
```

An **exit** statement may appear in any repetitive statement (i.e., **while**, **repeat**, **for** or **loop**). When executed, it always causes control to leave the immediately enclosing repetitive statement.

Note: There is no **goto** statement in CCNPascal.

Error Returns

When a procedure is called, it usually performs its actions and returns control to the statement following the procedure call. This is called a 'normal' return. A procedure can also be programmed to recognize unusual conditions in its execution and perform an 'error' return, with an error value.

A special statement **return error** is provided which, when executed within a procedure body, returns control to the caller with an error. An error return can be tested in an **iferror** clause associated with a procedure call. An **iferror** clause can have an optional **otherwise** clause to be executed when there is no error.

```
ProcedureCall(P1,...,PN)
  iferror {Control comes here on error return}
    S1 {and S1 will be executed}
  otherwise {Control comes here on normal return}
    S2 {and S2 will be executed}
```

The **return error** statement and the **iferror** clause allow exceptional conditions in a program to be detected and handled. When there is no **iferror** clause associated with a procedure call, an error return from the procedure has the same effect as a normal return.

As an example, let us look at the way a user at an interactive terminal gets a program compiled. The compiler first asks the user for the name of the program file and then invokes a file system procedure Open to open the file. If this call fails, the compiler must print an error message on the terminal and ask for another file name. These steps will be repeated until a program file is successfully opened.

The file system procedure, Open, must check if a file of the specified name exists and whether it can be accessed by the user.

```
procedure Open(Fname:Name);
   begin
      "Check if the file named Fname exists and is accessible";
      if "Not accessible"
         then return error
      else "Open the file Fname"
   end Open:
```

The calling program (i.e., the compiler, in this case) can check for an error return from the procedure Open. We use two procedures ReadTtyString and WriteTtyString to read and write strings from the terminal.

```
var
   FileName: Name;
begin
   loop
      ReadTtyString(FileName);
      Open(FileName)
         iferror WriteTtyString('File not found—type new file name')
         otherwise exit
   end;
   Compile;
end
```

In this example, the procedure Open is assumed to return a single error condition when the file cannot be opened.

It is also possible for a procedure to return different kinds of errors. Such errors must be values of an enumeration type (i.e. a user defined scalar type) that is declared as the **error** type for the procedure (declaration of an **error** type should immediately follow the procedure header). If a procedure declares an **error** type, each **return error** statement in the procedure body must supply an expression of this type. The value of this expression is available to the caller as the value of a standard function **errorval**. The function **errorval** is accessible only within an **iferror** clause and only if the called procedure has an error type.

Let us now rewrite the file system procedure Open to recognize two kinds of errors, both of which are propagated to the caller.

```
type
    ErrorsInOpen = (FileNotFound, EmptyFile);

procedure Open(Fname:Name)
    error ErrorsInOpen;
    begin
        "Check if the file Fname exists";
        if "no such file exists"
            then return error FileNotFound
        else
            if "the file is empty"
                then return error EmptyFile
            else "open the file Fname"
    end Open;
```

The compiler can now be more specific in its error messages to the user.

```
var
    FileName: Name;
    begin
        loop
            ReadTtyString(FileName);
            Open(FileName)
                iferror
                    case errorval of
                        FileNotFound: WriteTtyString('File not found');
                        EmptyFile: WriteTtyString('File empty')
                    end
                    otherwise exit;
                WriteTtyString('—Type new file name')
            end;
            Compile;
        end
```

Note: A function subprogram cannot return errors.

Data Abstraction: The Class

It is possible to design a file system which provides 'file' as a type. A user can then declare a variable of this type (we will refer to this as a file variable) and call the file system procedure, Open, to associate this variable with a physical file. If this association can be recorded in the file variable, it can serve to identify the physical file for subsequent Read or Write operations. Operations on this file can be terminated by a Close operation and the file variable can then be associated with some other physical file by once again using the Open operation.

There are two distinct purposes we are trying to accomplish: to provide a way for a user to associate a file variable with a physical file and, internally, to represent this association in the file variable. It is useful to go a little beyond this and ensure that the values of the file variable are not modified at all by any statements other than those in the Open, Read, Write and Close operations. This can be accomplished by encapsulating these procedures, and some variables that are accessible to them, in an abstraction called a **class** (Hoare,1972).

Assume the file system reads and writes information on disk in blocks of fixed size. User programs have different requirements, reading and writing data in sizes ranging from a single character to a whole line. Let us now provide a class, File, which has the operations Open, Read, Write and Close, and internal variables, Fname in which the file name is stored, FileBuf which is used for buffering transfers of data from and to the disk, and two Booleans Opened and EndOfFile. These variables should be inaccessible to the rest of the program.

```
type
  File = class;
    const
      FileBufSize = 512;
    var
      Fname: Name;
      FileBuf: Buffer(FileBufSize);
      Opened, EndOfFile: Boolean;

    procedure export Open(FileName:Name);
      begin
        "Call file system to open file FileName";
        if "successful" then
        begin
          Fname := FileName; Opened := true;
        end
      end Open;

    procedure export Read(var UserBuf:Buffer(?BufSize));
      begin
        if Opened then
          repeat
            if "FileBuf.Buf is empty"
              then "refill FileBuf.Buf from file Fname";
            "Copy data from FileBuf.Buf to UserBuf.Buf"
          until "UserBuf is full or no more data in file"
      end Read;
```

```
procedure export Write(UserBuf:Buffer(?BufSize));
  begin
    if Opened then
      repeat
        if "FileBuf.Buf is full"
          then "output FileBuf.Buf to file Fname";
          "Copy data from UserBuf.Buf to FileBuf.Buf"
        until "UserBuf is empty"
  end Write;

function export Empty return Boolean;
  begin
    return EndOfFile
  end Empty;

procedure export Close;
  begin
    "Call file system to close file Fname";
    Opened := false
  end Close;

begin
  Opened := false;
  Buf.Bufptr := 0;
  EndOfFile := false
end File;
```

A variable of type File can be used to access one file at a time. Only the subprograms designated by **export** are available to users. Any other subprogams in the class can only be called from within the class.

The following program reads data from a file in buffers of size 80 and prints the data. We will use a procedure Print to print a buffer.

```
var
  UserFile: File;
  UserBuf: Buffer(80);
begin
  UserFile.Open('DataFile');
  while not UserFile.Empty do
  begin
    UserFile.Read(UserBuf);
    Print(UserBuf)
  end;
  UserFile.Close
end
```

An exported subprogram of a class is called by prefixing the name of the subprogram with the name of the class variable or instance (e.g. the subprogram Open of the variable UserFile is referred to as UserFile.Open). A

with statement can be used to avoid such prefixing. Types and variables may also be exported from a class. An exported variable should not be modified outside the class.

A class is a simple programming language version of an abstract data type: its subprograms are like the operations of a data type, and its variables provide a representation for the data type. Since these variables can be modified only by subprograms defined within the class, they can be kept free of 'side effects' due to undisciplined use. The consistency of a class can be maintained by defining invariant conditions for the values of its variables and ensuring that these are preserved by all of its operations.

Let us now take another example of a class: this time, a generic class type to manage a first-in-first-out queue (FiFoQ). The elements of the queue are not defined by FiFoQ, but its operations can be used to obtain the positions of the first and last elements.

The FiFoQ class provides a procedure Put to determine the position in the queue where a new item can be inserted, and a function Get to determine the position from where the next item can be removed. If Put is called only when the queue is not full and Get is called only when the queue is not empty, then the variable Length represents the number of items in the queue.

```
type
    FiFoQ(QMax: integer) = class;
        var
            QHead, QTail, QLength: integer;

            { 1 ≤ QHead ≤ QMax }
            { 1 ≤ QTail ≤ QMax }
            { QLength = Total calls to Put – Total calls to Get }

        function export Put return integer;
            { to be called only when not Full }
            begin
                QTail := (QTail mod QMax) + 1;
                QLength := QLength + 1;
                return QTail
            end Put;

        function export Get return integer;
            { to be called only when not Empty }
            begin
                QHead := (QHead mod QMax) + 1;
                QLength := QLength – 1;
                return QHead
            end Get;
```

```
function export Top return integer;
  { to be called only when not Empty }
  begin
    return QHead;
  end Top;

function export Waiting return integer;
  begin
    return QLength;
  end Waiting;

function export Empty return Boolean;
  begin
    return (QLength = 0);
  end Empty;

function export Full return Boolean;
  begin
    return (QLength = QMax);
  end Full;

begin
  QHead := QMax; QTail := QMax; QLength := 0
end FiFoQ;
```

A line printer spooler, for example, can use the class FiFoQ to implement a queue of files to be printed. Two procedures QueueFile and PrintFile are used to enter files into the spooler and to print them.

```
const
  FileMax = 100;
var
  FileList: array [1 .. FileMax] of Name;
  FileQ: FiFoQ(FileMax);

procedure QueueFile(Fname:Name);
  begin
    if not FileQ.Full
      then FileList[FileQ.Put] := Fname;
    else return error
  end QueueFile;

procedure PrintFile;
  var
    Fname: Name;
  begin
    if not FileQ.Empty then
```

```
    begin
        Fname := FileList[FileQ.Get];
        "Print the file Fname"
    end
end PrintFile;
```

Multiview Records

So far, File is suitable only for dealing with text files. If the class is also to handle binary files, it must be extended to use a different type of buffer.

A buffer used for a binary file must hold a sequence of binary bytes, in contrast to a text buffer which holds a sequence of characters. Thus, the file buffer (FileBuf) should provide two different views: when it is used for text files, it should look like a text buffer and when used for binary files, it should look like a buffer of binary bytes. This is made possible in CCNPascal by the use of *multiview* records.

(The multiview records of CCNPascal serve the same purpose as the variant records of Pascal, but offer additional type protection. Special constructs are introduced to ensure that access to multiview records is type-safe.)

```
type
    FileKind = (Text, Binary);
    Buffer(BufSize: integer) =
        record
            BufPtr: 0 .. BufSize;
            case FileKind of
                Text: (TextBuf: array [1 .. BufSize] of char);
                Binary: (BinBuf: array [1 .. BufSize] of Byte)
        end Buffer;
```

We shall use the term *view* to mean a field list. A multiview record definition consists of an optional *common view* (e.g. BufPtr) and an optional *variant view*. The variant view is specified as one among a list of alternative views. When an instance of the multiview record is declared, one of these alternative views can be 'bound' to the variant view; this view is called the *actual variant view*. In the definition of a multiview record, each alternative view is identified with a value (e.g. Text or Binary) of an enumeration type (e.g. FileKind); this enumeration type is called the *viewtype* of the multiview record.

A buffer variable may be declared by binding either the Text or the Binary view as its actual variant view; this is done by supplying one of the two constants, Text or Binary, as an additional parameter to type Buffer.

```
var
    TextBuffer: Buffer(100, Text);
    BinBuffer: Buffer(200, Binary);
```

Both the common view and the actual variant view are made accessible for an instance of Buffer as if they together form a single large view. Thus, TextBuffer has two fields BufPtr and TextBuf, and BinBuffer has two fields BufPtr and BinBuf.

The type File can be safely used for both text and binary files if we follow three rules: (a) when a user declares an instance of type File, he should specify whether it is intended to be used as a text file or as a binary file, (b) FileBuf should be allocated in File class as a text or binary buffer depending on the intended use of the file, and (c) the procedures of File class should be programmed to allow a compile time check that buffers passed by users are consistent with the file declaration. These rules are further elaborated in the following paragraphs.

First, a particular instance of type File should be used for only one kind of file, Text or Binary; this should be specified at compile time. To accomplish this, File should be made a generic type with one parameter denoting the kind of file.

```
type
    File(Fkind: FileKind) = class;
        .
        .
    end File;
```

A user must declare instances of type File by specifying a particular view for each instance.

```
var
    File1: File(Text)
    File2: File(Binary);
```

Second, FileBuf, which is internal to File class, should be declared as a text or binary buffer depending on its intended use. This is possible if the actual variant view of FileBuf is determined by the value of the class parameter Fkind.

```
type
    File(Fkind: FileKind) = class;
        var
            FileBuf: Buffer(FileBufSize, Fkind);
            .
            .
    end File;
```

Without further specification, only the common view of a multiview record is accessible to a program. In order to access the actual variant view, a special form of **case** statement (the **case view** statement) is provided.

```
case view(FileBuf) of
    Text: "Statements to access the fields BufPtr and TextBuf";
    Binary: "Statements to access the fields BufPtr and BinBuf"
end
```

When this statement is executed, one of the case alternatives, Text or Binary, is selected depending on the actual variant view of FileBuf. Within each case of the **case view** statement, the fields of the corresponding alternative view of FileBuf are made available—these fields are directly available and need not be qualified with FileBuf (i.e., it is as if they appear inside a **with** FileBuf **do** statement).

Third, the procedure Read in File class should now require its parameter, UserBuf, to be either a text buffer or a binary buffer, depending on whether the File class was instantiated with the parameter value Text or Binary. This can be checked, at compile time, if UserBuf is specified to have the same variant view as that of the class parameter Fkind.

```
procedure Read(var UserBuf:Buffer(?BufSize,Fkind));
    begin
        case view(UserBuf) of
            Text: "Transfer characters to TextBuf and set BufPtr";
            Binary: "Transfer bytes to BinBuf and set BufPtr"
        end
    end Read;
```

UserBuf is to be filled with data from FileBuf which, of course, is refilled from the disk file whenever it is empty. We have already seen that to access FileBuf we need to use a **case view** statement. To write data into UserBuf we need to use a second **case view** statement. Thus, in this case, nested **case view** statements will be necessary to copy data from FileBuf to UserBuf. To simplify programming in such situations, a special form of **if** statement (the **if view** statement) is provided. Its general form is given below.

```
if view(R,V)
    then S1
    else S2
```

If V is the actual variant view of the multiview record variable R, statement S1 is executed; otherwise, statement S2 is executed. It is important to note that **view**(R,V) by itself has no significance (it is not a Boolean function): **if view**(R,V) is treated as a special statement.

The procedure Read can now be programmed as follows.

```
type
  File(Fkind: FileKind) = class;
    const
      FileBufSize = 512;
    var
      FileBuf: Buffer(FileBufSize, Fkind);
      EndOfFile: Boolean;
    procedure export Read(var UserBuf:Buffer(?BufSize,Fkind));
      begin
        case view(UserBuf) of
          Text:
            if view(FileBuf, Text) then
              repeat
                if "FileBuf.TextBuf is empty"
                  then "refill FileBuf.TextBuf from file";
                "Copy data from FileBuf.TextBuf to UserBuf.TextBuf"
              until (UserBuf.BufPtr = BufSize) or EndOfFile;
          Binary:
            if view(FileBuf, Binary) then
              repeat
                if "FileBuf.BinBuf is empty"
                  then "refill FileBuf.BinBuf from file";
                "Copy data from FileBuf.BinBuf to UserBuf.BinBuf"
              until (UserBuf.BufPtr = BufSize) or EndOfFile
        end {case}
      end Read;


  end File;
```

Multiview records can also have a different kind of use: to see the need for this, let us look at the implementation of directories in a file system. A directory is implemented as an array of entries and each entry can be for a file or for another directory. We do not want to reserve some entries for files and some for directories: it is more economical to be able to use any empty entry for either purpose. Then, if a particular entry is used for a file at some time, it may be used for a directory at a different time. We would still like some protection against a file entry being used as a directory entry, and vice versa. The directory can be programmed using multiview records as follows.

```
type
  EntryKind = (FileEntry, DirEntry);
  EntryType =
    record
      EntryName: Name; InUse: Boolean;
```

```
      case EntryKind of
         FileEntry: (FD: FileDescriptor);
         DirEntry: (DD: DirDescriptor)
      end EntryType;

const
   EntryMax = 50;
var
   EntryTable: array [1 .. EntryMax] of EntryType;

procedure MakeEntry(Entry:EntryType);
   begin
      for I in 1 to EntryMax do
         if not EntryTable[I].InUse then
         begin
            EntryTable[I] := Entry;
            EntryTable[I].InUse := true;
            exit
         end
   end MakeEntry;
```

An instance of a multiview record can be declared without binding an actual view to its variant view; we shall call such an instance a *union* record. In the example, components of the array EntryTable and the parameter Entry to procedure MakeEntry are union records. The fields of a union record can be selectively accessed or modified using the **case view** and **if view** statements discussed earlier.

An actual parameter to MakeEntry can have either the FileEntry view or the DirEntry view. For example,

```
var
   FileEnt: EntryType(FileEntry);
   DirEnt: EntryType(DirEntry);
begin
   MakeEntry(FileEnt);
   MakeEntry(DirEnt)
end
```

In the procedure MakeEntry, the parameter Entry is copied into EntryTable using the assignment statement; this sets the view of EntryTable[I] to be the actual view of Entry (the old view-value of EntryTable[I] is ignored).

Assignment is not allowed on a union record if it is a reference parameter to a subprogram. Relaxing this restriction can introduce a loophole in the protection provided in the language. For example, a procedure could specify a formal **var** parameter of EntryType and, within its codebody, it could assign a directory entry variable to the **var** parameter. A particular call to the procedure may supply a file entry variable (e.g. FileEnt) as the

actual parameter. The procedure would then return a directory entry while
the caller expects a file entry. This is a clear breach in protection; such
errors should be detected and signalled to the procedure attempting the
assignment.

To permit copying a value into a **var** parameter of a union record type, a
standard procedure **copyview** is provided. It takes two parameters, both of
which must be union records of the same type. The **copyview** procedure
tests if assignment is valid: if so, it performs the copy operation, and
otherwise it returns an error to the caller.

For example, the following procedure searches for a name in the directory;
if the type of its entry in the directory is the same as expected by the caller,
the entry is returned to the caller, otherwise, an error is returned.

```
procedure GetEntry(Fname:Name; var Entry:EntryType);
  begin
    for I in 1 to EntryMax do
      with EntryTable[I] do
        if InUse then
          if EntryName = Fname
            then copyview(Entry, EntryTable[I])
                 iferror return error
                 otherwise return
    end GetEntry;
```

A standard function **viewval** is provided: if R is a union record with
viewtype T, then **viewval**(R) gives the actual view of R and is of type T.

CONCURRENT PROGRAMMING

The classic example used to illustrate concurrent programming is the
bounded buffer of fixed capacity which is used to even out the rates of
output by a producer and input by a consumer. The producer inserts items
into the buffer and the consumer removes them for its use. The producer
and the consumer are active agents called *processes* which can execute
independently of each other. The bounded buffer is an example of a *shared
resource*. Notice the similarity between the requirements here and those
for FiFoQ; in fact, we will program the bounded buffer using FiFoQ.

Process

A CCNPascal program may consist of a number of processes: these
processes execute concurrently. For example, the producer and the
consumer described above are concurrent processes.

A process definition consists of a declaration part and a statement part.

```
var
   Producer: process;
      var
         Item: ItemType;
      begin
         "Manufacture Item";
         "Put Item in the bounded buffer"
      end Producer;
```

The statements of a process perform actions on the variables defined in the declaration part. These variables are not accessible outside the process. Processes can communicate with each other only in a carefully controlled way which we will describe later.

For a process to start execution, it must be initialized using an **init** statement.

```
begin
   .
   init Producer;
   .
end
```

When this statement is executed in a program P, the Producer will begin execution of its statements independently of, and concurrently with P. A process will continue execution until it has performed its last statement.

Monitor

Processes often need to communicate with each other and share resources (as, in our example, the producer and the consumer share a bounded buffer). We need a means by which sharing can be safely done. An obvious way for two processes to communicate with each other is for them to have commonly accessible (or shared) variables. But we know that processes execute independently, so shared variables would be liable to arbitrary modification and it would not in general be possible to give any guarantee for the values of shared variables. The alternative is for processes to follow a strict discipline (or a protocol) for reading or modifying shared variables.

A **monitor** (Hoare,1974) is an abstraction which has been designed to be safely shared between processes, as it can be accessed *only* in a disciplined way. A monitor is very similar to a class, in the sense that it hides the internal representation of its variables and provides to the outside world only the functional behavior defined by its *exported* subprograms. But a monitor provides more: it guarantees that at most one process will execute the monitor code at any time. This property, called *mutual exclusion*, ensures consistency of monitor data and makes it safe for concurrent processes to access a monitor. Thus, a monitor is well suited to represent shared resources: for example, the bounded buffer can be programmed as a monitor.

We can view the bounded buffer as a first-in-first-out queue of items. The producer inserts an item into the queue and the consumer removes an item from the queue. An instance of FiFoQ is used to manage the buffer.

```
var
   BoundedBuffer: monitor;
      const
         BufSize = 100;
      var
         Buffer: array [1 .. BufSize] of ItemType;
         Q: FiFoQ(BufSize);

      procedure export Insert(Item:ItemType);
         begin
            Buffer[Q.Put] := Item
         end Insert;

      procedure export Remove(var Item:ItemType);
         begin
            Item := Buffer[Q.Get]
         end Remove;

   end BoundedBuffer;
```

This monitor uses the array variable Buffer as a ring buffer. There is one snag, however. If the buffer is full when the producer attempts to insert an item, an item that is yet to be consumed is overwritten. Similarly, if the buffer is empty when the consumer attempts to remove an item, either an old item or an undefined value is returned. We shall consider these problems when we reprogram the bounded buffer in the next section.

A technique to implement the mutual exclusion required for a monitor is to lock the entire monitor whenever a process starts to perform any of its operations. The monitor is unlocked only when the process has completed its call. If the monitor is found locked when a process attempts to enter the monitor, that process is made to wait till the monitor is unlocked. When a process leaves a monitor, the monitor is unlocked and one of the waiting processes, if there are any, is selected to enter the monitor.

The Kernel (described in Chapter 12) provides a type MonitorGate, and two operations LockGate and UnlockGate which require a MonitorGate as a parameter. These are used in the implementation of mutual exclusion for monitors as follows:

1. for each monitor variable, an instance Gate of type MonitorGate is implicitly allocated;
2. at the beginning of each exported subprogram of a monitor, a call to LockGate(Gate) is implicitly inserted;
3. at the end of each exported subprogram of a monitor, a call to UnlockGate(Gate) is implicitly inserted.

Queues

The bounded buffer monitor described in the previous section works correctly only if we can guarantee that each item produced is consumed exactly once. More precisely, the following invariant condition should hold for the buffer at any time.

Total items in buffer = Total calls to Insert – Total calls to Remove

We have already seen that the FiFoQ has a similar property, provided that calls to Put and Get are made only after ensuring that the queue is not full and not empty, respectively. To ensure that the above invariant holds for the BoundedBuffer monitor, the producer should be delayed if the buffer is full and the consumer should be delayed if the buffer is empty.

When a process is delayed, this fact should be remembered so that the process can be continued as soon as it can proceed with its operation. This can be done quite simply if we reserve for each process what is called a **queue** variable (Brinch Hansen,1975) in which the relevant information can be stored. (Thus, we need two queue variables, one for the producer and the other for the consumer.) Two operations **delay** and **continue** are provided on a queue variable: **delay**(Q) temporarily stops a process from executing and delays it in the queue variable Q, and **continue**(Q) releases the process previously delayed in Q and gives it an opportunity to continue its execution.

```
var
  BoundedBuffer: monitor;
    const
      BufSize = 100;
    var
      Buffer: array [1 .. BufSize] of ItemType;
      BufQ: FiFoQ(BufSize);
      ProducerQ, ConsumerQ: queue;
```

```
procedure export Insert(Item:ItemType);
  begin
    if BufQ.Full
      then delay(ProducerQ);
    Buffer[BufQ.Put] := Item;
    continue(ConsumerQ)
  end Insert;

procedure export Remove(var Item:ItemType);
  begin
    if BufQ.Empty
      then delay(ConsumerQ);
    Item := Buffer[BufQ.Get];
    continue(ProducerQ)
  end Remove;

end BoundedBuffer;
```

With this version of the monitor, our earlier problem vanishes. The producer will be delayed when it attempts to add an item to a full buffer, and the consumer will be delayed when the buffer is empty.

The bounded buffer monitor is a typical example of a 'subprogram' used for resource management. In general, monitors are used to manage the allocation and release of resources. When a request for a resource is being processed, the resource manager (which is programmed as a monitor) may find that the requested resource cannot be granted immediately. In such cases, the requesting process can be delayed (using the **delay** operation) until the resource is released by some other process, and continued (using the **continue** operation) only when its request can be granted.

A **delay** operation stops the executing process temporarily and delays it in the specified queue variable—if another process has already been delayed in the queue variable, the **delay** operation has no effect. On executing a **delay** operation, the current monitor is unlocked, i.e., if another process is waiting for access to the monitor, it is allowed to begin its operation. Note that at most one process can be delayed on a queue variable at any time.

When a **continue** operation is performed on a queue variable on which a process has been delayed, the process is removed from the queue and made to wait until the monitor is unlocked by the currently executing process—if no process has been delayed on the queue variable, the **continue** operation has no effect. When an executing process unlocks the monitor before leaving it, one of the waiting processes is allowed to continue its execution. Of the waiting processes, those previously selected and rescheduled by **continue** operations are given preference over those waiting to enter the monitor anew.

A Boolean valued function, **delayed**, is provided to test if a process is delayed in a queue variable: if Q is a queue variable, **delayed**(Q) returns **true** only if a process is currently delayed in Q.

The Kernel provides a type ProcessHook, and two operations HookProcess and UnhookProcess which require a ProcessHook and a MonitorGate as parameters. These are used in the implementation of **queue** variables and the **delay** and **continue** operations. A **queue** variable Q is represented as an instance Hook of type ProcessHook, and the invocations **delay**(Q) and **continue**(Q) are treated as the Kernel calls HookProcess(Hook, Gate) and UnhookProcess(Hook, Gate) respectively, where Gate is the MonitorGate for the enclosing monitor.

Resource Scheduling

In the bounded buffer example discussed above, selection of the process that can continue next is very simple; in fact, after the producer inserts an item, the consumer is allowed to continue if it was waiting, and after the consumer removes an item, the producer is allowed to continue if it was waiting. There is no need to select one among competing processes. But more sophisticated resource management is often needed in operating system design as many processes usually compete for a resource. There may be a single resource (like a peripheral device), or a resource with an associated size (such as memory). A process requesting a resource should be delayed if the resource has already been acquired by some other process and not yet released. When the resource is released by the process, one of the delayed processes should be selected according to a scheduling algorithm and the selected process should be allowed to continue execution.

A typical example of a resource for which many processes compete is the disk access. Let us program a disk manager as a monitor representing an abstract shared resource. We assume that no request for disk transfers can ever be rejected and that each request should eventually succeed. As any process in the system can make disk requests, the disk monitor should have provision to delay any or all of these processes. This means the disk monitor should declare as many queue variables as there are processes in the system. When the disk is released by a process, we use the *elevator algorithm* (Wirth,1977) to select the next process that can access the disk.

Let ProcessMax denote the maximum number of processes that can be simultaneously *alive* in the system. Also let ProcId be a predefined function that returns the identification (an integer between 1 and ProcessMax) of the process that makes the call.

```
type
  DiskMonitor = monitor;
    type
      ProcessRange = 1 .. ProcessMax;
    var
      ProcessQ: array [ProcessRange] of
                          record
                            DskAdr: DiskAddress;
                            Q:queue
                          end ProcessQ;
      Up, {This gives the direction of head movement}
      Busy: Boolean;
      HeadPosition: DiskAddress;

    procedure export Request(Adr:DiskAddress);
      begin
        if Busy then
          with ProcessQ[ProcId] do
          begin
            DskAdr := Adr; delay(Q)
          end;
        HeadPosition := Adr; Busy := true
      end Request;

    procedure export Release;
      var
        P: ProcessRange; Found: Boolean;

      procedure NextRequest(var P:ProcessRange);
        begin
          "Search pending requests in the current
           direction of head movement and
           select process P whose request is closest";
          Found := "true if such P was found and false otherwise"
        end NextRequest;

      begin {Release}
        Busy := false;
        NextRequest(P);
        if not Found then
        begin
          Up := not Up; NextRequest(P)
        end;
        if Found
          then continue(ProcessQ[P].Q)
      end Release;

    begin
      Up := true; Busy := false
    end DiskMonitor;
```

Pure Class

Access to a single disk can be managed by an instance of DiskMonitor. Now consider an operating system which supports a number of (identical) disks. We then require an array of type DiskMonitor where each monitor in the array manages access to a separate disk.

```
const
  DisksMax = 5;
var
  Disks: array [1 .. DisksMax] of DiskMonitor;
```

A file system can be designed in two different ways:

(a) It can view the disk resource as an array of disk monitors (as above). Then, to perform a file data transfer, it is for the file system to select the disk unit on which the file is stored and to invoke the corresponding disk monitor. Thus, it will be the file system which decides where files are stored on disks, and files should not be moved around in the disk storage without the knowledge of the file system.

(b) The file system can view the disk as an abstract resource called a 'virtual disk'. The virtual disk is addressed using logical addresses, called virtual addresses. Implementation of the virtual disk interprets virtual addresses and maps them onto physical disk addresses.

Let us look at how access to a virtual disk can be programmed. It is desirable that the actual representation of the virtual disk (an array of disks) be hidden from the file system. For this, the principle of data abstraction should be used. As we permit different users to concurrently request disk operations, it appears natural to use another monitor to manage access to the virtual disk. Though a single disk cannot perform more than a single operation at a time, the virtual disk consisting of several physical disks should allow operations on different disks to be performed in parallel. But if access to the virtual disk is managed by a monitor, all disk accesses will be serialized. For example, even if two users have their files on different disks, the virtual disk monitor would perform their disk operations one after the other. This slows down disk accesses.

So access to the virtual disk should not be managed by a monitor if efficiency in disk access is sought. The only reason to use a monitor is to provide safe and consistent disk accesses to concurrent users. But access to each individual disk is managed by a disk monitor which, by itself, provides safe and consistent disk access. The procedures implementing access to the virtual disk need only route requests to one or the other of the disk monitors: there is no need for any data, other than the array of disk monitors, to be stored in the virtual disk abstraction, and hence, there is no reason for it to be programmed as a monitor.

In principle, the virtual disk could be programmed as a class, except that a class variable cannot be shared between concurrent processes. Thus, we require a different kind of abstraction (other than the **class** and the **monitor**) which can be shared by concurrent processes without serializing access. A **pure class** is such an abstraction. All the variables declared in a pure class must be monitors or other pure classes. This guarantees that concurrent access to a pure class is safe.

The virtual disk could be programmed as a pure class:

```
var
  VirtualDisk: pure class;
    const
      DisksMax = 5;
    var
      Disks: array [1 .. DisksMax] of DiskMonitor;

    procedure export Request(Adr:VirtualDiskAdr);
      begin
        "Decode the virtual disk address Adr into two parts:
        D, the disk number
        A, the address within the selected disk";
        Disks[D].Request(A)
      end Request;

    procedure export Release(Adr:VirtualDiskAdr);
      begin
        "Decode the virtual disk address Adr
         and get D, the disk number";
        Disks[D].Release
      end Release;

  end VirtualDisk;
```

A pure class is often useful when deadlocks between processes must be avoided. To illustrate this, let us develop a different kind of abstraction, DiskInterface, which implements read/write operations on a single disk which is managed by a monitor, Disk, of type DiskMonitor. DiskInterface defines two procedures Read and Write; procedure Read reads data from disk into a buffer and procedure Write writes data from a buffer to the disk. These procedures use the monitor Disk to serially perform disk operations. They also use a memory allocator to acquire and release buffers.

The memory allocator, Mem, is a monitor which defines two procedures Allot and Release; procedure Allot allocates a buffer if one is available, and otherwise delays the requesting process; procedure Release frees a buffer and (possibly) continues a waiting process.

```
var
   Mem: monitor;
      ..
      procedure export Get(BufSize:integer; var BufAdr:MemAddress);
         begin
            "Delay the requesting process if
             no buffer of size BufSize is available";
            "When continued, allocate buffer of size BufSize";
            "Return the buffer address in BufAdr"
         end Get;

      procedure export Free(BufSize:integer; BufAdr:MemAddress);
         begin
            "Release buffer of size BufSize and address BufAdr";
            "Continue as many processes waiting for buffers as possible"
         end Free;

   end Mem;
```

When the procedure DiskInterface.Read is called by a user, it first calls Mem to acquire a buffer and then calls Disk to perform the read operation to fill the buffer. To write data to the disk, the procedure DiskInterface.Write first calls Disk to perform the write operation and then returns the buffer to Mem. We shall program DiskInterface as a pure class.

```
var
   DiskInterface: pure class
                     import
                         var : Disk, Mem
                     end;

      procedure export Read(DskAdr:VirtualDiskAdr; BufSize:integer;
                              var BufAdr:MemAddress);
         begin
            Mem.Get(BufSize, BufAdr);
            Disk.Request(DskAdr);
            "Read BufSize bytes of data from disk into buffer";
            Disk.Release
         end Read;

      procedure export Write(DskAdr:VirtualDiskAdr; BufSize:integer;
                              BufAdr:MemAddress);
```

```
    begin
      Disk.Request(DskAdr);
      "Write BufSize bytes of data from buffer onto disk";
      Disk.Release;
      Mem.Free(BufSize,BufAdr);
    end Write;
  end DiskInterface;
```

(Note the use of the **import** clause: variables and subprograms declared outside an abstraction (i.e., **class, monitor, pure class** or **process**) are not available inside unless they are explicitly imported; types and constants are, however, available. Variables imported into a monitor, pure class or process can only be other monitors and pure classes.)

If DiskInterface were programmed as a monitor, we would be confronted with severe problems. It would be possible for a user calling the Read procedure to be blocked in Mem.Get, awaiting a free buffer. The monitor, DiskInterface, would be locked until this process completed its request. But the only way the waiting process could receive a buffer is for some other process to perform a Write call which releases a buffer. This can never occur, because the monitor, DiskInterface, will remain locked and no process can make any call until the first process left the monitor. This is a simple case of *deadlock*.

In general, deadlocks of this kind can occur if monitor calls are nested and if inner monitors can delay processes. Such deadlocks can usually be avoided if pure classes are used instead of nested monitor calls. Our DiskInterface programmed as a pure class is free from deadlocks of this kind.

Signals and Queues

We have seen that queue variables can be used for synchronization between processes. Let us compare this mechanism with *signal* variables first proposed by Hoare (Hoare,1974) and later used in Modula (Wirth,1977). In contrast to a queue variable, any number of processes, each performing a *wait* operation, can be suspended on a signal variable. The relative priorities of waiting processes can be specified by supplying a 'delayrank' along with each wait operation. A *send* operation is used to continue one of the waiting processes: the process selected is the one with the smallest delayrank. A send operation has no effect if no process is suspended on the associated signal variable.

There are several examples where the use of signal variables brings clarity and simplicity to program structure. But there are some important synchronization needs that are not met by them.

1. Signal variables can be used with advantage if waiting processes can be ordered when they are delayed, rather than when they are due for resumption. Though signal variables are well suited to algorithms such as the elevator algorithm for disk head scheduling, they are of no particular advantage for, say, best-fit memory allocation schemes.

2. With signal variables, waiting processes are ordered by one attribute, their delayranks (which are integer values). If more than one scheduling parameter should be considered to schedule a process for a particular resource, these parameters must be first converted to a delayrank. In contrast to this, any number of scheduling parameters can be used when programming with queue variables.

Signal variables can be efficiently built out of the more primitive queue variables. We shall now program a monitor abstraction which can simulate signal variables and the wait and send operations. Waiting processes are kept in a list in increasing order of their rank values. The list is implemented using arrays to accommodate all the processes in the system. It could also have been implemented using storage allocated through pointer variables and the standard procedure, New, available in CCNPascal: we do not do so here because these features are not usually implemented in versions of languages used for operating systems as it is the operating system itself which must decide on storage allocation policies.

```
    var
        Name: array [ProcessRange] of ProcessRange;
        Rank: array [ProcessRange] of integer;
        Q: array [ProcessRange] of queue;
        Link: array [ProcessRange] of 0 .. ProcessMax;
        Head, FreeHead: 0 .. ProcessMax;
```

For any item I, Name[I] denotes the identification of the process stored at the item, Rank[I] denotes its delayrank, Q[I] denotes the queue variable on which the process can be delayed, and Link[I] the index of the process with the next higher rank. The index of the process at the head of the list of waiting processes is denoted by Head. The free elements of the arrays, i.e., those not used for the list of waiting processes, are organized in a free-list and the index of the item at the head of this list is denoted by FreeHead.

A procedure WaitForSignal puts an executing process in the list of waiting processes at a position that depends on its delayrank.

```
procedure WaitForSignal(DelayRank:integer);
   begin
      if "List is empty"
         then "put the process identification at the head of the list"
      else
         if DelayRank ≤ "Delayrank of process at the head of the list"
            then "put the process identification at the head of the list"
         else
         begin
            "Search the list for the appropriate position, I";
            "Insert the process identification at Name[I]";
            "Delay the process on the queue Q[I]"
         end
   end WaitForSignal;
```

A procedure SendSignal releases the process at the head of the list of waiting processes (i.e. the one with the smallest delayrank), unless the list is empty. The freed list position is added to the free-list and the process is continued. The code for the monitor SignalType follows.

```
type
   SignalType = monitor;
      var
         Name: array [ProcessRange] of ProcessRange;
         Rank: array [ProcessRange] of integer;
         Q: array [ProcessRange] of queue;
         Link: array [ProcessRange] of 0 .. ProcessMax;
         Head, FreeHead: 0 .. ProcessMax;

      procedure export WaitForSignal(DelayRank:integer);
         var
            Previous, This, Current: ProcessRange;
         begin
            Current := FreeHead;
            if Head = 0 then
            begin
               Link[Current] := 0;
               Head := Current
            end
            else
               if DelayRank ≤ Rank[Head] then
               begin
                  Link[Current] := Head;
                  Head := Current
               end
               else
               begin
                  Previous := Head; This:= Head;
```

```
            while DelayRank > Rank[This] do
            begin
               Previous := This;
               This := Link[This];
               if This = 0
                  then exit
            end;
            Link[Current] := Link[Previous];
            Link[Previous] := Current
         end;
         Rank[Current] := DelayRank;
         Name[Current] := ProcId;
         FreeHead := Link[FreeHead];
         delay(Q[ProcId])
      end WaitForSignal;

   procedure export SendSignal;
      var
         OldHead: ProcessRange;
      begin
         if Head ≠ 0 then
         begin
            OldHead := Head;
            Head := Link[Head];
            Link[OldHead] := FreeHead;
            FreeHead := OldHead;
            continue(Q[OldHead])
         end
      end SendSignal;

   begin
      Head := 0; FreeHead := 1;
      for I in 1 to (ProcessMax – 1)
         do Link[I] := I + 1;
      Link[ProcessMax] := 0
   end SignalType;
```

Standard Subprograms

We have already discussed three standard functions: **errorval**, **viewval** and **delayed**, and three standard procedures: **copyview**, **delay** and **continue**. Two other standard functions are provided: one to get the size and the other to get the address of a variable. The function **varsize**(V) returns an integer value which is the number of memory units necessary to *store* the variable V. The function **varadr**(V) returns an integer value which is the *address* of the memory location assigned to the variable V.

To understand the need for **varsize** and **varadr**, visualize how data in the variable FileBuf of File class can be copied to and from disk. The subprograms that perform the actual data transfer require the source and destination addresses and the size of the data to be transferred. The functions **varsize** and **varadr** can be used to get the size and address of FileBuf. Such functions are not needed in the usual 'user' programming languages, but they become essential when programming an operating system. They must be used with care!

DISCUSSION

Compilation of Programs

Let us consider how user programs should be compiled so that they can be executed on a machine with the help of the operating system described in this book. User programs may be written in CCNPascal, or in any other language. When a program is compiled, the compiler can be instructed either to identify separately the instruction and data parts of the program or to treat them together as a single whole. In the former case the program file generated by the compiler is called 'separated' and in the latter case, it is called 'mixed'. When a separated program is called by different jobs, a single storage segment can be used for its instructions while separate data segments are used for each calling job. This can result in considerable saving of space for commonly used programs, such as system utilities. Separated programs are sometimes called 're-entrant' procedures, or 'pure' procedures. In Chapter 11, we shall see how this feature is used in the operating system.

The CCNPascal compiler translates the concurrent programming constructs of the language (i.e. **process**, **monitor**, **queue**, **delay**, **continue** and **delayed**) into primitives provided by the Kernel. The implementation of these Kernel primitives will be discussed in Chapter 12.

Summary

Although CCNPascal can be used as a general purpose programming language, it is primarily intended for system programming: that is why it provides certain special features to cater for system programming. The extreme case of a language with special features is an assembly language, which consists only of special features. What we require in a high-level system programming language are simple features which enforce some discipline on their use. Any discipline has its restrictions. A good discipline has both possibilities and restrictions, and allows 'good' things to be done and prevents 'bad' things from happening. In the design of CCNPascal, we have tried to balance flexibility with the protection desired in a good high-level language.

To evaluate the effectiveness of a language, it must be used for a non-trivial exercise that does not hide practical problems. A language encourages, and sometimes enforces, a pattern of use. In this book, we are concerned with the activity of designing an operating system in steps and in separate components. CCNPascal helps us to do this: the structure and the code of the complete operating system are written in the language.

CCNPascal has many similarities with other languages. The data abstraction mechanism **class** and the concurrent programming abstractions **process** and **monitor** are largely drawn from Concurrent Pascal (Brinch Hansen,1975). We have demonstrated that the *signal* variables of Modula (Wirth,1977) can be programmed using the **queue** variables of CCNPascal. *Generic* types and subprograms are provided in a variety of languages: e.g., Alphard (Wulf *et al.*,1976), Clu (Liskov *et al.*,1977), and Ada (Honeywell,1980); in fact, these languages provide generic types in their full generality as they also allow types as generic parameters. By contrast, the generic types allowed in CCNPascal are simple: this has been done deliberately to simplify implementation. This simplicity has another advantage: it would not be difficult to rewrite the operating system described in this book in any of the contemporary languages, for example, in Ada.

CCNPascal has been implemented on several machines: the DECSystem 10 and PDP-11, the TDC316 (manufactured in India), the Intel 8086, the Motorola 68000 and a hypothetical stack machine (based on the Pascal-P machine). The first compiler was written in Pascal as a cross compiler: it executes on the DECSystem 10 and produces assembly code for the target machine. A new version of the compiler, written in CCNPascal, is now available. The machine-dependent part of the compiler has been separated (this is about 1500 lines of Pascal code, or 20% of the whole compiler); only this needs modification to implement the compiler on a different machine.

EXERCISES

1. We described a program to search in a fixed size table of items.
    (a) Rewrite the program using a generic type and a generic subprogram which can be used to search in a table of any size.
    (b) We assumed that the item being searched for is present in the table. Rewrite the program to return an error if the item is not found.

2.   On entering a Computer Science department, each student has to join one of two task schemes for helping to run the department. In scheme A, the student undertakes to provide user consultancy at the Computer Center, to make announcements of new books, and to help with the annual picnic. In scheme B, the tasks are to deal with visitors to the department, to help prepare the annual report, and to buy coffee, milk and sugar for the lounge. Before graduation, each student must do each task in the scheme of his choice.

Write a program which can be used to keep a record of students and tasks. Use a multiview record to describe the two task schemes.

3.   A computer is equipped with a clock which sends interrupts every millisecond. These interrupts can be converted by the interrupt handler into calls to a procedure. Design a monitor, Timer, which performs the following operations:
   (a) receives calls from the clock interrupt handler and increments an internal counter, and
   (b) accepts calls from processes wishing to be delayed for periods of time specified in milliseconds.

Assume there are ten processes in the system and use queue variables to delay processes. Ignore arithmetic overflows in operations.

Why is it important in this case that each monitor procedure executes fast?

4.   For the computer and clock described in the previous question, design an abstraction to record the time of the day in hours, minutes and seconds. It should have two procedures: SetTime, to set the time of the day, and ReadTime, to return the current time of the day. Assume the computer has a 16 bit word and that integers are stored in single words.

Will the abstraction be a class or a monitor? Explain the reasons for your choice.

5.   A spooling program for a line printer accepts requests to print files. The program schedules printing according to the following rules:
   (a) small files are printed before larger ones,
   (b) once printing of a file starts, it is continued to completion (i.e., there is no pre-emption), and
   (c) no request must be delayed for more than one hour (i.e., there is no starvation).

Assume a request comes as a procedure call with the name of the file and its length in 'blocks' as parameters. The printer can print 10 blocks a minute and no file has more than 100 blocks. The spooler can have a maximum of 10 pending requests.

Design the spooler as a process, assuming that a time-of-the-day monitor is available.

6.   SignalType, as defined in this chapter, has an internal array of queue variables. Each instance of this type will therefore have one such array. We know that a process can be blocked at only one queue variable at any time.

Redesign SignalType so that it keeps a list of waiting processes and their delay ranks but, to delay or continue a process, uses a monitor variable, Hold. This must be the only monitor in the system that uses **queue** variables and the **delay** and **continue** operations.

3 MULTIPROCESSOR ARCHITECTURE

Concurrency in the Operating System

Using CCNPascal, we can describe the concurrent operations of the operating system in terms of *processes* which communicate (or interact) with each other through *monitors*. Processes can be simultaneously executed, if there are enough processors, or executed in any order if there are fewer processors than processes. A process is like a virtualization of a processor, so it is sometimes called a virtual processor. In a multiprocessor system, several processes are likely to be simultaneously in execution and special attention must be paid to the mechanisms used to guarantee that the operations of a monitor are executed in strictly serial order.

If we look more closely at the operating system, anticipating what we will do from Chapter 4 onwards, we can distinguish a few important functions that its processes must perform:

1. The major processes in the operating system are

    (a)   those that perform the functions of resource allocation—allotting memory space, processor time and input–output devices to user programs;

    (b)   those that execute user programs.

We have seen a few simple examples of such processes in Chapter 2. Let us call these *general* processes, as they conform closely to what we would expect CCNPascal processes to do.

2.   The operating system must also control the execution of input–output
      devices which perform their operations autonomously, i.e., once
      started, each such device will execute independently of a processor in
      the system until the operation is completed (or an error is
      encountered). A device is therefore like a separate processor, though
      it is one that can perform only certain operations. The part of the
      operating system that controls the execution of a device 'processor'
      will typically have a structure such as:

```
begin loop
    loop
        "Wait for I/O request from a general process";
        "Initiate device operation";
        "Wait for device to complete operation";
        "Check for possible errors";
    end;
end;
```

This looks remarkably like the structure of a *process* that waits for a
request from some other process, initiates the device operation and then
waits again until this is over. We can refer to routines like this as *device*
processes. The operating system will need one of these for each device in
the system. (As we will see in later chapters, device processes are part of
the Kernel of the operating system.)

Broadly speaking, the operating system consists of a number of general
processes to perform the tasks of resource allocation and user program
execution, and a set of device processes (one for each device) to control
input and output operations. In the rest of this chapter, we shall examine
how such processes can be executed on different computer architectures
and the mechanisms that must be provided for mutual exclusion between
processes.

SYSTEM ARCHITECTURES

Processors are needed for the execution of processes, and storage is used to
house 'objects' like programs and data. Computer architectures can be
classified by the alternatives chosen for providing physical resources to
represent processes and objects. The operating system has the task of
sharing the physical resources of the system among its users. The resource
allocation techniques available to the operating system will vary considerably with the architecture of the system and the kind of use for which it is
intended.

If one storage unit is used to house all active objects and one processor is shared between all processes, the configuration is a *multiprogrammed uniprocessor*. The processor can be multiplexed between various processes in the following way: a process which either completes execution, or which cannot continue execution (i.e., is blocked) because some resource is not available, relinquishes control of the processor to another process. This transfer of control is referred to as a *context switch*. Processes must be scheduled so that no unblocked process is indefinitely delayed before it is scheduled for execution. The processor may therefore need to be switched quite frequently between processes and the speed with which a context switch can be performed becomes crucial to the performance of such a system.

Uniprocessors have existed from the days of the earliest computers. Until recently, it appeared to be felt (at least among computer manufacturers) that reasons of technology and cost ruled out any drastic deviations from this ruling standard. A lot of effort was therefore directed to improving the components and assemblies that went into building uniprocessor computers, and successive models featured faster circuitry, faster memories and faster disks, more compact assemblies that consumed less power or that were easier to cool, etc. Techniques of organizing memory were improved so that a single memory could be divided into 'banks', to reduce the average access time of the memory; small, high-speed scratch-pad memories were added to processors to hold the contents of the most recently, or the most frequently, accessed memory locations. Multiprogrammed uniprocessors are by far the most common systems in use even today, but developments in semiconductor technology make several other kinds of systems viable. We shall describe some of these systems in the following sections.

Multiprocessors

In a *multiprocessor*, there are several processors, each accessing some common storage. The advantage in introducing multiple processing elements is that this permits true concurrency, i.e., several instructions can be simultaneously executed. This can be used

1. to reduce the execution time of a *single* program, if it can be split into several parts that can be independently executed as processes,
2. to increase the throughput of the system, through parallel execution of *several* user programs;
3. to build a highly reliable system, using the availability of many processors to provide redundancy in case of failures.

Case 1 is rarely used in practice because fairly advanced programming methodology is needed for a large program to be decomposed into several small units that can be executed concurrently. Such a methodology has been used for a certain class of programs, such as operating systems or real-time systems, but not often in the design of user programs. Thus, while the general processes of an operating system can be executed independently on separate processors, a user program will usually run on one processor at a time, as in (2). Note that to allow a single user program to be run as a set of processes on different processors would also require the operating system to recognize and provide mechanisms for supporting user programs with concurrent processes. Most commercial operating systems do not yet provide such facilities.

Case 2 is the most prevalent mode of using a multiprocessor. The reduction in 'turn-around' time achieved by multiprocessing enables a large user community to share expensive but relatively slow peripherals (such as the disk subsystems, printers, etc), and makes the use of such a system economical. Considering that it has long been said that multiprocessors are just a logical extension of single processor systems, it is surprising that relatively few multiprocessor systems have ever been built (and many of these only for special purposes). Symmetric multiprocessors, those in which the functions of different processors are indistinguishable, are even fewer.

For real-time applications, where reliability is of great importance, (3) has often been used. It is quite common for such a system to have two processors, one for normal use and one serving as a 'hot' standby. We shall not be considering the design of such systems in this book.

Processor–Memory Interconnection

The distinguishing characteristic of a multiprocessor is the use of common storage for the processors. For this to be possible, processors and memory units have to be interconnected. The architectures of multiprocessors vary primarily in the way this interconnection is made.

The simplest way to interconnect processors and memory is through multiple *memory ports*. As shown in Fig.3.1, the shared memory of the multiprocessor is divided into several banks with each bank having several ports. Each processor is connected to one port of every bank. It is possible for different processors to concurrently access *different* memory banks, but access to a *single* bank must be in serial order. The hardware controller within each bank schedules multiple access requests according to some fixed algorithm (either 'round robin', or based on processor priority). This

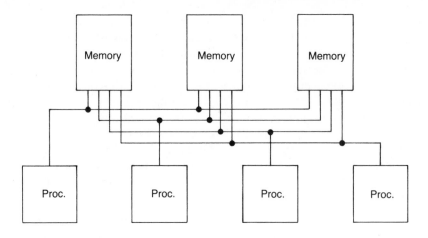

Fig. 3.1 A multiprocessor with multiported memory.

kind of interconnection is extremely simple. Typically, each memory bank comes with a certain fixed number of ports. To add a processor, all that is necessary is to connect the processor to one port of every bank. This simplicity is also the limitation of this scheme. The number of ports is fixed and this determines the maximum number of processors that can be connected. Hence, this scheme is used when the number of processors is small (typically 2).

The limitation of the ported memory scheme can be overcome by replacing the logic contained in each bank controller by a centralized switch. This is illustrated in Fig.3.2.

The centralized switch, called a *crossbar switch*, routes an access request from a processor to the appropriate bank of memory. The switch arbitrates between multiple requests to the same bank but, as in the previous scheme, concurrent access to different banks is allowed. The advantage of the centralized switch is its *conceptual* simplicity, and it can be designed to support many more processors than is possible through ported memory. The main disadvantage is that it needs the introduction of a fairly complex centralized component, and this can affect the reliability of the system. If there are m banks and n processors, the number of interconnections is $m \times n$ and the switch must handle all these switching elements without appreciable delay.

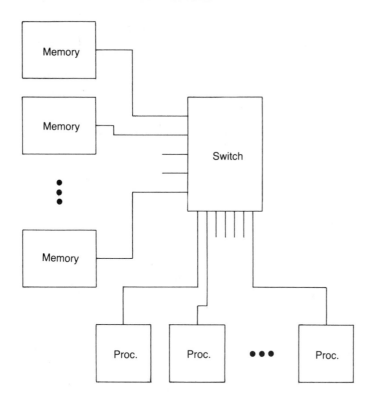

Fig. 3.2 A multiprocessor with a centralized switch.

In general, multiprocessors have one serious limitation: when processors compete for access to shared storage, they may delay each other and the average memory access time will increase for each processor. This puts a practical limit to the number of processors that can be connected to a single shared storage unit. Several design improvements have been proposed to alleviate this problem of *memory contention.* By introducing multiple memory banks, the contention in access to a single bank can be reduced. A further refinement is to introduce *cache* storage between each processor and the switch. A cache retains a copy of the locations of the shared storage that have been recently accessed by a processor. When a processor makes a memory reference, the data is retrieved from the cache, if it is there; otherwise, the access request is forwarded to memory through the switch and a copy of the data received is stored in the cache. With this refinement, processors need less frequent access to shared stoarge. But, the cache introduces a new problem: since there are several processors, copies of a single location of shared memory may be simultaneously present in several cache units. Hence, whenever a processor alters a memory location, it is necessary for it also to 'inform' other processors so that they may update their caches, if necessary. Rather than designing special hardware for this purpose, it is easier to follow the simple convention of only caching read-only data (e.g., instructions).

Another way of reducing contention is to to attach *local storage* to each processor, as illustrated in Fig.3.3.

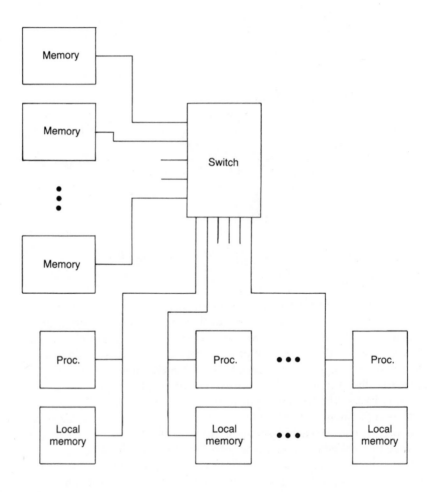

Fig. 3.3 A multiprocessor with local memory.

The introduction of local storage reduces memory contention (as with a cache) but results in some asymmetry in the memory: no processor will be able to access the entire memory. Each processor can access only the shared storage and *its own* local storage. With this asymmetry, objects shared between processes have (in general) to be in shared storage, and local storage can be used for storing data private to a process. Allocation of local storage can be controlled dynamically by the operating system. The operating system can use local storage to achieve the effect of a cache by allocating frequently used data that is private to a process in local storage. However, it has to be careful to execute a process on a processor that can access the memory allocated to the instructions and data of that process. There is an added overhead in executing a process first on one processor and then on another.

The centralized switching element has another limitation: the number of interconnections is determined when the switch is designed and it is not possible to add more processors than this predetermined number. To allow extensibility, and to improve reliability, a *distributed switching* scheme can be used. This is illustrated in Fig.3.4.

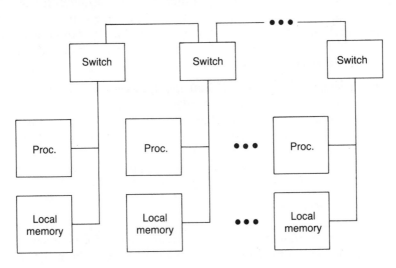

Fig. 3.4 A distributed multiprocessor.

In this scheme, there are several switches, each associated with a processor and its local storage. The local storage of every processor is accessible to any other processor. Thus, all processors share a common address space but storage units are physically distributed, each unit connected to one processor. A processor can access its local storage directly, but access to non-local storage must be routed through its switch. The switching strategy is called *packet switching*, in contrast to the crossbar switch which uses *circuit switching*.

In packet switching, there is no direct electrical path between a processor and non-local memory. Instead, the local switch communicates the request as a message (or packet) to the destination switch. It is not even necessary that all switches be directly connected: a request can be routed to the destination switch through intermediate switches. When a request is received by a destination switch, it retrieves the data from its local memory and returns this as a packet to the source switch. After issuing a non-local memory request, the processor waits for the data to arrive. But, during this time, it does not 'hold' its local bus and the local switch can handle requests from other processors.

The structure of this organization, called a *distributed multiprocessor*, is similar to that of a network of computers interconnected through telephone lines or coaxial cables. But there is an important difference: all the processors of a distributed multiprocessor share the entire memory. In contrast, each processor in a computer network has its own local storage and there is no shared storage. The operating system we describe in this book is not applicable to this class of architecture.

The main advantage of a distributed multiprocessor is that there is no single component that can be a bottleneck in the system. Distributed switching introduces a variable delay in memory access, the delay being proportional to the remoteness of the memory being accessed. In such a system, the processes of the operating system must be distributed in a way that minimizes the delay in accessing common data.

Input/Output Structure

In the previous section, we described various schemes for interconnecting processors and memory units. Similar schemes have to be provided for connecting processors and input/output devices. We can think of

  (a) devices with multiple ports,
  (b) devices and processors connected by a crossbar switch,
  (c) devices connected to only one processor and inaccessible to other processors, or
  (d) devices connected to only one processor but also accessible to all other processors.

In scheme (a), each port of a device would be connected to the bus of one processor and the device would use the port for data transfers and interrupt transactions. The device could use different ports for different transactions. However, unlike memory banks, device controllers are rarely designed with multiple ports and so this scheme is not commonly used.

The crossbar switch of scheme (b) has similarities to a crossbar processor-memory switch. But the device switch is more complicated, since a device must remain connected to a processor during a transaction which may take quite long (e.g., a disk read). It is usually more convenient to arbitrate between requests involving considerable delay at the software level, rather than through a centralized switch.

In scheme (c), which is quite common, a processor can only access devices to which it is connected. Access to non-local devices is only possible by software mediation: a process on one processor must send a request to a process on the other processor, asking for an operation to be performed on the device.

Scheme (d) is used when distributed switching is employed and where devices are accessed through memory addresses, rather than through input/output instructions. In this case, since an input/output operation is initiated by writing some data into a location, the distributed switching scheme does not need any special extension to allow processors to access remote devices. But the path from a device to processors is usually non-symmetric. So, though any processor may initiate input/output operations on any device, data transfers and interrupts from the device must be handled only by the processor to which it is connected. This asymmetry is the outcome of two considerations:

1. Interrupts from the device will need quick attention, which is difficult to ensure if interrupt-handling is done by a remote processor.
2. Data transfers to or from non-local memory have variable delay, which may be larger than the rate at which data must be read from or written to the device.

Each of these schemes makes slightly different demands on the device processes of the operating system. In schemes (a) and (b), device processes may be executed on any processor. In scheme (c), a device process must execute only on the processor from which the device is accessible. Scheme (d) requires rather different device processes: in fact, the operations of each device process must be divided into those that can be executed on any processor and those that can be executed only on the processor to which the device is connected.

Interprocessor Communication

The shared storage of a multiprocessor can be used to implement interprocess communication. For example, two processes can communicate with each other through a monitor residing in shared storage. But there are occasions when interprocess communication through monitors (using shared storage) is not very convenient. For example, if the input/output structure is asymmetric, a general process executing on one processor can initiate input/output on a non-local device only by communicating with the device process controlling that device. If communication is through a monitor, the input/output can be initiated only when the device process is scheduled for execution. This has the drawback that a request from a process may not get immediate attention.

To allow communication between processes when immediate response is required, a different technique is used to implement interprocess communication. An interprocessor interrupt (IPI) mechanism allows a processor to interrupt any other processor with an interrupt message. When a processor receives an IPI interrupt, the message is received and delivered to the appropriate process. Interrupt-based communication assures immediate response. Different systems have variations of this scheme. In some systems, IPI hardware is organized pairwise, i.e. when processor A interrupts processor B, processor C also can interrupt B etc. In other systems, IPI is like a shared device and processor A can interrupt processor B only if there is no other interrupt request for B.

PROGRAMMING ISSUES

Mutual Exclusion

In the previous chapter, we described how concurrent processes interact with each other through monitors. Different executions of the exported procedures of a monitor must mutually exclude each other in time: i.e., at any given time only one process can be inside a monitor. In a uniprocessor, mutual exclusion can be achieved by setting a single global variable on entry to a monitor, and clearing it on exit from the monitor. This will be adequate for mutual exclusion among general processes, since only one of these can be executing at any time. To ensure mutual exclusion between device processes requires a more powerful mechanism: disabling all interrupts on entry to a monitor, and enabling them on exit from the monitor. Unfortunately, even this solution cannot guarantee mutual exclusion in a multiprocessor environment.

To achieve mutual exclusion between general processes in a multi-processor, we require an *indivisible read–modify–write* operation on a single memory location in shared storage. There are two ways of achieving this:

(a) Having a 'read–modify–write' cycle for the memory, so that a memory location will remain exclusively assigned to a processor while it is read and written into, or

(b) Using an indivisible 'test-and-set' instruction, by which a processor can both test the contents of a memory location and alter it (perhaps conditionally) without interference from other processors.

Both these features provide basic mutual exclusion at the level of single (indivisible) machine instructions and they can then be used for ensuring mutual exclusion between general processes for access to monitors. (In Chapter 12, we describe the implementation of mutual exclusion assuming an indivisible read–modify–write cycle). Mutual exclusion between general and device processes on the same processor must still be ensured. This can be done, as before, by disabling the interrupts of the processor.

Resource Allocation

A multiprocessor architecture introduces a few special problems in resource allocation which are not encountered in a uniprocessor system.

An important factor that complicates resource allocation in a multi-processor is asymmetry in the hardware. For example, processors may have local storage: a process that has been allocated space in some local memory can be executed only on the processor that can access the local memory. Similarly, there may be input/output asymmetry. It is then more efficient to execute a process that performs frequent input/output on a processor that can access the necessary devices. A crucial issue in the design of an operating system for a multiprocessor is whether the asymmetry in the hardware should be made 'visible' to the user. In some cases, visibility has advantages. For example, when only some processors have floating point hardware, a user can be asked to provide information to the operating system on whether his program uses floating point operations. This can eliminate the need to monitor the dynamics of user program execution for efficient resource allocation. But, if some memory banks in the system were faster than others, it would be merely confusing to ask a user to choose where his program should be allotted space.

Having a multiplicity of processing elements can complicate processor scheduling. The goal of the scheduler is to optimize throughput by balancing the processing 'load' among processors and ensure, as far as possible, that no processor is idle. This goal is not difficult to achieve if a single user program is executed as one process. But, if a user program consists of several concurrent processes, the scheduling strategy has to take into account the process structure of a user program. For example, consider the following situation. A user program has two processes, P1 and P2, and process P1 is blocked while waiting for a signal from process P2; since a blocked process cannot continue execution, the processor is allocated (by a context switch) to another process. When P2 is scheduled, it signals P1 and waits for a signal from P1. Once again, another process must be scheduled and there is one more context switch. Thus, processes that communicate often are also 'context switched' often (this is sometimes referred to as processor thrashing) and this may defeat the very purpose of concurrent programming, which is to reduce execution time. A simple scheduling strategy, called *co-scheduling*, reduces this effect by simultaneously scheduling (on different processors) processes that communicate often with each other. A blocked process will not be immediately context-switched but is permitted to wait for 'some time' in the expectation that its execution can soon be resumed (after receiving a message from another process). Such a strategy will reduce the number of context switches, at some cost in processor time.

One of the oft-stated merits of a multiprocessor is its potential for increased reliability. Certainly, after a failure in a processor or some bank of memory is discovered, the system can easily be reconfigured to eliminate the faulty unit. But it requires a very sophisticated operating system to perform such reconfiguration automatically. For example, recovery from a processor failure involves identification of the process that was being executed by the failed processor and 'backtracking' the process to a consistent state so that it can be executed on another processor. Such error recovery schemes can be quite elaborate.

A MODEL ARCHITECTURE

The design of the operating system we shall study in this book is based on a multiprocessor with some shared memory and some local memory for each processor. A possible system could consist of several homogeneous, or similar, processors. Access to the shared memory is controlled by some form of crossbar processor–memory switch which ensures that only one processor at a time is given access to a bank of memory. Simultaneous requests from different processors must be sequenced fairly so that no processor has to wait indefinitely long for memory access.

While we assume that all the processors are similar, we do allow asymmetry in the configuration of each processor. The asymmetry is of two kinds:

1. The amount of local memory available to each processor may differ (and some processors may have none).
2. Each processor has exclusive access to a set of input/output devices and, in general, the configuration of input/output devices for each processor may differ.

There must be primitives at the hardware level for mutual exclusion between processors. We also require a mechanism for a processor to communicate with other processors. The simplest feature that is needed is an interprocessor interrupt (IPI) which is accessible to all processors. Given this basic facility, it is possible to build any interprocessor communication scheme.

We will assume that processors have memory protection mechanisms to ensure that a user program cannot access the memory allocated to other user programs or data. We will also assume that the address space of a program can be divided into two segments, an instruction segment and a data segment, which can be independently positioned in memory.

We assume that there is an interval timer with each processor. The interval can be set by program and the timer interrupts the processor when the interval elapses. This is required for processor scheduling. In addition to these interval timers, we also assume there is a real time clock that can be accessed by all processors. The real time clock will be set at system initialization time and used later for computing the time of the day, as well as for accounting purposes.

DISCUSSION

We have described several alternative multiprocessor architectures using various possible schemes for processor–memory and processor–device interconnection. Many experimental and some commercial multiprocessors have been built using such interconnection schemes.

The DEC-10 (DEC, 1977) has versions with dual-processors, using ported memory. In one version, all devices are connected to one processor, called the master. In another version, fast devices such as disks are dual-ported and slower peripherals are connected through a switch. The B-7700 (Burroughs Corp., 1973) is another multiprocessor that uses ported memory. In this system, there are three major units: processors, memory modules and input/output modules (IOM). Each processor, and IOM, is connected to all memory modules through ports. Some peripherals are connected to all IOMs through a centralized switch and others are private to different IOMs. IOMs and processors communicate with each other through an interrupt bus.

C.mmp (Fuller and Harbison, 1978) is a multiprocessor with local storage. The processors (PDP-11s) are connected to a shared memory through a crossbar switch. Each peripheral is connected to only one processor. Interprocessor communication takes place through an interprocessor interrupt bus. There are several function registers on this bus using which a processor can start, stop or continue any other processor. Cm* (Swan *et al.*, 1977) is a distributed multiprocessor that uses a hierarchy of switches. Several computer modules, each consisting of a processor, storage, some peripherals and a local switch, are connected to form a cluster. A cluster is controlled by a unit, called a KMap, and intracluster communication is through a bus. Each cluster is connected to other clusters through cluster buses. Non-local memory access by a processor is routed (packet-switched) through a collection of local switches and KMaps. The processors are LSI-11s, and all devices and processors are accessed through memory addresses. Since a processor can access all the memory in the system, the same packet-switching mechanism is used for accessing remote devices as for inter-processor communication. An interesting aspect of Cm* is that the switches are processors that can be microprogrammed to provide different address structures.

Most commercial systems use multiprocessors only for increasing through-put. User-level concurrency is not generally supported. Hydra (Wulf *et al.*, 1981), the kernel of an operating system for C.mmp, and StarOS (Jones *et al.*, 1979) and Medusa (Ousterhout *et al.*, 1979), operating systems for Cm*, provide facilities for user programs to be composed of multiple processes. StarOS and Medusa allow user programs to be constructed as 'task forces'. A task force is a collection of processes that cooperate with each other. In StarOS, a user can control the placement of the code and data of a task force, taking into account the asymmetry in the hardware. In Medusa, all the processes of a task force are co-scheduled to minimize context switching.

The memory protection scheme we have assumed for the model architecture is quite minimal and many commercial systems provide more elaborate features. In the DEC-10, the program address space is divided into two segments and each segment is divided into several pages. Relocation and access control is at page level but the operating system restricts sharing to instruction segments. In the PDP-11, the program address space is divided into two parts (instructions and data) each of which is further subdivided into many segments. In both these systems, the program address space is smaller than the possible physical memory size. This is not so in the IBM 370 systems, or in Multics (Organick, 1972), each of which has different versions of segmentation and paging schemes.

Most commercial systems restrict a user program to one address space. But there is a class of *domain-based* architectures, where programs can be composed as 'domains'. Each domain is a separate address space. During execution, a process can switch execution from one domain to another. Examples of this kind of architecture are CAP (Wilkes and Needham, 1979) and the Plessey 250 (England,1974). Domain-based architectures provide a fine degree of protection and are designed to support the programming methodology of data abstraction and modularity.

The operating system described in this book makes relatively few demands on the architecture, and so it can be used on many different systems.

EXERCISES

1. PLURIBUS (Katsuki, 1978) is a multiprocessor that has been designed to operate in environments where high reliability is important (e.g., an interface to a computer network). PLURIBUS is a flexibly-configurable collection of three types of modules:
   (a) a *processor bus* consisting of two processors and a local storage for each processor,
   (b) a *memory bus* containing shared storage units and
   (c) an *I/O bus* containing I/O and special purpose devices.

   These modules are interconnected by bus couplers so that every processor bus can reference every memory and I/O bus. There is no interrupt mechanism. Interprocessor and processor-device communication is achieved by placing *tokens* into a special purpose, hardware maintained priority queue called the *Pseudo-Interrupt Device*.

   Is the architecture of PLURIBUS adequately covered by the interconnection schemes described in this chapter? If not, suggest a more general classification of interconnection schemes to include architectures like PLURIBUS.

2. Assuming a read–modify–write cycle for the memory, outline a program for ensuring mutual exclusion between general processes.

3. (Group Exercise.) Suppose you have a sequential program for solving a problem. What are the broad guidelines that you would follow while transforming the sequential program into a concurrent program capable of executing on a multiprocessor? Your solution should consider aspects of decomposition of the sequential program as well as the implications of various architectural attributes on the placement of code and data of the concurrent program.

4 OVERVIEW OF THE OPERATING SYSTEM

Introduction

There are two important aspects to the design of any system: *what* it must do, and *how* this can be done. The first of these defines the external view, in terms of functions of a system that are visible to a user. *How* the functions are to be performed is the subject of interest to a designer, who must work out the *specifications* for the design and an *implementation*. For example, a requirement for a process control computer may be that it must operate at temperatures up to 50°C. The hardware designer of the system must define specifications for the system and implement the design, using components that will withstand operation at high temperatures and a mechanical structure that can be adequately cooled with ambient air at 50°C. When this has been done, we can say that

    (a) A *specification* of the system asserts that it will operate at temperatures up to 50°C, and

    (b) This specification meets a particular *requirement*.

In the same way, the specifications of an operating system must meet certain requirements. A special-purpose operating system may be designed to meet particular requirements: to provide, say, a guaranteed response time to external events. A general-purpose operating system, such as the one we shall be describing in this book, is usually designed to meet the requirements of a broad class of users. Naturally, the computer system for which the operating system is designed must have the necessary basic capabilities—it is not possible to build a general-purpose, time-sharing system using an 8-bit microprocessor!

The specifications of the operating system must be derived from the requirements so that each requirement is met by some function of the system. These specifications provide the goal for the design of the whole system. At this level, the specifications define broad functional characteristics for the system, without indicating how they are to be provided. In designing the system, we must look for groupings of functions which can be used to mark out coherent areas in the structure. These groupings will allow us to decompose the large structure into smaller components, each of which has well-defined external functions. We can call such a component an *abstraction*, because its functions can be understood independently of its internal structure.

The next step is to design each component. Once again, we can examine the specifications for a component and design subcomponents, or smaller abstractions, that can be assembled together to meet these specifications. If we systematically repeat this step, decomposing each abstraction into smaller abstractions, we will come finally to the abstractions defined by the machine architecture. The operating system must use these abstractions to implement its operations.

In practice, it is unusual for any design to be completed in quite so systematic a manner. More often, the abstractions designed at one level are found unsuitable (for any of several reasons) for implementation at some other level. When this happens, it is necessary to re-design some abstractions so that their implementations can be programmed with greater ease. The process of design can thus be repetitive, with a certain amount of re-tracing of paths in the light of hindsight. In a design that is composed of abstractions, the side-effects of re-design can be minimized and often only one abstraction, or perhaps a few, will need to be altered each time.

Requirements

The operating system presented in this book is intended to support batch and time-sharing use of a multiprocessor system: this allows us to put down some general requirements.

1. It should allow a set of users to be 'registered' with the system, and should provide a means of authenticating users.
2. Registered users should be allowed to execute programs submitted through batch input devices, such as card readers, or through interactive terminals.
3. Users should be allowed to create and store files of information, to modify these files, and to share files with other users; files must be stored over long periods, and access to files must be controlled.

4. The operating system must continue to operate correctly in the presence of errors in user programs.
5. The operating system should execute on a multiprocessor system.

Requirements such as these are fairly typical for a general-purpose operating system. In addition, there will usually be more specific requirements, such as the number of user jobs that can be simultaneously executed, or the way files can be shared between users. Our first task is to look at the general requirements and see if we can identify units, or components, that can broadly perform the functions to meet these requirements. We can then consider the detailed design of each functional component and, at that time, take possible specific requirements into account.

To give these rather general requirements more definite form, we shall illustrate them with short excerpts from the dialogue between a hypothetical user and the operating system. This will provide the 'user view' of the system. Once this is done, the internal organization of the operating system can be considered and we must answer the question: "what program structures must be used to preserve the external character of the system"? The outcome will be a 'first level' design specification, with a broad decomposition of functions into components that appear to meet the requirements. Later chapters of the book will examine the design of these components in much greater detail and, as can be expected, the functional decomposition will then have to be altered to take account of implementation details and to provide greater efficiency in execution.

JOB MANAGEMENT

The User View

User programs executing in the system will be called *jobs*: many user jobs will simultaneously compete for the resources of the system.

The first function required is to allow users to be registered with the system, with a unique identification for each user and a means of authenticating user jobs. Authentication is usually done by means of *passwords*: a password is a string of characters which is kept confidential by the system. The name and password for a user must be preserved as long as that user is registered. Such information cannot be stored in the main memory (as that will be erased whenever the system is switched off) so data on user registration must be stored in a *file* on the disk.

User jobs may be presented through a *batch* input device, such as a card reader, or through interactive terminals. For example, a registered user with the name ZETA, may 'log-in' on an interactive terminal as follows:

```
LOGIN ZETA                    – user identification
password:                     – user password
logged-in at 10:20:46 on 15 August 19XX
```

where only the text in capitals is typed by the user. Note that the password is not visible because it is not printed when typed (i.e., passwords are not 'echoed'). Given the user's name (ZETA) and a password, the Job Manager can check that the user has been registered and that the password is correct. Assuming this is so, the user is ready to execute programs, e.g.

```
*RUN PASCAL                   – execute the Pascal compiler
file:EIGHTQ                   – and compile the program in the file,
                                EIGHTQ
compiling eightq              – these three lines
no errors                     – are printed by
end of compilation            – the Pascal compiler
*EXECUTE EIGHTQ               – the user executes the compiled program
...
```

A user executes programs by typing instructions (e.g., RUN PASCAL) to the Command program. The Command program is ready to accept instructions, or commands, when it types a 'prompt' character '*'. Most commands work with files: how files are created and manipulated is described in the next section.

Experience tells us that many programs cause machine errors when they are first tested. Such errors must be intercepted by the operating system and reported to the user. Let us assume that the execution of a program is automatically terminated when an error occurs and that the Command program reports the error.

```
*EXECUTE EIGHTQ
***error in execution         – Error detected by the
  illegal memory reference    – operating system and message
  execution terminated        – typed by the Command program.
*                             – Ready for next command
```

The user can then check his program, edit the program file to change the program, and repeat the steps of compilation and execution. When the user has completed his work, the session can be terminated by 'logging-out':

```
*LOGOUT
logged out at 11:32:40 on 15 August 19XX
```

This allows the operating system to release the resources assigned to the job.

Batch jobs are executed in a similar way, using commands supplied in a deck of cards. A system process, called the *input spooler*, reads batch jobs and stores them in a file from where they can be taken for execution.

The Internal View

Every user job must be allocated resources, such as processor time and memory space, for its execution. When there are competing requirements for resources, and resources are limited, a Job Manager must decide how they must be allocated; e.g., whether memory is to be allotted to one user job or another. The Job Manager must take decisions on the allocation of resources to jobs, and it must also keep an account of the resources used by each job.

Within the operating system, which is programmed in CCNPascal, the unit for concurrent execution is the **process**. So, several user jobs can be simultaneously executed if they are processes in the operating system. If the system has a pre-declared number of *job processes*, a new user job can be 'created' by attaching it to one of these processes. The job process can then execute the commands in the user program, on behalf of the user.

```
type
  JobProcess: process;
    begin
      loop
        "Wait for a user job to appear";
        if "the job is interactive"
          then "input will come from terminal"
        else "input will come from the spooler file";
        "Execute the user job";
          {authenticate user}
          ... {execute user commands}
        "Do finalization work";
        "Update accounting file for user";
      end;
    end JobProcess;
```

The Job Initiator is a system process which has the responsibility for recognizing when an interactive user is attempting to log-in and of associating a new user job with a job process in the system. It also looks in the input spooler's file for batch jobs that are ready to be executed.

```
var
  JobInitiator: process;
    begin
```

```
loop
  if "an interactive user wants to log-in"
    or "there is a batch job waiting for execution" then
  begin
    if "there is a free job process"
      then "associate this job process with the new job";
  end;
  end;
end JobInitiator;
```

The Job Manager, and other system processes, will need to be able to access information about each user job. Two kinds of information are needed:

1. Identification of the user associated with the process, and an account of the resources used by the job.
2. Details of the program being executed by the job, and an execution *frame* which contains definitions of the storage areas assigned to the job and the value of the instruction counter when it was last executed.

The first of these is stored in the monitor, JobTable.

```
var
  JobTable: monitor;

    { declarations }

    procedure export SetId("Identification for user job");
      begin
        "Store identification of a new user job";
      end SetId;

    function export GetData("Job Number") return JobData;
      begin
        "Return data about a user job";
      end GetData;

    procedure export MarkRun("Job Number");
      begin
        "Mark job data to show that the job has been scheduled";
      end MarkRun;

    procedure export SetTime("Job Number"; "Time Used");
      begin
        "Add Time Used to the processor time used by the job";
        "Mark job data to show that the job is not being executed";
      end SetTime;

      ...

  end JobTable;
```

Different user jobs may use the same programs, e.g., the Command program is executed by all user jobs, and other programs may similarly be shared. When we say a program is shared, we really mean that its instruction part is shared: each job using the same program must have its own data part. Thus, the mapping from jobs to programs is not 1:1. A separate monitor, ProgTable, is used to keep information on the program and data parts being used, and the frame for each job.

```
var
    ProgTable: monitor;

      { declarations }

      procedure export NewProgram(...);
        begin
           "Record details of a new program being used by a job";
        end NewProgram;

      procedure export NewData(...);
        begin
           "Record details of a new data part being used by a job";
        end NewData;

      procedure export EnterProgram(...);
        begin
           "Execute the new program";
        end EnterProgram;

      procedure export LeaveProgram(...);
        begin
           "Remove entries for the program and data parts and
              return to the Command program";
        end LeaveProgram;

      procedure export GetFrames(...);
        begin
           "Supply the execution frame for a job";
        end GetFrames;

    end ProgTable;
```

The operations NewProgram and NewData are called when the user decides to execute a program. Once the details of the instruction and data parts of this program are recorded by these procedures, the job process calls the procedure EnterProgram to start the execution of the program. On completing this execution, the procedure LeaveProgram is called to return control to the Command program; this procedure is also called when a fault occurs during the execution of the called program.

For many utility programs, it would be convenient if one program could *call* another program, much as a procedure calls another procedure. This would require program calls to be nested, and for exit from one program to resume the execution of the previous program. At present, we can assume this requirement will be met by the design of the monitor, ProgTable.

A job process can be in one of three states: Runnable, when it can be executed on a processor, Blocked when it is waiting to enter a monitor or delayed on a queue variable, and IOWait when it is waiting for the completion of an input/output request. The Job Manager has the task of allocating runnable jobs to processors in a manner that is fair (i.e., no runnable process should wait indefinitely long to be executed), and that uses the system resources most effectively. Since the system has several processors, the Job Manager can schedule more than one process at a time.

```
var
    JobManager: process;

    { declarations }

    begin
    loop
        if "there is a runnable user job that is not scheduled"
        and "all processors are not busy" then
            for I in 1 to CPUMax do
                if Processor[I] "can accommodate process" then
                begin
                    ProgTable.GetFrames(CurrentFrame);
                    "Schedule chosen user job for execution
                    with CurrentFrame on Processor[I]";
                    JobTable.MarkRun("chosen user job");
                    exit;
                end;
        if "some user job has completed execution"
            then JobTable.SetTime("user job", "time used");
        if "user jobs need more memory than is available"
            then "select some program or data parts to be
                    swapped to the disk";
        if "user jobs are waiting for memory to load program or
                data parts" and "memory is now available"
            then "select program and data parts to be swapped
                    into memory";
    end;
    end JobManager;
```

A scheduled job may complete its execution because it has nothing more to do, or because it is no longer runnable. JobManager retrieves all jobs that complete execution and alters the entries in JobTable to record the processor time used by the process. When user jobs require more memory than is available, JobManager must select some program and data parts to be swapped to the disk. Similarly, when memory is available, JobManager must select swapped-out program and data segments that can be brought into memory. The actual swapping operations can be performed by a separate process, the Swapper.

FILE MANAGEMENT

The User View

Files are needed to store information that must be preserved over periods that are longer than a single job session (which is the time for which a job is logged-in). The Job Manager uses a file to store the list of registered users and their passwords, and users store programs, data and text in files. Files are managed by the File System and stored on non-volatile storage media such as disks.

Consider the following command typed by an interactive user:

```
*RUN FILECOPY(SOURCEFILE, DESTFILE)
```

which asks for the program in the file named FILECOPY to be executed. Let us assume that this program copies the contents of one file to another; in this case, the user wants the contents of the file named SOURCEFILE to be copied into the file named DESTFILE.

The program in FILECOPY will treat the strings 'SOURCEFILE' and 'DESTFILE' as names of files. The program must be able to perform operations on the files with these names. A file is represented in a program as a CCNPascal class of type SeqFile (which stands for sequential file). A program must declare a variable of this type to access a file. Operations on a file are then performed as operations on a class variable.

```
var
    Infile, OutFile: SeqFile;
```

Each variable of type SeqFile must first be associated with a file in the File System. This is done by the operation, Open. After this has been successfully done, the other operations of the class can be invoked. Let us describe the class, SeqFile.

```
type
  Access = (Read, Write, Append, Execute);
  Buffer(Size: integer) = string(Size);
  Name = string(10);

type
  SeqFile = class;

  { declarations }

  procedure export Open(Fname:Name; Facc:Access;
                        var Status:CallStatus);
    begin
      "Associate the file class with the file named by Fname";
      if "access mode Facc is permissible for file Fname"
        then Status := "success"
        else Status := "failure";
    end Open;

  procedure export Get(var UsrBuf:Buffer(?N); var Size:integer;
                       var Status:CallStatus);
    begin
      if "there are at least Size units of information
          left in the file"
        then "copy Size units to UsrBuf"
        else "copy what is left in the file into UsrBuf";
      Size := "number of units actually copied";
      if "operation was successful"
        then Status := "success"
        else Status := "failure";
    end Get;

  procedure export Put(UsrBuf:Buffer(?N); Size:integer;
                       var Status:CallStatus);
    begin
      "Copy Size units of information from the buffer, UsrBuf,
      into the file";
      if "operation was successful"
        then Status := "success"
        else Status := "failure";
    end Put;

  procedure export Close(var Status:CallStatus);
    begin
      "Terminate association between this class and the file";
      if "a file had been opened" and "it has been closed"
        then Status := "success"
        else Status := "failure";
    end Close;

end SeqFile;
```

Since the class handles sequential files, the first call to Get will read information from the start of the file and a subsequent call will read information from the point following what was last read. Similarly, the first call to Put will write information to the start of the file, and later calls will append information to what has been written.

The program in FILECOPY or, for short, the FILECOPY program, could perform its function as follows:

```
program FileCopy(SourceName, DestName: Name);

var
    InFile, OutFile: SeqFile; LengthRead: integer;
    Buf: Buffer(80); Status: CallStatus;

begin
    InFile.Open(SourceName, Read, Status);
    OutFile.Open(DestName, Write, Status);
    InFile.Get(Buf, LengthRead, Status);
    while Status ≠ "end of file" do
    begin
        OutFile.Put(Buf, LengthRead, Status);
        InFile.Get(Buf, LengthRead, Status);
    end;
end FileCopy.
```

A less trusting version of this program would, of course, check that the variable Status has the value Success, after each operation.

A file is accessed by a program, but the File System will treat every file as if it 'belongs' to some user. A program executed by a user may open only those files to which the user has access: these will include files created by the user, and files to which the user is granted access by other users. When opening a file, the kind of access required must be specified (e.g., Read access, Write access, etc) so that it can be checked against the kind of access permitted on the file (e.g., a file belonging to another user may, perhaps, be only available with Read access).

Files belonging to a user are grouped together in *directories*. A user may have a number of directories and one of these is called the *root* directory. All the directories of a user can be accessed from the root directory and every file appears in some directory. Each user has a special directory, called the 'Share' directory, which is used to access files belonging to other users. To allow another user to access a file, a user must store the file identification, and the kind of access permitted, in the Share directory of the other user.

A user refers to a file by means of a symbolic name. Corresponding to the name, a directory records the kind of access permitted on the file. At any time, a user can access files in only one directory, which is then called the 'current' directory. Any directory accessible by a user can be made the current directory. The operations to choose the current directory, and to share files, are provided in FileOps, which is a pure class as it needs to make calls to monitors in the File system.

```
var
    FileOps: pure class:

      type
        AccessRights = set of Access:

      procedure export SetCurDir(DirName:Name; var Status:CallStatus);
        begin
          "Set the directory named DirName as the current directory";
        end SetCurDir;

      procedure export SetRoot;
        begin
          "Set the root directory as the current directory";
        end SetRoot;

      procedure export SetShrDir;
        begin
          "Set the Share directory as the current directory";
        end SetShrDir;

      procedure export Share(ShrdFil,DestName:Name; Rts:AccessRights;
                             var Status:CallStatus);
        begin
          "Place an entry for the file, ShrdFil, in the
          Share directory for the user, DestName, permitting
          access according to Rts";
        end Share;

      procedure export Lookup(Fname:Name; var Status:CallStatus);
        begin
          "Check that the file Fname exists in
          the current directory for the user";
        end Lookup;

      procedure export Delete(Fname:Name; var Status:CallStatus);
        begin
          if "file Fname exists in the current directory" then
          begin
            "Delete the file Fname";
            "Delete the entry for Fname in the current directory";
          end
        end Delete;
```

procedure export NewUser(UsrName,Pswrd:Name; Quota:**integer**;
                                      var Status:CallStatus);
   begin
     "Register a new user, UsrName, with password, Pswrd,
     and set the limit for file space that can be
     allotted to this user as Quota";
   end NewUser;

procedure export Authenticate(UsrName,Pswrd:Name;
                                      var Status:CallStatus);
   begin
     "Check that the user with name, UsrName, and
     password, Pswrd, is a registered user";
   end Authenticate;

  end FileOps;

In the operations of FileOps, the variable parameter Status is set when calls are made to the File System.

The last two operations, NewUser and Authenticate, are used when a new user is to be registered and when a user is to be authenticated. Naturally, these operations must only be used by a responsible person, often called the System Administrator.

The Internal View

A file appears to a user as if it is stored contiguously in disk memory. Internally, it is more convenient to store a file in pieces, called *segments*, that can be stored wherever there is place on the disk. This makes it easier to perform operations (such as Write) that alter the size of the file. A segment is subdivided into a number of *sectors*. A segment is a unit of disk space allocation, while a sector is the unit of information that can be transferred to or from a disk. Let us assume that, for each file, there is a table giving the disk positions of the segments in that file; this table is also stored on the disk.

Since there will be many concurrent users of the system, each executing as a process, control must be exercised over access to data structures that can be shared between users. This can be done if these data structures are declared as monitors. For the operations of the file system, two monitors are needed: FileHandler, to control access to files, and DirHandler, to control access to directories. The operations performed in a user program on instances of the class, SeqFile, or by calls to the pure class, FileOps, will result in calls being made to these monitors.

```
var
  FileHandler: monitor;

    { declarations }

    procedure export Open(Fname:Name; AccMode:Access;
                          var Status:CallStatus);
      begin
        if "file Fname does not exist in current directory"
          then "create file Fname in current directory";
        if AccMode = Read
          then "wait if some other user is writing to the file"
        else
          if (AccMode = Write) or (AccMode = Append)
            then "wait if any other user is using the file";
        if "no error in operation"
          then Status := Success
        else Status := "kind of error";
      end Open;

    procedure export Read(Fname:Name; SegNum,SectorNum:integer;
                          var Buf:Buffer(?); var Status:CallStatus);
      begin
        "Using the file Fname, read into Buf
          the contents of sector SectorNum from segment SegNum";
        if "no error in operation"
          then Status := Success
        else Status := "kind of error";
      end Read;

    procedure export Write(Fname:Name; SegNum,SectorNum:integer;
                          Buf:Buffer(?); var Status:CallStatus);
      begin
        if "SegNum is the number of a new segment"
          and "there is still quota available for one segment" then
          begin
            "Allocate a new segment";
            "Decrement the quota for the current directory
              by the size of one segment";
            "Using the file Fname, write the contents of Buf
              to sector SectorNum of segment SegNum";
          end;
        if "quota was available" and "no error in operation"
          then Status := Success
        else Status := "kind of error";
      end Write;

    procedure export Close(Fname:Name);
      begin
        "Terminate operations on the file Fname";
        if "the open file Fname has been closed"
```

```
        then Status := Success
        else Status := "kind of error";
      end Close;

   procedure export Delete(Fname:Name);
      begin
        if "any other user is using the file" then "wait";
        "Delete the segments of the file";
        if "file has been deleted" then
        begin
           "Increment the quota available for
           the current directory";
           Status := Success;
        end
        else Status := "kind of error";
      end Delete;

  end FileHandler;

var
   DirHandler: monitor;

      { declarations }

   procedure export Lookup(Fname:Name; var Status:CallStatus);
      begin
        "Check if the file Fname is in the
        current directory for the user";
        if "no error in operation"
           then Status := Success
           else Status := "kind of error";
      end Lookup;

   procedure export NewEntry(Fname:Name; var Status:CallStatus);
      begin
        "Make a new entry for the file Fname
        in the current directory for the user";
        if "no error in operation"
           then Status := Success
           else Status := "kind of error";
      end NewEntry;

   procedure export DeleteEntry(Fname:Name; var Status:CallStatus);
      begin
        "Delete the entry for the file Fname
        from the current directory for the user";
        if "no error in operation"
           then Status := Success
           else Status := "kind of error";
      end DeleteEntry;
```

```
procedure export CreateDir(DirName:Name; Quota:integer;
                           var Status:CallStatus);
  begin
    "Create a new directory with the name DirName
     and a disk space allocation of Quota";
    if "the directory has been created"
      then Status := Success
    else Status := "kind of error";
  end CreateDir;

procedure export SetCurrentDir(DirName:Name;
                               var Status:CallStatus)
  begin
    "Make the directory DirName the current directory";
    if "the directory of that name can be accessed"
      then Status := Success
    else Status := "directory cannot be accessed";
  end SetCurrentDir;

procedure export SetShareDir(var Status:CallStatus);
  begin
    "Make the Share directory the current directory";
    if "Share directory can be accessed"
      then Status := Success
    else Status := "directory cannot be accessed";
  end SetShareDir;

procedure export SetRoot(var Status:CallStatus);
  begin
    "Make the root directory the current directory";
    if "root directory can be accessed"
      then Status := Success
    else Status := "directory cannot be accessed";
  end SetRoot;

procedure export DecQuota(Amount:integer; var Status:CallStatus);
  begin
    "Decrease the available quota of the current directory
     by Amount";
    if "available quota greater than Amount"
      then Status := Success
    else Status := "quota exhausted";
  end  DecQuota;

procedure export IncQuota(Amount:integer);
  begin
    "Increase the available quota of the current directory
     by Amount";
  end IncQuota;

end DirHandler;
```

There is almost overcautious use of the variable parameter, Status, in calls to the File System components. This is because these components make use of information on a disk and there is some probability (though it may be small) that hardware errors are encountered in disk read and write operations. Users set great store upon the reliability of a File System so it is prudent to make thorough checks for errors, and to report them as soon as they are noticed.

INPUT/OUTPUT ON DEVICES

The User View

A file resembles an input/output device because it can be used for writing and reading information. But a file is an abstract device, as many files are collected together (by the File System) on one physical disk. In contrast to this, there are physical devices (like card readers and terminals) that can be directly used by a program for input and output of information.

A physical device can also be represented by an abstraction if operations on the abstraction result in operations being performed on the device. We could have a different abstraction for each type of device, or one abstraction for all devices that perform sequential transfers. But an even more useful abstraction would be one that could be used either with files or with physical devices. SeqIO is a 'device independent' class type for performing sequential transfers on files or devices. In the same way that files were manipulated using instances of the class SeqFile, this class type must be instantiated in a program and each instance must be associated with a file or a physical device using the Open operation.

```
type
   CharSet = set of char;
   DevKind = (CardReader, Terminal, LinePrinter, DiskFile);

type
   SeqIO = class;

      var
         Device: DevKind;
         TermSet: CharSet;

      procedure export Open(Dev:DevKind; Fname:Name; Acc:Access;
                            var Status:CallStatus);
         begin
            Device := Dev;
```

```
    if Device = DiskFile
      then FileHandler.Open(Fname, Acc, Status)
    else
    begin
      "Acquire a physical device of kind Dev
      for access Acc";
      if "no error in operation"
        then Status := Success
      else Status := "kind of error";
    end;
  end Open;

procedure export SetEndChars(TSet:CharSet);
  begin
    TermSet := TSet;
    {The Read operation will treat characters in TermSet
    as terminating characters for input}
  end SetEndChars;

procedure export Read(var Buf:Buffer(?N); var Size:integer;
                      var Status:CallStatus);
  begin
    repeat
      if Device = DiskFile
        then FileHandler.Read(.. parameters ..)
      else "read from physical device"
    until "Size characters have been read"
      or "the last character is in TermSet";
    Size := "number of characters read";
    if "no error in operation"
      then Status := Success
    else Status := "kind of error";
  end Read;

procedure export Write(Buf:Buffer(?N); var Size:integer;
                       var Status:CallStatus);
  begin
    if Device = DiskFile
      then FileHandler.Write(.. parameters ..)
    else "write from Buf to physical device";
    if "no error in operation"
      then Status := Success
    else Status := "kind of error";
  end Write;

procedure export Close(var Status:CallStatus);
  begin
    if Device = DiskFile
      then FileHandler.Close(.. parameters ..)
    else "release physical device";
```

```
        if "no error in operation"
          then Status := Success
          else Status := "kind of error";
        end Close;

    end SeqIO;
```

Different users may simultaneously attempt to acquire the same physical device. The first user to acquire the device (using the operation, Open) will use it and other users must wait until this user releases the device (using the operation, Close).

Similar to the program, FILECOPY, there could be a program, COPY, that copies information from a file or a device to another file or device.

```
    program Copy(SourceDev, DestDev: DevKind; SName, DName: Name);
    var
        InDev, OutDev: SeqIO; CharsRead: integer;
        Status: CallStatus; Buf: Buffer(80);
    begin
        InDev.Open(SourceDev, SName, Read, Status);
        OutDev.Open(DestDev, DName, Write, Status);
        InDev.SetEndChars(Charset["Line Feed character"]);
        {A line feed character will terminate a read operation}
        InDev.Read(Buf, CharsRead, Status);
        while Status ≠ "end of file" do
        begin
            OutDev.Write(Buf, CharsRead, Status);
            InDev.Read(Buf, CharsRead, Status);
        end;
        InDev.Close(Status);
        OutDev.Close(Status);
    end Copy.
```

Once again, a more cautious program would test the value returned in the variable parameter, Status, after each call.

The Internal View

There is a fixed number of physical devices connected to a system at any time and each device can be allocated to only one user. When users perform the Open operation on the class, SeqIO, a physical device can be allotted only if it is not already in use. If the device is not free, the user must wait until it is released.

Device allocation is done in a monitor, DevAlloc.

```
var
   DevAlloc: monitor;

   type
      DevIndex = 1 .. DevMax;

   {declarations}

   procedure export Acquire(Dev:DevKind; var Num:DevIndex);
      begin
        loop
          if "device of kind Dev is free" then
          begin
            "Allot the device to this user";
            Num := "number of allotted device";
            exit;
          end
          else "Delay the user on a queue variable";
        end;
      end Acquire;

   procedure export Release(Dev:DevKind; Num:DevIndex);
      begin
        "Release device number Num of kind Dev";
        if "any other users are waiting for this device"
           then "Continue one user";
      end Release;

   end DevAlloc;
```

MEMORY MANAGEMENT

The User View

Users of the system are only indirectly aware of the way main memory and disk memory are managed. An interactive user will notice that there is a delay in response from a program when it is swapped out, but the user cannot decide either when it is to be swapped out or when it will be brought into memory. No user has need to deal with memory addresses, either for the disk or for main memory. In many respects, memory management is transparent to users. The only property of memory that the user does need to be concerned with is the allotted size: there are usually limits to the main memory and the disk memory that can be allotted to each user.

The Internal View

Memory management is one of the most important functions of resource management that the operating system has to perform. The overall efficiency of the system is closely dependent on the way main memory is allocated to user jobs, and the speed of access to information on the disk is affected by the way disk space is managed.

All physical memory can be characterized by two attributes: the starting address of a *segment* of memory, and its size. In the kind of multiprocessor system we shall be considering (which is described in Chapter 3), main memory is composed of some shared memory and some local memory for each processor. Similarly, disk memory is composed of separate packs, each characterized by the identification of the pack. But once the kind of memory (i.e., the kind of main memory, or the particular disk pack) is selected, space within the memory has enough similarity for us to consider a common abstraction to perform the operations of allocation and release of segments of memory. These operations will deal with memory in terms of segments.

A simple and basic allocator which can be used for administering both the main memory and disk memory would have the structure:

```
type
  Allocator = class;
    type export
      Seg =
        record
          Loc,                    {Starting address of segment}
          SegSize: integer {Size of segment}
        end Seg;

    var
      Chunk: Seg; {Memory available for allocation}

    procedure export Allot(SSize:integer; var ReqSeg:Seg);
      begin
        if "a segment of size SSize can be taken from Chunk"
          then "set its starting address and size in ReqSeg"
          else return error;
        end Get;

    procedure export Release(OldSeg:Seg);
      begin
        "Add the segment OldSeg to Chunk";
        end Release;
```

```
     begin
        "Set the address and initial size of memory in Chunk";
     end Allocator;
```

This simple allocator has some notable deficiencies, such as the fact that the Release operation cannot just add the returned segment to Chunk unless they happen to be contiguous. But these limitations can be overcome by adding more detail to the internal structure of the class so, for the moment, we can ignore them.

A main memory allocator can be built using this class.

```
var
   MemAlloc: monitor;
     type
        MemKind = (Shared, Local1, Local2, ... LocalN);
     var
        MemArray: array [MemKind] of Allocator;

     procedure export Allot(Where:MemKind; Size:integer;
                                 var ReqSeg:Seg);
        begin
        loop
          MemArray.Allot[Where](Size, ReqSeg)
             iferror "wait for memory of this kind to be released"
             otherwise exit;
          end;
        end Allot;

     procedure export Release(Where:MemKind; OldSeg:Seg);
        begin
          MemArray[Where].Release(OldSeg);
          if "some user is waiting for memory of this kind"
             then "Continue one user";
        end Release;

   end MemAlloc;
```

A similar monitor can be built for disk space allocation.

```
var
   DiskAlloc: monitor;
     type export
        PackId = "identification for disk packs";

     var
        DiskArray: array [1 .. DriveMax] of Allocator;

     procedure export Allot(Pack:PackId; Size:integer; ReqSeg:Seg;
                                 var Found:Boolean);
```

```
    begin
      DriveNum := "drive on which Pack is mounted";
      DiskArray[DriveNum].Allot(Size, ReqSeg);
      if "segment was Allotted"
        then Found := true
        else Found := false;
    end Allot;

  procedure export Release(Pack:PackId; OldSeg:Seg);
    begin
      DriveNum := "drive on which Pack is mounted";
      DiskArray[DriveNum].Release(OldSeg);
    end Release;

end DiskAlloc;
```

Since disk space is allotted for relatively long periods, it would not serve any purpose to delay a user if space cannot be found for a request. So a Boolean, Found, is set to **true** if space has been found and to **false** if no space is available. Disk packs can be mounted on any available disk drive, so the drive number for a pack must be found by looking up a table of all the mounted packs.

THE KERNEL

The Kernel of the operating system is not 'visible' at all to user programs so we need consider only its internal view. The Kernel has two main purposes:

1. To provide the basic operations necessary to support concurrency in CCNPascal, and
2. To perform machine-dependent operations that cannot be done within the rest of the operating system.

The operations required for the first purpose will be evident from Chapter 2. The machine-dependent operations required for the operating system are those that deal with input and output on devices, and those that manipulate the internal registers of each processor in the system.

To the operating system, the Kernel is a pure class with a number of operations. Many of these operations can be written in CCNPascal but some will need to be programmed in assembly language.

```
    var
      Kernel: pure class;
```

```
procedure export Run("Process Number"; "Process Descriptor";
                     "Time Allotted");
  begin
    "Execute the process for a specified time";
  end Run;

procedure export Suspend;
  begin
    "Suspend the process' execution";
  end Suspend;

procedure export ProgramCall("New Program");
  begin
    "Call a new program for execution";
  end ProgramCall;

procedure export ProgramReturn;
  begin
    "Return from a program to the previous program";
  end ProgramReturn;

procedure export DiskRead("Drive"; "Disk Address";
                          "Memory Address"; "Size";
                          var "Status");
  begin
    "Read from the disk into memory";
  end DiskRead;

procedure export DiskWrite("Drive"; "DiskAddress";
                           "Memory Address"; "Size";
                           var "Status");
  begin
    "Write from memory to the disk";
  end DiskWrite;

procedure export Read("Device Kind"; "Device Number";
                      "Memory Address"; "Size";
                      var "Status"; var "Count");
  begin
    "Read from a device into memory";
  end Read;

procedure export Write("Device Kind"; "Device Number";
                       "Memory Address"; "Size";
                       var "Status"; var "Count");
  begin
    "Write from memory to a device";
  end Write;

end Kernel;
```

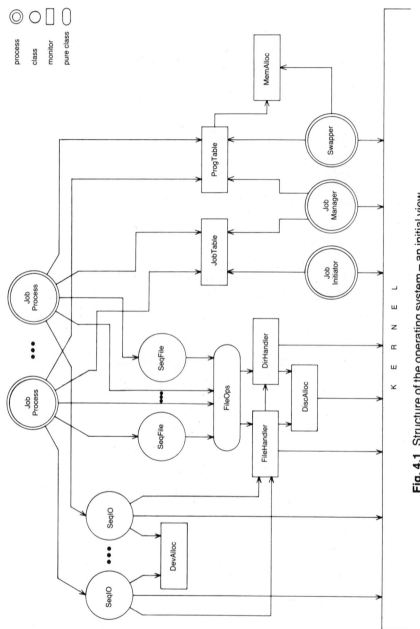

Fig. 4.1 Structure of the operating system – an initial view.

DISCUSSION

We can now collect together the components described in this chapter and present them diagrammatically in Fig. 4.1 to give a structural overview of the whole operating system.

The design of each component has emerged from a study of the requirements. Starting with the question "What does the operating system need to do?" we have tried to answer the question, "How does it perform its functions?". The user view describes the answer to the first question and the internal view the answer to the second.

As we mentioned earlier, the structure that has been designed here has to be modified to take account of several factors. Problems of implementation, and reasons of efficiency, require us to redesign many of the abstractions of this chapter. Some abstractions will merely be slightly altered, as a result of more careful design. Others may change their form considerably, and still others may need to be broken up into different abstractions altogether.

In the design of any large system, this degree of redesign is not surprising. As more considerations come into focus, and as there is a better understanding of the problems, it is inevitable that major changes take place in a design.

EXERCISES

1. In the outline of ProgTable given in this chapter, a user job can call one program at a time. How would the structure of this monitor need to be altered if user jobs are permitted to call a program which can then call another program, and so on? Assume that when it completes its work, each program must return control to the previous program. Is it necessary to set an upper limit to the number of program calls that can be nested in this way?

    (*Hint*: Assuming program names are unique, use a stack to save the name of the calling program and the address to which control must be returned after a call is over.)

2. The program FileCopy allows a user to copy information from one file to another. However, it has been assumed that both files are in the same directory, and that this directory is the current directory. Modify this program to be able to copy from a file in one directory to a file in another directory. Note that only one directory can be the current directory at any time.

3. Assume two user programs, A and B, each need a card reader and a line printer and that there is only one of each of these devices in the system. If

program A acquires the line printer and program B acquires the card reader, each program will wait for the other to release its device before it can proceed, and the programs will be 'deadlocked'. How can you alter the monitor **DevAlloc** to avoid this problem?

(*Hint*: Insist that a program is either allotted *all* the devices it needs or none at all, and that it must release all the devices it has acquired before it can ask for any more.)

4.   Assume S1 and S2 are two records of type **Seg** which represent segments of memory. What conditions must be satisfied by the values of their fields, **Loc** and **SegSize**, for the segments to be contiguous? Also, write a procedure to merge two segments if they are contiguous.

5   A BASIC MEMORY ALLOCATOR

Introduction

An important resource in a computer system is memory—in single processor systems it was probably the most important resource and operating systems have sometimes succeeded, or failed, merely because of the techniques they used to manage memory.

For purposes of resource management in an operating system, memory can be divided into segments, each of which is characterized by its location and size. In a multiprocessor system, we have also to consider that the entire main memory may not be accessible to every processor. A process running on a processor can then only be allotted memory from what can be addressed by that processor (conversely, a process can only be scheduled to execute on a processor that can access the memory in which the program's instructions and data are stored). Another attribute, though less critical in our case, is that of speed : the execution time of a program can usually be reduced if it has been allotted faster memory (assuming, of course, that there is a choice). And, apart from the basic speed of the memory, the *effective* access time for memory may differ depending on the path on which it is connected to a processor. For example, there will be fewer delays in access to local memory than for shared memory which has to be multiplexed between several processors through a switch.

We shall not consider differences in memory speeds in our basic memory allocator as we will assume that memory can be classified into large disjoint partitions and that all locations within a partition have the same access time for a processor. For example, the local memory of a processor is a partition that can be accessed only by that processor; shared memory is a partition that can be accessed by any processor. In this chapter, we will design a basic allocator for one partition of memory. In two succeeding chapters, we will show how such an allocator can be used for different partitions of memory and for allocating space on a disk.

Representing Memory in an Operating System

The two attributes of a single partition of memory that can be used in the allocator are its starting address, or location, and its extent, or size. If we divide a partition into *segments*, we can initially assume that the whole partition is one segment and define a record, Seg, with two fields to represent memory:

```
type
  Seg =
    record
      Loc, SegSize: integer
    end Seg;
```

and we can describe a variable of type Seg in terms of the values of its fields Loc and SegSize. If the smallest and largest values of Loc in a partition of memory are denoted by the constants MinLoc and MaxLoc, for any variable, Frag, of type Seg there are some invariant properties that must be maintained:

$$\text{MinLoc} \leq \text{Frag.Loc} \leq \text{Frag.Loc} + \text{Frag.SegSize} \leq \text{MaxLoc}$$

Let us assume the allocator starts with all the memory in a partition being represented by a variable, MainChunk, with the pair of values

```
MainChunk.Loc = MinLoc
MainChunk.SegSize = MaxLoc – MinLoc + 1
```

A request for a segment of memory can be met if the required size is not greater than MainChunk.SegSize. We can treat the allocation of a segment of memory as the result of an operation that splits a segment into two: in this case, MainChunk will be split and a new segment, Frag, made of the requested size. Similarly, when a segment Frag is freed, we can assume that there is an operation by which it is merged with MainChunk, provided it is adjacent; i.e., if

```
MainChunk.Loc = Frag.Loc + Frag.SegSize
```

or

```
Frag.Loc = MainChunk.Loc + MainChunk.SegSize
```

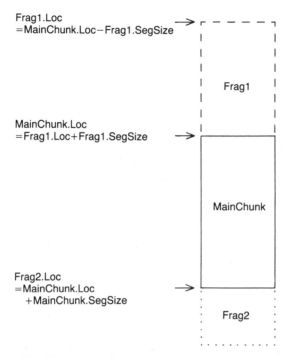

Frag1.Loc
=MainChunk.Loc−Frag1.SegSize

MainChunk.Loc
=Frag1.Loc+Frag1.SegSize

Frag2.Loc
=MainChunk.Loc
+MainChunk.SegSize

Fig. 5.1 Three adjacent memory segments.

We give below a Boolean function, Adjacent, and two procedures, Split and Merge, which can be used to operate on variables of type Seg. It will be seen that the procedure Split makes a new segment from the 'lower' (i.e., low address) end of a larger segment.

```
function Adjacent(X,Y:Seg) return Boolean;
  begin
    return (X.Loc = Y.Loc + Y.SegSize) or (Y.Loc = X.Loc + X.SegSize)
  end Adjacent;

procedure Split(var Chunk,Frag:Seg; ReqSize:integer);
  begin
    with Frag do
    begin
      Loc := Chunk.Loc;
      SegSize := ReqSize;
    end;
    with Chunk do
    begin
      SegSize := SegSize − ReqSize;
      Loc := Loc + ReqSize;
    end
  end Split;
```

```
procedure Merge(var Chunk,Frag:Seg);
  begin
    with Frag do
    begin
      Chunk.SegSize := Chunk.SegSize + SegSize;
      if Chunk.Loc = Loc + SegSize
        then Chunk.Loc := Loc;
      SegSize := 0;
    end
  end Merge;
```

Note that the operations Split and Merge do not check that the preconditions necessary for their correct operation do, in fact, hold: e.g., when Split is called, it is assumed that

Chunk.SegSize ⩾ ReqSize

and the statements of Merge are only valid if Chunk and Frag are adjacent (which can be tested using the function Adjacent).

Outline of a Memory Allocator

The memory allocator needs two primary operations which can be called Allot, to allocate memory, and Release, to return memory. Let us assume the variable, MainChunk, has been initialized. (We shall freely use the names of variables of type Seg as if they *are* segments, instead of merely representing them: thus we may refer to the initial block of memory as MainChunk.)

The basic memory allocator should be easily usable for managing any of several partitions of memory. We can assume for the moment that a complete memory allocator is a monitor within which there are instances (or *instantiations*) of the basic allocator, one for each partition of memory. If this is so, the basic allocator can be declared as a class.

```
type
  Allocator = class;

    type export
      Seg =
        record
          Loc, SegSize: integer
        end Seg;

    var
      MainChunk: Seg;

    function Adjacent(X,Y:Seg) return Boolean;
```

procedure Split(**var** Chunk,Frag:Seg; ReqSize:**integer**);

procedure Merge(**var** Chunk,Frag:Seg);

procedure export Allot(**var** Slot:Seg; Size:**integer**);

procedure export Release(**var** Slot:Seg);

end Allocator;

The parameters for a call to the procedure Allot are a variable, Slot, which will be set to represent the allocated segment if the call is successful, and a value, Size, to specify how much storage is required; there will be an error return from the procedure if the request cannot be honored. Similarly, a call to Release requires a variable, Slot: if this call is successful, Slot will be cleared, but if it is unsuccessful, Slot will be unchanged and an error will be returned. We shall deal with the case of unsuccessful calls in the next chapter.

From the point of view of the allocator, calls to Allot are honored as long as there is memory available, and calls to Release cause space to be added to the pool of available memory. Unfortunately, though, segments are rarely released in the *order* in which they were allocated. To take an extreme example, if all the available memory were allocated as segments $S_1,...S_n$, in that order, and segments $S_1,S_3,S_5,...$ are then released, we would have

$$\text{total memory available} = \Sigma S_i.\text{SegSize} \quad \text{for } i = 1, 2, 3, ...$$

The *total* memory available for allocation at this point may then be an appreciable fraction of the size of the partition. But the size of the largest request that can be honored will be restricted to that of the largest of $S_1,S_3,S_5,...$ Hence, though it may appear that the total space available is adequate for a request, there may be no single segment large enough to meet the request. In this example, none of the returned segments is adjacent to any other so we cannot even merge two segments to produce a larger segment. Such *fragmentation* of memory is an important concern in memory management and we shall describe ways in which its effects can be reduced.

As a first step, we can distinguish between requests for 'large' and 'small' amounts of memory: large segments of memory are typically required for programs or data, while small segments often serve different needs, such as those for file directories etc. We can therefore expect small segments to have a significantly different pattern of use from that of large segments and different allocation techniques will be needed to meet these two requirements. Let a small segment be one whose size is less than or equal to the value of a constant, Small.

```
procedure export Allot(var Slot:Seg; Size:integer);
  begin
    if Size ≤ Small then
      if MainChunk.Size > Size
        then "allocate small segment"
        else return error
      else
      if MainChunk.Size > Size
        then "allocate large segment"
        else return error;
  end Allot;

procedure export Release(var Slot:Seg);
  begin
    if Slot.SegSize ≤ Small then
      if "small segment is adjacent to MainChunk"
        then "add small segment to MainChunk"
        else return error
      else
      if "large segment is adjacent to MainChunk"
        then "add large segment to MainChunk"
        else return error;
  end Release;
```

Allocating Segments from a Large Chunk

The procedure Split is the operation to divide a large chunk in two, with one piece of a specified size. We can use it to allocate storage for segments from MainChunk. This is done in the procedure TryMainChunk.

```
procedure TryMainChunk(var Slot:Seg; ReqSize:integer;
                              var Found:Boolean);
  begin
    if MainChunk.SegSize ≥ ReqSize then
    begin
      Split(MainChunk, Slot, ReqSize);
      Found := true;
    end
    else Found := false;
  end TryMainChunk;
```

The next step is to decide how large and small segments are to be made from the single variable, MainChunk. Having already distinguished between these segments because of the differences in their use, we should plan different techniques for their allocation and release.

If each segment were to be used for the same length of time, any technique of allocation would work: but we expect small segments to be used and released at a rate different from that of large segments. If segments of either size were arbitrarily created by splitting MainChunk, we would encounter the familiar problem of fragmentation when they were returned—though there may be enough memory available, it may be dispersed in fragments that are each too small to meet the allocation requests. A simple preventive for this would be to allocate small and large segments from different parts of the memory; but we must do this without dividing memory by a rigid boundary or else we may find there is memory available on one side of the boundary when there is none on the other.

We can get the advantages of having a boundary, without its disadvantages, by a very simple technique: small segments can be allocated from the low address end of MainChunk and large segments from the high address end, so that any unallocated memory is in the middle and available for use as either small or large segments. This can be visualized as a scheme with a floating boundary between the memory used for small and large segments. The modified form of the procedure TryMainChunk performs this allocation.

```
procedure TryMainChunk(var Slot:Seg; ReqSize:integer;
                       var Found:Boolean);
var
    Temp: Seg;
begin
    if MainChunk.SegSize ⩾ ReqSize then
    begin
        Found := true;
        if ReqSize ⩽ Small
            then Split(MainChunk, Slot, ReqSize)
        else
        begin
            Split(MainChunk, Temp, MainChunk.SegSize – ReqSize);
            Slot := MainChunk;
            MainChunk := Temp;
        end;
    end
    else Found := false;
end TryMainChunk;
```

The Split operation makes new segments from the low end of a chunk so it can be directly used to make small segments. To make large segments from the high end of MainChunk, we first create a temporary segment of size equal to (MainChunk.SegSize – ReqSize) from the low end of MainChunk. MainChunk will then be left with the required large segment which is copied into the parameter, Slot. The temporary segment is then copied back to MainChunk. An initial test (MainChunk.SegSize ⩾ ReqSize) ensures that the operations are only performed when there is enough memory available.

Returning Memory—Fragmentation Problems

The technique of allocating small segments from one end of a chunk and large segments from the other helps to reduce fragmentation—it still does not prevent it altogether. The reason is that segments, whether small or large, will often (or even usually) be returned in an order quite different from that in which they were allocated. A returned segment may therefore not be adjacent to MainChunk and cannot then be merged with it. But, assuming all allocated memory is returned at some time, each segment will eventually be found adjacent either to MainChunk or to some other segment.

To handle such 'unmergeable' segments, we can hold them in a list. But as we should still keep small and large segments apart, we shall declare two separate lists, SmallSegs and LargeSegs, of type Segments:

```
type
  Segments(Max: integer) =
    record
      Last: 0 .. Max;
      List: array [1 .. Max] of Seg
    end Segments;
```

(Segments is a generic record type: when it is instantiated, an integer constant defines the actual value corresponding to the formal name, Max. Different instances of Segments may have different instantiation parameters, and will then differ in the range for the field, Last, and in the size of the array field, List.)

Unmerged segments can be stored as elements of the array field, List. The field, Last, is the index of the last element to be filled; we must take care to ensure that the filled elements are at one end of the array and empty elements, if there are any, at the other end.

If SMax and LMax are integer constants, the two variables could be declared as

```
var
  SmallSegs: Segments(SMax); LargeSegs: Segments(LMax);
```

Choosing from a Set of Segments

The procedure Allot can now allocate memory in two ways: from

MainChunk, as before, or from one of the unmerged segments in the lists. But if an unmerged segment is allocated, it could leave an empty 'hole' in the list. To avoid this, a procedure Contract is used to copy the last element of the list into the hole.

```
procedure Contract(var Segs:Segments(?); Posn:integer);
  begin
    with Segs do
    begin
      List[Posn] := List[Last];
      Last := Last – 1;
    end
  end Contract;
```

An economical way to choose a segment from the list would be to select one of size closest to (but not smaller than) the required size. This is done in the procedure, BestFit, where we assume an integer constant, Largest, is the largest permissible size for any segment.

```
procedure BestFit(var Segs:Segments(?); var Slot:Seg;
                  ReqSize:integer; var Found:Boolean);
  var
    Trial, Fit, Piece, Best: integer;
  begin
    Piece := 0; Best := 0; Fit := Largest; Found := false;
    with Segs do
    begin
      repeat
        Piece := Piece + 1;
        Trial := List[Piece].SegSize;
        if (Trial ≥ ReqSize) and (Trial < Fit) then
        begin
          Fit := Trial; Best := Piece;
        end
      until (Trial = ReqSize) or (Piece = Last);
      if Best ≠ 0 then
      begin
        if Fit = ReqSize then
        begin
          Slot := List[Best];
          Contract(Segs, Best);
        end
        else Split(List[Best], Slot, ReqSize);
        Found := true;
      end
    end
  end BestFit;
```

The first part of the procedure has a loop in which ReqSize is compared with the sizes of segments in the list. The segment chosen for allocation is either

1. The first in the list with size equal to ReqSize, or
2. The first in the list with the smallest size that is larger than ReqSize.

In (1), the new segment is made by copying the old one; this will leave an empty entry in the list which must be removed by calling the procedure Contract. In (2), the chosen segment is split to make the new segment.

It should be noted that the procedure BestFit takes a parameter of type Segments: it can therefore be used to find segments in either SmallSegs or LargeSegs. A similar pattern can be followed for other procedures.

There are other ways in which to find space for the required segment from those in the list.

1. A simple change to BestFit would be to stop the search when the *first* segment of adequate size was found (if we did this, we should probably also change the name of the procedure to FirstFit!). This would give us a procedure that was faster in execution. The cost to be paid would be that some segments would unnecessarily be split into smaller units that may each be too small to meet any request.
2. Another way would be to add a field, MaxSize, to the record type Segments. This field could then be set to the size of the largest segment in the list, and the list would not need to be scanned at all unless MaxSize was at least as large as the required size. There would, however, be the added cost of updating the value of MaxSize when a segment was added to, or allocated from, the list.
3. An alternative organization would be to have one list, rather than two, storing small segments from one end and large segments from the other. This would have the advantage that instead of each list being of fixed size, there would only be a limit to the sum of the numbers of small and large segments in the list. But to avoid small and large segments getting interspersed, we would still need to store the positions of the last entry for each kind of segment.

To choose between these possibilities we need to know more about the typical sizes of segments that the basic allocator will handle. Remembering that different requirements could be met by one of these techniques, the rest of the basic allocator will be developed using the procedure BestFit. This is a reasonable choice, especially if we note that when segments on a list are of only one size, BestFit functions exactly as a 'first-fit' procedure.

Compaction of Segments

The next possibility we have to consider is that two entries in a list may represent segments that are adjacent. If this is so, these segments can be compacted to produce larger segments from which allocation is easier. The procedure Compact scans a list of segments, merges adjacent segments, and then calls the procedure Contract to remove any holes that may have formed.

```
procedure Compact(var Segs:Segments(?); var Merged:Boolean);
  var
    Piece, NextPiece: integer;
  begin
    Piece := 1; Merged := false;
    with Segs do
      while Piece < Last do
      begin
        NextPiece := Piece + 1;
        while NextPiece ≤ Last do
        begin
          if Adjacent(List[Piece], List[NextPiece]) then
          begin
            Merge(List[Piece], List[NextPiece]);
            Contract(Segs, NextPiece);
            Merged := true;
            NextPiece := Piece + 1;
          end
          else NextPiece := NextPiece + 1;
        end;
        Piece := Piece + 1;
      end;
  end Compact;
```

The Boolean parameter Merged is set to **true** if any adjacent segments are merged. Compact can also be used on either of the two segment lists.

Merging Segments with MainChunk

The last step in combatting fragmentation is to merge segments back into MainChunk; this reduces the lengths of the segment lists and increases the size of MainChunk, making it easier to meet demands for larger segments. It is this step that has the effect of creating the floating boundary between small and large segments: when segments are released after peaks of activity, they can be added to MainChunk so that the storage is made available for other requests.

```
procedure Remerge(var Segs:Segments(?); var Merged:Boolean);
  begin
    Merged := false;
    with Segs do
      for Piece in 1 to Last do
        if Adjacent(MainChunk, List[Piece]) then
        begin
          Merge(MainChunk, List[Piece]);
          Contract(Segs, Piece);
          Merged := true; exit;
        end;
  end Remerge;
```

The procedure Remerge has a single loop to test if any segment is adjacent to MainChunk; the loop terminates either when the whole list has been scanned, *or when a segment has been merged with* MainChunk. There is, however, the possibility that after one segment has been merged, another segment may be adjacent to the new value of MainChunk. This suggests that we repeat the loop until no segment is found to be adjacent to MainChunk. We can avoid this if we take care that each call to Remerge is preceded by a call to Compact as we can then be sure that all adjacent segments in the list have been merged, leaving no more than one segment that can be adjacent to MainChunk.

Operation of the Whole Allocator

We have assumed that the traffic in small segments will be different from that of large segments. Also, it is evident that when segments are small there can only be small differences in their sizes. To avoid the overhead of frequently allocating similar-sized small segments and then, on release, attempting to merge them into MainChunk, it would be useful to keep as many returned small segments as possible in SmallSegs.List and to merge them only when this list is full. On the other hand, large segments can vary considerably in size and allocation of new large segments will be more successful if the returned large segments are merged, whenever possible, with MainChunk. With the procedures we have already described, this strategy is easily programmed.

```
procedure export Allot(var Slot:Seg; Size:integer);
  var
    Found, Merged: Boolean;
  begin
    Found := false;
    if Size ≤ Small then
      if SmallSegs.Last = 0
      then TryMainChunk(Slot, Size, Found)
      else
```

```
      begin
        BestFit(SmallSegs, Slot, Size, Found);
        if not Found
           then TryMainChunk(Slot, Size, Found);
        if not Found then
        begin
           Compact(SmallSegs, Merged);
           if Merged
              then BestFit(SmallSegs, Slot, Size, Found);
           if not Found then
           begin
              Remerge(SmallSegs, Merged);
              if Merged
                 then TryMainChunk(Slot, Size, Found)
           end
        end
      end
    else
    begin
      if LargeSegs.Last ≠ 0
         then BestFit(LargeSegs, Slot, Size, Found);
      if not Found
         then TryMainChunk(Slot, Size, Found);
    end;
    if not Found
       then return error;
  end Allot;
```

The alternative ways of finding the required space are examined in the following order:

If there is at least one segment on a list, call BestFit.

If there are no segments on a list, or if none of the segments is large enough, call TryMainChunk to see if a segment of the right size can be made from MainChunk.

If neither of these attempts succeeds, and a large segment is required, the call must be rejected; if, however, a small segment is required, then try again after calling Compact to merge adjacent segments and, if that fails, call Remerge to merge a segment with MainChunk, if that is possible, and try again.

The Release operation has to complement the strategy used in Allot by keeping small segments in SmallSegs.List unless it is full, and by merging large segments whenever possible.

One possibility we have not yet considered is that a list may be full with unmergeable segments, so that no more segments can be returned: this will result in a kind of deadlock as the only way segments in a full list can be merged will be with segments that are to be returned. We must therefore ensure that the last place on each list is always kept empty so that every returned segment will have a chance of being merged either with segments on a list or with MainChunk. This is done in the procedure Release. When a segment supplied in a call to Release cannot be merged with a segment in a list or with MainChunk, and the list is full, the segment is removed from the list and the call returns with an error. The procedure NewSeg is used to add a segment to a list, and Remove to take the last segment off a list.

```
procedure export Release(var Slot:Seg);
   var
      Space: integer; Done, Merged: Boolean;

   procedure NewSeg(var Segs:Segments(?));
      {When this procedure is called
       Last is always < size of Segs.List}
      begin
        with Segs do
        begin
          Last := Last + 1;
          List[Last] := Slot;
        end
      end NewSeg;


   procedure Remove(var Segs:Segments(?));
      {Remove the last segment to be added
       i.e., the segment supplied in Slot}
      begin
        with Segs
          do Last := Last – 1
      end Remove;
   begin {Release}
      Done := true; Space := Slot.SegSize; Merged := false;
      if Space ≤ Small then
      begin
        NewSeg(SmallSegs);
        if SmallSegs.Last = SMax then
        begin
          Compact(SmallSegs, Merged);
          if not Merged then
          begin
            Remerge(SmallSegs, Merged);
            if not Merged then
            begin
              Remove(SmallSegs);
              Done := false;
            end
          end
        end
      end
end
```

```
      else
      begin
        NewSeg(LargeSegs);
        Compact(LargeSegs, Merged);
        Remerge(LargeSegs, Merged);
        if LargeSegs.Last = LMax then
        begin
          Remove(LargeSegs);
          Done := false;
        end
      end;
      if not Done
        then return error;
    end Release;
```

Whenever possible, a returned segment will be added to the memory being managed by the allocator. When a segment cannot be returned, its representation in Slot is left unchanged. In the next chapter, we shall discuss how rejected requests to Allot or Release will be handled.

In order for the allocator to get its initial values for MainChunk, we need a procedure to which these values are passed. MainChunk is then initialized by entering these values into its Loc and SegSize fields. We shall see in the two succeeding chapters that these values can vary between different instances of the allocator or, at different times, even for the same instance. According to the technique used to allocate and free memory, the value of MainChunk.SegSize will only represent the total memory available when there are no segments on any of the lists.

```
    procedure export SetMem(InitAdd,InitSize:integer);
      begin
        with MainChunk do
        begin
          Loc := InitAdd; SegSize := InitSize;
        end;
      end SetMem;
```

The allocator is initialized with the block

```
    begin
      SmallSegs.Last := 0; LargeSegs.Last := 0;
      with MainChunk do
      begin
        Loc := 0; SegSize := 0;
      end;
    end Allocator;
```

Making the Allocator Generic

Looking only at declarations in the type Allocator, we have

```
type Allocator = class;

    const
        Small = ...; SMax = ...; LMax = ...;

    type export
        Segments(Max : integer) =
                        record
                            Last : 0 .. Max;
                            List : array[1 .. Max] of Seg
                        end Segments;

    var
        MainChunk : Seg;
        SmallSegs : Segments(SMax); LargeSegs : Segments(LMax);

        ...

    end Allocator;
```

In the declaration of the type, Segments, the parameter Max determines the range of values that can be taken by Last, and the number of entries there can be in List. As we wished to have differently sized data structures for small and large segments, the constants SMax and LMax were used in the variable declarations for SmallSegs and LargeSegs.

But if we wish to use the same allocator type for different kinds of memory, we have an additional requirement. The sizes of these memories may vary considerably, and we would expect large memories to have many more fragments than smaller memories. Is it then realistic to use the same constant values for SMax and LMax? Ideally, we would like to be able to use instances of the same allocator with values of SMax and LMax chosen appropriately for the size of memory to be administered. We must therefore make these generic parameters of the type Allocator, so that actual values are supplied at the time of declaration. This would also be true for the choice of value for Small (and, in fact, for the value of Largest, but we can ignore this if its value is kept sufficiently high). With these changes, the type Allocator becomes:

```
type Allocator(Small, SMax, LMax:integer) = class;

    ... type, variable and procedure declarations ...

    end Allocator;
```

The complete listing is given at the end of the chapter.

DISCUSSION

The design of the basic allocator illustrates one way in which memory allocation can be handled in an operating system. Each segment of memory is represented by a record with fields for the starting address and size. This *indirect* representation allows the allocator to deal with memory that it need not (and perhaps cannot) address directly. Without this constraint, the allocator could use locations in the segments themselves to chain them into a list and procedures similar to those we have described could then be used for allocation and release of segments. This technique has often been used in operating systems. It has one advantage: it does not require fixed size arrays, such as SmallSegs and LargeSegs, to hold the representation of segments so that there would never be need to reject requests to release memory. It shares another advantage with our basic allocator, as in both cases the allocator needs to represent only the memory that is available for allocation and not the memory that has been allocated. Thus, if a large fraction of memory is usually allocated to user programs, the arrays SmallSegs and LargeSegs need only be used to store the unmerged segments that remain.

When the operating system is in a 'steady state', i.e. when the pattern of jobs it is executing is not changing, we would expect the array SmallSegs to contain the number of small segments that are cycled through allocation and release. When the job load changes, this number could also change. The parameter SMax must therefore be set to be the largest number of small segments that is normally required. If this is done, these segments can be rapidly allocated and released without any delay for compaction. The parameter LMax must, on the other hand, be set to the value of the maximum number of large segments that are liable to be unmergeable at any time. To be safe, this parameter must be set to a reasonably large value. We have already discussed alternative ways of handling segment lists, which may reduce or avoid the effects of these limitations (but usually with some other price to be paid).

Another well known way of representing memory is by a 'bit-map', with one bit, whose value indicates if the associated segment is allocated or free, being used to represent the smallest segment that can be allocated. To represent memory of N such segments, we would need a Boolean array

```
var
  Free: array [1 .. N] of Boolean;
```

with an element being **true** if the corresponding segment is free. In an actual implementation, such an array would be declared as *packed*, so that the Booleans occupied successive bits in words of storage. We can re-write the procedures Allot and Release to use this data structure to allocate small and large segments starting from opposite ends of the memory.

```
procedure export Allot(var Slot:Seg; Size:integer);
  var
    Qty: integer;
  begin
    Qty := 0;
    if Size ≤ Small then
      for Posn in 1 to N do
        if Free[Posn] then
        begin
          Qty := Qty + 1;
          if Qty = Size then
          begin
            for Start in Posn – Size + 1 to Posn
              do Free[Start] := false;
            with Slot do
            begin
              Loc := Posn – Qty + 1; Size := Qty;
            end;
            return ;
          end;
        end
        else Qty := 0
    else
      for Posn in N downto 1 do
        if Free[Posn] then
        begin
          Qty := Qty + 1;
          if Qty = Size then
          begin
            for Start in Posn to Posn + Size – 1
              do Free[Start] := false;
            with Slot do
            begin
              Loc := Posn; Size := Qty;
            end;
            return ;
          end;
        end
        else Qty := 0;
    return error;
  end Allot;
```

```
procedure export Release(var Slot:Seg);
  begin
    with Slot do
      for Posn in Loc to Loc + Size – 1
        do Free[Posn] := true;
  end Release;
```

The relative simplicity of these procedures is appealing, especially when compared with the procedures of the basic allocator. And there are many cases when the 'bit-map' technique would be far preferable, especially as there is never a problem of calls to Release being rejected. But what are its disadvantages?

A minor problem is that the simple allocation technique can result in small and large segments being interspersed as there is no 'boundary' between them. A more important disadvantage is that the 'bit-map' technique requires storage to represent *both* allocated and free segments. Even if only one bit is needed for each segment, this can amount to a substantial requirement if segments are small. For example, if the smallest segment size is 32 words, memory of just 64K words would need an array of 2048 bits (or 128 words on a 16 bit computer). With larger memory sizes, which we will encounter when designing the disk space allocator, this requirement becomes appreciable (e.g., 32,000 bits for memory of 1M words).

Another disadvantage is that, though the Allot procedure is simple, it is also relatively slow. The *average* search time in a table of N bits is of the order of $N/2$. With values of N being in the thousands, $N/2$ is large and the average search time could easily amount to several milliseconds. On the other hand, the Release procedure is almost trivially simple and extremely fast.

Some computers have instructions that make 'bit-map' operations particularly fast. The DEC System 10 and the Vax 11/780 each have a single instruction that will find the first bit set in a word and use of this will speed up the outer loop of the Allot procedure given above by a large factor. If there are B bits per word, the average search time is reduced to about $N/2B$. This technique is used primarily in operating systems that are coded in assembly language. By performing an arithmetic test for non-zero on a word *before* using the bit searching instruction, and combining this with loop counting in index registers, the actual search time can be made quite low. We could use this technique by calling a specially coded assembly language procedure to perform this operation. The 'bit-map' allocator can be made more efficient by increasing the size of the smallest allocatable unit: this will reduce its storage requirement and speed up its execution. But such a step could also be used to reduce the list handling problems of the basic allocator. In both these cases, we would then be trading-off the internal fragmentation in users' programs against the speed and storage of the allocator.

We could combine the advantages of both techniques in an allocator which used lists for allocation but which also represented storage in a bit map. At the cost of increasing storage for the allocator, we would then be able to allocate segments *and* release segments quickly. We leave the actual choice of technique open at this point and, in the two subsequent chapters, when we refer to the 'basic' allocator we shall mean an allocator such as one of those we have discussed here.

Summary

The problem of fragmentation of memory was discussed by Randell (1969) who made the distinction between internal and external fragmentation, i.e., between using a large segment size which will result in some wastage for most programs, and using a small segment size which leaves unmergeable fragments with the allocator. Knuth (1969) describes several techniques for allocating variable size segments. He considers the question of whether to allocate the best or the first fit for a segment and concludes that the latter is usually preferable. In general, the first fit method is suited to the case when no distinction can be made in the patterns of use of different sizes of segments. It also assumes that when the first suitable segment is split to meet the request, there is a high probability of using the remaining piece. There is a great body of literature on studies of memory allocation in systems that have paging and segmentation (also called virtual storage), but much of this is particular to the system studied. McKeag and Hoare (1972) describe several important memory management techniques and provide a good summary. Parmelee *et al.* (1972) give an account of the virtual storage and virtual machine concepts of CP-67 for the IBM System/360 Model 67 and conclude their paper with an extensive annotated bibliography of most of the publications in the area.

EXERCISES

1.   Problems of memory fragmentation occur whenever allocation of variable size segments is allowed. The basic allocator assumes memory sizes fall into just two groups—small and large—and the method we adopted is to allocate small segments from one side of the memory and large units from the other side. Assume a performance analysis shows that memory is usually allocated

in one of *four* different sizes. Is the same method of allocation effective? If memory is *only* allocated in one of four different sizes, how will you alter the basic allocator?

2. Consider the management of segment lists in our basic allocator.
    (a) Segments in the lists SmallSegs and LargeSegs are not ordered according to size. The procedure BestFit therefore has to search through the whole list unless it finds a segment of exactly the right size. Maintaining a list with segments ordered by size would require only half the list to be searched, on the average. Why is this method not used here?
    (b) Why is compaction not always attempted when a segment is added to a list? This will certainly minimize the list length. Are there any drawbacks in doing so?
    (c) Assume we replace the two lists, SmallSegs and LargeSegs, by one list in which we add small segments at one end and large segments at the other. How will the procedure, BestFit, need to be changed?

3. (Group Exercise.) Two other memory allocation techniques have been suggested in this chapter: (a) assuming the whole memory is addressable by the allocator, segments are chained together using storage in each segment to store the links, and (b) the bit-map method. Write complete basic allocators for these two different schemes and compare their memory requirements.

4. A particular system executes jobs that each require memory in the following sizes and order:

    10, 2, 50, 4, (4), .. repeat .. 4, (4), (50), (2), (10)

    | .. Start .. | .. Main Execution .. | .. End .. |

    where the numbers are in units of *blocks* and a number in parentheses indicates return of memory to the allocator. After the short starting phase, the job repeatedly requires a 4 block buffer for input and output during its execution phase. Jobs are initiated at random intervals and the system must execute as many jobs as possible with memory limited to 1000 blocks. Design a memory allocator for the system.

    Suppose now that the system is extended to include a new kind of job with the following sequence of memory requests:

    5, 1, 20, 8, (8), .. repeat .. 8, (8), (20), (1), (5)

    If jobs of this kind are interleaved with the other jobs, how will you need to alter your design?

THE BASIC MEMORY ALLOCATOR PROGRAM

```
{***                        ***}
{*** The Memory Allocator ***}
{***        – Outline      ***}

type
    Allocator(Small, SMax, LMax: integer) = class;

        function Adjacent(X,Y:Seg) return Boolean;
        procedure Split(var Chunk,Frag:Seg; ReqSize:integer);
        procedure Merge(var Chunk,Frag:seg);
            {The function and the two procedures are used for
            operations on objects of type Seg}
        procedure Contract(var Segs:Segments(?); Posn:integer);
            {Removes the segment at Posn from the list Segs}
        procedure BestFit(var Segs:Segments(?); var Slot:Seg;
                                ReqSize:integer; var Found:Boolean);
            {Puts in Slot the index of the segment with size
            which best fits the ReqSize: else sets Found to false}
        procedure Compact(var Segs:Segments(?); var Merged:Boolean);
            {Merges together adjacent segments in Segs, if possible}
        procedure Remerge(var Segs:Segments(?); var Merged:Boolean);
            {Merges segments in Segs with MainChunk, if possible}
        procedure TryMainChunk(var Slot:Seg; ReqSize:integer;
                                var Found:Boolean);
            {Gets a segment of ReqSize from MainChunk, if possible}
        procedure export Allot(var Slot:Seg; Size:integer);
            {Puts in Slot a segment of Size; returns error if no space}
        procedure export Release(var Slot:Seg);
            {Releases the segment in Slot; returns error if not released}
        procedure export SetMem(InitAdd,InitSize:integer);
            {Sets initial values for the starting address
            and size of MainChunk}
    end Allocator;


{***                        ***}
{*** The Memory Allocator ***}
{***    – Implementation   ***}

type
    Allocator(Small, SMax, LMax: integer) = class;

        type export
            Seg =
                record
                    Loc, SegSize: integer
                end Seg;
```

```
type
  Segments(Max: integer) =
    record
      Last: 0 .. Max;
      List: array [1 .. Max] of Seg
    end Segments;

var
  MainChunk: Seg;
  SmallSegs: Segments(SMax); LargeSegs: Segments(LMax);

function Adjacent(X,Y:Seg) return Boolean;
  begin
    return (X.Loc = Y.Loc + Y.SegSize)
           or (Y.Loc = X.Loc + X.SegSize)
  end Adjacent;

procedure Split(var Chunk,Frag:Seg; ReqSize:integer);
  begin
    with Frag do
    begin
      Loc := Chunk.Loc;
      SegSize := ReqSize;
    end;
    with Chunk do
    begin
      SegSize := SegSize – ReqSize;
      Loc := Loc + ReqSize;
    end
  end Split;

procedure Merge(var Chunk,Frag:Seg);
  begin
    with Frag do
    begin
      Chunk.SegSize := Chunk.SegSize + SegSize;
      if Chunk.Loc = Loc + SegSize
        then Chunk.Loc := Loc;
      SegSize := 0;
    end
  end Merge;

procedure Contract(var Segs:Segments(?); Posn:integer);
  begin
    with Segs do
    begin
      List[Posn] := List[Last];
      Last := Last – 1;
    end
  end Contract;
```

```
procedure BestFit(var Segs:Segments(?); var Slot:Seg:
                   ReqSize:integer; var Found:Boolean):
  var
    Trial, Fit, Piece, Best: integer;
  begin
    Piece := 0; Best := 0; Fit := Largest; Found := false;
    with Segs do
    begin
      repeat
        Piece := Piece + 1;
        Trial := List[Piece].SegSize;
        if (Trial ≥ ReqSize) and (Trial < Fit) then
        begin
          Fit := Trial; Best := Piece;
        end
      until (Trial = ReqSize) or (Piece = Last);
      if Best ≠ 0 then
      begin
        if Fit = ReqSize then
        begin
          Slot := List[Best];
          Contract(Segs, Best);
        end
        else Split(List[Best], Slot, ReqSize);
        Found := true;
      end
    end
  end BestFit;

procedure Compact(var Segs:Segments(?); var Merged:Boolean);
  var
    Piece, NextPiece: integer;
  begin
    Piece := 1; Merged := false;
    with Segs do
      while Piece < Last do
      begin
        NextPiece := Piece + 1;
        while NextPiece ≤ Last do
        begin
          if Adjacent(List[Piece], List[NextPiece]) then
          begin
            Merge(List[Piece], List[NextPiece]);
            Contract(Segs, NextPiece);
            Merged := true;
            NextPiece := Piece + 1;
          end
          else NextPiece := NextPiece + 1;
        end;
        Piece := Piece + 1;
      end;
  end Compact;
```

```
procedure Remerge(var Segs:Segments(?); var Merged:Boolean);
  begin
    Merged := false;
    with Segs do
      for Piece in 1 to Last do
        if Adjacent(MainChunk, List[Piece]) then
        begin
          Merge(MainChunk, List[Piece]);
          Contract(Segs, Piece);
          Merged := true;
        end;
  end Remerge;


procedure TryMainChunk(var Slot:Seg; ReqSize:integer;
                       var Found:Boolean);
  var
    Temp: Seg;
  begin
    if MainChunk.SegSize ≥ ReqSize then
    begin
      Found := true;
      if ReqSize ≤ Small
        then Split(MainChunk, Slot, ReqSize)
      else
      begin
        Split(MainChunk, Temp, MainChunk.SegSize − ReqSize);
        Slot := MainChunk;
        MainChunk := Temp;
      end;
    end
    else Found := false;
  end TryMainChunk;

procedure export Allot(var Slot:Seg; Size:integer);
  var
    Found, Merged: Boolean;
  begin
    Found := false;
    if Size ≤ Small then
      if SmallSegs.Last = 0
        then TryMainChunk(Slot, Size, Found)
      else
      begin
        BestFit(SmallSegs, Slot, Size, Found);
        if not Found
          then TryMainChunk(Slot, Size, Found);
        if not Found then
        begin
          Compact(SmallSegs, Merged);
          if Merged
            then BestFit(SmallSegs, Slot, Size, Found);
          if not Found then
```

```
          begin
            Remerge(SmallSegs, Merged);
            if Merged
              then TryMainChunk(Slot, Size, Found)
          end
        end
      end
    else
    begin
      if LargeSegs.Last ≠ 0
        then BestFit(LargeSegs, Slot, Size, Found);
      if not Found
        then TryMainChunk(Slot, Size, Found);
    end;
    if not Found
      then return error;
  end Allot;

procedure export Release(var Slot:Seg);
  var
    Space: integer; Found, Merged: Boolean;

  procedure NewSeg(var Segs:Segments(?));
    begin
      with Segs do
      begin
        Last := Last + 1;
        List[Last] := Slot;
      end
    end NewSeg;

  procedure Remove(var Segs:Segments(?));
    begin
      with Segs
        do Last := Last − 1
    end Remove;

  begin {Release}
    Done := true; Space := Slot.SegSize; Merged := false;
    if Space ≤ Small then
    begin
      NewSeg(SmallSegs);
      if SmallSegs.Last = SMax then
      begin
        Compact(SmallSegs, Merged);
        if not Merged then
        begin
          Remerge(SmallSegs, Merged);
          if not Merged then
```

```
                begin
                  Remove(SmallSegs);
                  Done := false;
                end
              end
            end
          end
          else
          begin
            NewSeg(LargeSegs);
            Compact(LargeSegs, Merged);
            Remerge(LargeSegs, Merged);
            if LargeSegs.Last = LMax then
            begin
              Remove(LargeSegs);
              Done := false;
            end
          end;
          if not Done
            then return error;
        end Release;

procedure export SetMem(InitAdd,InitSize:integer);
  begin
    with MainChunk do
    begin
      Loc := InitAdd; SegSize := InitSize;
    end;
  end SetMem;

begin
  SmallSegs.Last := 0; LargeSegs.Last := 0;
  with MainChunk do
  begin
    Loc := 0; SegSize := 0;
  end;
end Allocator;
```

6 THE MAIN MEMORY ALLOCATOR

Introduction

The basic storage allocator of Chapter 5 handles requests for allocating and releasing segments of storage in sizes that are multiples of a small unit. These segments are pieces of one large partition which is administered by the allocator. The allocator is basic, in the sense that it has not been designed for any particular kind or amount of storage. From the overview of the operating system in Chapter 4, we know that one requirement of such an allocator is to be able to allocate and release segments of the main, or primary, memory of the system. We have already seen in Chapter 3 that the main memory of our system is not a monolithic unit (as is often the case in single processor systems) but consists of one partition that is shared among all the processors and some partitions that are each accessible by only one processor. In other words, no processor can access the entire memory of the system.

Since the basic allocator only deals with managing the memory in one partition, we will need separate allocators for the shared and local memories in the system. What are the system level consequences of this decision? Does it mean, for example, that each local memory allocator must run on its own processor and the shared memory allocator on one (or any) processor?

A useful characteristic of the basic allocator is that it does not need to access the storage it handles. Storage is represented in the allocator in terms of the abstraction, Seg, which only contains the starting address and size of a segment. This means that the allocation of the local memory of one processor need not be performed on that processor. Therefore, the answer to the question is that though we will need as many allocators as there are partitions of memory they can, in principle, be executed on any processor. The choice of processor on which an allocator can be run does not depend on the partition of memory it is managing, but on where the data structures for the allocator are stored. We could decide this at the time of generating the operating system or, if we wished to copy the data structures from one local memory to another, at run time. As explained in Chapter 3, we can retain flexibility in the execution of the operating system if important structures such as these are always kept in shared memory so that they are accessible from any processor.

We can declare the main memory allocators for the system by a declaration such as

```
var
    Shared: Allocator("generic parameters");
    Local: array [1 .. CPUMax] of Allocator("generic parameters");
```

which will give us one allocator for each partition of memory.

Outline of the Main Memory Allocator

The functional view of the basic allocator would be in terms of its externally visible procedures:

```
type
    Allocator(Small, SMax, LMax: integer) = class;

        procedure export Allot(var Slot:Seg; Size:integer);
            begin
                "Get a segment of memory";
                "if space not allotted then return error";
            end Allot;

        procedure export Release(var Slot:Seg);
            begin
                "Return a segment of memory";
                "if space not returned then return error";
            end Release;

        procedure export SetMem(InitAdd,InitSize:integer);
            begin
                "Initialize MainChunk";
            end SetMem;

    end Allocator;
```

At this level, we can ignore differences between a list-based allocator and a 'bit-map' allocator and just assume that both the procedures Allot and Release return with an error if the operations are unsuccessful. When there is no error return, there is really nothing further that needs to be done. But otherwise, we come up with a problem: do we just reject the call, or can we automatically retry the call later when (hopefully) it may be more successful?

The feature offered by the language to allow a process to be delayed is the queue variable, upon which the operations **delay** and **continue** can be performed. But queue variables can only be declared in monitors, or in other structures that are used only in monitors, while Allocator is of type **class**. If this were the only problem, we could of course convert the type Allocator into a monitor and, within this monitor, delay processes whose requests are unsuccessful and resume them when space became available. For main memory, this would be a satisfactory solution because memory is certain to be released when jobs cease execution. This is not true of disk memory which is used for 'pervasive' objects, such as files which outlive the programs that create them and which may be retained for days or months. It would be greatly inconvenient, and unrealistic, to keep requests for disk space pending until file space is released. (In the next chapter, we shall also see that the handling of disk errors is another reason for a disk space allocator to differ from a main memory allocator.)

Another alternative is to define a main memory allocation monitor for *each* kind of memory. This is perfectly workable and, in many cases, would be the ideal choice. It does have the disadvantage that we would need many monitors, each with its own queues to delay processes. For this reason, we shall not make this choice here but it should be noted that there may be situations where this alternative would be preferable. However, let us instead declare a new monitor, MainMem, within which *all* the instances of Allocator for main memory allocation are declared. Requests that fail at the first attempt can be delayed and continued for subsequent attempts, using queue variables declared in this monitor. Assume the kinds of memory are represented by the values of the enumerated type

    type
      MemKind = (Share, Loc1, Loc2, ... , LocN);

where N = CPUMax, the maximum number of processors in the system, and the ellipses (...) denote other elements of the enumeration.

    type
      MainMem(SmallSize, ShdMax1, ShdMax2, LocMax1, LocMax2: **integer**)
      = **monitor**;
        ...

```
var
    Shared: Allocator(SmallSize, ShdMax1, ShdMax2);
    Local: array [Loc1 .. LocN]
            of Allocator(SmallSize, LocMax1, LocMax2);

    ...

end MainMem;
```

MainMem is also a generic type, and the values of its generic parameters are used in the declarations of the variables, Shared and Local. SmallSize is the limit to the size of small segments, and the other parameters are used to define the maximum lengths of the lists in each instance of Allocator. A request for allocation or release of memory must now specify the kind of memory it relates to, apart from the parameters required for the procedures Allot and Release of the basic allocator.

Delaying Requests

Requests to get memory can fail because there is no single piece of the necessary size, and requests to return memory can fail if the lists of memory segments are full and segments cannot be merged because of fragmentation. In both these cases, failed requests must be delayed and retried later when conditions have changed. We use a record, MemReq, to represent a delayed request.

```
type
    MemReq =
    record
        Mem: MemKind;
        MemQ: queue
    end MemReq;
```

The number of delayed requests can be at most equal to ProcMax, the maximum number of processes in the system, so we can declare a table of delayed requests as an array

```
var
    Requests: array [1 .. ProcMax] of MemReq;
    Pending: integer;
```

where Pending is used to count the number of requests that have been delayed. The procedures Hold and Resume can be used to delay and continue requests.

```
procedure Hold(Place:MemKind);
  begin
    with Requests[ProcId] do
    begin
      Mem := Place;
      Pending := Pending + 1;
      delay(MemQ);
      Pending := Pending - 1;
    end
  end Hold;

procedure Resume(Place:MemKind);
  begin
    if Pending > 0 then
      for Indx in 1 to ProcMax do
        with Requests[Indx] do
          if delayed(MemQ) and (Mem = Place)
            then continue(MemQ);
  end Resume;
```

The Kernel function, ProcId, returns the unique number of the process making the call, and this number is used to choose an entry in the table, Requests. The parameters and local variables of a delayed process retain their values until execution of the process is resumed, and these variables are not accessible to any other process. The procedure Hold will keep a record of the kind of memory being requested and increment the count of pending requests before the process is delayed. The procedure Resume will continue the execution of *all* processes waiting for one kind of memory.

We now have all the data structures needed for the monitor, MainMem, and the statements of its procedures Allot and Release can now be composed. Note that we are free to use the same names for these procedures as were used for Allocator: since calls to these procedures will always be qualified by the name of the variable of which they are part, there will be no confusion.

```
procedure export Allot(Choice:MemKind; Amount:integer;
                       var Allotment:Allocator.Seg);
  var
    Found: Boolean;
  begin
    Found := true;
    repeat
      case Choice of
        Share: Shared.Allot(Allotment, Amount)
                 iferror Found := false;
        otherwise: Local[Choice].Allot(Allotment, Amount)
                 iferror Found := false
      end;
```

```
            if not Found
                then Hold(Choice)
                else Resume(Choice);
            until Found;
        end Allot;

    procedure export Release(Which:MemKind; var Piece:Allocator.Seg);
    var
        Done: Boolean;
    begin
        Done := true;
        repeat
            case Which of
                Share: Shared.Release(Piece)
                            iferror Done := false;
                otherwise: Local[Which].Release(Piece)
                            iferror Done := false
            end;
            if not Done
                then Hold(Which)
                else Resume(Which)
        until Done;
    end Release;
```

A successful call to Release will return memory and may also reduce some of the internal fragmentation in the allocator. This could result in

1. A memory segment of a larger size being available for allocation, or
2. The number of segments in lists in the allocator being reduced, so that more entries are now available for returned segments.

A successful call to Allot will reduce the memory available for allocation but it may also have the effect described in 2.

As we cannot predict the effects of successful calls, since these will depend on the internal data structures of the allocator, we follow a simple rule: after every successful call to return one kind of memory, resume the execution of *all* pending requests, for that kind of memory. An unsuccessful call to Allot will be delayed (possibly more than once) until its request can be met: a successful call, on the other hand, may reduce the length of a segment list in the allocator so that a pending call to return memory can then succeed. To be strict, it is only the pending calls in Release that need to be resumed at this point but we have taken the simpler alternative of resuming all calls. A refinement would be to have a more selective procedure that performed just the necessary resumptions.

Finally, we need a procedure in which the starting address and size of each kind of memory is initialized. If each local memory has the same starting address and size, this procedure could take the form

```
procedure export SetMem(ShdAddr,ShdSize,LocAddr,LocSize:integer);
   begin
      Shared.SetMem(ShdAddr, ShdSize);
      for I in Loc1 to LocN
         do Local[I].SetMem(LocAddr, LocSize);
      end SetMem;
```

where we have used the (partial) definition of the enumerated type, MemKind.

DISCUSSION

The advantages of designing an 'abstract' memory allocator have been that different instances of the allocator can be used for different purposes, with each instance retaining the basic properties of the allocator. Once each allocator has been initialized for the partition of memory it is to handle, details of the allocation and release of segments of memory can be largely ignored. In practical terms, it means that there is considerable saving in program size, since just one copy of the instructions of the allocator is required and only the data structures of different instances need separate space. Moreover, reducing the program size has the other advantage that program maintenance and modification become easier.

There are, of course, some disadvantages too. While the advantage of abstraction should always be that a level of detail can be ignored, this is only accomplished by some loss of fine control. We can see evidence of this in the way pending requests are handled, as we have no way of assuring that a request that is continued after a delay will be successful. In fact, a request may be retried several times before it is honoured. To avoid this, we could add a number of additional checks but, unless they were planned with great care, they would make the program more obscure and have doubtful advantage. To have real effect, we would need to monitor the performance of the system in practical use and then add just enough checks to improve the efficiency. At the same time, the trade-off between the degree of internal and external fragmentation must be balanced and sizes for allocation chosen so that memory can be efficiently used and quickly allocated and released. Such fine tuning is an important part of implementing operating systems.

The memory allocator described in this chapter serves as a kind of 'envelope', collecting in one place the allocators for different partitions of memory. It does little by way of implementing policies. Simple extensions to this allocator would allow waiting processes to be ordered by priority, or by the sizes of their requests for memory. In Chapter 11, where we discuss job management, we shall see how policies at a higher level can be applied to alter the rate of execution, or the response times, of jobs. It is at that level that memory allocation decisions must be coordinated with scheduling policies. Here, we shall just assume that higher level decisions take account of the total memory in the system and that long queues for memory are not built up. This will justify fairly simple techniques for resuming pending requests for memory. As mentioned earlier, it is also possible to break up the single memory monitor into separate monitors for each kind of memory, improving the degree of concurrency. We did not do this here, largely to avoid the extra overhead of managing several sets of queues.

EXERCISES

1. Some operating system processes may need to be able to ask for memory *without* being delayed if memory is not available. Write a new procedure, OSAllot, which performs allocation in this way. How can you also ensure that these processes are not delayed when returning memory? [*Hint*: keep a separate list of segments returned by operating system processes, for which release is still pending].

2. Sketch the broad procedure-level outline and give the details of queue handling that will be required if the single monitor described here is replaced by one monitor for each kind of memory.

3. Assume delayed requests for memory are to be ordered according to the size of the request, so that smaller requests are serviced before larger requests. How can this be accomplished while ensuring that there is no 'starvation', i.e., that no request is kept waiting indefinitely long?

THE MAIN MEMORY ALLOCATOR PROGRAM

```
{***                          ***}
{*** Main Memory Allocator ***}
{***          – Outline        ***}

type
    MainMem(SmallSize, ShdMax1, ShdMax2, LocMax1, LocMax2) =
    monitor;

        procedure Hold(Place:MemKind);
            {Delay a process for memory of kind MemKind}
        procedure Resume(Place:MemKind);
            {Continue all processes waiting for memory of kind MemKind}
        procedure export Allot(Choice:MemKind; Amount:integer;
                            var Allotment:Allocator.Seg);
            {Allocate memory space of size Amount and kind Choice}
        procedure export Release(Which:MemKind; var Piece:Allocator.Seg);
            {Return the memory segment Piece of kind Which}
        procedure export SetMem(ShdAddr,ShdSize,LocAddr,
                            LocSize:integer);
            {Set limits to the sizes of shared and local memories}

    end MainMem;


{***                          ***}
{*** Main Memory Allocator ***}
{***     – Implementation     ***}

{The following enumeration type must be defined according to the}
{system configuration; Share refers to the shared memory and there}
{must be one value, LocM, for each of M local memories}
type
    MemKind = (Share, Loc1, Loc2, ... , LocN);

type
    MainMem(SmallSize, ShdMax1, ShdMax2, LocMax1, LocMax2) =
    monitor;

        {SmallSize = largest size of small segment}
        {ShdMax1,ShdMax2 = lengths of the lists of small and large segments}
        { for the shared memory}
        {LocMax1,LocMax2 = lengths of the lists of small and large segments}
        { for each local memory}

        type
            MemReq =
```

```
          record
            Mem: MemKind;
            MemQ: queue
          end MemReq;

var
    Shared: Allocator(SmallSize, ShdMax1, ShdMax2);
    Local: array [Loc1 .. LocN]
              of Allocator(SmallSize, LocMax1, LocMax2);
    Requests: array [1 .. ProcMax] of MemReq;
    Pending: integer;

procedure Hold(Place:MemKind);
   begin
     with Requests[ProcId] do
     begin
       Mem := Place;
       Pending := Pending + 1;
       delay(MemQ);
       Pending := Pending − 1;
     end
   end Hold;

procedure Resume(Place:MemKind);
   begin
     if Pending > 0 then
        for Indx in 1 to ProcMax do
          with Requests[Indx] do
             if delayed(MemQ) and (Mem = Place)
                then continue(MemQ);
   end Resume;

procedure export Allot(Choice:MemKind; Amount:integer;
                       var Allotment:Allocator.Seg);
   var
      Found: Boolean;
   begin
     Found := true;
     repeat
       case Choice of
          Share: Shared.Allot(Allotment, Amount)
                       iferror Found := false;
          otherwise: Local[Choice].Allot(Allotment, Amount)
                       iferror Found := false
       end;
       if not Found
          then Hold(Choice)
          else Resume(Choice)
     until Found;
   end Allot;
```

```
procedure export Release(Which:MemKind; var Piece:Allocator.Seg);
var
   Done: Boolean;
begin
   Done := true;
   repeat
      case Which of
         Share: Shared.Release(Piece)
                     iferror Done := false;
         otherwise: Local[Which].Release(Piece)
                     iferror Done := false
      end;
      if not Done
         then Hold(Which)
      else Resume(Which)
   until Done;
end Release;


procedure export SetMem(ShdAddr,ShdSize,LocAddr,
                        LocSize:integer);
begin
   Shared.SetMem(ShdAddr, ShdSize);
   for I in Loc1 to LocN
      do Local[I].SetMem(LocAddr, LocSize);
   end SetMem;

begin
   Pending := 0;
end MainMem;
```

A variable of this type can now be declared, giving values for the generic
parameters SmallSize, ShdMax1, ShdMax2, LocMax1, LocMax2; e.g.

```
var
   MemorySpace: MainMem(... parameter values ...);
```

7 THE DISK SPACE ALLOCATOR

Introduction

The next use for the basic memory allocator is to administer requests for disk space. There are obvious similarities between main memory and memory on a disk, such as the facts that space on the disk has contiguous addresses and that it can be allotted in small units (usually called *sectors* or *blocks*, but we will sometimes use the term segments to refer both to them and to contiguous areas of main memory). These similarities make it possible to use the basic allocator for disk space allocation. But, compared to main memory, access to disk storage is relatively slow and radical improvements in the performance of a system can often be accomplished by minimizing the average seek time to the disk. The techniques used for disk space allocation, and for access to the disk, must therefore also take account of the essential characteristics of disk memory devices.

Apart from their differences with main memory, disk memories themselves vary considerably in their capacity and seek time. The table below gives some performance figures for typical disk drives; these figures are only indicative, because products from different manufacturers may have different characteristics, and disk technology is rapidly improving.

Disk Type	Capacity in Mbytes	Av. Seek Time in ms
Floppy disk	0.25–2	300
Disk cartridge	2–20	40–60
Disk pack	29–300	30–60
Winchester pack	600	25–30

(An interesting feature of this technology is that while improvements in packing density allow disk capacity to be doubled every two years or so, the reliability also shows improvement and 600 Mbyte Winchester technology disk drives have greater capacity *and*, often, greater reliability than, say, 100 Mbyte disk pack drives!)

A disk pack has several disks, or *platters*, stacked one above the other; a disk cartridge has a single platter. A platter has two recording surfaces and most present-day disk drives have read–write heads that move over a surface.

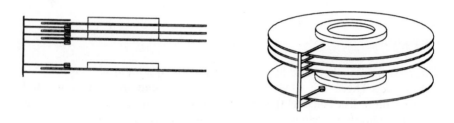

Fig. 7.1 Two views of a disk pack with some disks removed to show the position of the read/write heads.

We shall consider the characteristics of such moving head drives in the design of the disk space allocator, ignoring fixed head disks that are, in any case, becoming less popular (some recent Winchester drives also have fixed heads on one surface, in addition to moving heads for the other surfaces, but we shall ignore this feature).

For moving head disks, the time to access a sector of a track is the sum of the seek time, or the time it takes the heads to move to the right track, and the latency time, which is the rotational delay before the right sector comes under the heads. The average seek time is approximately one-half the time it takes the read–write heads to move from one extreme position to another. The average revolution time is around 160 ms for a floppy drive and 16 ms for a Winchester drive, and the average latency time is one-half the revolution time.

There is little that can be done to minimize the latency time in disk access (though special disk drives and controllers have been built to do this, they have not proved to be particularly reliable). But we can obviously reduce the seek time if information can be arranged on the disk so that it is clustered together near the mean, or middle, position of the heads. This will combine effectively with the well known 'elevator algorithm' to bring the average access time close to the minimum (a CCNPascal version of this algorithm was given in Chapter 2; another version, in Modula, can be found in Wirth, 1977).

Rather than consider each of the wide variety of disks available, let us design our disk space allocator for an 'abstract' disk so that we can temporarily ignore differences in performance and capacity. The abstract disk will be accessed in terms of *cylinders*, where a cylinder is defined as consisting of tracks with the same track number on each surface. There is no disk head movement needed to access different sectors in one cylinder. Let this disk have a total capacity of T bytes, which is divided into C cylinders of S sectors. If each sector holds m bytes, we have

$$T = C \times S \times m$$

We can view this disk as having C cylinders, numbered from 0 to CMax (where CMax = C − 1). The maximum seek time will be required when the heads move from one end to the other, i.e. from cylinder 0 to cylinder CMax or vice versa, and the mean position of the heads will be over cylinders (CMax/2) or (CMax/2)+1. On many disks, especially the smaller ones, the storage space on a cylinder may not be very large when compared to the average size of files that are to be stored on the disk. So the abstract disk will be divided into sets of N consecutive cylinders, and each such set will be called a *group*. Assuming C is a multiple of N, if there are G groups (numbered from 0 to GMax) the capacity T can be written as

$$T = G \times N \times S \times m$$

Allocation in a Group

Space in a group can be treated as a contiguous area over which the seek time is roughly uniform (when N = 1, the seek time will be exactly equal for any sector in the cylinder, and for small values of N the approximation is still reasonable). Within a group, space can then be allocated in any units that are multiples of a sector in size. Once again, space will usually be required in two or more sizes, one of which is small and the others larger. For example, file directories will typically occupy small fixed size units of space while user files may be spread over larger units. These requirements match well with the provisions in the basic allocator, so there should be no difficulty in using it for allocation of space within a group.

Disk memory differs from main memory primarily in having far larger capacity and a relatively slower rate of use. It is therefore impractical to keep the allocation data for all groups in main memory at one time. Further, disk packs are removable and, even if main memory space were available, it would be altogether an extravagance to keep such information about every disk pack in the main memory. Obviously then, we must plan to keep the bulk of the information on the disk, in specially identified areas. How do we partition the allocation data into convenient units? The answer will depend on the size (in bytes) of the group and on a judicious trade-off between the main memory space that can be spared for storing part of the allocation data and the time it will take to get another part of the data from the disk, when necessary. With the wide range of disk capacities that is available, it is difficult to provide a single good answer.

Let us assume that the allocation data for just one group is kept in main memory at any time, which is a reasonable choice if the size of the group is appropriately chosen. For a group Ki ($0 \leq i \leq$ GMax) the disk space allocator can then allot space for an area that has a starting address consisting of a cylinder number (equal to Ki $\times$ N) and a segment number within that group.

The division of the disk into groups is a logical partitioning done for reasons of disk space allocation. Outside the allocator, groups will have no meaning and disk addresses will be represented in a single, uniform way. A disk address has the following fields: Pack, to store the identification of the pack, Cyl, to represent the cylinder number within that pack, and DiskSeg, which has the starting sector number in that cylinder, and the size of the segment.

```
type
  DiskAdr =
    record
      Pack: PackId;
      Cyl: integer;
      DiskSeg: Allocator.Seg
    end DiskAdr;
```

PackId is a type whose values are the identification names of disk packs. A distinguished value of PackId, BlankName, is used during initialization and in case of errors. (The term 'pack' is used here to refer to the storage medium on a disk drive, irrespective of whether it is a floppy disk, a cartridge or a disk pack.)

For the allocator, disk addresses can be converted from the form in DiskAdr into group numbers and sector numbers within a group. Let G groups on the disk be numbered from 0 to GMax (note GMax = G − 1). If D is a variable of type DiskAdr, the group number Ki can be found by the expression

$$Ki = D.Cyl \ \textbf{div} \ N$$

and the sector SN within this group will be

$$SN = (D.Cyl \ \textbf{mod} \ N) * S + D.DiskSeg.Loc$$

Conversely, given a sector SN within a group Ki, we have

$$D.Cyl = (Ki * N) + (SN \ \textbf{div} \ S)$$
$$D.DiskSeg.Loc = SN \ \textbf{mod} \ S$$

Outline of the Disk Allocator

The disk subsystem consists of a number (DiskMax) of disk drives on which disk media (e.g., packs, cartridges or floppies) can be mounted. At any time, as many disk space allocators will be needed as there are drives. The allocation data for each pack will be stored on the disk itself at fixed locations, and the data for each group will be brought into the main memory as needed.

Requests for disk space allocation and release can come from different concurrent processes so the disk allocator must be a monitor. There will be one instance of this monitor to administer space for each mounted pack and the identification of the pack will be stored in a variable, ThisPack. Another variable, ThisGroup, will be set to the number of the group (within this pack) for which allocation data is in the main memory—this will sometimes be referred to as the 'current' group. To allocate and release space within the current group, we will use an instantiation, GroupAlloc, of type Allocator.

Each group in the pack will be identified by an integer in the range 0 .. GMax. During the execution of the system, disk space will be allocated and released in response to calls from users and, naturally, some groups will be fully allocated. Searching through every group to see if space is available for a request will be a slow business as it will require the allocation data for each group to be brought into main memory from the disk. To avoid this, a request to allocate or return space is classified by its size as a value (Small, Large) of type RequestKind. Every group has an associated array of type GroupStatus, consisting of two Boolean elements which indicate when there is no space on the group for small or large requests. The values of the Booleans in this array can be used to choose a group which may have space of the required size, and to avoid unnecessary searching in groups that are full.

To distinguish between small and large requests, the monitor has a parameter, SmallSize, as the limit for the size of a small segment. Two other parameters, SSectMax and LSectMax, determine the lengths of the queues in the basic allocator. GMax is the highest group number, CMax the highest cylinder number, N the number of cylinders in a group and S the number of sectors in a cylinder.

```
type
    DiskAlloc(GMax, CMax, N, S, SmallSize, SSectMax, LSectMax: integer)
    = monitor;

    type export
        DiskAdr =
            record
                Pack: PackId;
                Cyl: integer;
                DiskSeg: Allocator.Seg
            end DiskAdr;
    type
        RequestKind = (Small, Large);
        GroupStatus = array [RequestKind] of Boolean;

    var
        ThisPack: PackId;
        GroupFull: array [0 .. GMax] of GroupStatus;
        ThisGroup: integer;
        GroupAlloc: Allocator(SmallSize, SSectMax, LSectMax);

    procedure export Allot(var Place:DiskAdr; Size:integer;
                           var Done:Boolean);
    var
        Kind: RequestKind;
    begin
        Done := false;
        "Set Kind to be Small or Large, according to Size";
        while not Done and "all groups have not been tried" do
        begin
            "Call GroupAlloc.Allot to get space"
            iferror
                begin
                    GroupFull[ThisGroup][Kind] := true;
                    "Replace ThisGroup with another for which
                    GroupFull[Group number][Kind] ≠ true";
                end
```

```
        otherwise Done := true
   end;
 end Allot;
```

```
procedure export Release(var Place:DiskAdr);
  begin
    if ThisGroup ≠ "Group number of address in Place"
      then "replace ThisGroup with the required group";
      "Call GroupAlloc.Release to return space";
    end Release;
```

```
end DiskAlloc;
```

Choosing Groups for Allocation

The simplest way to find a group in which space can be allotted for a request is to choose any group that is not full. If this is done randomly, space will also be randomly allocated all over the disk and our objective of reducing the seek time by clustering the allocated blocks near the middle group will not be met. To devise a better way of choosing a group, let us examine how requests for disk access are handled by the Kernel.

The elevator algorithm used in the Kernel for minimizing the average access time to a disk has three main steps:

1. Start the disk heads moving to the position of the first request that is received and perform the disk transfer,
2. After this, serve all waiting requests whose positions can be reached with the same direction of head movement, starting with the position closest to the present position, and
3. When there are no more such requests, reverse the direction of head movement and go to Step 2.

This algorithm is of most use when there is a queue of disk requests, as otherwise it never proceeds beyond Step 1. If there is a queue, the average access time is reduced if the interval between the furthest requests is small. If there is no queue, the access time can still be reduced if successive requests are close together.

In order to cluster disk space allocation near the centre of the disk, we shall follow two rules:

(a) Always allocate space for a *new* file or directory as close to the middle group as possible.
(b) When more space is required for an *existing* file, allot it in the same group if possible, or else in the closest group in which there is space.

The first rule will help in keeping files close to each other and to the middle group, thereby reducing the time needed to access different files. When successive accesses are to the same file, the delay in access can be further reduced if the segments of a file are kept close together: this is the purpose of the second rule. Naturally, these rules serve their purposes best when space on the disk is not fully used. If the disk is often full and there is a great deal of activity with files, the allocated space on the disk can still be scattered over all cylinders. The only way to bring the access time down again will be to 'refresh' the pack by reorganizing the allocation of space to files. Refreshing a pack is time-consuming but will usually pay for itself by the time subsequently saved in disk access. It can be done either incrementally or for the whole pack. An objective of our rules is to increase the interval between successive 'refreshments'.

We need two procedures to implement these rules. The first, GetGroup, is a simple procedure which brings in the data for a specified group; this procedure uses two other procedures, ReadGroup and WriteGroup, for actually reading allocation data and writing it back to the disk. The Boolean parameter, Completed, is set to **true** only when each operation is successful.

```
procedure GetGroup(NewGroup:integer; var Completed:Boolean);
  begin
    Completed := true;
    if NewGroup ≠ ThisGroup then
    begin
      WriteGroup(Completed);
      if Completed
        then ReadGroup(NewGroup, Completed);
      if Completed
        then ThisGroup := NewGroup;
    end;
  end GetGroup;
```

The procedure FindNewGroup has to find the group closest to a specifed group where space of the right kind (i.e., Small or Large) can be found. It does this by searching on either side of the group whose number is in the parameter, Preference. Completed is set to **true** if a group is found and its map has been successfully loaded. If no such group can be found, it calls an error procedure, Report.

```
procedure FindNewGroup(var Preference:integer; Kind:RequestKind;
                       var Completed:Boolean);
  var
    LowerFull, HigherFull, TryLower: Boolean;
    Trial, Inc: integer;
```

```
begin
  TryLower := true;
  LowerFull := false; HigherFull := false;
  Trial := Preference; Inc := 0;
  while not Completed and not (LowerFull and HigherFull) do
  begin
    if TryLower then
    begin
      if (Preference – Inc) ⩾ 0
        then Trial := Preference – Inc
      else LowerFull := true;
      if not HigherFull
        then TryLower := false
      else Inc := Inc + 1;
    end
    else
    begin
      if (Preference + Inc) ⩽ GMax
        then Trial := Preference + Inc
      else HigherFull := true;
      if not LowerFull
        then TryLower := true
      else Inc := Inc + 1;
    end;
    Completed := not GroupFull[Trial][Kind];
    if Completed
      then GetGroup(Trial, Completed):
  end;
  if Completed
    then Preference := Trial
  else Report(0, PackFull);
end FindNewGroup;
```

To distinguish between calls for space for new files and calls to extend existing files, two separate procedures called AllotNew and AllotNext can be used. Apart from the initial choice of group, these two procedures will share a common set of operations that can be performed in a procedure Allot: this tries to find space by calling the procedure FindNewGroup. Let the middle group be represented by the variable, MidGroup, which is initialized by the statement MidGroup := GMax **div** 2;

```
procedure Allot(var Place:DiskAdr; Size,Group:integer;
                var Done:Boolean);
var
  Kind: RequestKind; Completed: Boolean;
begin
  Done := false; Completed := false;
  if Size ⩽ SmallSize
    then Kind := Small
  else Kind := Large;
```

```
      FindNewGroup(Group, Kind, Completed);
      while not Done and Completed do
      begin
        GroupAlloc.Allot(Place.DiskSeg, Size)
          iferror
            begin
              GroupFull[ThisGroup][Kind] := true;
              FindNewGroup(Group, Kind, Completed);
            end
          otherwise
            with Place, DiskSeg do
            begin
              Cyl := (ThisGroup * N) + (Loc div S);
              Loc := Loc mod S;
              Done := true;
            end;
      end;
    end Allot;


  procedure export AllotNew(var Place:DiskAdr; Size:integer);
    var
      Done: Boolean;
    begin
      Allot(Place, Size, MidGroup, Done);
      if not Done
        then return error;
    end AllotNew;


  procedure export AllotNext(OldPlace:DiskAdr; var NewPlace:DiskAdr;
                             Size:integer);
    var
      Done: Boolean;
    begin
      Allot(NewPlace, Size, OldPlace.Cyl div N, Done);
      if not Done
        then return error;
    end AllotNext;


  procedure export Release(var Place:DiskAdr);
    var
      Completed: Boolean; Kind: RequestKind;
      Group: integer;
    begin
      with Place, DiskSeg do
      begin
        Group := Cyl div N;
        Loc := (Cyl mod N) * S + Loc;
        if SegSize ≤ SmallSize
          then Kind := Small
          else Kind := Large;
```

```
        GetGroup(Group, Completed);
        if Completed
          then GroupAlloc.Release(DiskSeg)
                  iferror Completed := false;
        if Completed
          then GroupFull[ThisGroup][Kind] := false;
          else LostSpace := LostSpace + SegSize;
      end;
    end Release;
```

In the procedure AllotNew, MidGroup is chosen as the starting group so that the space will be allocated as close to the middle of the disk as possible. Similarly, the procedure AllotNext chooses the group of the previous part of the file (OldPlace) as the starting group. In the procedure Allot, procedure FindNewGroup is called to find the closest group where space may be found. This procedure calls GetGroup when necessary to replace the allocation data of the current group, ThisGroup, by that for the requested group (i.e., Group). Both these procedures return a Boolean value, Completed, which is **true** when they have successfully performed their tasks. Note that a group that is not already marked as full may, in fact, be found to be full when a request is made; the **while** loop in Allot is therefore repeated until space is found or until the procedure FindNewGroup is not able to complete its work. A request for disk space will be rejected if there is no space on the disk (or, as we shall see later, if there are errors while transferring allocation data to and from the disk).

Unlike the case of the main memory allocator, the Release procedure here only *attempts* to return space to the allocator. If this is not possible, either because the group allocation data cannot be read, or because the allocation lists are full, the calling process is not delayed. The variable, LostSpace, keeps an account of the amount of space that has been 'lost' in this way. (Though lost space will reduce the space available for subsequent allocation, it does not cause any conflicts with allocation). The value of LostSpace can be used as an indicator of the need to refresh a pack.

Reporting Errors

Errors in transferring information from and to the disk can result in inconsistencies in the allocation data in main memory, or on the disk. Procedures that require disk transfers must be coded to detect such errors and the errors must be recorded so that they can later be examined.

Errors in transferring disk information in the disk space allocator are classified as values of an enumerated type, DiskMapError. The errors are recorded by a procedure, Report, which stores the information in a FiFoQ (see Chapter 2). A function, IsError, can be used to check if any error has occurred, and the procedure GetError used to retrieve error information.

```
type export
  DiskMapError = (BadPack, WrongPack, MapReadFail, MapWriteFail,
                  PackFull);
  DiskErr =
    record
      WhichCyl: integer;
      WhatFault: DiskMapError
    end DiskErr;

var
  ErrorPtr: FiFoQ(MaxErrors);
  Errors: array [1 .. MaxErrors] of DiskErr;

procedure Report(Cylind:integer; Err:DiskMapError);
  begin
    if not ErrorPtr.Full then
      with Errors[ErrorPtr.Put] do
      begin
        WhichCyl := Cylind;
        WhatFault := Err;
      end;
  end Report;

function export IsError return Boolean;
  begin
    return not ErrorPtr.Empty;
  end IsError;

procedure export GetError(var CylNum:integer; var Err:DiskMapError);
  begin
    if not ErrorPtr.Empty then
      with Errors[ErrorPtr.Get] do
      begin
        CylNum := WhichCyl; Err := WhatFault;
      end;
  end GetError;
```

Note that the functions Put and Get in the class FiFoQ have the side-effects of incrementing and decrementing (respectively) the number of entries in Errors (see Chapter 2).

Storing Allocation Data on the Disk

We shall use the simple convention of storing the allocation data for a group in the first part of the group; as security against disk errors, a copy of this data will also be kept in the last part of the group. The first part of the first group will also be used to store the identification for the pack (in practice, this area would include information about the pack, such as the date and time it came into use, when it was last refreshed, the amount of lost space and, possibly, a record of the areas where errors were found on the disk). Again, this information can be replicated in the last group. For simplicity, let the allocation data and the identification information be stored in one sector each. The disk addresses of this information will be:

for the whole pack
identification stored at cylinder 0, sector 1
                    and at cylinder CMax, sector S − 2

for a group GN
allocation data stored at cylinder GN * N, sector 0
                    and at cylinder (GN * N) + N − 1, sector S − 1

We assume that a single disk error is unlikely to damage both copies of such data, unless it is of catastrophic proportions (archiving of files by the filing system is intended to reduce the effects of even such failures—see Chapters 8, 9).

Calls to read and write information from or to the disk go through the pure class, Disk (see Chapter 10), and have the form

   Disk.Read(<DiskAddress>, <SectNum>, <Size>, <MemoryAddress>);

DiskAddress is the address at which the segment of information *begins*, and SectNum is the number of the sector *within* the segment from where information is to be transferred. The call will return an error if the transfer operation fails, and we can use the error checking features of the language to detect this case and to take appropriate action. The call to write disk information has a similar form.

In our use of CCNPascal, we have so far never needed to refer to the physical addresses of variables or even to use pointers to them but this is one clear case where we do need some help from the language and the compiler. We must make use of the standard functions of the language, **varadr** and **varsize**, that return as values the address and size of a variable. Such functions are often called 'unsafe', because they can be misused to undermine the assumptions on which the abstract features of the language are built. We must be cautious in their use, but it is worth noting that they do not have inverses: i.e., there are no functions that, given an arbitrary address, will cause a variable to appear there.

There is one main use for the physical addresses and sizes of variables: to use them to transfer information to and from the disk or other input–output device. In this case, we will be transferring the allocation data for groups so that we can avoid keeping more than one set of data in the main memory. Later, we will see that there is a similar requirement for 'overlaying' file directories and, indeed, for doing a variety of input–output that is otherwise not possible.

The parameters MemoryAddress and Size for the two disk calls can be found using the functions, **varadr** and **varsize**. (As allocation data often needs to be transferred, the address and size of the data area of GroupAlloc will be stored in the variables DataAdd and DataSize, and of ThisPack in the variables IdAdd and IdSize.)

The procedures WriteGroup and ReadGroup can now be written.

```
procedure WriteGroup(var Completed:Boolean);
  var
    Addr: DiskAdr;
  begin
    with Addr do
    begin
      Pack := ThisPack;
      Cyl := ThisGroup * N;
      DiskSeg.Loc := 0;
    end;
    Completed := false;
    Disk.Write(Addr, 0, DataSize, DataAdd)
      iferror Report(Addr.Cyl, MapWriteFail)
      otherwise
        begin
          with Addr
            do Cyl := Cyl + N – 1;
          Disk.Write(Addr, S – 1, DataSize, DataAdd)
            iferror Report(Addr.Cyl, MapWriteFail)
            otherwise Completed := true;
        end;
  end WriteGroup:

procedure ReadGroup(NewGroup:integer; var Completed:Boolean);
  var
    Addr: DiskAdr;
  begin
    with Addr do
    begin
      Pack := ThisPack;
      Cyl := NewGroup * N;
      DiskSeg.Loc := 0;
    end;
    Completed := true;
    Disk.Read(Addr, 0, DataSize, DataAdd)
      iferror
        begin
```

```
        with Addr
          do Cyl := Cyl + N - 1;
        Disk.Read(Addr, S - 1, DataSize, DataAdd)
          iferror
            begin
                Report(Addr.Cyl, MapReadFail);
                Completed := false;
            end;
      end;
  end ReadGroup;
```

Notice that when writing allocation data, Completed is not set to **true** unless *both* copies have been correctly written. This allows us to be less severe when reading allocation data: as both disk copies will be consistent, Completed will be **true** if either of them can be correctly read. There still remains the question of whether the allocator should continue its operations at all when WriteGroup sets Completed to **false**, and we leave this to the section on Crash Recovery.

Mounting and Initializing a Disk Pack

The system operator has the responsibility of mounting packs on disk drives. This can be done when there are specific requests from users, or at other times. A pack that is in use will have an identification and its allocation data will show how much space has been allotted to files. A new pack has no information whatsoever on it, and an old pack that is to be re-used will have its previous identification and allocation data written on it; before such packs can be used, they must be mounted on drives, assigned new identification and have their allocation data properly initialized. The monitor DiskMount, described in Chapter 10, maintains the mapping between packs and drives.

When a pack is mounted on a drive, its identification must be provided to the disk space allocator so that it can be checked against the name of the pack stored on the disk. The allocator must then read in the allocation data for one group and reset the values in the array GroupFull.

```
    procedure export MountPack(PackName:PackId);
        var
          Addr: DiskAdr; Completed: Boolean;
        begin
          if ThisPack = BlankName then
          begin
            with Addr do
            begin
              Pack := PackName;
              Cyl := 0;
              DiskSeg.Loc := 0;
```

```
        end;
    Disk.Read(Addr, 1, IdSize, IdAdd)
      iferror
        begin
          Addr.Cyl := CMax;
          Disk.Read(Addr, S – 2, IdSize, IdAdd)
            iferror
              begin
                Report(Addr.Cyl, BadPack);
                ThisPack := BlankName;
                return error;
              end;
        end;
    if ThisPack = PackName then
    begin
      ReadGroup(MidGroup, Completed);
      if Completed
        then "reset values in array GroupFull"
      else
      begin
        ThisPack := BlankName;
        return error;
      end;
    end
    else
    begin
      Report(0, WrongPack);
      ThisPack := BlankName;
      return error;
    end;
  end;
end MountPack;
```

In this procedure, we have assumed that the pack identification and allocation data are already available on the pack. For a new pack, this information must first be written there, using the procedure InitPack.

The allocatable space in group 0 and GMax of a pack will be S – 3 sectors: in group 0 the first two and the last sector and in group GMax the first and the last two sectors will be used for storing this allocation and identification information. For other groups, the allocatable space will be S – 2 sectors.

The allocation data for each group must be initialized by calling GroupAlloc.SetMem and then written to the places reserved on the pack; in doing so, the initial allocatable address in each group is appropriately set to ensure that the areas reserved for allocation data and pack identification will not be allocated to users.

```
    procedure export InitPack(PackName:PackId);
      var
        Addr: DiskAdr; Completed: Boolean;
```

```
begin
  ThisPack := PackName; ThisGroup := 0;
  GroupAlloc.SetMem(2, N * S – 3);
  WriteGroup(Completed);
  if Completed then
  begin
    ThisGroup := GMax;
    WriteGroup(Completed);
    if Completed then
    begin
      with Addr do
      begin
        Pack := PackName;
        Cyl := 0;
        DiskSeg.Loc := 0;
      end;
      Disk.Write(Addr, 1, IdSize, IdAdd)
        iferror Completed := false
        otherwise
          begin
            Addr.Cyl := CMax;
            Disk.Write(Addr, S – 2, IdSize, IdAdd)
              iferror Completed := false
              otherwise
                begin
                  GroupAlloc.SetMem(1, N * S – 2);
                  for I in 1 to GMax – 1 do
                  begin
                    ThisGroup := I;
                    WriteGroup(Completed);
                    if not Completed
                      then exit;
                  end;
                end;
          end;
    end;
  end;
  if Completed
    then "reset values in array GroupFull"
  else
  begin
    ThisPack := BlankName;
    return error;
  end;
end InitPack;
```

Checking for errors during pack initialization is fairly exhaustive so that packs with errors are not brought into use. The more tolerant error checking in MountPack is justifiable because it permits at least some files (i.e., those on groups without errors) to be retrieved. In the full version of the disk space allocator, a variable, AllErrors, keeps a count of the number of error reports that have been made. This variable, and the variable LostSpace, can be read using the procedure Status.

Finally, we need a small procedure to be called when a pack is to be dismounted. All this requires is to write out the data for the current group and to set ThisPack to BlankName.

```
procedure export DisMount;
  var
    Completed: Boolean;
  begin
    WriteGroup(Completed);
    ThisPack := BlankName;
  end DisMount;
```

Each monitor of type DiskAlloc can be used to manage space on one disk pack. As a typical system will have several disk drives, we shall need many instances of DiskAlloc. In the program listing at the end of this chapter, these instances are declared as elements of an array, within the pure class, DiskSpace. For the rest of the operating system, this pure class serves as a single abstraction representing all the available disk packs.

Crash Recovery

The hardware faults that have been accounted for so far are those relating to disk storage. Hardware faults in processors and main memory, software faults in the operating system and power failures can each cause considerably more damage as they may result in inconsistencies in information stored on the disk. This is a consequence of our neglect to write the group map back to the disk whenever it is modified. For example, if the system crashes after space is allotted for a file and before the group allocation data is written back to the disk, the disk copy of the allocation data will have no record of the recent allocation of space (and the same space may then be allotted to some other request). A number of changes must be made in the disk space allocator to ensure that it has provision to tolerate system and disk failures.

1. The procedure GetGroup copies the allocation data for one group, say G1, to the disk and replaces it by allocation data for another group, say G2. If the first action is satisfactorily completed and there is a failure during the second, an error is reported. However, the second operation may have partially or completely overwritten the old group allocation data; the variable ThisGroup will still be set to G1, even though the data in GroupAlloc is

corrupted. To avoid this, we must be able to recognize when there is no allocation data in GroupAlloc. Just as we use the value, BlankName, to denote that there is no pack mounted on a drive, a distinguished value (say –1) can be assigned to ThisGroup to indicate this situation and special action can be taken whenever ThisGroup has this value.

2. To avoid inconsistencies between the disk and the main memory versions of group allocation data, the main memory copy of this data can be written to the disk whenever it is modified (i.e., when space is allocated or released in that group); this must be done for calls to AllotNew, AllotNext and Release.

3. Two copies of group allocation data are always written to the disk in the procedure WriteGroup. If one of these copies is incorrectly written, it should be possible to guarantee that an error will be encountered when it is subsequently read (hardware checking will usually ensure this). If neither copy is correctly written, some indication must be preserved so that this group is never again used: for example, the group can be marked as full.

4. The array, GroupFull, must be written to the disk and the main memory and disk copies must be kept consistent. Suppose a group is marked as full in the disk copy and that, due to the release of some space, the main memory copy shows that it is not full. If there is a system crash, a new copy of GroupFull will be read from the disk in which the group will still appear as full. Hence, no space will be allocated in this group unless a later Release operation for this group is successfully completed. As for group allocation data, the contents of GroupFull should therefore be written to the disk whenever the main memory copy is altered.

DISCUSSION

When main memory was limited and expensive and the most important backing store device was the drum, considerable effort and ingenuity was expended in finding ways to reduce the latency time by carefully positioning data around the drum. Of course, drums being fixed head devices, there was no seek time to be minimized. The early disks had larger capacity than drums, but far greater access times, so attention moved to reducing the seek time and the elevator algorithm passed into the folklore as a simple and efficient way by which to schedule disk requests. The first analysis of this technique appears in Denning (1967), where it is called the SCAN algorithm and is compared with the first-come-first- served and shortest-seek-time-first techniques. Programmed versions of the elevator algorithm can be found in Hoare (1974) and Wirth (1977).

It is useful to contribute to the minimization of seek time that the elevator algorithm attempts, by clustering disk space allocations near the mean position of the heads. The allocator in this chapter does this by allotting space for new files in or near the middle group of cylinders, and by finding the available space closest to the last allotted segment for existing files. Despite this, after a period of use, files may be scattered all over the disk: it is impossible to prevent this unless there are predictable patterns of file use that can be studied to move heavily used files to the mean position of the heads. A good analysis of the problem of combining a placement algorithm with a seek algorithm can be found in Wong (1980).

There are many different ways in which disk space allocation is recorded, perhaps the most common of these being the 'bit-map' which we have already discussed in Chapter 5. As we pointed out there, efficient allocation of variable size requests using bit-maps requires good bit-manipulation instructions in the machine. Storage requirements and segment size also play an important role in deciding how disk space is represented: it is hardly feasible to use 32 word segments for a 600Mb disk, and the usual compromise is to use very large segments (of the order of 1K words). Even then, the number of segments may be as large as 100,000 for which 4K words of allocation data would be required on a 32 bit machine. Dividing the disk into groups helps to break this requirement into smaller units of which only one need be resident in main memory. At the other extreme, a floppy disk of 0. 25Mb could, at some loss of efficiency in access, be considered to be a single group.

One advantage of using a common allocator is the saving of main memory space: a single copy of the code of the allocator can serve for all instances of the allocator. With several local memories attached to processors, and many disk drives, this saving can be substantial.

Disks are mainly used for storing information required over long periods and it would be imprudent to expect them to be free of errors. The disk space allocator is designed to recognize errors and to avoid using information that may be corrupted. Writing critical information (such as allocation data) to two well-separated places on the disk is fairly common practice but even such measures of caution cannot take account of major 'head- crashes'. We have chosen to report all significant errors and to leave it to the managers of the system to decide when the disk performance warrants more effective recovery action. It must be noted that we have assumed that calls to read and write disk information result in a number of automatic re-tries to overcome transient errors, and that the errors reported are those that persist.

EXERCISES

1. Suppose the disk space allocator is to be used for a system with a single disk drive where about 256 words (of 32 bits) are available for storing allocation data in main memory. A disk pack has a capacity of 100Mbytes, and space is allotted in sizes of 256 words (for file directories), and in segments of 1 Kwords, 2 Kwords and 4 Kwords for files (a file may contain an arbitrary number of such segments). Which basic allocator would you choose for the disk space allocator? If each cylinder has a capacity of 0.5 Mbytes, how many cylinders should be combined in a group? Note: the space available for storing allocation data should be effectively used to reduce the number of times allocation data has to be brought from the disk.

2. Assuming that group allocation data that is incorrectly written to the disk is also incorrectly read (i.e., there is a disk error while reading), modify the disk space allocator so that no further attempts are made to allot space in a group for which both copies of the allocation data have been incorrectly written to the disk.

3. Modify the disk space allocator so that the contents of the array, GroupFull, and the group allocation data are always written to the disk when the main memory copies are modified. Using the value − 1 for ThisGroup to indicate that no valid copy of the allocation data is available in main memory, ensure that when calls to AllotNew and AllotNext are successful, the disk and main memory copies of GroupFull and the allocation data are always consistent. Will your method also ensure that these copies are always consistent for calls to Release?

4. Write a program which retrieves errors using the procedure, GetError, and classifies them according to the kind of error and the position at which they occur on the disk pack. When the results are printed out, they should clearly show if errors are clustered in the same cylinder, or in neighboring cylinders. It should also be possible to see if multiple errors occur on the same disk surface. (The same program can be used to analyse disk errors reported by the File System—see Chapters 8, 9.)

THE DISK SPACE ALLOCATOR PROGRAM

Note: the type PackId and the constant BlankName are provisionally defined
here as

```
type
    PackId = string(8);
    BlankName = ' ';
```

Suitable, possibly implementation dependent, definitions of this type must
be provided for a system. The definitions of the calls to Disk are provided in
Chapter 10.

```
{****                                ****}
{**** The DiskPack Space Allocator ****}
{****              – Outline         ****}

type
    DiskAlloc(GMax, CMax, N, S, SmallSize, SSectMax,
              LSectMax: integer)
    = monitor;
      procedure Report(Cylind:integer; Err:DiskMapErr);
      function export IsError return Boolean;
      procedure export GetError(var CylNum:integer; var Err:DiskMapErr);
          {Report is used to store errors and IsError and GetError are
           for use by system processes to retrieve error reports}
      procedure export Status(var Lost,Err:integer);
          {To find out the extent of lost space and the number of errors}
      procedure WriteGroup(var Completed:Boolean);
      procedure ReadGroup(NewGroup:integer; var Completed:Boolean);
          {To read and write group allocation maps from and to disk}
      procedure GetGroup(NewGroup:integer; var Completed:Boolean);
          {To replace the current group allocation map by that for NewGroup}
      procedure FindNewGroup(var Preference:integer; Kind:RequestKind;
                             var Completed:Boolean);
          {To find the closest group to Preference where space may be found}
      procedure export AllotNew(var Place:DiskAdr; Size:integer);
          {To get disk space for a new file}
      procedure export AllotNext(OldPlace:DiskAdr; var NewPlace:DiskAdr;
                                 Size:integer);
          {To get disk space to extend a file}
      procedure export Release(var Place:DiskAdr);
          {To release disk space}
      procedure export MountPack(PackName:PackId);
          {For initialising the allocator data with data from a freshly
           mounted pack}
      procedure export InitPack(PackName:PackId);
          {For writing a new identification and fresh group maps to a pack}
      procedure export DisMount;
          {To clear the allocator when a pack is dismounted}
    end DiskAlloc.
```

```
{****                          ****}
{**** The Disk Space Allocator ****}
{****     –    Implementation   ****}
```

type
   DiskAlloc(GMax, CMax, N, S, SmallSize, SSectMax,
               LSectMax: **integer**)
  = **monitor**;

  const
     MaxErrors = 10;

  type export
     DiskAdr =
      record
        Pack: PackId;
        Cyl: **integer**;
        DiskSeg: Allocator.Seg
      end DiskAdr;
     DiskMapError = (BadPack, WrongPack, MapReadFail,
                 MapWriteFail, PackFull);
  type
     DiskErr =
      record
        WhichCyl: **integer**;
        WhatFault: DiskMapError
      end DiskErr;
     RequestKind = (Small, Large);
     GroupStatus = **array** [RequestKind] **of Boolean**;

  var
     ThisPack: PackId;
     GroupFull: **array** [1 .. G] **of** GroupStatus;
     ThisGroup, MidGroup: **integer**;
     GroupAlloc: Allocator(SmallSize, SSectMax, LSectMax);
     IdAdd, IdSize, DataAdd, DataSize: **integer**;
     ErrorPtr: FiFoQ(MaxErrors);
     Errors: **array** [1 .. MaxErrors] **of** DiskErr;
     LostSpace, AllErrors: **integer**;

  procedure Report(Cylind:**integer**; Err:DiskMapErr);
    begin
      if not ErrorPtr.Full **then**
        with Errors[ErrorPtr.Put] **do**
        begin
          WhichCyl := Cylind;
          WhatFault := Err;
          AllErrors := AllErrors + 1;
        end;
    end Report;

```
function export IsError return Boolean;
  begin
    return not ErrorPtr.Empty;
  end IsError;

procedure export GetError(var CylNum:integer;
                                    var Err:DiskMapErr);
  begin
    if not ErrorPtr.Empty then
      with Errors[ErrorPtr.Get] do
      begin
        CylNum := WhichCyl; Err := WhatFault;
      end;
  end GetError;

procedure export Status(var Lost,Err:integer);
  begin
    Lost := LostSpace; Err := AllErrors;
  end Status;

procedure WriteGroup(var Completed:Boolean);
  var
    Addr: DiskAdr;
  begin
    with Addr do
    begin
      Pack := ThisPack;
      Cyl := ThisGroup * N;
      DiskSeg.Loc := 0;
    end;
    Completed := false;
    Disk.Write(Addr, 0, DataSize, DataAdd)
      iferror Report(Addr.Cyl, MapWriteFail)
      otherwise
        begin
          with Addr
            do Cyl := Cyl + N - 1;
          Disk.Write(Addr, S - 1, DataSize, DataAdd)
            iferror Report(Addr.Cyl, MapWriteFail)
            otherwise Completed := true;
        end;
  end WriteGroup;

procedure ReadGroup(NewGroup:integer; var Completed:Boolean);
  var
    Addr: DiskAdr;
  begin
    with Addr do
    begin
      Pack := ThisPack;
      Cyl := NewGroup * N;
      DiskSeg.Loc := 0;
    end;
```

```
          Completed := true;
          Disk.Read(Addr, 0, DataSize, DataAdd)
            iferror
              begin
                with Addr
                  do Cyl := Cyl + N − 1;
                Disk.Read(Addr, S − 1, DataSize, DataAdd)
                  iferror
                    begin
                      Report(Addr.Cyl, MapReadFail);
                      Completed := false;
                    end;
              end;
      end ReadGroup;

  procedure GetGroup(NewGroup:integer; var Completed:Boolean);
    begin
      Completed := true;
      if NewGroup ≠ ThisGroup then
      begin
        WriteGroup(Completed);
        if Completed
          then ReadGroup(NewGroup, Completed);
        if Completed
          then ThisGroup := NewGroup;
      end;
    end GetGroup;

  procedure FindNewGroup(var Preference:integer; Kind:RequestKind;
                         var Completed:Boolean);
    var
      LowerFull, HigherFull, TryLower: Boolean;
      Trial, Inc: integer;
    begin
      TryLower := true;
      LowerFull := false; HigherFull := false;
      Trial := Preference; Inc := 0;
      while not Completed and not (LowerFull and HigherFull) do
      begin
        if TryLower then
        begin
          if (Preference − Inc) ⩾ 0
            then Trial := Preference − Inc
          else LowerFull := true;
          if not HigherFull
            then TryLower := false
          else Inc := Inc + 1;
        end
        else
        begin
          if (Preference + Inc) ⩽ GMax
            then Trial := Preference + Inc
```

```
        else HigherFull := true;
        if not LowerFull
            then TryLower := true
            else Inc := Inc + 1;
       end;
      Completed := not GroupFull[Trial][Kind];
      if Completed
          then GetGroup(Trial, Completed);
     end;
     if Completed
        then Preference := Trial
        else Report(0, PackFull);
   end FindNewGroup;


 procedure Allot(var Place:DiskAdr; Size,Group:integer;
                     var Done:Boolean);
   var
     Kind: RequestKind; Completed: Boolean;
   begin
     Done := false; Completed := false;
     if Size ≤ SmallSize
        then Kind := Small
        else Kind := Large;
     FindNewGroup(Group, Kind, Completed);
     while not Done and Completed do
     begin
        GroupAlloc.Allot(Place.DiskSeg, Size, Done);
        iferror
           begin
             GroupFull[ThisGroup][Kind] := true;
             FindNewGroup(Group, Kind, Completed);
           end
        otherwise
           with Place, DiskSeg do
           begin
             Cyl := (ThisGroup * N) + (Loc div S);
             Loc := Loc mod S;
           end;
     end;
   end Allot;


 procedure export AllotNew(var Place:DiskAdr; Size:integer);
   var
     Done: Boolean;
   begin
     Allot(Place, Size, MidGroup, Done);
     if not Done
        then return error;
   end AllotNew;
```

```
    procedure export AllotNext(OldPlace:DiskAdr; var NewPlace:DiskAdr;
                               Size:integer);
var
    Done: Boolean;
begin
    Allot(NewPlace, Size, OldPlace.Cyl div N, Done);
    if not Done
        then return error;
end AllotNext;

procedure export Release(var Place:DiskAdr);
    var
        Completed: Boolean; Kind: RequestKind;
        Group: integer;
    begin
        with Place, DiskSeg do
        begin
            Group := Cyl div N;
            Loc := (Cyl mod N) * S + Loc;
            if SegSize ≤ SmallSize
                then Kind := Small
            else Kind := Large;
            GetGroup(Group, Completed);
            if Completed
                then GroupAlloc.Release(DiskSeg)
                        iferror Completed := false;
            if Completed
                then GroupFull[ThisGroup][Kind] := false
            else LostSpace := LostSpace + SegSize;
        end;
    end Release;

procedure SetGroupMap;
    begin
        for I in 0 to GMax do
        begin
            GroupFull[I][Small] := false;
            GroupFull[I][Large] := false;
            LostSpace := 0; AllErrors := 0;
        end;
    end SetGroupMap;

procedure export MountPack(PackName:PackId);
    var
        Addr: DiskAdr; Completed: Boolean;
    begin
        if ThisPack = BlankName then
        begin
            with Addr do
```

```
        begin
          Pack := PackName;
          Cyl := 0;
          DiskSeg.Loc := 0;
        end;
        Disk.Read(Addr, 1, IdSize, IdAdd)
          iferror
            begin
              Addr.Cyl := CMax;
              Disk.Read(Addr, S – 2, IdSize, IdAdd)
                iferror
                  begin
                    Report(Addr.Cyl, BadPack);
                    ThisPack := BlankName;
                    return error;
                  end;
            end;
        if ThisPack = PackName then
        begin
          ReadGroup(MidGroup, Completed);
          if Completed
            then SetGroupMap
          else
          begin
            ThisPack := BlankName;
            return error;
          end
        end
        else
        begin
          Report(0, WrongPack);
          ThisPack := BlankName;
          return error;
        end;
      end;
    end MountPack;

procedure export InitPack(PackName:PackId);
  var
    Addr: DiskAdr; Completed: Boolean;
  begin
    ThisPack := PackName; ThisGroup := 0;
    GroupAlloc.SetMem(2, N * S – 3);
    WriteGroup(Completed);
    if Completed then
    begin
      ThisGroup := GMax;
      WriteGroup(Completed);
      if Completed then
      begin
        with Addr do
```

```
          begin
            Pack := PackName;
            Cyl := 0;
            DiskSeg.Loc := 0;
          end;
          Disk.Write(Addr, 1, IdSize, IdAdd)
            iferror Completed := false
            otherwise
              begin
                Addr.Cyl := GMax;
                Disk.Write(Addr, S – 2, IdSize, IdAdd)
                  iferror Completed := false
                  otherwise
                    begin
                      GroupAlloc.SetMem(1, N * S – 2);
                      for I in 1 to GMax – 1 do
                      begin
                        ThisGroup := I;
                        WriteGroup(Completed);
                        if not Completed
                          then exit;
                      end;
                    end;
              end;
          end;
        end;
        if Completed
          then SetGroupMap
        else
        begin
          ThisPack := BlankName;
          return error;
        end;
      end InitPack;


    procedure export DisMount;
      var
        Completed: Boolean;
      begin
        WriteGroup(Completed);
        ThisPack := BlankName;
      end DisMount;

  begin {DiskAlloc}
    ThisPack := BlankName;
    ThisGroup := 0; MidGroup := GMax div 2;
    DataAdd := varadr(GroupAlloc); DataSize := varsize(GroupAlloc);
    IdAdd := varadr(ThisPack); IdSize := varsize(ThisPack);
    SetGroupMap;
  end DiskAlloc;
```

An array of disk space allocators can now be declared in a pure class which presents a single interface to the rest of the system. The operating system will use the convention of using the physical number of the disk drive as the index in the table where the pack identification is stored.

```
{****                          ****}
{**** The Disk Space Allocator ****}
{****           – Outline       ****}

var
   DiskSpace: pure class;
      procedure export MountPack(Pk:PackId; Ind:integer);
         {Set the allocator Ind to deal with pack Pk}
      procedure export RemovePack(Ind:integer);
         {Reset the allocator Ind}
      procedure export AllotNew(var Addr:DiskAdr; Size:integer);
      procedure export AllotNext(OldAddr:DiskAdr; var NewAddr:DiskAddr;
                                 Size:integer);
      procedure export Release(var Addr:DiskAddr);
         {These procedures perform the operations of the
          disk allocator whose PackId is in the disk address}
      function export IsError(Ind:integer);
      procedure export GetError(Ind:integer; var Cyl:integer;
                                var ErrKind:DiskMapError);
         {To test for and retrieve errors for allocator Ind}
      procedure export Status(Ind:integer; var Lost,Errs:integer);
      procedure export InitPack(Pk:PackId; Ind:integer);
         {To perform the associated operations on allocator Ind}
   end DiskSpace.


{****                          ****}
{**** The Disk Space Allocator ****}
{****        – Implementation   ****}

var
   DiskSpace: pure class;

      var
         PackSpace: array [1 .. DiskMax] of DiskAlloc(< parameters >);

      procedure export MountPack(Pk:PackId; Ind:integer);
         begin
            PackSpace[Ind].MountPack(Pk, Done)
               iferror return error;
         end MountPack;

      procedure export RemovePack(Ind:integer);
         begin
            PackSpace[Ind].Dismount;
         end Remove;
```

```
procedure export AllotNew(var Addr:DiskAdr; Size:integer);

  var
    Ind: integer;
  begin
    Ind := DiskMount.IsMounted(Addr.Pack);
    if Ind ≠ 0
      then PackSpace[Ind].AllotNew(Addr, Size)
           iferror return error
    else return error;
  end AllotNew;


procedure export AllotNext(OldAddr:DiskAdr; var NewAddr:DiskAdr;
                           Size:integer);
  var
    Ind: integer;
  begin
    Ind := DiskMount.IsMounted(Addr.Pack);
    if Ind ≠ 0
      then PackSpace[Ind.].AllotNext(OldAddr, NewAddr, Size)
           iferror return error
    else return error;
  end AllotNext;


procedure export Release(var Addr:DiskAdr);
  var
    Ind: integer;
  begin
    Ind := DiskMount.IsMounted(Addr.Pack);
    if Ind ≠ 0
      then PackSpace[Ind].Release(Addr)
    else return error;
  end Release;

function export IsError(Ind:integer) return Boolean;
  begin
    return PackSpace[Ind].IsError;
  end IsError;


procedure export GetError(Ind:integer; var Cyl:integer;
                          varErrKind:DiskMapError);
  begin
    PackSpace[Ind].GetError(Cyl, ErrKind);
  end GetError;

procedure export Status(Ind:integer; var Lost,Errs:integer);
  begin
    PackSpace[Ind].Status(Lost, Errs);
  end Status;
```

```
procedure export InitPack(Pk:PackId; Ind:integer);
  begin
    PackSpace[Ind].InitPack(Pk)
      iferror return error;
  end InitPack;

end DiskSpace;
```

8 THE FILE SYSTEM—PART I

Introduction

We now come to the first, and the most major, facility provided in the operating system for user programs. This is the file system which allows user jobs to create, read, write and delete files of information. For each user program, the file system appears as a repository in which files that outlive the program can be created. Files must therefore be associated, not with user programs but with *users* whose identities do not change between sessions. To make this relationship quite clear, we could say that a file 'belongs' to a user and that it can normally be manipulated only by programs that are run by that user. The security of the file system depends critically on the method used for authenticating a user.

To make identification possible, files belonging to a user will be grouped in one or more directories. This serves two purposes. First, files can be collected in directories according to any grouping decided by a user: for example, a user may choose to keep all the program files for a project in one directory and text files in another. Second, the association of files with directories allows a user to *share* a file, by explicitly specifying that a particular user (or a set of users) can access that file. Files then become the medium for the exchange of information between users. A particularly important use of such sharing is for files in the System Library directory (which contains all the programs that are commonly available) to be made accessible to all users. Once again, secure sharing of files relies on the method of authenticating users.

In this chapter, we shall describe the basic features of the file system that are necessary to allow user programs to create, manipulate and share files. In the next chapter, we will add the mechanisms that are needed for implementing the operations of the file system.

FILES

From the point of view of an individual user, a file is an abstract object with an associated set of operations. We require (at least) two kinds of files: text files to store symbolic information as characters, and binary files to store non-textual data as 'bytes'. We distinguish between files of these kinds as they will be accessed in different ways.

```
type
    FileKind = (Text, Binary);
```

Each kind of file can be organized in one of two modes, Sequential and Random.

```
type
    FileMode = (Sequential, Random);
```

Sequential Files

A *sequential* file is an ordered sequence of characters or bytes and it can be accessed in one of four ways.

```
type
    SeqAccess = (Read, Write, Append, Execute);
```

Read access is used for retrieving data from existing files, Write access for creating new files, Append access for adding information to the end of an existing file, and Execute access for running a program stored as a binary file.

Every sequential file can be treated as an instance of an abstract data type, SeqFile, which has the following outline.

```
type
    Buffer(Size: integer) =
        record
            case FileKind of
                Text: (TextBuf: array [1 .. Size] of char);
                Binary: (BinaryBuf: array [1 .. Size] of Byte)
        end Buffer;
```

```
type
  SeqFile(Kind: FileKind) = class;

    procedure export Open(Fname:Name; Facc:SeqAccess;
                          var Status:CallStatus);

    procedure export Get(var UsrBuf:Buffer(?N,Kind);
                         var Size:integer;
                         var Status:CallStatus);

    procedure export Put(var UsrBuf:Buffer(?N,Kind);
                         var Size:integer;
                         var Status:CallStatus);

    procedure export Close(var Status:CallStatus)

  end SeqFile;
```

To manipulate a sequential file, a user will need to instantiate a variable of type SeqFile and invoke its operations, as illustrated in the following example.

```
var
  MyFile: SeqFile(Text);
  MyBuf: Buffer(100, Text);
  Status: CallStatus;
  Size: integer;

begin
  MyFile.Open('Test', Read, Status);
  MyFile.Get(MyBuf, Size, Status);
  while "there is data in the file Test" do
  begin
    "Process data";
    MyFile.Get(MyBuf, Size, Status)
  end;
  MyFile.Close(Status)
end;
```

Operations on a sequential file begin with the Open operation and end with the Close operation. The sequence of file operations enclosed between an Open and a Close is called a *file transaction*.

Procedure Open binds the file variable to an object of the file system, of the specified kind and name. This must be the first operation to be invoked. Get and Put are data transfer operations. Access to a sequential file starts from the *current* position, which is initially at the beginning of the file, except for Append access, for which it is at the end of the file. Get transfers the specified amount of data starting from the current position of the file to

UsrBuf and updates the current position. Put transfers data in the opposite direction, i.e. from UsrBuf to the file, and updates the current position. The purpose of the Close operation is to install, or make permanent, the effects of the transaction and to delink the object from the file variable. If Close is not done for some reason (perhaps due to program error or a system crash), the effects of the transaction may not be made permanent. The parameter, Status, gives the status of each operation: whether it has been successfully completed, or aborted due to errors.

Random Files

A *random* file is an array of segments, where a segment is

```
type
  Segment =
    record
      case FileKind of
        Text: (TextSeg: array [1 .. Segsize] of char);
        Binary: (BinarySeg: array [1 .. Segsize] of Byte)
    end Segment;
```

All random files have segments of equal size, denoted by the constant Segsize. Data stored in random files must be accessed in two steps: by first positioning to a segment and then accessing the data contained in that segment. A random file can be accessed in one of four ways.

```
type
  RandAccess = (Read, Write, Update, Execute);
```

Read, Write and Execute have the same functions as in sequential files. Update access is used for creating new segments or for updating old segments of an existing file.

Every random file can be treated as an instance of an abstract data type, RandFile, defined in outline as

```
type
  RandFile(Kind: FileKind) = class;

    procedure export Open(Fname:Name; Facc:RandAccess;
                          var Status:CallStatus);

    procedure export Get(var UsrSeg:Segment(Kind); SegNum:integer;
                         var Status:CallStatus);

    procedure export Put(var UsrSeg:Segment(Kind); SegNum:integer;
                         var Status:CallStatus);
```

    procedure Close(**var** Status:CallStatus)

  end RandFile;

A transaction on a random file is broadly similar to one on a sequential file. But, in contrast to SeqFile, RandFile allows positioning at any segment boundary within a file and restricts data transfer to be in fixed size units of segments.

When a user creates a new file (by opening a file with Write access), the mode of the file (sequential or random) is determined implicitly by the type of the file variable. After creation, the mode of a file cannot be changed. We have used two different types, SeqAccess and RandAccess, to describe access to the two modes of files. We shall now use a single type access which defines the access possible in either mode.

  type
    Access = (Read, Write, Update, Append, Execute);

Internal Structure of a File

Irrespective of its mode, the file system represents a file as a collection of segments, where a segment is a group of contiguous disk blocks (or sectors). The advantage of such a representation is that while each segment needs contiguous storage, this is not essential for the entire file. Space for segments can be allocated using the disk space allocator (Chapter 7), which attempts to cluster segments of a file together to reduce access time. The organization of a file as a collection of segments also allows a file to grow (in units of segments) and it conveniently provides a common representation for implementing operations on sequential and random files.

Each segment of a file has two attributes: a Boolean, Used, to indicate if the segment is present, and SegAdr of type DiskAdr:

  type
    SegAttr =
     record
       Used: **Boolean**;
       SegAdr: DiskAdr
     end SegAttr;

The Boolean Used helps in making consistency checks, e.g. for the existence of a segment in a random file.

We have described a file as a *collection* of segments. Note that it is not possible to represent a file as an *array* of segments since that would require contiguous storage for the file. Instead, a file is implemented at two levels, using a file descriptor which is an array containing the attributes of individual segments.

```
type
    FileDescriptor = array [1 .. SegMax] of SegAttr;
```

The constant, SegMax, is the maximum number of segments possible for a file. The file descriptor contains the necessary information for retrieving data from segments and it can be considered as the 'header' segment for a file.

The attributes of a file are its kind, its mode, the amount of disk space occupied by the file, and the disk address of the file descriptor. Further, for sequential files we need to know the index and size of the last segment to determine the end of the file.

```
type
    FileAttr =
    record
        Kind: FileKind; Mode: FileMode;
        BlkAlloc, LastSeg, LastSegsize: integer;
        FileDescAdr: DiskAdr
    end FileAttr;
```

(Note that FileAttr does not contain an instance of FileDescriptor, but only the disk address of the descriptor. We will see later that attributes of a file are stored within the directory that contains the file.)

IMPLEMENTATION OF FILE OPERATIONS

Sequential Files

The user views a sequential file as an instance of the class SeqFile. SeqFile allows transfer of data of different sizes between the user's data space and the file. But it would not be very efficient to have a physical transfer to or from the disk for every Get and Put operation. Instead, we should buffer data in main memory and initiate a disk data transfer when the buffer is empty (or full). Let us call this buffer FilBuf. If the size of FilBuf is chosen to be a multiple of the disk sector (block) size, data transfer from or to FilBuf can be performed through a single device command. Here, we choose the size of FilBuf as equal to the size of a disk block, BlkSize.

```
var
    FilBuf: Buffer(BlkSize, Kind);
```

FilBuf is a component of SeqFile and each instance of SeqFile will have its own private buffer. This avoids having to manage a central buffer pool and simplifies accounting, since each user can be charged for the memory he uses.

Access to a sequential file always starts from the current position in the file. We need the following variables to maintain the current position.

```
var
    CurrSeg: 0 .. SegMax;
    CurrBlk, CurrPtr, LastSeg, LastBlk,
    CurrSegsize, LastSegsize, CurrBlksize, LastBlksize: integer;
```

The variables CurrSeg, CurrBlk and CurrPtr together denote the current position in the file. CurrSeg denotes the index of the current segment, CurrBlk the index of the current block within the current segment and CurrPtr indicates the position within the current block. LastBlk has the number of the last block of the current segment and LastSeg has the number of the last segment of the file. The variable, CurrSegsize, will be used to record the size of the current segment: this is needed as the segment may become the last segment of the file, and in that case it may not be full.

Using these variables, we define certain boundary conditions for the current position in a file. The current position is

1. at the beginning of a segment when (CurrBlk=1) **and** (CurrPtr=0),
2. at the end of a segment when (CurrBlk=LastBlk) **and** (CurrPtr=CurrBlksize),
3. at the beginning of the file, i.e. at the end of a hypothetical 'zeroth' segment, when (CurrSeg=0) **and** (CurrBlk=LastBlk) **and** (CurrPtr=CurrBlksize), and
4. at the end of the file when (CurrSeg=LastSeg) **and** (CurrBlk=LastBlk) **and** (CurrPtr=CurrBlksize).

While writing data into a file, we encounter two conditions. If we assume the maximum block number possible for a segment to be BlkMax, and the maximum segment number to be SegMax,

1. the current segment is full when (CurrBlk=BlkMax) **and** (CurrPtr=BlkSize), and
2. the file is full when (CurrSeg=SegMax) **and** (CurrBlk=BlkMax) **and** (CurrPtr=BlkSize).

Since data is written sequentially, all segments of a sequential file except (possibly) the last will be full.

While reading data from a sequential file, whenever a segment boundary is crossed, we have to recompute LastBlk and LastBlksize so that we can recognize the boundary conditions described above. The procedure MakeCurrent performs this computation.

```
procedure MakeCurrent(SegNum:integer);
  begin
    CurrSeg := SegNum;
    if (SegNum ≠ 0) and (SegNum = LastSeg) then
    begin
      LastBlk := (LastSegsize – 1) div BlkSize + 1;
      LastBlksize := LastSegsize mod (BlkSize + 1)
    end
    else
    begin
      LastBlk := BlkMax; LastBlksize := BlkSize
    end
  end MakeCurrent;
```

Opening a Sequential File

The Open operation binds the file variable of the user program to a file of the file system. It also makes access control checks to see whether the file is of the proper kind and mode, and whether the access attempted is possible for the file. We need the following variables to do this.

```
var
  FileOpened: Boolean;
  AccMode: Access;
```

FileOpened is a Boolean which is **true** when the file variable is associated with a file. AccMode is set to the access specified when the file is opened. If the access is legal and is either Read or Write, Open sets the current position to the beginning of the file; for Append access, the current position is set to the end of the file. Also, for Append access, if the last block of the file is not full, it is read into FilBuf so that subsequent Put operations may append data to that block.

```
procedure export Open(Fname:Name; Facc:Access;
                      var Status:CallStatus);
  begin
    if FileOpened
      then Status := DuplicateOpen
    else
    begin
      "Check legality of access";
      "Get index and size of the last segment
```

```
        in LastSeg and LastSegsize";
      FileOpened := true;
      ˆAccMode := Facc;
      if AccMode = Append
        then MakeCurrent(LastSeg)
      else MakeCurrent(0);
      CurrBlk := LastBlk; CurrBlkSize := LastBlkSize;
      CurrPtr := CurrBlkSize;
      if AccMode = Append then
      begin
        if CurrPtr ≠ BlkSize
          then "Read the last block of data into FilBuf from disk";
        CurrSegsize := LastSegsize
      end
      else CurrSegsize := 0
    end
  end Open;
```

Transferring Data in a Sequential File

The procedure Get transfers the required amount of data from FilBuf to the
user's area. If FilBuf is empty, it reads a block of data from the disk.

```
  function Min(X,Y:integer) return integer;
  begin
    if X < Y
      then return X
    else return Y
  end Min;

  procedure export Get(var UsrBuf:Buffer(?N,Kind); var Size:integer;
                       var Status:CallStatus);
  var
    ReqSize, DataInBuf, Tsize: integer;
  begin
    if not FileOpened
      then Status := FileNotOpened
    else
      if AccMode ≠ Read
        then Status := NotOpenedForRead
      else
      begin
        Status := Success;
        ReqSize := Min(N, Size); Size := 0;
        repeat
          DataInBuf := CurrBlkSize – CurrPtr;
          if (ReqSize ≠ Size) and (DataInBuf ≠ 0) then
```

```
      begin
        Tsize := Min(DataInBuf, ReqSize - Size);
        case view(UsrBuf) of
          Text:
            if view(FilBuf, Text) then
              for I in 1 to Tsize
                do UsrBuf.TextBuf[Size + I]
                      := TextBuf[CurrPtr + I];
          Binary:
            if view(FilBuf, Binary) then
              for I in 1 to Tsize
                do UsrBuf.BinaryBuf[Size + I]
                      := BinaryBuf[CurrPtr + I]
        end;
        Size := Size + Tsize; CurrPtr := CurrPtr + Tsize
      end;
      if ReqSize ≠ Size then
      begin
        if CurrBlk ≠ LastBlk
          then CurrBlk := CurrBlk + 1
        else
          if CurrSeg ≠ LastSeg then
          begin
            MakeCurrent(CurrSeg + 1); CurrBlk := 1
          end
          else Status := Eof;
        if Status ≠ Eof then
        begin
          "Read the next block of data into FilBuf from disk";
          if CurrBlk := LastBlk
            then CurrBlksize := LastBlksize
          else CurrBlksize := Blksize;
          CurrPtr := 0
        end
      end
    until (RegSize = size) or (Status = Eof)
  end
end Get;
```

The value of Size on entry specifies the limit to the amount of data to be transferred: on return, Size indicates the actual amount of data transferred. Get returns when either the specified amount of data is read or end-of-file is encountered.

Note that the specification of the parameter UsrBuf includes Kind, the parameter to the class type SeqFile. This ensures that the views of UsrBuf and FilBuf are identical. But the actual views of UsrBuf and FilBuf will be known only at runtime and hence we use **case view** and **if view** constructs to access the fields of the proper variant.

Put transfers data in the opposite direction, creating segments on disk whenever necessary. After a segment is created, data is written in units of disk blocks.

```
procedure export Put(var UsrBuf:Buffer(?N,Kind); var Size:integer;
                        var Status:CallStatus);
   var
      ReqSize, EmptyBufSize, Tsize: integer;
   begin
      if not FileOpened
         then Status := FileNotOpened
      else
         if AccMode = Read
            then Status := OpenedForRead
         else
         begin
            Status := Success;
            ReqSize := Min(Size, N); Size := 0;
            repeat
               EmptyBufSize := Blksize – CurrPtr;
               if (ReqSize ≠ Size) and (EmptyBufSize ≠ 0) then
               begin
                  Tsize := Min(EmptyBufSize, ReqSize – Size);
                  case view(UsrBuf) of
                     Text:
                        if view(FilBuf, Text) then
                           for I in 1 to Tsize
                              do TextBuf[CurrPtr + I]
                                    := UsrBuf.TextBuf[Size + I];
                     Binary:
                        if view(FilBuf, Binary) then
                           for I in 1 to Tsize
                              do BinaryBuf[CurrPtr + I]
                                    := UsrBuf.BinaryBuf[Size + I]
                  end;
                  Size := Size + Tsize;
                  CurrSegsize := CurrSegsize + Tsize;
                  CurrPtr := CurrPtr + Tsize;
                  if CurrPtr = Blksize then
                  begin
                     "Write data in FilBuf onto the current
                     block of the current disk segment"
                  end
               end;
               if ReqSize ≠ Size then
               begin
                  if CurrBlk ≠ BlkMax then
                  begin
                     CurrBlk := CurrBlk + 1; CurrPtr := 0
                  end
```

```
            else
            begin
              if CurrSegsize ≠ 0
                then "Add the completed segment to the file";
              if CurrSeg ≠ SegMax then
              begin
                CurrSeg := CurrSeg + 1;
                " Create a new disk segment";
                CurrSegsize := 0;
                CurrPtr := 0; CurrBlk := 1
              end
              else Status := FileFull
            end
          end
        until (ReqSize = Size) or (Status = FileFull)
      end
    end Put;
```

The parameter Size is used in the same way as in Get. The procedure terminates either when the specified amount of data has been transferred, or when the file is too big, i.e. when it requires more segments than the maximum possible (SegMax).

Closing Sequential Files

When a sequential file is closed after Write or Update access, there may still be data in FilBuf that has not been written to the disk (this will happen if CurrPtr ≠ BlkSize). It is then necessary to flush this out into its disk segment. After this is over, the number and the size of the current segment must be recorded as this will now be the last segment in the file. This information will be used in subsequent transactions for recognizing the end of the file.

```
    procedure export Close(var Status:CallStatus);
    begin
      Status := Success;
      if FileOpened then
      begin
        if (AccMode = Write) or (AccMode = Append) then
        begin
          if CurrPtr ≠ BlkSize then
          begin
            "Flush out the remaining data in FilBuf"
          end;
          "Make the current segment the last"
```

```
      end;
         FileOpened := false
      end
   end Close;
```

Random Files

The implementation of random files is very similar to that of sequential files, but much simpler. There is no need to do any buffering since data is transferred in units of fixed size segments. The data transfer is directly between main memory and the disk segments.

```
var
   AccMode: Access; SegUsed: Boolean;
   FileOpened: Boolean;

procedure export Open(Fname:Name; Facc:Access;
                             var Status:CallStatus);
   begin
      if FileOpened
         then Status := DuplicateOpen
      else
      begin
         "Check legality of access";
         FileOpened := true;
         AccMode := Facc
      end
   end Open;

procedure export Get(var UsrSeg:Segment(Kind); SegNum:integer;
                             var Status:CallStatus);
   begin
      if not FileOpened
         then Status := FileNotOpened
      else
         if AccMode ≠ Read
            then Status := NotOpenedForRead
         else
         begin
            "Get the Used attribute of the segment in SegUsed";
            if SegUsed then
            begin
               Status := Success;
               "Read data from the disk segment to UsrSeg"
            end
            else Status := SegmentNotFound
         end
   end Get;
```

```
procedure export Put(var UsrSeg:Segment(Kind); SegNum:integer;
                     var Status:CallStatus);
  begin
    if not FileOpened
      then Status := FileNotOpened
    else
      if AccMode = Read
        then Status := OpenedForRead
      else
      begin
        "Get the Used attribute of the segment in SegUsed";
        if not SegUsed then
        begin
          "Create a new disk segment and add it to the file"
        end;
        "Write data onto the segment"
        Status := Success
      end
  end Put;

procedure export Close(var Status:CallStatus);
  begin
    FileOpened := false
  end Close;
```

DIRECTORIES

So far, we have said that an individual user views a file as an abstract object
and the file system as a repository for these objects. This view is adequate if
there is just one user. But, typically, a system will have multiple users and
this requires more levels in the structure of the file system. Files belonging
to one user must be collected in groups, and a user should have complete
control in organizing his files. At the same time, the file system should
provide facilities for files to be shared across groups (i.e. between users) in
a controlled manner.

To allow files to be grouped, we introduce *directories*. A directory is a
collection of *objects*. An object can either be a file or another directory.
Directories induce a name structure: objects within a directory must be
uniquely named, but objects in different directories may have the same
name. Since a directory can have another directory as an element, it is
possible to have a hierarchic structure of directories and files.

In our system, every job belongs to a user. Each user has a *root* directory
and each job has a *current* directory. A user's job starts with his root

directory as its current directory. A job can access only objects contained in its current directory. To access other objects, it has to make a directory object within the current directory as its next current directory. The procedure for this is

procedure SetCurDir(DirName:Name; **var** Status:CallStatus);

A directory can be made current only if it can be named from the current directory.

There is a special operation to make the root as the current directory.

procedure SetRoot;

This is necessary since the root is not contained in any directory that a user can access.

Sharing Objects

Each object is contained in (or 'owned by') only one directory, but if the object is to be shared, it should be possible to access it from other directories. This can be achieved in two ways.

(a) by associating with the object a list, called an *Access Control List*, which specifies the directories that can access the object, or

(b) by associating with the directory the list of objects it can access.

We choose the latter scheme, in which each entry in the directory can be called a *capability*. An object can be accessed through a directory if that directory has a capability for the object. We said earlier that a directory is a collection of objects. We now see that a directory is just a collection of capabilities. Each capability in a directory specifies the name and the other attributes of the object to which it refers.

Since an object can be accessed from several directories, it is necessary to selectively control access to the object. To do this, we associate access rights with each capability.

type
  AccessRights = **set of** Access;

A value of type AccessRights indicates the operations permissible on the object when accessed through the associated capability. We have already described five access modes for a file, but not all of these are applicable to directories. A directory can only be accessed for Read, Write or Update accesses. Read access is used for directory lookup, either to check if a capability is contained in a directory or to list all the capabilities contained in the directory. Write access is used for creating new capabilities. Update access is used for changing the attributes of an existing capability. A capability can be used to access an object only if that access is contained in its access rights.

Initially, when an object is created by a job, a capability with full access rights is entered into the current directory of the job. This directory then 'owns' the object; the initial capability is called the *owner capability* and the directory is called the *owner* of the object. Later, new capabilities, called *links*, for the object can be created with restricted rights and passed to other users. Thus, through links, an object can also be accessed through directories other than its owner.

Creating Links

There are two ways of creating links. One way is to invoke

procedure CopyLink(Object,DestDir,NewLink:Name; Rts:AccessRights;
var Status:CallStatus);

CopyLink creates a link with the name NewLink for the specified object and enters it into the directory named by the capability DestDir. The object may be either an owner capability or a link. Thus, through CopyLink, links can either be created or propagated to directories that can be named directly.

But it is not always possible to name directories into which links have to be stored. Consider the case of two users who wish to share a file. Such sharing should be possible with each user being unaware of the directory structure of the other. This is essential since a user may wish to have complete control, flexibility and guaranteed protection in organizing his file structure. To facilitate such unplanned sharing among users, we introduce the notion of *shared directories*.

Each user has an associated shared directory. The purpose of a shared directory is to act as a 'mail box' between users. Any one who wishes to share an object with another user invokes

procedure Share(Object,DestName,NewLink:Name; Rts:AccessRights;
var Status:CallStatus);

DestName is the name of the destined user. The procedure creates a link with the name NewLink, and enters it into the shared directory of the destined user. It is important to note that the current directory does *not* need to have a capability for DestName.

At a later time, the destined user can copy that link into his current directory by invoking

procedure GetLink(ShrdObj,NewLink:Name; **var** Status:CallStatus);

where ShrdObj is the name of the link in the shared directory, and NewLink the name it will have when it is put into the current directory.

It is not always necessary to copy the link from the shared directory. A shared object can also be accessed by making the shared directory as the current directory and naming the object through the link contained in it. The shared directory can be made current by invoking

procedure SetShrDir(**var** Status:CallStatus);

However, since the purpose of the shared directory is only to act as a mail box, it does not own any object.

Managing Objects and Names

To check for the existence of a capability with a given name, the procedure

procedure Lookup(Fname:Name; **var** Status:CallStatus);

can be invoked. Capabilities can be renamed through

procedure Rename(OldName,NewName:Name; **var** Status:CallStatus);

Renaming links does not affect the shared object. But renaming owner capabilities has an important side effect. When a shared object is accessed through a link, access is routed through the owner directory and the owner capability contained in it. In fact, a link does not address the object directly but only through the owner capability for the object named by the pair

<Owner Directory, Owner Capability Name>

When an object is accessed through a link, the file system checks for the existence of the named owner capability in the owner directory. So when an owner capability is renamed, all links addressing the capability through the old name become invalid and can no longer be used to access the shared object. Thus, by renaming an owner capability, it is possible to revoke access to an object that may otherwise be permitted through links.

To create a file, the file has to be opened through a file transaction with Write access. But a directory is created by calling

```
procedure DirGen(DirName:Name; Quota:integer;
             var Status:CallStatus);
```

Capabilities can be deleted by calling

```
procedure Delete(Fname:Name; var Status:CallStatus);
```

Deletion of a link merely gives up the right to access an object, but deletion of owner capabilities results in the deletion of the associated object. When a owner capability is deleted, all links for the object become invalid.

A file can be deleted at any time. But a directory can be deleted only when it does not contain any capability, i.e. it should be empty. Further, a directory cannot be deleted if it is currently being used in some file transaction.

Quite often, a user would like to know the capabilities contained in a directory and their attributes, like the date of creation, access rights etc. The attributes of a capability can be retrieved through

```
procedure ListEntry(Index:integer; var Ent:DirEntry;
              var Status:CallStatus);
```

By repeatedly calling this procedure with values of Index from 1 to FileMax, all capabilities of a directory can be listed.

Let us illustrate the use of the file system procedures described above through a few examples. Let us assume that all file system procedures are contained in a class, FileSys.

Example 1

Suppose a user A wishes to grant three other users X, Y, Z access (with different access rights) to a file named F in a directory D. This can be achieved by the following piece of code:

```
begin
   ...
   with FileSys do
   begin
     SetCurDir('D', Status);
     Share('F', 'X', 'FLink', AccessRights[Read, Write, Append],
           Status);
     Share('F', 'Y', 'FLink', AccessRights[Read, Append], Status);
     Share('F', 'Z', 'FLink', AccessRights[Read], Status);
   end;
   ...
end;
```

The program creates a link, FLink, in the shared directories of X, Y and Z. Note that the three users are granted different access rights. (In CCNPascal, set constants and expressions must be prefixed with the name of the corresponding set type.)

Example 2

User A now wishes to revoke the access granted to user X but is willing to let users Y and Z continue to access file F. This is done as follows:

```
begin
   ...
   with FileSys do
   begin
      SetCurDir('D', Status);
      Rename('F', 'F1', Status);
      Share('F1', 'Y', 'NewLink', AccessRights[Read, Append], Status);
      Share('F1', 'Z', 'NewLink', AccessRights[Read], Status);
   end;
   ...
end;
   ...
```

Selective revocation is achieved by renaming the owner capability and creating new links. Now, user X cannot access file F but users Y and Z can access the file through NewLink in their shared directories. We assume that users Y and Z are somehow 'informed' of this change so that they access file F through NewLink instead of FLink.

Example 3

User A now wishes to grant user Z both Read and Append access to another file F1, in directory D. This is done by the code

```
begin
   ...
   with FileSys do
   begin
      SetCurDir('D', Status);
      Share('F1', 'Z', 'NLink', AccessRights[Read, Append], Status);
   end;
   ...
end;
```

Example 4

Suppose user A wishes to create a subdirectory S within the directory D and to grant user X access to S with the constraint that while A can create or update files in S, X can only read files contained in S. This is achieved by

```
begin
    ...
    with FileSys do
    begin
        SetCurDir('D', Status);
        Dirgen('S', 1000, Status);
        Share('S', 'X', 'SLink', AccessRights[Read], Status);
    end;
    ...
end;
```

Note that X has only Read access to S. If X is given both Read and Update access, it can read or modify files but can still not create files in S.

INTERNAL STRUCTURE OF DIRECTORIES

The Representation of a Capability

A directory consists of capabilities: owner capabilities for some objects, and links for shareable objects owned by other directories. Objects owned by a directory may either be files or directories.

When a user registers with the system, a new root directory is created. Owner capabilities for root directories are contained in a distinguished system directory, called the *Master File Directory* (MFD). A user's job may create directories, called *sub-directories*. Irrespective of how a directory is created, its structure is always a collection of capabilities.

A capability in a directory can be of one of four types.

```
type
    Entry = (File, SubDir, Root, Link);
```

Capabilities of the first three kinds are owner capabilities and the last is a link capability. Each capability has a name, access rights and other attributes. A skeleton of the description of a capability would be

```
type
    DirEntry =
        record
            Used: Boolean;
            LocalName: Name; Rights: AccessRights;
```

```
        CreationDate, CreationTime: integer;
        case Entry of
            File: (...);
            SubDir: (...);
            Root: (...);
            Link: (...)
        end DirEntry;
```

When created, a directory has only empty (null) entries: the Boolean Used indicates whether an entry contains a capability or is empty. The creation date and time are set when a capability is entered into the directory and this data can be used by users to keep track of versions of files.

In addition to the common attributes of capabilities, such as the name, rights etc., the representation of a capability includes information that depends on the type of the capability.

The owner capability for a file contains the attributes of the file.

```
    type
        DirEntry =
            record
                ...
                case Entry of
                    File: (Fattr: FileAttr);
                ...
            end DirEntry;
```

We could similarly define a structure for the owner capability for a directory. Then, a directory capability would have the name, rights and the disk address of the directory. But this would have a severe limitation. To understand the reason for this, we must look at the implementation of links.

We mentioned earlier that links are used to access objects from non-owner directories and that such accesses are routed through the owner capability (in the owner directory) for the object. To achieve this indirection, links should point to their owner capabilities. An obvious implementation of links would be

```
    type
        DirEntry =
            record
                ...
                case Entry of
                    ...
                    Link: (OwnerCap: Name; OwnerDir: DiskAdr)
            end DirEntry;
```

This implementation has the restriction that as long as a link exists, the disk address of the owner directory of the object must not change (though revocation of access is still possible). This is a severe limitation since, in practice, disks have to be refreshed periodically. This refreshing is done both for preventive maintenance and to restore files from backup in case of disk crashes. When files and directories are reconstructed during such refreshes, it would be very difficult to ensure that they are restored to the same place they occupied before refreshing. Hence it is essential to allow the disk addresses of objects to be changed.

To accommodate this requirement, while retaining the need for sharing and revocation, we introduce a distinguished object called the *System Indirectory*, or just *Indirectory*. Every directory (root or subdirectory) in the system has a unique name, in addition to its external (user visible) name, and for every directory there is an entry in Indirectory of the form

```
type
  IndirEntry =
    record
      Used: Boolean;
      DirId: integer; DirPtr: DiskAdr
    end IndirEntry;
```

where the field DirId contains the unique name (an integer) of the directory. The Indirectory is then declared as

```
type
  Sindex = 1 .. IndirMax;

var
  Indir: array [Sindex] of IndirEntry;
```

An element of Indir provides a mapping between a directory's unique name and its disk address. Now when a directory is created or refreshed, only its entry in Indir needs to be updated. The entry for a directory will occupy the same position in Indir as long as the directory exists. Hence a directory must be addressed as

```
type
  DirAdr =
    record
      Id: integer; Index: Sindex
    end DirAdr;
```

Note that the Id and Index for a directory do not change after it is created, so there is an invariant address for a directory. The implementation of directory capabilities and links must use DirAdr and not absolute disk addresses. We can now define a directory entry in complete detail.

```
type
   DirEntry =
      record
         Used: Boolean;
         LocalName: Name; Rights: AccessRights;
         CreationDate, CreationTime: integer;
         case Entry of
            File: (Fattr: FileAttr);
            SubDir: (Adr: DirAdr);
            Root: (Password: Name; Adr, ShrDirAdr: DirAdr);
            Link: (OwnerCap: Name; OwnerDirAdr: DirAdr)
      end DirEntry;
```

Files are still accessed through disk addresses. This does not pose any problem during refreshing, since there is only one capability (i.e. the owner capability) that has to be altered to contain the new disk address.

The Structure of a Directory

In addition to capabilities, a directory contains disk quota information: how many disk blocks this directory can use and how many have been used.

```
type
   Directory =
      record
         Quota, Consumed: integer;
         FileArr: array [1 .. FileMax] of DirEntry
      end Directory;
```

FileMax, a constant, is the maximum number of capabilities that a directory can contain. The field, Quota, is initialized when the directory is created and is never altered thereafter. When objects are created within a directory, or when new segments are added to a file owned by the directory, Consumed is incremented by the number of disk blocks used by the object or segment. When objects are deleted, the value of Consumed is decremented accordingly. Before creating new objects and segments, it is necessary to check that the value of Consumed will not become larger than the value of Quota.

Implementation of the Indirectory

Since directories need to be accessed by several processes, a monitor, SysIndir, implements operations on the Indirectory.

```
type
  IndirEntry =
    record
      Used: Boolean;
      DirId: integer; DirPtr: DiskAdr
    end IndirEntry;
type export
  Sindex = 1 .. IndirMax;
  DirAdr =
    record
      Id: integer; Index: Sindex
    end DirAdr;

var export
  SysIndir: monitor;
    var
      Indir: array [Sindex] of IndirEntry;
      Counter: integer;

    procedure export GetDiskAdr(Adr:DirAdr; var Ptr:DiskAdr;
                                var Found:Boolean);
      begin                          .
        with Indir[Adr.Index] do
          if Used and (DirId = Adr.Id) then
          begin
            Found := true; Ptr := DirPtr
          end
          else Found := false
      end GetDiskAdr;

    procedure export SetDiskAdr(Adr:DirAdr; Ptr:DiskAdr;
                                var Done:Boolean);
      begin
        with Indir[Adr.Index] do
          if Used and (DirId = Adr.Id) then
          begin
            Done := true; DirPtr := Ptr
          end
          else Done := false
      end SetDiskAdr;

    function GetUname return integer;
      begin
        Counter := Counter + 1;
        return Counter
      end GetUname;

    procedure export NewDir(Ptr:DiskAdr; var Adr:DirAdr;
                            var Done:Boolean);
      begin
        Done := false;
```

```
        for I in 1 to IndirMax do
          with Indir[I] do
            if not Used then
            begin
              Used := true; Done := true;
              DirId := GetUname; DirPtr := Ptr;
              Adr.Id := DirId; Adr.Index := I;
              exit
            end
        end NewDir;

    procedure export RemoveDir(Adr:DirAdr);
      begin
        with Indir[Adr.Index] do
          if Used and (DirId = Adr.Id)
            then Used := false
        end RemoveDir;


    begin {SysIndir}
      for I in 1 to IndirMax
        do Indir[I].Used := false;
      Counter := 0
    end SysIndir;
```

As can be seen, the field Index in DirAdr is used only to avoid having to search through Indir. Whenever a directory is addressed through DirAdr, SysIndir compares the unique name field, Id, with that of the indexed entry in Indir to ensure that the directory exists. Procedure NewDir is invoked when a directory is created and SetDiskAdr is called during disk refreshes.

This implementation requires Indir to be in main memory. Indir must be loaded from disk when the system starts and unloaded when the system shuts down. If IndirMax is large, it may not be practical to keep the entire indirectory in main memory. Further, if a crash occurs, all updates to Indir since the system start will be lost. The disk copy of Indir can be maintained up-to-date if the main memory copy is written to disk whenever an IndirEntry is updated. To avoid having to copy the entire structure, Indir can be split into many parts. Each part can then be brought into main memory from disk on demand and copied back onto disk if any entry is updated. This would be similar to the way the group allocation maps are maintained on disk, as discussed in Chapter 7.

ACTIVE FILES

Let an *active* file be one that has been opened and is being used in a transaction. We must keep a record of all active files for controlling concurrent accesses to files. We shall first define the operations of a monitor, ActFiles, which maintains this data. We can then examine the conditions that must hold for concurrent accesses to a file to be consistent.

```
type export
  FileIndex = 1 .. ActFileMax;
var export
  ActFiles: monitor
            import
                var : SysIndir
            end;
        var
      OpenFiles: array [FileIndex] of
                 record
                     UseCount: integer;
                     FileName: Name;
                     OwnerDir: DirAdr
                 end OpenFiles;
```

The DirAdr of the owner directory is kept to ensure the uniqueness of file names. When a file is opened, it is entered into the array OpenFiles if it is not already there, and the index of the entry is returned. This index then serves as a unique identification for that active file. Translating passive file names to active file indices is an important function of the monitor ActFiles.

```
procedure Lookup(Owner:DirAdr; Fname:Name;
                 var Findex:FileIndex; var Found:Boolean);
    begin
      Found := false;
      for I in 1 to ActFileMax do
        with OpenFiles[I] do
          if (UseCount ≠ 0) and (OwnerDir = Owner)
              and (FileName = Fname) then
          begin
            Findex := I; Found := true;
            exit
          end
    end Lookup;


procedure export IsActive(Owner:DirAdr; Fname:Name;
                          var Findex:FileIndex;
                          var Active:Boolean);
    begin
       Lookup(Owner, Fname, Findex, Active)
    end IsActive;

procedure export Activate(Owner:DirAdr; Fname:Name;
                          var Findex:FileIndex;
                          var Done:Boolean);
```

```
begin
  Done := false;
  Lookup(Owner, Fname, Findex, Done);
  if Done then
    with OpenFiles[Findex]
      do UseCount := UseCount + 1
  else
    for I in 1 to ActFileMax do
      with OpenFiles[I] do
        if UseCount = 0 then
        begin
          UseCount := 1; OwnerDir := Owner;
          FileName := Fname; Findex := I;
          Done := true;
          exit
        end
end Activate;
```

When a transaction closes a file, the file is deactivated but it becomes inactive only if no other transaction has opened the file.

```
procedure export DeActivate(Findex:FileIndex;
                        var Inactive:Boolean);
  begin
    with OpenFiles[Findex] do
    begin
      UseCount := UseCount – 1;
      Inactive := UseCount = 0
    end
  end DeActivate;
```

When an active file is renamed, its entry in OpenFiles has to be updated.

```
procedure export Rename(Owner:DirAdr; OldName,NewName:Name;
                        var Found:Boolean);
  var
    Findex: FileIndex;
  begin
    Lookup(Owner, OldName, Findex, Found);
    if Found
      then OpenFiles[Findex].FileName := NewName
  end Rename;

begin {ActFiles}
  for I in 1 to ActFileMax
    do OpenFiles[I].UseCount := 0
end ActFiles;
```

Concurrency Control of File Transactions

The need to coordinate concurrent accesses on files is well known. In our implementation, we enforce a discipline that is followed when files are opened, closed or deleted. All Open, Close and Delete operations on files are mediated through a monitor, Arbiter, which enforces a concurrency control policy by delaying processes (transactions) when necessary.

For purposes of concurrency control, we distinguish between three kinds of transactions: readers, writers and 'deleters'. A reader is one who has opened the file for read access, a writer is one who has opened the file for all other accesses and a deleter is one who is attempting to delete the file. Arbiter implements the following synchronization rule:

(a) A reader transaction is delayed only if a writer is already using the file.

(b) A writer is delayed if a reader or a writer is using the file.

(c) A deleter is delayed until no transaction is using, or waiting to use, the file.

To specify the synchronization rule formally, we identify three *events* in the course of a file transaction. Req(T) is the event of a transaction T requesting an operation (Read, Write or Delete) on the file, Use(T) is the event of T using the file and Exit(T) is that of T completing its operation on the file. We use a temporal ordering relation, "precedes", denoted as $<$, with the following meaning: E1 $<$ E2 if the event E1 occurs before E2. If we denote a reader, writer and a deleter transaction as TR, TW and TD respectively, and logical implication by $\Rightarrow$, we can specify the rule as

$$(a)\ \text{Use(TR)} < \text{Req(TW)} \Rightarrow \text{Exit(TR)} < \text{Use(TW)}$$
$$(b)\ \text{Use(TW)} < \text{Req(TR)} \Rightarrow \text{Exit(TW)} < \text{Use(TR)}$$
$$(c)\ \text{Use(TW)} < \text{Req(TW1)} \Rightarrow \text{Exit(TW)} < \text{Use(TW1)}$$
$$(d)\ (\text{Use(TR)} < \text{Req(TD)})\ \text{or}\ (\text{Req(TR)} < \text{Req(TD)})$$
$$\Rightarrow \text{Exit(TR)} < \text{Use(TD)}$$
$$(e)\ (\text{Use(TW)} < \text{Req(TD)})\ \text{or}\ (\text{Req(TW)} < \text{Req(TD)})$$
$$\Rightarrow \text{Exit(TW)} < \text{Use(TD)}$$

Condition (a) can be read as saying that if a reader transaction TR begins to use a file before a writer transaction TW requests the file, then TR must complete using the file before TW starts using the file. The other conditions can be interpreted similarly.

To implement this rule for an active file, let us associate two variables, ReadCount and WriteFlag, with the file. ReadCount denotes the number of concurrent readers using the file and WriteFlag is **true** if a writer is using the file. We can then restate the synchronization rule using these variables as

1. a transaction (reader, writer or deleter) is delayed if WriteFlag is **true**,
2. a writer transaction is delayed if ReadCount is non-zero and
3. a deleter transaction is delayed if readers or writers are waiting to use the file.

To implement the rule, we must use queue variables on which processes can be delayed.

```
var export
  Arbiter: monitor
              import
                 var : SysIndir, ActFiles
              end;

      type
        Request = (Reader, Writer);
      var
        ShrdFiles: array [FileIndex] of
                       record
                           ReadCount: integer;
                           WriteFlag: Boolean;
                           DeleteQ: queue
                       end ShrdFiles;
        RWq: array [ProcIndex] of
                  record
                    Q: queue;
                    Findex: FileIndex;
                    Req: Request
                  end RWq;
```

For each active file, Arbiter keeps a count of the concurrent readers and a Boolean variable to indicate whether a writer is using the file. For each process, there is a queue variable in RWq on which the process may be delayed, whenever necessary. For each active file, there is a separate queue, DeleteQ, on which the deleter for that file waits. (There can be at most one deleter for a file, and having a separate queue simplifies scheduling.) Before a reader or writer transaction is delayed, it enters the FileIndex of the file and the nature of the request in RWq. When one reader is resumed, it resumes another waiting reader, if there is any. In this way, multiple waiting readers are made concurrent users of the file. When a writer is resumed, it sets WriteFlag to indicate that a writer is active.

```
      procedure Suspend(Index:FileIndex; CurrReq:Request);
      begin
        with RWq[ProcId] do
        begin
          Findex := Index; Req := CurrReq;
```

```
       delay(Q)
     end;
     if CurrReq = Reader then
     begin
       with ShrdFiles[Index]
         do ReadCount := ReadCount + 1;
       for I in 1 to ProcMax do
         with RWq[I] do
           if delayed(Q) then
             if (Findex = Index) and (Req = Reader) then
             begin
               continue(Q); exit
             end
     end
     else ShrdFiles[Index].WriteFlag := true
   end Suspend;
```

When requests for accessing a file arrive, the arbiter first checks if the file is already being used and, depending on the request, the transaction is either delayed or allowed to proceed. Procedures Enter and Mark receive requests to open and delete files.

```
       procedure export Enter(Findex:FileIndex; AccMode:Access;
                              var Status:CallStatus);
     var
       CurrReq: Request;
     begin
       Status := Success;
       if AccMode = Read
         then CurrReq := Reader
       else CurrReq := Writer;
       with ShrdFiles[Findex] do
         if WriteFlag or (ReadCount ≠ 0) then
           if WriteFlag then
             if AccMode = Write
               then Status := DuplicateName
             else Suspend(Findex, CurrReq)
           else
             if CurrReq ≠ Reader
               then Suspend(Findex, CurrReq)
             else
             begin
               ReadCount := ReadCount + 1;
               RWq[ProcId].Req := Reader
             end
         else
         begin
           if CurrReq = Reader
             then ReadCount := 1
```

```
            else WriteFlag := true;
            RWq[ProcId].Req := CurrReq
       end
   end Enter;

procedure export Mark(Owner:DirAdr; Fname:Name);
   var
       Findex: FileIndex; Active: Boolean;
   begin
       ActFiles.IsActive(Owner, Fname, Findex, Active);
       if Active
           then delay(ShrdFiles[Findex].DeleteQ)
   end Mark;
```

Notice that creation of a file is considered as a writer transaction and, if the creation request happens to be a duplicate, the transaction is not delayed but signalled as an error. This situation arises when more than one user attempts to create files in a directory with the same name. We assume that the first create operation will be the most likely one to succeed and signal errors to the other creation requests. Alternatively, we could delay the duplicate creation requests and signal an error only when the first creation is successfully completed.

When a file is closed, the arbiter is informed through the procedure Close. The closing transaction deactivates the file and, if the file actually becomes inactive, the deleter is resumed, if one is waiting. If the file is active and if the closing transaction is a writer, or the last reader, Arbiter schedules a waiting transaction to open the file by searching through RWq and resuming the first found waiting transaction. Since RWq is searched sequentially, process numbers induce a priority. But if we assume there is random arrival of open requests, this simple policy is quite fair.

```
       procedure Schedule(Index:FileIndex);
           begin
               for I in 1 to ProcMax do
                   with RWq[I] do
                       if delayed(Q) and (Findex = Index) then
                       begin
                           continue(Q); exit
                       end
           end Schedule;

       procedure export Close(Findex:FileIndex);
           var
               Inactive: Boolean;
           begin
               with ShrdFiles[Findex] do
```

```
begin
    ActFiles.DeActivate(Findex, Inactive);
    if Inactive and delayed(DeleteQ)
        then continue(DeleteQ);
    if not Inactive then
        if RWq[ProcId].Req = Reader then
        begin
            ReadCount := ReadCount - 1;
            if ReadCount = 0
                then Schedule(Findex)
        end
        else
        begin
            WriteFlag := false;
            Schedule(Findex)
        end
    end
end Close;


begin {Arbiter}
    for I in 1 to ActFileMax do
        with ShrdFiles[I] do
        begin
            ReadCount := 0; WriteFlag := false
        end
end Arbiter;
```

In this implementation, the deleter of a file waits until there is no transaction using the file. However, unlike readers and writers, there is no absolute need for a deleter to wait. It would be more convenient if the deleter needed only to record the decision to delete the file and left the responsibility of actually deleting the file to the system. A simple way to achieve this automatic deletion would be to introduce a process, say FileDeleter, within the file system.

With the introduction of this process, a deleter transaction merely has to mark the entry for the file in ActFiles as Delete if there is no transaction using or waiting to use the file. However, if there is a transaction using or waiting to use the file, the deleter marks the entry as ToDelete and, when a reader or writer transaction closes, it remarks the entry as Delete if there is no transaction using or waiting to use the file. FileDeleter waits on a queue variable and is continued when an entry is marked as Delete; when it resumes, it deletes all files marked as Delete. We leave the programming of this asynchronous file deleter as an exercise.

DISCUSSION

In this design, we view directories and files as separate kinds of objects.

This difference is apparent in the structure of the file system where there are distinct abstractions to implement the two types of objects using different schemes. Thus, for example, file descriptors are identified by disk addresses whereas directory names go through the Indirectory.

There is an alternative design in which this distinction is not made. Here, files are viewed as basic objects and directories are files whose contents have a specific structure. This design is structurally more appealing but it has some deficiencies. For instance, operations on directories have to be implemented using operations on files. Not only is this inconvenient, but it results in performance degradation. Further, this design will require a uniform naming scheme for files and directories and there will be an overhead for maintaining the large Indirectory that would result.

This alternative design is a natural choice in 'pure' capability-based systems. But our design is not a true capability-based system though it does use some similar ideas. The concept of ownership, which we have used, is not intrinsic to a pure capability-based system; this is the reason why revocation of access in capability systems is difficult. Most capability systems use the notion of 'aliases' for purposes of revocation, and this is quite similar to the use of links in our design. The concept of ownership provides a simple mechanism for revocation of access, while retaining the basic property of capability systems, i.e. access control is enforced at the point of reference and not after accessing the object.

The decision to use capability-based access control has considerable effect on the way users organize and share information (Newell and Robertson,1975). Since a job cannot access any object that is not named in the current directory, it is necessary for users to plan sharing of objects before access. A limited amount of unplanned sharing, e.g. the ability to name any root, is provided through shared directories and this can serve as a bootstrap to implement further planned sharing.

Summary

The idea of using capabilities for access control first appeared in a paper by Dennis and Van Horn (1966). Later systems refined this idea. Hydra (Wulf *et al.*,1981), a multiprocessor operating system, made extensive use of capabilities for its protection mechanisms. There are several machine architectures that incorporate hardware support for capabilities, e.g. the Plessey 250 (England 1974), the Cambridge CAP (Wilkes and Needham,1979), the IBM System/38 (Hondek *et al.*,1981), and the Intel 432 (Intel, 1981). But most commercially available systems enforce protection through access control lists rather than capabilities. To keep such a list compact, users are divided into groups and the list for each object specifies the access rights each group has for the object. For example, the DEC System 10 file system (DEC, 1977) classifies users in three groups: the owner, members of a project, or 'others'.

The problem of controlling concurrent access to a file is a refinement to the classical problem of synchronizing multiple readers and writers of shared data (Courtois *et al.*,1971; Hoare, 1974). In our design, in addition to readers and writers, we also have the deleter. Our synchronization rule does not specify any priority for either readers or writers, but the implementation enforces a priority scheme which is usually quite fair.

EXERCISES

1. Suppose you are a user of the file system described in this chapter. Your shared directory has a link, Source, for a sequential file owned by some other directory. Write a program to copy the contents of the file addressed by Source to another file, Destination, within your current directory. If a file named Destination exists already in the current directory, the copy operation should overwrite the old file.

2. Let Path be a sequence of Name.

    type
        Path(N: **integer**) = **array** [1 .. N] **of** Name;

    The first element of Path names either a directory in the current directory or the root if it is 'ROOT'. Each successive element of Path names a directory within the directory named by its preceding subsequence. Design a procedure, SetPath as

    procedure SetPath(PathName:Path(?N); **var** Status:CallStatus)

    to make the directory named by PathName as the current directory.

3. While creating a link in the shared directory of another user, a user has to ensure that the name of the link is not a duplicate. To facilitate this, design a procedure ListShrDir, with the outline given below, to list the names of links contained in a user's shared directory.

    type
        LinkArr = **array** [1 .. FileMax] **of** Name;

    procedure ListShrDir(UserName:Name; **var** Links:LinkArr;
                        var Status:CallStatus);

4. A link contained in a directory becomes useless if access through that link has been revoked. Write a procedure for deleting all revoked links in a directory.

5. Using **CopyLink** and **Share**, a user can grant another user a link for an object either owned by him or granted to him by some other user. These procedures permit uncontrolled propagation of links. Suggest a way for restricting this propagation. (It should be possible for a user, while granting access, to specify if the grantee can, in turn, grant others access to the object.)

6. In the implementation of **SeqFile** given in this chapter, FilBuf is filled from, or emptied to, disk when a block boundary is crossed. This has the disadvantage that further transfer between FilBuf and UsrBuf has to wait till the disk input/output is complete. Suppose we allow the size of FilBuf to be a multiple of the size of a disk block and organize FilBuf as a ring buffer. Then, when a block boundary is crossed, disk input/output can be initiated and, in parallel, transfer between FilBuf and UsrBuf can continue and has to wait only when it reaches that part that is being emptied or filled from disk. Modify the current implementation to include this multiple buffering technique. How will you handle concurrency? How will you allow different file transactions to have different ring buffer sizes?

7. Extend the implementation of **SysIndir** given in this chapter, to allow parts of Indir to be brought into main memory from disk on demand. The implementation should be crash-resistant.

8. Program the asynchronous file deleter described in the text.

9 THE FILE SYSTEM—PART II

In the previous chapter, we described the implementation of file operations largely from the point of view of an individual user. In this chapter, we design the additional mechanisms needed for implementing operations on files taking multiple users into account. We have already described one aspect of this, i.e. controlling concurrent access to a file. It still remains to implement the name structure used for accessing a file. A job can access a file only if there is a capability for the file in its current directory. We have to maintain the relationship between jobs and directories and provide operations for reading and writing capabilities into directories.

JOBS AND DIRECTORIES

Associating Directories with Jobs

In our design, every job has an associated root directory and a current directory. Let us assume that before a job actually starts execution, the operating system finds its root (from the MFD) and sets it as the current directory. During execution, the job can make a different directory as its current directory. When a job initiates a file transaction, the current directory of the job must have either the owner capability or a link for the file. In the latter case, the owner directory of the file is *implicitly* made part of the transaction. Thus, there is one set of directories that are either roots or current directories for jobs, and another set of directories that is implicitly brought into use through links. All such directories are called *active directories*.

A monitor, JobDir, associates jobs with directories, keeping a list of active directories.

```
var
  JobDir: monitor;

    type
      DirIndex = 1 .. ActDirMax;
      DirCap =
        record
          Adr: DirAdr; DirPtr: DiskAdr;
          Rights: AccessRights
        end DirCap;
      JobRec =
        record
          Root, ShrDir, Current: DirCap;
          CurInd: DirIndex
        end JobRec;
      DirRec =
        record
          Adr: DirAdr; UseCount, Credit: integer
        end DirRec;

    var
      DirArr: array [DirIndex] of DirRec;
      JobArr: array [ProcIndex] of JobRec;
```

DirArr is the array of active directories. For each active directory, JobDir maintains its address and the disk space, Credit, that is available for objects to be created or extended in that directory. Since a job will change its current directory less often than altering its files, it is faster to perform quota checks using the value of Credit than to retrieve the directory from the disk merely for computing the available space.

For each job, JobArr keeps the addresses of its root, shared and current directories and the access rights the job has for those directories. This is necessary, as different users may have different rights for a directory. In addition, we also keep in CurInd the index of the current directory in DirArr. Keeping the index in CurInd avoids having to search through DirArr for the directory.

To activate a directory, either when it is made current for a job or when it is used in a file transaction, DirArr is first checked to see if the directory is already active. If it is active, its UseCount is incremented; otherwise, a new entry is made in DirArr. When a directory is deactivated, its UseCount is

decremented. If the value in UseCount drops to zero, the corresponding
entry in DirArr becomes free.

```
procedure ChkActive(AdrDir:DirAdr; var Index:DirIndex;
                    var Active:Boolean);
begin
  Active := false;
  for I in 1 to ActDirMax do
    with DirArr[I] do
      if (UseCount ≠ 0) and (Adr = AdrDir) then
      begin
        Active := true; Index := I; exit
      end
end ChkActive;

procedure MakeActive(AdrDir:DirAdr; Quota:integer;
                     var Index:DirIndex;
                     var Done:Boolean);
begin
  Done := false;
  ChkActive(AdrDir, Index, Done);
  if Done then
    with DirArr[Index]
      do UseCount := UseCount + 1
  else
    for I in 1 to ActDirMax do
      with DirArr[I] do
        if UseCount = 0 then
        begin
          Done := true; Index := I;
          UseCount := 1; Credit := Quota;
          Adr := AdrDir;
          exit
        end
end MakeActive;

procedure MakeInactive(Address:DirAdr);
begin
  for I in 1 to ActDirMax do
    with DirArr[I] do
      if (UseCount ≠ 0) and (Adr = Address) then
      begin
        UseCount := UseCount − 1; exit
      end
end MakeInactive;
```

A directory used in a file transaction is activated through the procedure
Activate. When the transaction closes, the directory is deactivated through
DeActivate. The function IsActive can be used to check if a directory is
active.

```
procedure export Activate(Adr:DirAdr; Credit:integer;
                                 var Done:Boolean);
  var
    Index: DirIndex;
  begin
    MakeActive(Adr, Credit, Index, Done)
  end Activate;

procedure export DeActivate(Adr:DirAdr);
  begin
    MakeInactive(Adr)
  end DeActivate;

function export IsActive(Adr:DirAdr) return Boolean;
  var
    Index: DirIndex; Active: Boolean;
  begin
    ChkActive(Adr, Index, Active); return Active
  end IsActive;
```

Setting the Current Directory

When a user logs in, the procedure NewJob is invoked to initialize JobRec
for that job, and to set the root as the current directory.

```
procedure export NewJob(ProcNum:ProcIndex;
                        DirDesc,ShrDesc:DirCap;
                        Credit:integer; var Done:Boolean);
  begin
    with JobArr[ProcNum] do
    begin
      Root := DirDesc; Current := Root;
      ShrDir := ShrDesc;
      MakeActive(DirDesc.Adr, Credit, CurInd, Done)
    end
  end NewJob;
```

For a job to set a new current directory, the previous current directory is
deactivated and the new directory is activated. The root is never
deactivated since, at any time, the user can reset his current directory to
the root.

```
procedure export SetCurrent(DirDesc:DirCap; Credit:integer;
                                 var Done:Boolean);
  begin
    with JobArr[ProcId] do
    begin
      if Current.Adr ≠ Root.Adr
```

```
        then MakeInactive(Current.Adr);
        MakeActive(DirDesc.Adr, Credit, CurInd, Done);
        if Done
            then Current := DirDesc
    end
end SetCurrent;
```

When a user resets the root as the current directory, since the root is always active, its index in DirArr is retrieved through GetIndex.

```
function GetIndex(AdrDir:DirAdr) return DirIndex;
var
    Index: DirIndex;
begin
    with JobArr[ProcId] do
        if Current.Adr = AdrDir
            then Index := CurInd
        else
            for I in 1 to ActDirMax do
                with DirArr[I] do
                    if (UseCount ≠ 0) and (Adr = AdrDir) then
                    begin
                        Index := I; exit
                    end;
        return Index
end GetIndex;

procedure export SetRoot;
    begin
        with JobArr[ProcId] do
        begin
            CurInd := GetIndex(Root.Adr);
            Current := Root
        end
    end SetRoot;
```

A job can also set its shared directory as the current directory. When a shared directory is activated, its credit is set to zero. This effectively prevents the creation of files and directories in the shared directory.

```
procedure export SetShrDir(var Done:Boolean);
    begin
        with JobArr[ProcId] do
        begin
            MakeActive(ShrDir.Adr, 0, CurInd, Done);
            if Done
                then Current := ShrDir
        end
    end SetShrDir;
```

Procedures for retrieving the address and access rights for the current and shared directories of a job are simple to implement.

```
procedure export GetDir(var DirDesc:DirCap);
  begin
    DirDesc := JobArr[ProcId].Current
  end GetDir;

procedure export GetShrDir(var ShrDesc:DirCap);
  begin
    ShrDesc := JobArr[ProcId].ShrDir
  end GetShrDir;
```

Checking Space Quota Limits

Procedures for retrieving and updating the quota manipulate Credit after getting the index of the directory by calling GetIndex.

```
procedure export DecQuota(DirDesc:DirCap; Amount:integer;
                          var Done:Boolean);
  begin
    with DirArr[GetIndex(DirDesc.Adr)] do
      if Credit – Amount < 0
        then Done := false
      else
      begin
        Credit := Credit – Amount; Done := true
      end
  end DecQuota;

procedure export IncQuota(DirDesc:DirCap; Amount:integer);
  begin
    with DirArr[GetIndex(DirDesc.Adr)]
      do Credit := Credit + Amount
  end IncQuota;

function export GetQuota(DirDesc:DirCap) return integer;
  begin
    with DirArr[GetIndex(DirDesc.Adr)]
      do return Credit
  end GetQuota;
```

There is a procedure which, given a directory, returns its status, a Boolean showing whether it is active, and the value of its Credit.

```
procedure export GetStatus(Adr:DirAdr; var Credit:integer;
                           var Active:Boolean);
  var
    Index: DirIndex;
```

```
begin
  ChkActive(Adr, Index, Active);
  if Active
    then Credit := DirArr[Index].Credit
end GetStatus;
```

The Master File Directory

Capabilities to various root directories are contained in a distinguished system directory, called the Master File Directory (MFD). The MFD is made active when the system starts and then always remains active. We can define procedures for setting and retrieving the address of the MFD. The address is set at system generation time and is subsequently required for system administration activities like authenticating a user, registering a new user, etc.

```
var
  MFDDesc: DirCap;

procedure export GetMFD(var MFDCap:DirCap);
  begin
    MFDCap := MFDDesc
  end GetMFD;

procedure export SetMFD(MFDCap:DirCap);
  begin
    MFDDesc := MFDCap
  end SetMFD;
```

The initialization code of this monitor sets UseCount to zero for all entries in DirArr.

```
begin {JobDir}
  for I in 1 to ActDirMax
    do DirArr[I].UseCount := 0
end JobDir;
```

MAINTAINING DIRECTORIES

A directory consists of capabilities and we need procedures for manipulating them when objects are created, deleted, renamed etc. Since we cannot allow concurrent access to a directory, we encapsulate these procedures in a monitor, DirHandler.

```
var
   DirHandler: monitor
                  import
                     var : JobDir, SysIndir, ActFiles, Disk, FileErr
                  end;

      type
         Directory =
            record
               Quota, Consumed: integer;
               FileArr: array [1 .. FileMax] of DirEntry
            end Directory;

      var
         Dir: Directory; Loaded: Boolean; PresentDir: DiskAdr;
         Vadr, Vsize: integer;
```

We have only one monitor, DirHandler, operating on all directories. For every request, DirHandler operates on a directory by reading it into main memory, performing the action, and writing it back to the disk.

A directory need only be read in if it is not already in main memory. The Boolean Loaded indicates if a directory is loaded and, if so, PresentDir contains its disk address. The variables Vadr and Vsize contain the address and size of the variable Dir, and they are used in the procedure LoadDir which loads a directory if it is not already loaded.

```
procedure LoadDir(DirPtr:DiskAdr);
   begin
      if not Loaded or (DirPtr ≠ PresentDir) then
      begin
         Disk.Read(DirPtr, 0, Vsize, Vadr);
         Loaded := true; PresentDir :=DirPtr
      end
   end LoadDir;
```

Error Reporting

In the procedure LoadDir, we have assumed that there will not be any disk transfer errors. In practice, this is grossly optimistic and any of several errors may occur. It is particularly important for the file system to record such errors so that some action can be taken for recovery. Within the file system, the only recovery action possible is to abort the file system procedure that initiated the disk transfer and to report the error to the caller. But further recovery actions, such as aborting the user job, or even temporarily shutting the system down, can be taken by modules responsible for job management or system administration.

In addition to reporting the error to the calling modules, the file system logs the errors encountered, describing the nature of error and indicating which object (file descriptor, directory, or MFD) has become inaccessible due to the error. The errors logged by the file system are

```
type
    FileSysErr = (BadDescriptor, BadDirectory, BadMFD, PackOffLine);
```

(We have defined FileSysErr as a scalar type just to enumerate the various errors possible. In our subsequent discussion, we will treat FileSysErr as a subrange of CallStatus.)

A monitor, FileErr, stores errors in a queue of messages that can be later retrieved for examination.

```
var
    FileErr: monitor;

        var
        ErrQ: FiFoQ(ErrQMax);
        ErrMsg: array [1 .. ErrQMax] of
                        record
                            Err: FileSysErr; Posn: DiskAdr
                        end ErrMsg;

        procedure export PutError(Msg:FileSysErr; DiskPosn:DiskAdr);
            begin
                if not ErrQ.Full then
                    with ErrMsg[ErrQ.Put] do
                    begin
                        Err := Msg; Posn := DiskPosn
                    end
            end PutError;

        function export IsError return Boolean;
            begin
                return not ErrQ.Empty
            end IsError;

        procedure export GetError(var Msg:FileSysErr;
                                    var DiskPosn:DiskAdr);
            begin
                if not ErrQ.Empty then
                    with ErrMsg[ErrQ.Get] do
                    begin
                        Msg := Err; DiskPosn := Posn
                    end
            end GetError;

    end FileErr;
```

We can now rewrite the procedure LoadDir taking errors into account. If the disk transfer returns with an error, we log the error as BadDirectory or PackOffLine, as appropriate, and return to the caller with an error.

```
procedure LogError(Err:IoErr; Posn:DiskAdr; var Msg:FileSysErr);
  begin
    case Err of
      NotAvail: Msg := PackOffLine;
      Fail: Msg := BadDirectory
    end;
    FileErr.PutError(Msg, Posn)
  end LogError;

procedure LoadDir(DirPtr:DiskAdr)
  error FileSysErr;
  var
    Msg: FileSysErr;
  begin
    if not Loaded or (DirPtr ≠ PresentDir) then
    begin
      Disk.Read(DirPtr, 0, Vsize, Vadr)
        iferror
          begin
            Loaded := false;
            LogError(errorval, DirPtr, Msg);
            return error Msg
          end;
      Loaded := true; PresentDir := DirPtr
    end
  end LoadDir;
```

Similar checks for errors will be made in many of the procedures and functions in this chapter. They can be ignored on a first reading, because they do not alter the structure of the program. But checking for errors is an important activity in an operating system and, though often tiresome in detail, such checks must be placed at strategic points in the program.

Directory Lookup

There are three kinds of retrieval operations on a directory. One is to check if there is a capability in the directory with a given name. This is needed when we create new objects as no two objects in the same directory can have the same name. This operation is implemented by the procedure Lookup. Another retrieval operation, performed by the procedure GetEntry, is to retrieve a capability with the given name from the directory. Here, we also have to ensure that the named capability is of the proper type. The third retrieval operation, ListEntry, merely returns a capability in a directory.

```
procedure CheckEntry(DirPtr:DiskAdr; Fname:Name;
                     var Index:integer; var Found:Boolean)
  error FileSysErr;
  begin
    Found := false;
    LoadDir(DirPtr)
      iferror return error errorval;
    for I in 1 to FileMax do
      with Dir.FileArr[I] do
        if Used and (LocalName = Fname) then
        begin
          Found := true; Index := I; exit
        end
  end CheckEntry;

procedure export Lookup(DirPtr:DiskAdr; Fname:Name;
                        var Status:CallStatus);
  var
    Index: 1 .. FileMax; Found: Boolean;
  begin
    CheckEntry(DirPtr, Fname, Index, Found)
      iferror Status := errorval
      otherwise
        if Found
          then Status := Success
          else Status := ObjNotFound
  end Lookup;

procedure export GetEntry(DirPtr:DiskAdr; Fname:Name;
                          var Fentry:DirEntry;
                          var Status:CallStatus);
  var
    Index: 1 .. FileMax; Found: Boolean;
  begin
    CheckEntry(DirPtr, Fname, Index, Found)
      iferror
        begin
          Status := errorval; return
        end;
    if Found
      then copyview(Fentry, Dir.FileArr[Index])
              iferror Found := false;
    if Found
      then Status := Success
      else Status := ObjNotFound
  end GetEntry;

procedure export ListEntry(DirPtr:DiskAdr; Index:integer;
                           var Fentry:DirEntry;
                           var Status:CallStatus);
```

```
begin
  Status := Success;
  if Index > FileMax
    then Status := FileNotFound
  else LoadDir(DirPtr)
         iferror Status := errorval
         otherwise Fentry := Dir.FileArr[Index]
end ListEntry;
```

Note that the check that the named capability is of the proper type is implicitly achieved through the procedure **copyview**. For example, in an invocation of GetEntry, if the actual parameter for Fentry is of type DirEntry(Link) and the entry with the given name in the directory is not a link, **copyview** returns an error.

Creating a New Capability

Capabilities are entered in a directory when newly created files are closed, when directories are created, or when objects are to be shared. When a new capability is entered, it is necessary to ensure that the name of the capability is not a duplicate. Also, if the capability is the owner capability for an object, we have to update the field, Dir.Consumed, which records the number of blocks used. Performing this update at this time, rather than at the time of the creation of files and segments, improves the performance. It also ensures that if there is a system failure before a file is closed, the value of Consumed is consistent with the fact that the creation of the file is not recorded.

```
procedure WriteEntry(DirPtr:DiskAdr; Fentry:DirEntry;
                     var Done:Boolean)
  error FileSysErr;
  var
    Msg: FileSysErr;
  begin
    Done := false;
    with Dir do
    begin
      for I in 1 to FileMax do
        if not FileArr[I].Used then
        begin
          copyview(FileArr[I], Fentry);
          FileArr[I].Used := true; Done := true;
          exit
        end;
      if Done then
      begin
```

```
            case view(Fentry) of
              File: Consumed := Consumed + Fentry.Fattr.BlkAlloc;
              Root, SubDir: Consumed := Consumed + Dirsegsize
            end;
            Disk.Write(DirPtr, 0, Vsize, Vadr)
              iferror
                begin
                  LogError(errorval, DirPtr, Msg);
                  return error Msg
                end
          end
        end
      end WriteEntry;

    procedure export NewEntry(DirPtr:DiskAdr; Fentry:DirEntry;
                              var Status:CallStatus);
      var
        Found, Done: Boolean; Index: 1 .. FileMax;
      begin
        Status := Success;
        CheckEntry(DirPtr, Fentry.LocalName, Index, Found)
          iferror Status := errorval
          otherwise
            if Found
              then Status := DuplicateName
            else WriteEntry(DirPtr, Fentry, Done)
                  iferror Status := errorval
                  otherwise
                    if not Done
                      then Status := DirFull
      end NewEntry;
```

Updating an Existing Capability

An existing capability may sometimes have to be updated. For instance,
when new segments are added to a file, the owner capability for the file has
to be updated to include the changed attributes of the file.

```
    procedure export UpdateEntry(DirPtr:DiskAdr; Fentry:DirEntry;
                                 var Status:CallStatus);
      var
        OldEntry: DirEntry; Index: integer;
        Found: Boolean; Msg: FileSysErr;
      begin
        Status := Success;
        CheckEntry(DirPtr, Fentry.LocalName, Index, Found)
          iferror
            begin
              Status := errorval;
```

```
                return
              end;
        if not Found
          then Status := ObjNotFound
        else
        begin
          copyview(OldEntry, Dir.FileArr[Index]);

          if view(Fentry, File) then
            if view(OldEntry, File)
              then Dir.Consumed := Dir.Consumed
                                   + Fentry.Fattr.BlkAlloc
                                   − OldEntry.Fattr.BlkAlloc;
          copyview(Dir.FileArr[Index], Fentry);
          Disk.Write(DirPtr, 0, Vsize, Vadr)
            iferror
              begin
                LogError(errorval, DirPtr, Msg);
                Status := Msg
              end
        end
      end UpdateEntry;
```

Renaming a Capability

Renaming a capability changes the name of the capability but, as we discussed earlier, it also has an important side effect: revocation of access. In addition, there is a subtle problem when active files are renamed. We described in the previous chapter how Arbiter enforces concurrency control for an active file by checking if a requested operation is in conflict with a transaction in progress. To check whether a file is active, ActFiles uses only the name of the file (more precisely, the name of the owner capability of the file). So, if an active file is renamed and only the owner capability in the owner directory is altered, it is possible for a job to initiate a new transaction using the renamed capability. In such a case, Arbiter cannot enforce proper control since it would use only the new name and cannot detect conflicts even if the file is active with the old name. Notice that this problem arises because, unlike directories, there is no unique internal name for a file. Hence, renaming active files should change both the directory entry as well as the file entry in ActFiles. The two changes should be done atomically (i.e. indivisibly).

```
        procedure export Rename(DirDesc:DirCap;
                                OldName,NewName:Name;
                                var Status:CallStatus);
```

```
var
  Index: 1 .. FileMax; Found: Boolean;
  Msg: FileSysErr;
begin
  Status := Success;
  CheckEntry(DirDesc.DirPtr, OldName, Index, Found)
    iferror
      begin
        Status := errorval;
        return
      end;
  if not Found
    then Status := ObjNotFound
  else
  begin
    if viewval(Dir.FileArr[Index]) = File
      then ActFiles.Rename(DirDesc.Adr, OldName, NewName,
                           Found);
    Dir.FileArr[Index].LocalName := NewName;
    Disk.Write(DirDesc.DirPtr, 0, Vsize, Vadr)
      iferror
        begin
          LogError(errorval, DirDesc.DirPtr, Msg);
          Status := Msg
        end
  end
end Rename;
```

Handling Links

When an object is accessed through a link, we have to retrieve the owner
capability for the object. The procedure FetchObj, given below, follows the
link, reads in the owner directory (if it exists) and fetches the owner
capability. Notice that revocation is possible either by renaming or deleting
the owner capability, or by deleting the owner directory. FetchObj takes
these possibilities into account and, when possible, fetches the owner
capability and the address of the owner directory.

```
procedure FetchObj(DirDesc:DirCap; Fname:Name;
                   var OwnerDir:DirCap;
                   var Fentry:DirEntry; var Found:Boolean)
error FileSysErr;
var
  Index: 1 .. FileMax; Rts: AccessRights;
begin
  CheckEntry(DirDesc.DirPtr, Fname, Index, Found)
    iferror return error errorval;
  if Found then
```

```
   begin
     Rts := Dir.FileArr[Index].Rights;
     if view(Dir.FileArr[Index], Link) then
     begin
       SysIndir.GetDiskAdr(OwnerDirAdr, OwnerDir.DirPtr, Found);
       if Found then
       begin
         OwnerDir.Adr := OwnerDirAdr;
         CheckEntry(OwnerDir.DirPtr, OwnerCap, Index, Found)
           iferror return error errorval
       end
     end
     else OwnerDir := DirDesc
   end;
   if Found
     then copyview(Fentry, Dir.FileArr[Index])
           iferror Found := false
           otherwise Fentry.Rights := Rts
 end FetchObj;
```

When a file is accessed through a link, the file and the owner directory have
to be made active. The procedure GetFile fetches the owner capability and
activates the owner directory, and the file (if it is found). For making a
directory active, JobDir requires Credit, the amount of free disk space
available for that directory. To supply this data, we check if the directory is
already active and, if so, retrieve Credit from JobDir; otherwise, we
compute the value of Credit from the values of Quota and Consumed
contained in the directory.

```
   procedure export GetFile(DirDesc:DirCap; Fname:Name;
                            var Fentry:DirEntry; var OwnerDir:DirCap;
                            var Findex:FileIndex;
                            var Status:CallStatus);
     var
       Credit: integer; Found, Active: Boolean;
     begin
       FetchObj(DirDesc, Fname, OwnerDir, Fentry, Found)
         iferror
           begin
             Status := errorval; return
           end;
       JobDir.GetStatus(OwnerDir.Adr, Credit, Active);
       if not Active
         then Credit := Dir.Quota – Dir.Consumed;
       JobDir.Activate(OwnerDir.Adr, Credit, Active);
       if not Active
         then Status := ActDirTooMany
       else
         if not Found
           then Status := FileNotFound
```

```
        else
        begin
            ActFiles.Activate(OwnerDir.Adr, Fentry.LocalName,
                              Findex, Active);
            if not Active
                then Status := ActFilesTooMany
                else Status := Success
        end
    end GetFile;
```

Deletion of Capabilities

Deletion of links and file capabilities is quite simple and can always be done. But the owner capability for a directory cannot be deleted if the directory is not empty. This rule is enforced so that the file system need not perform any implicit deletion of objects. For the same reason, deletion of active directories is not allowed. In the case of active files, Arbiter delays the job requesting the deletion. We should not insist on such arbitration for active directories since, usually, a directory is active for a longer duration than a file. Hence, to simplify the implementation, an attempt to delete an active directory is signalled as an error.

```
    function IsEmpty(Adr:DirAdr) return CallStatus;
    var
        Found: Boolean; DirPtr: DiskAdr;
    begin
        SysIndir.GetDiskAdr(Adr, DirPtr, Found);
        LoadDir(DirPtr)
            iferror return errorval;
        for I in 1 to FileMax do
        if Dir.FileArr[I].Used
            then return DirNonEmpty;
        return Success
    end IsEmpty;

    procedure export DeleteEntry(DirPtr:DiskAdr; Fname:Name;
                                 var Fentry:DirEntry;
                                 var Status:CallStatus);
    var
        Index, Size: integer; Found: Boolean;
        Msg: FileSysErr;
    begin
        Status := Success;
        CheckEntry(DirPtr, Fname, Index, Found)
            iferror
                begin
                    Status := errorval; return
                end;
```

```
            if not Found
              then Status := ObjNotFound
            else copyview(Fentry, Dir.FileArr[Index])
                    iferror Status := ObjNotFound
                    otherwise
                      case view(Fentry) of
                        File: Size := Fentry.Fattr.BlkAlloc;
                        SubDir:
                          begin
                            Size := DirSegsize;
                            if JobDir.IsActive(Adr)
                               then Status := DirActive
                               else Status := IsEmpty(Adr)
                          end;
                        Root:
                          begin
                            Size := DirSegsize;
                            if JobDir.IsActive(Adr)
                                or JobDir.IsActive(ShrDirAdr)
                               then Status := DirActive
                               else Status := IsEmpty(Adr)
                          end;
                        Link: Size := 0
                      end;
        if Status = Success then
        begin
           LoadDir(DirPtr)
             iferror
               begin
                 Status := errorval;
                 return
               end;
           with Dir do
           begin
             Consumed := Consumed – Size;
             FileArr[Index].Used := false
           end;
           Disk.Write(DirPtr, 0, Vsize, Vadr)
             iferror
               begin
                 LogError(errorval, DirPtr, Msg);
                 Status := Msg
               end
        end
      end DeleteEntry;
```

Setting the Current Directory

To set a directory as the current one for a job, we have to fetch its owner
capability and make the directory active.

```
procedure export SetCurDir(DirDesc:DirCap; DirName:Name;
                           var Status:CallStatus);
var
  NewDir, OwnerDir: DirCap; Done, Active: Boolean;
  Credit: integer;
  Fentry: DirEntry(SubDir);
begin
  FetchObj(DirDesc, DirName, OwnerDir, Fentry, Done)
    iferror
      begin
        Status := errorval;
        return
      end;
    if not Done
      then Status := DirNotFound
    else
    begin
      NewDir.Adr := Fentry.Adr;
      NewDir.Rights := Fentry.Rights;
      SysIndir.GetDiskAdr(NewDir.Adr, NewDir.DirPtr, Done);
      JobDir.GetStatus(NewDir.Adr, Credit, Active);
      if not Active then
      begin
        LoadDir(NewDir.DirPtr)
          iferror
            begin
              Status := errorval;
              return
            end;
        Credit := Dir.Quota − Dir.Consumed
      end;
      JobDir.SetCurrent(NewDir, Credit, Done);
      if Done
        then Status := Success
        else Status := ActDirTooMany
    end
  end SetCurDir;
```

We must also provide a procedure, GetDirData, for retrieving quota information directly from the directory. This information will be required, for example, when printing the contents of a directory.

```
procedure export GetDirData(DirPtr:DiskAdr;
                            var Qta,Used:integer;
                            var Status:CallStatus);
begin
  LoadDir(DirPtr)
    iferror Status := errorval
    otherwise
      with Dir do
```

```
            begin
                Status := Success; Qta := Quota; Used := Consumed
            end
        end GetDirData;
```

The procedure, InitDir, initializes a directory.

```
        procedure export InitDir(Qta:integer; DirPtr:DiskAdr;
                            var Status:CallStatus);

        var
            Msg: FileSysErr;
        begin
            Status := Success;
            with Dir do
            begin
                Quota := Qta; Consumed := 0;
                for I in 1 to FileMax
                    do FileArr[I].Used := false
            end;
            Disk.Write(DirPtr, 0, Vsize, Vadr)
                iferror
                    begin
                        LogError(errorval, DirPtr, Msg);
                        Status := Msg
                    end
        end InitDir;
```

The initialization code of DirHandler sets Vadr and Vsize to the address and size of Dir and initializes the Boolean Loaded.

```
        begin
            Vadr := varadr(Dir); Vsize := varsize(Dir);
            Loaded := false
        end DirHandler;
```

We have only one monitor, DirHandler, for manipulating all directories. This design has the disadvantage that it prevents concurrent operations on different directories. To improve performance, we can redefine DirHandler as a type and declare an array of DirHandler, each handling one directory at a time, e.g. as

```
        var
            Directories: array [1 .. N] of DirHandler;
```

We have to prevent concurrent operations on the same directory and this could be done by defining a monitor, say Controller, which keeps a table giving the array index in Directories of the monitor for each directory. We can encapsulate all these monitors in a pure class, say DirMan. Then, all operations on directories will be routed through DirMan, which first requests Controller to 'allocate' a DirHandler monitor for its use, invokes that monitor to perform the desired operation and, after completion, 'releases' the DirHandler monitor.

This extension illustrates the way the basic design can be easily modified for performance improvement. However, in our further discussion, we will not consider this two-level structure and we assume there will be only one monitor, DirHandler, for handling all directories.

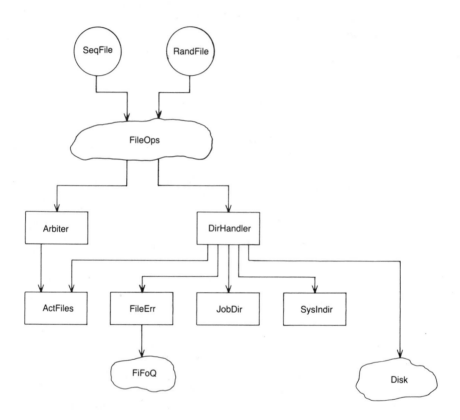

Fig. 9.1 A skeleton structure of the file system.

MANAGING FILE OPERATIONS

Until now, we have described two kinds of components of the file system: the user-level file classes, SeqFile and RandFile, form one kind and the

internal monitors, ActFiles, Arbiter, SysIndir, JobDir and DirHandler, consti-
tute the other. The internal monitors implement individual functions, like
controlling concurrent access to files, providing basic operations on
directories etc. However, there are still several requirements to be met for
implementing operations on files. Many of the functions common to all
files, like access control checks, creation and deletion of files and segments,
invoking Arbiter to enforce concurrency control etc., still remain to be
provided (see Fig. 9.1). We now describe the modules implementing these
functions.

Managing File Descriptors

The information in a file descriptor is needed both to retrieve the addresses
of segments and to add segments to a file. We use a single monitor,
FileDesc, for managing all file descriptors. At any given time, the monitor
procedures manipulate only one descriptor, which is read from disk into
the variable Desc and written back to disk after it has been modified. The
technique used is similar to the one used in DirHandler.

```
var
   FileDesc: monitor
               import
                     var : FileErr, Disk, DiskSpace
                  end;
         type export
           SegAttr =
              record
                 Used: Boolean; SegAdr: DiskAdr
              end SegAttr;
           FileDescriptor = array [1 .. SegMax] of SegAttr;
         var
           Desc: FileDescriptor;
           DescAdr, DescSize: integer;
           Loaded: Boolean; CurrentDesc: DiskAdr;
```

DescAdr and DescSize are set to the address and size of Desc and are used
during transfers to the disk. The Boolean Loaded indicates if a descriptor
has been loaded, and CurrentDesc has the address of the descriptor
currently loaded in the monitor.

To create a descriptor on the disk, the variable Desc is first initialized and
written to a specified address on the disk. If the disk transfer returns with
error, we log the error as BadDescriptor or PackOffLine, as before, and
report the error to the caller.

```
procedure LogError(Err:IoErr; Posn:DiskAdr; var Msg:FileSysErr);
  begin
    case Err of
      NotAvail: Msg := PackOffLine;
      otherwise: Msg := BadDescriptor
    end;
    FileErr.PutError(Msg, Posn)
  end LogError;


procedure export InitDesc(FileAdr:DiskAdr; var Status:CallStatus);
  var
    Msg: FileSysErr;
  begin
    Status := Success;
    for I in 1 to SegMax
      do Desc[I].Used := false;
    Disk.Write(FileAdr, 0, DescSize, DescAdr)
      iferror
        begin
          LogError(errorval, FileAdr, Msg);
          Status := Msg
        end
  end InitDesc;
```

A file descriptor must be loaded into main memory when a segment of the
file is accessed, or when a new segment is created. Note that the descriptor
need only be loaded into memory if it is not already there. Procedure
LoadDesc performs this check and loads the descriptor when necessary.

```
procedure LoadDesc(FileAdr:DiskAdr)
  error FileSysErr;
  var
    Msg: FileSysErr;
  begin
    if not Loaded or (CurrentDesc ≠ FileAdr) then
    begin
      Disk.Read(FileAdr, 0, DescSize, DescAdr)
        iferror
          begin
            Loaded := false;
            LogError(errorval, FileAdr, Msg);
            return error Msg
          end;
      Loaded := true;
      CurrentDesc := FileAdr
    end
  end LoadDesc;
```

```
procedure export GetSegAttr(FileAdr:DiskAdr; SegNum:integer;
                            var Attr:SegAttr;
                            var Status:CallStatus);
begin
   LoadDesc(FileAdr)
      iferror Status := errorval
      otherwise
         begin
            Attr := Desc[SegNum]; Status := Success
         end
end GetSegAttr;
```

When a new segment is to be added to a file, the descriptor is read into main memory, appropriately modified and written back.

```
procedure export AddSeg(FileAdr:DiskAdr; SegNum:integer;
                        Adr:DiskAdr; var Status:CallStatus);
var
   Msg: FileSysErr;
begin
   Status := Success;
   LoadDesc(FileAdr)
      iferror
         begin
            Status := errorval; return
         end;
   with Desc[SegNum] do
   begin
      Used := true; SegAdr := Adr
   end;
   Disk.Write(FileAdr, 0, DescSize, DescAdr)
      iferror
         begin
            LogError(errorval, FileAdr, Msg); Status := Msg
         end
end AddSeg;
```

A file is deleted by first deleting its component segments and then the file descriptor.

```
procedure export Delete(FileAdr:DiskAdr; var Status:CallStatus);
begin
   Status := Success;
   LoadDesc(FileAdr)
      iferror Status := errorval;
   if Status = Success then
   begin
      for I in 1 to SegMax do
         if Desc[I].Used
```

```
            then DiskSpace.Release(Desc[I].SegAdr);
         DiskSpace.Release(FileAdr)
      end
   end Delete;
```

The initialization code sets the address and size of the data area of Desc
and initializes the Boolean Loaded.

```
   begin
      DescAdr := varadr(Desc); DescSize := varsize(Desc);
      Loaded := false
   end FileDesc;
```

Maintaining File Attributes

When a file participates in a transaction, certain of its attributes have to be
retained in memory until the transaction closes. For example, we should
know the owner directory of the file, because when the transaction closes
we may have to update the capability in the owner directory. We define a
monitor, FileBase, for maintaining the attributes of all active files.

```
var
   FileBase: monitor;
      var
      FileArr: array [FileIndex] of
               record
                  Owner: DirAdr;
                  Fentry: DirEntry(File);
                  CurrentSeg: integer;
                  CurSegAttr: SegAttr
               end FileArr;
```

For every active file, we keep the address of the owner directory, the
owner capability of the file and the attributes of the current segment of the
file. The current segment attributes are needed when data is read from or
written to the file. FileBase provides procedures for retrieving and
modifying the attributes of active files.

```
            procedure export GetFileAttr(Findex:FileIndex;
                                          var OwnerDir:DirAdr;
                                          var Ent:DirEntry(File));
         begin
            with FileArr[Findex] do
            begin
               OwnerDir := Owner;
               Ent := Fentry
            end
         end GetFileAttr;
```

```
procedure export PutFileAttr(Findex:FileIndex; OwnerDir:DirAdr;
                             Ent:DirEntry(File));
  begin
    with FileArr[Findex] do
    begin
      Owner := OwnerDir; Fentry := Ent
    end
  end PutFileAttr;

procedure export GetCurrentSeg(Findex:FileIndex;
                          var SegNum:integer;
                          var Attr:SegAttr);
  begin
    with FileArr[Findex] do
    begin
      SegNum := CurrentSeg; Attr := CurSegAttr
    end
  end GetCurrentSeg;

procedure export SetCurrentSeg(Findex:FileIndex;
                          SegNum:integer;
                          Attr:SegAttr);
  begin
    with FileArr[Findex] do
    begin
      CurrentSeg := SegNum; CurSegAttr := Attr
    end
  end SetCurrentSeg;

end FileBase;
```

Implementing File Operations

We now have all the monitors necessary to control operations on files. We can encapsulate them in a pure class, FileMan, to manage these operations.

When a file is to be opened, operations in the classes SeqFile and Randfile invoke the procedure OpenFile in FileMan. This procedure checks if there is a capability in the current directory for the file and, if so, whether it has adequate rights to perform the specified access. It also checks if the mode and kind of the file are proper. If the specified file does not exist, OpenFile creates a new file after ensuring that the current directory has a large enough quota. Finally, OpenFile invokes Arbiter to enforce concurrency control.

```
var
  FileMan: pure class
           import
```

```
              var : JobDir, Arbiter, FileDesc, FileBase, DirHandler,
                    ActFiles, DiskSpace, SysIndir, Disk
          end;

procedure CreateFile(DirDesc:DirCap; var FileAdr:DiskAdr;
                              var Status:CallStatus);
  var
    Done: Boolean;
  begin
    JobDir.DecQuota(DirDesc, FileDescsize, Done);
    if not Done
      then Status := QuotaFull
    else
    begin
      FileAdr.Pack := DirDesc.DirPtr.Pack;
      DiskSpace.AllotNew(FileAdr, FileDescsize)
        iferror Status := PackFull
        otherwise FileDesc.InitDesc(FileAdr, Status)
    end
  end CreateFile;

procedure export OpenFile(Fname:Name; Fkind:FileKind;
                              Fmode:FileMode;
                              AccMode:Access; var Status:CallStatus;
                              var Findex:FileIndex;
                              var Lastseg,LastSegsize:integer);
  var
    Fentry: DirEntry(File); DirDesc, OwnerDir: DirCap;
    Found, Created, Active: Boolean;
  begin
    Status := Success;
    Created := false; Active := false;
    JobDir.GetDir(DirDesc);
    DirHandler.GetFile(DirDesc, Fname, Fentry, OwnerDir, Findex,
                       Status);
    if Status = FileNotFound then
    begin
      if AccMode = Write then
        if not (Write in DirDesc.Rights)
          then Status := RightsCheck
        else
        begin
          Status := Success;
          with Fentry do
          begin
            LocalName := Fname;
            if Fmode = Sequential
              then Rights := AccessRights[Read, Write, Append,
                                          Execute]
              else Rights := AccessRights[Read, Write, Update,
                                          Execute];
```

```
                with Fattr do
                begin
                   Kind := FKind; Mode := Fmode; BlkAlloc := 0;
                   LastSeg := 0; LastSegsize := 0
                end
             end;
             Createfile(DirDesc, Fentry.Fattr.FileDescAdr, Status);
             if Status = Success then
             begin
                Created := true;
                ActFiles.Activate(DirDesc.Adr, Fname, Findex, Active);
                if not Active
                   then Status := ActFilesTooMany
             end
          end
       end
       else
          if Status = Success then
          begin
             Active := true;
             if AccMode = Write
                then Status := DuplicateName
             else
                with Fentry do
                begin
                   if Fkind ≠ Fattr.Kind
                      then Status := IllegalKind
                   else
                      if Fmode ≠ Fattr.Mode
                         then Status := IllegalMode
                      else
                         if not (AccMode in Rights)
                            then Status := RightsCheck
                end
          end;
          if Status = Success
             then Arbiter.Enter(Findex, AccMode, Status);
          if Status ≠ Success then
          begin
             if Created then
             begin
                DiskSpace.Release(Fentry.Fattr.FileDescAdr);
                JobDir.IncQuota(DirDesc, FileDescsize)
             end;
             if Active
                then ActFiles.DeActivate(Findex, Active);
             JobDir.DeActivate(OwnerDir.Adr)
          end
          else
          begin
             FileBase.PutFileAttr(Findex, OwnerDir.Adr, Fentry);
```

```
        with Fentry do
        begin
            LastSeg := Fattr.LastSeg; LastSegsize := Fattr.LastSegsize
        end
    end
end OpenFile;
```

Note that the file being opened and its owner directory are both made active while retrieving the owner capability through GetFile. In case the operation fails, the file and the directory are deactivated.

A file is closed by calling CloseFile to install the file in the directory, either by entering a new capability, in the case of Write access, or by updating an existing capability, in the case of Append or Update access. The owner directory can be deactivated and Arbiter informed of the closing event.

```
        procedure export CloseFile(Findex:FileIndex; AccMode:Access;
                                var Status:CallStatus);
        var
            Fentry: DirEntry(File); OwnerDir: DirCap; Found: Boolean;
        begin
            if AccMode ≠ Read then
            begin
                FileBase.GetFileAttr(Findex, OwnerDir.Adr, Fentry);
                SysIndir.GetDiskAdr(OwnerDir.Adr, OwnerDir.DirPtr, Found);
                if AccMode = Write
                    then DirHandler.NewEntry(OwnerDir.DirPtr, Fentry, Status)
                    else DirHandler.UpdateEntry(OwnerDir.DirPtr, Fentry, Status)
            end;
            JobDir.DeActivate(OwnerDir.Adr);
            Arbiter.Close(Findex)
        end CloseFile;
```

When a file is to be deleted, a check is made that there is no transaction pending on the file before the descriptor for the file is deleted.

```
        procedure export DeleteFile(Owner:DirAdr; Fname:Name;
                                FileAdr:DiskAdr;
                                var Status:CallStatus);
        begin
            Arbiter.Mark(Owner, Fname);
            FileDesc.Delete(FileAdr, Status)
        end DeleteFile;
```

A segment becomes current for a file when the previous segment boundary is crossed in a sequential file, or when a random file is positioned to that segment. When a segment becomes current, FileMan retrieves the attributes of that segment from the file descriptor and stores them in FileBase.

```
       procedure export SetSegCurrent(Findex:FileIndex;
                               SegNum:integer;
                               var SegUsed:Boolean;
                               var Status:CallStatus);
   var
       Fentry: DirEntry(File); Owner: DirAdr;
       Attr: SegAttr;
   begin
       Status := Success;

       FileBase.GetFileAttr(Findex, Owner, Fentry);
       FileDesc.GetSegAttr(Fentry.Fattr.FileDescAdr, SegNum, Attr,
                           Status);
       if Status = Success then
       begin
         if Attr.Used
            then FileBase.SetCurrentSeg(Findex, SegNum, Attr);
            SegUsed := Attr.Used
       end
   end SetSegCurrent;
```

When a segment of a file is to be created, the procedure CreateSeg is called to check if there is sufficient space in the owner directory and, if so, to invoke DiskSpace to allocate a segment. The created segment becomes the current one for that file.

```
       procedure export CreateSeg(Findex:FileIndex; SegNum:integer;
                               var Status:CallStatus);
   var
       Owner: DirCap; Fentry: DirEntry(File);
       Attr: SegAttr; Done: Boolean;
   begin
       Status := Success;
       FileBase.GetFileAttr(Findex, Owner.Adr, Fentry);
       SysIndir.GetDiskAdr(Owner.Adr, Owner.DirPtr, Done);
       JobDir.DecQuota(Owner, Segsize, Done);
       if not Done
          then Status := QuotaFull
       else
       begin
          DiskSpace.AllotNext(Fentry.Fattr.FileDescAdr, Attr.SegAdr,
                              Segsize)
          iferror Status := PackFull
          otherwise
             begin
                Attr.Used := true;
                FileBase.SetCurrentSeg(Findex, SegNum, Attr)
             end
       end
   end CreateSeg;
```

To add a new segment to a file, the address of the descriptor is retrieved
from FileBase, the descriptor is read into main memory, updated and
written back. The added segment now becomes the last segment of the file
and this changed attribute is recorded in FileBase. Note that the attributes
of the file (LastSeg etc.) are changed only in main memory to avoid
frequent disk transfers. When the file is closed, these attributes are written
into the owner directory.

```
        procedure export AddSeg(Findex:FileIndex; DataSize:integer;
                                var Status:CallStatus);
          var
            Owner: DirAdr; Fentry: DirEntry(File); SegNum: integer;
            Attr: SegAttr;
          begin
            FileBase.GetFileAttr(Findex, Owner, Fentry);
            FileBase.GetCurrentSeg(Findex, SegNum, Attr);
            FileDesc.AddSeg(Fentry.Fattr.FileDescAdr, SegNum, Attr.SegAdr,
                            Status);
            if Status = Success then
            begin
              with Fentry.FAttr do
              begin
                LastSeg := SegNum; LastSegsize := DataSize
              end;
              FileBase.PutFileAttr(Findex, Owner, Fentry)
            end
          end AddSeg;
```

FileMan provides procedures for transferring data from or to the current
segment of a file. The procedures allow transfer of parts of a segment in
units of blocks, and provide common operations for both sequential and
random files.

```
        procedure export Read(Findex:FileIndex;
                              BlkNum,MemAdr,Size:integer;
                              var Status:CallStatus);
          var
            SegNum: integer; Attr: SegAttr;
          begin
            Status := Success;
            FileBase.GetCurrentSeg(Findex, SegNum, Attr);
            Disk.Read(Attr.SegAdr, BlkNum, Size, MemAdr)
              iferror
                if errorval = NotAvail
                  then Status := PackOffLine
                  else Status := BadSegment
          end Read;
```

```
procedure export Write(Findex:FileIndex;
                      BlkNum,MemAdr,Size:integer;
                      var Status:CallStatus);
   var
      SegNum: integer; Attr: SegAttr;
   begin
      Status := Success;
      FileBase.GetCurrentSeg(Findex, SegNum, Attr);
      Disk.Write(Attr.SegAdr, BlkNum, Size, MemAdr)
         iferror
            if errorval = NotAvail
               then Status := PackOffLine
               else Status := BadSegment
      end Write;

   end FileMan;
```

IMPLEMENTING FILE SYSTEM PROCEDURES

SeqFile and RandFile, described earlier, provided the procedures Open, Get, Put and Close for implementing file transactions. Other file system procedures invoked by users for directory and file management are implemented by a single module, FileSys. FileSys is a pure class and it implements these operations using the various modules described thus far.

Setting Directories

Procedures for setting current, root and shared directories are simple to implement.

```
var
   FileSys: pure class
            import
               var : Disk, JobDir, SysIndir, DirHandler, DiskSpace,
                     FileMan, FileErr
            end;

   procedure export SetCurDir(DirName:Name; var Status:CallStatus);
      var
         DirDesc: DirCap;
      begin
         JobDir.GetDir(DirDesc);
         DirHandler.SetCurDir(DirDesc, Dirname, Status)
      end SetCurDir;
```

```
procedure export SetRoot;
  begin
    JobDir.Setroot
  end SetRoot;

procedure export SetShrDir(var Status:CallStatus);
  var
    Done: Boolean;
  begin
    JobDir.SetShrDir(Done);
    if not Done
      then Status := ActDirTooMany
      else Status := Success
  end SetShrDir;
```

Creating a Subdirectory

For a job to create a subdirectory, its current directory must have sufficient
disk space and the job must have Write access for its current directory. If
these requirements are satisfied, the disk space for the directory segment is
acquired, the directory is initialized and entered in Indir, and the owner
capability for the directory is entered in the current directory. The
operation may still fail if there are disk errors or if the name is a duplicate
in the current directory. In such cases, each of the previous steps must be
undone.

```
procedure export Dirgen(DirName:Name; Quota:integer;
                        var Status:CallStatus);
  var
    DirDesc: DirCap; Fentry: DirEntry(SubDir); Done: Boolean;
    DirPtr: DiskAdr;
  begin
    JobDir.GetDir(DirDesc);
    Status := Success;
    JobDir.DecQuota(DirDesc, Quota + DirSegsize, Done);
    if not Done then
    begin
      Status := QuotaFull; return
    end;
    if not (Write in DirDesc.Rights)
      then Status := RightsCheck
    else
    begin
      DirPtr.Pack := DirDesc.DirPtr.Pack;
      DiskSpace.AllotNew(DirPtr, DirSegsize)
        iferror Status := PackFull
        otherwise DirHandler.InitDir(Quota, DirPtr, Status);
      if Status = Success then
```

```
         with Fentry do
         begin
           LocalName := DirName;
           Rights := AccessRights[Read, Write, Update];
           SysIndir.NewDir(DirPtr, Adr, Done)
           if not Done
             then Status := DirTooMany
           else
           begin
             DirHandler.NewEntry(DirDesc.DirPtr, Fentry,
                                           Status);
               if Status ≠ Success
                 then SysIndir.RemoveDir(Adr)
           end
         end;
       if (Status ≠ Success) and (Status ≠ PackFull)
         then DiskSpace.Release(DirPtr)
     end;
     if Status ≠ Success
       then JobDir.IncQuota(DirDesc, Quota + DirSegsize)
   end Dirgen;
```

Name Management

The check for the existence of a name in the current directory, and the operation of renaming an object, are implemented as follows.

```
   procedure export Lookup(Fname:Name; var Status:CallStatus);
     var
       DirDesc: DirCap;
     begin
       Status := Success;
       JobDir.GetDir(DirDesc);
       if not (Read in DirDesc.Rights)
         then Status := RightsCheck
       else DirHandler.Lookup(DirDesc.DirPtr, Fname, Status)
     end Lookup;

   procedure export Rename(OldName,NewName:Name;
                             var Status:CallStatus);
     var
       DirDesc: DirCap;
     begin
       Status := Success;
       JobDir.GetDir(DirDesc);
       if not (Update in DirDesc.Rights)
         then Status := RightsCheck
       else DirHandler.Rename(DirDesc, OldName, NewName, Status)
     end Rename;
```

The procedure ListEntry retrieves a capability contained in the current directory.

```
procedure export ListEntry(Index:integer; var Ent:DirEntry;
                                var Status:CallStatus);
  var
    DirDesc: DirCap;
  begin
    Status := Success;
    JobDir.GetDir(DirDesc);
    if not (Read in DirDesc.Rights)
      then Status := RightsCheck
      else DirHandler.ListEntry(DirDesc.DirPtr, Index, Ent, Status)
  end ListEntry;
```

Deletion of Objects and Links

Since an object is owned by only one directory and others have only links to that object, deletion of capabilities should not require any special rights. But careful analysis reveals a subtle fact. Directories can be set current either through links or through owner capabilities. Hence, a job may not have all access rights over its current directory. We must insist that the job should have Update rights for its current directory, if it has to delete objects from this directory. If the job has sufficient rights, deletion is done by first deleting the entry from the directory. In the case of files, deletion requires permission from Arbiter. When a directory is deleted, its entry in Indir has to be removed.

```
procedure export Delete(Fname:Name; var Status:CallStatus);
  var
    DirDesc: DirCap; Fentry: DirEntry; DirPtr: DiskAdr;
    Found: Boolean;
  begin
    Status := Success;
    JobDir.GetDir(DirDesc);
    if not (Update in DirDesc.Rights)
      then Status := RightsCheck
    else
    begin
      DirHandler.DeleteEntry(DirDesc.DirPtr, Fname, Fentry,
                                Status);
      if Status = Success then
        case view(Fentry) of
          File: FileMan.DeleteFile(DirDesc.Adr, Fname,
                                Fentry.Fattr.FileDescAdr,
                                Status);
```

```
                SubDir:
                   begin
                      SysIndir.GetDiskAdr(Fentry.Adr, DirPtr, Found);
                      SysIndir.RemoveDir(Fentry.Adr);
                      DiskSpace.Release(DirPtr)
                   end
               end
            end
         end Delete;
```

Sharing

To enter a link for an object in the shared directory of another user, the address of the shared directory has to be retrieved. This is done by searching through the MFD for the capability for the receiving user's root directory. Having retrieved the address, it should be checked that the disk pack in which the shared directory is created is currently on-line. Procedure GetShrDir performs these functions.

```
         procedure GetShrDir(DirName:Name; var ShrDesc:DirCap;
                             var Status:CallStatus);
            var
               MFDDesc: DirCap; Fentry: DirEntry(Root);
               Found: Boolean;
            begin
               Status := Success;
               JobDir.GetMFD(MFDDesc);
               DirHandler.GetEntry(MFDDesc.DirPtr, DirName, Fentry, Status);
               if Status = BadDirectory then
               begin
                  FileErr.PutError(BadMFD, MFDDesc.DirPtr);
                  Status := BadMFD
               end;
               if Status = Success then
               begin
                  SysIndir.GetDiskAdr(Fentry.ShrDirAdr, ShrDesc.DirPtr, Found);
                  if not Found
                     then Status := DirNotFound
               end;
               if Status = Success then
                  if Disk.IsMounted(ShrDesc.DirPtr.Pack)
                     then ShrDesc.Adr := Fentry.ShrDirAdr
                  else Status := PackOffLine
            end GetShrDir;
```

Procedure Share retrieves the shared directory using GetShrDir, and invokes DirHandler to enter a link for the shared object in the shared directory.

```
procedure export Share(ShrdObj,DestDir,DestLink:Name;
                              Rts:AccessRights; Status:CallStatus);
var
  SdirDesc, DdirDesc: DirCap; Fentry: DirEntry(Link);
  Obj: DirEntry;
begin
  JobDir.GetDir(SdirDesc);
  DirHandler.GetEntry(SdirDesc.DirPtr, ShrdObj, Obj, Status);
  if Status = Success then
  begin
    GetShrDir(DestDir, DdirDesc, Status);
    if Status = Success then
    begin
      with Fentry do
      begin
        LocalName := DestLink; Rights := Rts;
        case view(Obj) of
          Link:
            with Fentry do
            begin
              OwnerDirAdr := Obj.OwnerDirAdr;
              OwnerCap := Obj.OwnerCap
            end;
          otherwise:
            begin
              OwnerDirAdr := SdirDesc.Adr;
              OwnerCap := ShrdObj
            end
        end
      end;
      DirHandler.NewEntry(DdirDesc.DirPtr, Fentry, Status);
    end
  end
end Share;
```

Note that the procedure takes into account the fact that the current directory may either have the owner capability or a link for the shared object. If the current directory only has a link, the address of the owner directory is retrieved from the link and entered in the newly created link.

The complementary operation of retrieving a link from a user's shared directory is performed by GetLink. Since this procedure is invoked by a user to operate on his shared directory, the address of the shared directory is retrieved from JobDir and there is no need to search through the MFD.

```
procedure export GetLink(OldLink,NewLink:Name;
                              var Status:CallStatus);
var
  DirDesc, ShrDirDesc: DirCap; Fentry: DirEntry(Link);
```

```
begin
  Status := Success;
  JobDir.GetDir(DirDesc);
  if not (Write in DirDesc.Rights)
    then Status := RightsCheck
  else
  begin
    JobDir.GetShrDir(ShrDirDesc);
    DirHandler.GetEntry(ShrDirDesc.DirPtr, OldLink, Fentry,
                          Status);
    if Status = Success then
    begin
      Fentry.LocalName := NewLink;
      DirHandler.NewEntry(DirDesc.DirPtr, Fentry, Status);
    end
  end
end GetLink;
```

Procedure CopyLink, for entering a link directly in another directory (called the destination), is slightly more complicated. First, the destination directory is made current and a new link is entered in the directory, and then the previous directory is reset to be the current one.

```
procedure export CopyLink(ShrdObj,DestDir,NewLink:Name;
                          Rts:AccessRights;
                          var Status:CallStatus);
var
  Obj: DirEntry; NewEntry: DirEntry(Link);
  DirDesc, DestDirDesc: DirCap; Credit: integer;
  Done: Boolean;
begin
  Status := Success;
  JobDir.GetDir(DirDesc);
  Credit := JobDir.GetQuota(DirDesc);
  DirHandler.GetEntry(DirDesc.DirPtr, ShrdObj, Obj, Status);
  if Status = Success then
  begin
    DirHandler.SetCurDir(DirDesc, DestDir, Status);
    if Status = Success then
    begin
      JobDir.GetDir(DestDirDesc);
      if not (Write in DestDirDesc.Rights)
        then Status := RightsCheck
      else
      begin
        NewEntry.LocalName := NewLink; NewEntry.Rights := Rts;
        case view(Obj) of
          Link:
            with NewEntry do
```

```
              begin
                 OwnerDirAdr := Obj.OwnerDirAdr;
                 OwnerCap := Obj.OwnerCap
              end;
           otherwise:
              with NewEntry do
              begin
                 OwnerDirAdr := DirDesc.Adr;
                 OwnerCap := ShrdObj
              end
           end;
           DirHandler.NewEntry(DestDirDesc.DirPtr, NewEntry,
                                Status);
        end
      end;
      JobDir.SetCurrent(DirDesc, Credit, Done)
    end
  end CopyLink;

 end FileSys;
```

By first making the destination directory the current directory, a lot of
housekeeping, like activating the directory, is implicitly achieved. It is
necessary to make the destination directory active to ensure that it is not
deleted before the link is entered.

FILE SYSTEM ADMINISTRATION

SeqFile, RandFile and FileSys provide the user interface to the file system.
But a system administrator requires some additional facilities to register a
new user, authenticate a user at login time, etc. We provide a pure class,
FileAdmn, to implement these facilities.

Registering a New User

Registering a new user involves creation of a root directory with the
specified name, and a shared directory. A password for checking
authentication, and the disk quota for the user also have to be specified.

```
    var
       FileAdmn: pure class
                 import
                       var : JobDir, SysIndir, DirHandler, Disk, DiskSpace,
                             FileErr
                 end;
```

```
procedure export NewUser(PackName:PackId;
                              DirName,Pswrd:Name;
                              Quota:integer; var Status:CallStatus);
var
   MFDDesc, DirDesc, ShrDesc: DirCap; Fentry: DirEntry(Root);
   Done: Boolean;
begin
   if not Disk.IsMounted(PackName) then
   begin
      Status := PackOffLine;
      return
   end;
   Status := Success;
   JobDir.GetMFD(MFDDesc);
   DirDesc.DirPtr.Pack := PackName;
   ShrDesc.DirPtr.Pack := PackName;
   DiskSpace.AllotNew(DirDesc.DirPtr, DirSegsize)
      iferror Status := PackFull
      otherwise DiskSpace.AllotNew(ShrDesc.DirPtr, DirSegsize)
         iferror
            begin
               DiskSpace.Release(DirDesc.DirPtr);
               Status := PackFull
            end;
   if Status = Success then
   begin
      SysIndir.NewDir(DirDesc.DirPtr, DirDesc.Adr, Done);
      if Done then
      begin
         SysIndir.NewDir(ShrDesc.DirPtr, ShrDesc.Adr, Done);
         if not Done
            then SysIndir.RemoveDir(DirDesc.Adr)
      end;
      if not Done then
      begin
         DiskSpace.Release(DirDesc.DirPtr);
         DiskSpace.Release(ShrDesc.DirPtr);
         Status := DirTooMany
      end
      else
      begin
         DirHandler.InitDir(Quota, DirDesc.DirPtr, Status);
         if Status = Success
            then DirHandler.InitDir(0, ShrDesc.DirPtr, Status);
         if Status = Success then
         begin
            with Fentry do
            begin
               LocalName := DirName;
               Rights := AccessRights[Read, Write, Update];
               Password := Pswrd;
```

```
              Adr := DirDesc.Adr; ShrDirAdr := ShrDesc.Adr
            end;
            DirHandler.NewEntry(MFDDesc.DirPtr, Fentry, Status);
            if Status = BadDirectory then
            begin
               FileErr.PutError(BadMFD, MFDDesc.DirPtr);
               Status := BadMFD
            end
         end;
         if Status ≠ Success then
         begin
            DiskSpace.Release(DirDesc.DirPtr);
            DiskSpace.Release(ShrDesc.DirPtr);
            SysIndir.RemoveDir(DirDesc.Adr);
            SysIndir.RemoveDir(ShrDesc.Adr)
         end
      end
   end
end NewUser;
```

Authentication

When a user attempts to log-in, it is necessary to ensure that he or she is a registered user. This authentication check is done by requiring the user to specify the name of the root directory and a password, and comparing them with the associated entry in the MFD. The authentication procedure also has to ensure that the disk pack on which the user has quota is currently on-line.

It is important to note that only this initial authentication requires the identity of the user. Once a user is successfully logged in, protection is enforced through capabilities contained in the directories that can be accessed from the root directory.

```
      procedure export Authenticate(DirName,Pswrd:Name;
                                    ProcNum:ProcIndex;
                                    var Status:CallStatus);
   var
      MFDDesc: DirCap; Fentry: DirEntry(Root);
      Found, Done: Boolean;
      DirDesc, ShrDesc: DirCap; Qta, Used: integer;
   begin
      Status := Success;
      JobDir.GetMFD(MFDDesc);
      DirHandler.GetEntry(MFDDesc.DirPtr, DirName, Fentry, Status);
      if Status = BadDirectory then
```

```
      begin
        FileErr.PutError(BadMFD, MFDDesc.DirPtr);
        Status := BadMFD
      end
      else
        if Status = DirNotFound
          then Status := NoSuchUser;
      if Status = Success then
        if Fentry.Password ≠ Pswrd
          then Status := IncorrectPassword
        else
        begin
          DirDesc.Adr := Fentry.Adr;
          DirDesc.Rights := Fentry.Rights;
          ShrDesc.Adr := Fentry.ShrDirAdr;
          ShrDesc.Rights := AccessRights[Read, Update];
          SysIndir.GetDiskAdr(DirDesc.Adr, DirDesc.DirPtr, Found);
          if Found
            then SysIndir.GetDiskAdr(ShrDesc.Adr, ShrDesc.DirPtr,
                                     Found);
          if not Found
            then Status := DirNotFound
          else
            if not Disk.IsMounted(DirDesc.DirPtr.Pack)
              then Status := PackOffLine
            else
            begin
              DirHandler.GetDirData(DirDesc.DirPtr, Qta, Used,
                                    Status);
              if Status = Success then
              begin
                JobDir.NewJob(ProcNum, DirDesc, ShrDesc,
                              Qta – Used, Done);
                if not Done
                  then Status := ActDirTooMany
              end
            end
        end
    end Authenticate;
```

Pack and MFD Creation

To create a new pack, the procedure CreatePack has to be invoked. This calls DiskSpace.InitPack to initialize and write the disk allocation data on the pack.

```
        procedure export CreatePack(PackName:PackId;
                              var Status:CallStatus);
```

```
begin
  Status := Success;
  DiskSpace.InitPack(PackName)
    iferror Status := BadPack
end CreatePack;
```

Another system administration activity is the creation of the MFD. This is done only at system generation time.

```
procedure export CreateMFD(PackName:PackId;
                            var Status:CallStatus);
var
  MFDDesc: DirCap; Done: Boolean;
begin
  with MFDDesc do
  begin
    DirPtr.Pack := PackName;
    DiskSpace.AllotNew(DirPtr, DirSegsize);
    DirHandler.InitDir(0, DirPtr, Status);
    if Status = BadDirectory then
    begin
      Status := BadMFD;
      FileErr.PutError(BadMFD, DirPtr);
      DiskSpace.Release(DirPtr)
    end
    else
    begin
      SysIndir.NewDir(DirPtr, Adr. Done);
      JobDir.SetMFD(MFDDesc)
    end
  end
end CreateMFD;

end FileAdmn;
```

DISCUSSION

The File System Structure

The complete structure of the file system is given in Fig. 9.2. The structure is not entirely hierarchic. The basic units of the file system are monitors and pure classes: typically, a pure class contains calls to several monitors. Wherever there is a call from one monitor to another, we have ensured

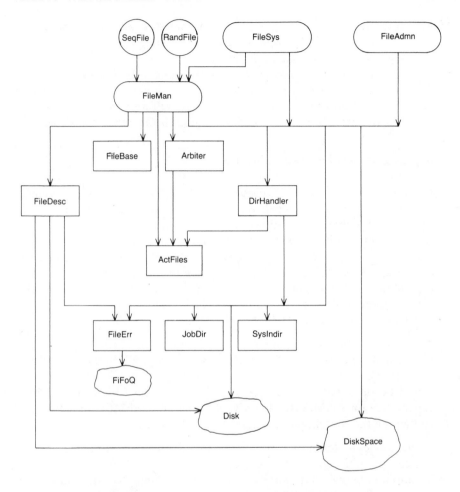

Fig. 9.2 The complete structure of the file system.

that a job is never suspended within the inner monitor. Thus, we consciously avoid deadlocks arising from 'nested monitor calls'.

One of the crucial issues in the design of the file system is the proper choice of language abstraction for a component. We can summarize the guidelines we have followed in making our choices.

   (a) A component that is not shared across processes need only be a class, e.g. SeqFile and RandFile.
   (b) A component that is just a collection of procedures shared by many processes can be a pure class, e.g. FileSys.

(c) Only atomic actions need be contained in monitors. Compound (nonatomic) actions which use atomic actions can be implemented through pure classes.

(d) The degree of concurrency is determined by the granularity of the operations in monitors. Except for reasons of atomicity, a procedure in a monitor should not call a procedure in another monitor. Monitor procedures should be as small as possible.

Representation of Files and Directories

In our design, there are limits (SegMax, FileMax) to the number of segments in a file and the number of capabilities in a directory. This may be a severe restriction for some applications. To overcome this, we could have a tree structure for an object. Here, the leaf nodes of a file would contain data and the nonleaf nodes would be descriptors pointing either to descriptors or to data nodes. Similarly, the leaf nodes of a directory would contain capabilities and non-leaf nodes would contain descriptors. Even in this design, there will be limits but they will be quite high and will not be restrictions in practice.

Another possible improvement is to distribute the MFD over several packs. Instead of placing all root directories in a single MFD, it would be more convenient if the MFD were implemented at two levels. The MFD would be on a distinguished pack, called the System Pack, and contain capabilities for subMFDs. There would then be a subMFD on each pack containing the root directories allocated in that pack.

In our implementation, we have taken care not to keep any sensitive data in user program space. For example, SeqFile and RandFile (which are instantiated by users) do not contain any critical data like disk addresses. We have taken this decision to support user programs written in several languages. Some of these languages may not provide sufficient compile-time and run-time checks to ensure that errors in one module do not propagate to others. If the underlying hardware supports a domain-based architecture, guaranteeing that errors in a domain (module) do not affect other domains, we can simplify the design and place sensitive data even in user-instantiated modules. However, current architectures do not efficiently support domains with such fine grain. Typically, they support only two domains, user and supervisor, so we have kept all sensitive data in what would be the supervisor domain.

A domain-based architecture relieves the designer from problems like those above, providing a simpler system structure. For example, in a domain architecture, we can replace the monitors FileDesc and FileBase and the pure class FileMan by the following structure. Let FileDesc be a class type implementing operations on a descriptor. Another class type, File, implements operations on a file (currently implemented by FileMan) using an instance of FileDesc. SeqFile and RandFile can then create instances of File to implement their operations.

Crash Recovery

It would be very desirable for operations on files and directories to have the property that they either complete successfully or, if they fail due to processor or disk failures, the file system reverts to the state that existed before the operation commenced. If all operations on files and directories have this property, called *atomicity*, users can recover from crashes by simply repeating their actions.

Let us examine the effects of crashes on file operations in our implementation. Recall that the capability for a file is created or updated in the owner directory only when the file is closed. If a crash occurs after a sequential or random file is created, but before it is closed, the file becomes inaccessible since there is no capability for the file. However, disk blocks allocated to the created segments remain allocated. Blocks allocated to such inaccessible segments will be 'lost'. If a crash occurs while a sequential file is being appended to, blocks allocated to the newly created segments are lost. Thus, in these two cases, the file transactions seen by the user are atomic and a crash may only cause some disk blocks to be lost.

However, the effect of a crash is quite different when an existing random file is being updated. A Put operation on an existing segment overwrites the old data. Thus, after a crash, a random file may have a mix of old and new data and the transaction is not atomic. To achieve atomicity, a segment should never be updated 'in-place'. Rather, when a segment is created or updated, a *shadow* segment has to be created and data written on it. Only when the file is closed should the shadow segments be made *real*. We leave the implementation of shadow segments as an exercise.

To ensure that operations on directories are atomic, we have to guarantee that a directory can be modified atomically through a single write command to disk. This can be achieved by maintaining two copies of each directory and modifying both copies whenever the directory is updated. If a crash occurs while one copy is being written, we recover from the crash by copying data from the other copy. This technique of implementing atomic disk writes is called *stable storage* (Lampson, 1981). The implementation of stable storage for crucial objects like the MFD, roots and subdirectories is left as an exercise.

The crash recovery procedures discussed above assume that data can be read from disk even after a crash. However, this may not always be the case (e.g. after disk head misalignment). Under those circumstances, we rely on the periodic backup of files (typically on magnetic tapes). In the event of failures, files have to be restored from the most recent backup. Further, these recovery procedures are adequate only to ensure that a transaction on a single file is atomic. But this atomicity is inadequate for database systems where a transaction may involve updating several files. Recently, there have been several proposals for robust file storage to facilitate the construction of multi-file transactions (Lampson, 1981; Sturgis *et al.*,1980).

EXERCISES

1.   Quite often, a system administrator may need to change the attributes of a user such as, quota, password etc. Design a new file system procedure, AlterUser, to alter the attributes of a user.

2.   Only a system administrator should be able to create new users or modify the attributes of registered users. How can this be ensured by the procedures NewUser and AlterUser?

3.   Re-program the current implementation of RandFile to include shadow segments. The implementation should take into account the possibility that a crash may occur while shadow segments are being made into real segments.

4.   Design an abstraction for stable storage which can be used for implementing directories, Indir and group allocation tables.

5.   Represent a file as a tree of segments, as described in the text, and reimplement the operations on files.

6.   (Group Exercise.) Assuming the underlying hardware is domain-based, suggest an alternative structure for the file system.

7.   Design a backup facility for the file system by which files and directories can be stored on magnetic tape and restored onto disk when their current disk copies are inaccessible. (See Chapter 10 for an abstraction, SeqIO, for input/output using assigned devices. Design an abstraction for operations on magnetic tapes using SeqIO.)

8.   (Group Exercise.) Study the literature on multifile transactions and implement a technique for atomic multifile transactions using this file system.

THE COMPLETE FILE SYSTEM PROGRAM

{The following constants must be set to appropriate values}

const
    Segsize = ... ; {Size of a data segment in bytes (8 bit)}
    Blksize = ... ; {Size of a disk block in bytes}
    BlkMax = ... ; {Number of blocks in a data segment}
    ActFileMax = ... ; {Maximum number of active files}
    IndirMax = ... ; {Maximum number of directories}
    ActDirMax = ... ; {Maximum number of active directories}
    ErrQMax = ... ; {Maximum number of errors that can be stored}
    FileMax = ... ; {Maximum number of caps. in a directory}
    SegMax = ... ; {Maximum number of segments in a file}
    DirSegSize = ... ; {Size of a directory segment (in blocks)}
    FileDescSize = ... ; {Size of a file descriptor segment (in blocks)}

type
    FileMode = (Sequential, Random);
    FileKind = (Text, Binary);
    Access = (Read, Write, Update, Append, Execute);
    AccessRights = **set of** Access;
    Byte = 0 .. 255;
    Buffer(Size: **integer**) =
      record
        case FileKind **of**
          Text: (TextBuf: **array** [1 .. Size] **of char**);
          Binary: (BinaryBuf: **array** [1 .. Size] **of** Byte)
      end Buffer;
    Segment =
      record
        case FileKind **of**
          Text: (TextSeg: **array** [1 .. Segsize] **of char**);
          Binary: (BinarySeg: **array** [1 .. Segsize] **of** Byte)
      end Segment;
    CallStatus = (BadDescriptor, BadDirectory, BadMFD, PackOffLine,
                   DuplicateOpen, FileNotOpened, NotOpenedForRead,
                   Eof, OpenedForRead, FileFull, SegmentNotFound,
                   RightsCheck, IllegalKind, IllegalMode, QuotaFull,
                   ActFilesTooMany, DuplicateName, ObjNotFound,
                   DirFull, FileNotFound, ActDirTooMany, DirNonEmpty,
                   DirActive, DirnotFound, PackFull,
                   BadPack, BadSegment, NoSuchUser,
                   IncorrectPassWord, DirTooMany, Success);
    FileSysErr = BadDescriptor .. PackOffLine;

```
{***                    ***}
{*** The Indirectory ***}
{***     –Outline     ***}
```

var
  SysIndir: **monitor**;
    type
      IndirEntry;
    type export
      Sindex, DirAdr;
    var
      Indir: **array** [Sindex] **of** IndirEntry;
      Counter: **integer**;
    function GetUname **return integer**;
      {creates unique names for directories}

    procedure export GetDiskAdr(Adr:DirAdr; **var** Ptr:DiskAdr;
                          var Found:**Boolean**);
    procedure export SetDiskAdr(Adr:DirAdr; Ptr:DiskAdr;
                          var Done:**Boolean**);
      {procedures for getting and defining the mapping between
      DirAdr and DiskAdr of a directory}

    procedure export NewDir(Ptr:DiskAdr; **var** Adr:DiskAdr;
                          var Done:**Boolean**);
    procedure export RemoveDir(Adr:DirAdr);
      {procedures for creating or deleting the IndirEntry
      of a directory)
  end SysIndir;

```
{***                              ***}
{***      The Indirectory  ***}
{***    –Implementation   ***}
```

var
  SysIndir: **monitor**;
    type
      IndirEntry =
        record
          Used: **Boolean**;
          DirId: **integer**; DirPtr: DiskAdr
        end IndirEntry;
    type export
      Sindex = 1 .. IndirMax;
      DirAdr =
        record
          Id: **integer**; Index: Sindex
        end DirAdr;

```
var
  Indir: array [Sindex] of IndirEntry;
  Counter: integer;

procedure export GetDiskAdr(Adr:DirAdr; var Ptr:DiskAdr;
                            var Found:Boolean);
  begin
    with Indir[Adr.Index] do
      if Used and (DirId = Adr.Id) then
      begin
        Found := true; Ptr := DirPtr
      end
      else Found := false
  end GetDiskAdr;

procedure export SetDiskAdr(Adr:DirAdr; Ptr:DiskAdr;
                            var Done:Boolean);
  begin
    with Indir[Adr.Index] do
      if Used and (DirId = Adr.Id) then
      begin
        Done := true; DirPtr := Ptr
      end
      else Done := false
  end SetDiskAdr;

function GetUname return integer;
  begin
    Counter := Counter + 1;
    return Counter
  end GetUname;

procedure export NewDir(Ptr:DiskAdr; var Adr:DirAdr;
                        var Done:Boolean);
  begin
    Done := false;
    for I in 1 to IndirMax do
      with Indir[I] do
        if not Used then
        begin
          Used := true; DirId := GetUname; DirPtr := Ptr;
          Adr.Id := DirId; Adr.Index := I;
          Done := true; exit
        end
  end NewDir;

procedure export RemoveDir(Adr:DirAdr);
  begin
    with Indir[Adr.Index] do
      if Used and (DirId = Adr.Id)
        then Used := false
  end RemoveDir;
```

```
    begin
      for I in 1 to IndirMax
        do Indir[I].Used := false;
      Counter := 0
    end SysIndir;
```

```
{***              ***}
{*** ActFiles ***}
{*** –Outline ***}
```

```
var
  ActFiles: monitor;
    var
      OpenFiles: array [FileIndex] of
                    record
                      UseCount: integer; FileName: Name;
                      OwnerDir: DirAdr
                    end OpenFiles;
    procedure Lookup(Owner:DirAdr; Fname:Name; var Findex:FileIndex;
                  var Found:Boolean);
      {check if the specified file is in OpenFiles}

    procedure export IsActive(Owner:DirAdr; Fname:Name;
                  var Findex:FileIndex;
                  var Active:Boolean);
    procedure export Activate(Owner:DirAdr; Fname:Name;
                  var Findex:FileIndex;
                  var Done:Boolean);
      {to activate a file, an entry is made in OpenFiles
      if it is not already there; otherwise the UseCount
      of the entry is incremented}

    procedure export DeActivate(Findex:FileIndex;
                  var Inactive:Boolean);
      {the UseCount of the file is decremented and Inactive
      is true if UseCount=0}

    procedure export Rename(Owner:DirAdr; OldName,NewName:Name;
                  var Found:Boolean);
  end ActFiles;
```

```
{***                        ***}
{***        ActFiles        ***}
{***     –Implementation    ***}
```

```
var
  ActFiles: monitor
              import
                var : SysIndir
              end;
```

```
type export
   FileIndex = 1 .. ActFileMax;
var
   OpenFiles: array [FileIndex] of
                     record
                        UseCount: integer; FileName: Name;
                        OwnerDir: DirAdr
                     end OpenFiles;


procedure Lookup(Owner:DirAdr; Fname:Name;
                    var Findex:FileIndex; var Found:Boolean);
   begin
      Found := false;
      for I in 1 to ActFileMax do
         with OpenFiles[I] do
            if (UseCount ≠ 0) and (OwnerDir = Owner)
                and (FileName = Fname) then
               begin
                  Findex := I; Found := true; exit
               end
   end Lookup;


procedure export IsActive(Owner:DirAdr; Fname:Name;
                             var Findex:FileIndex;
                             var Active:Boolean);
   begin
      Lookup(Owner, Fname, Findex, Active)
   end IsActive;


procedure export Activate(Owner:DirAdr; Fname:Name;
                             var Findex:FileIndex;
                             var Done:Boolean);
   begin
      Done := false;
      Lookup(Owner, Fname, Findex, Done);
      if Done then
         with OpenFiles[Findex]
            do UseCount := UseCount + 1
      else
         for I in 1 to ActFileMax do
            with OpenFiles[I] do
               if UseCount = 0 then
               begin
                  UseCount := 1; OwnerDir := Owner;
                  FileName := Fname;
                  Findex := I; Done := true;
                  exit
               end
   end Activate;
```

```
procedure export DeActivate(Findex:FileIndex;
                            var Inactive:Boolean);
  begin
    with OpenFiles[Findex] do
    begin
      UseCount := UseCount - 1;
      Inactive := UseCount = 0
    end
  end DeActivate;


procedure export Rename(Owner:DirAdr; OldName,NewName:Name;
                        var Found:Boolean);
  var
    Findex: FileIndex;
  begin
    Lookup(Owner, OldName, Findex, Found);
    if Found
      then OpenFiles[Findex].FileName := NewName
  end Rename;


  begin
    for I in 1 to ActFileMax
      do OpenFiles[I].UseCount := 0
  end ActFiles;




{***            ***}
{*** Arbiter ***}
{*** –Outline ***}

var
  Arbiter: monitor;
    type
      Request = (Reader, Writer);
    var
      ShrdFiles: array [FileIndex] of
                        record
                          ReadCount: integer;
                          WriteFlag: Boolean; DeleteQ: queue
                        end ShrdFiles;
      RWq: array [ProcIndex] of
                  record
                    Q: queue; Findex: FileIndex;
                    Req: Request
                  end RWq;
```

```
    procedure Suspend(Index:FileIndex; CurrReq:Request);
       {the calling process is delayed in RWq[ProcId].Q;
        when continued the process, if it is a reader, will
        continue another waiting reader}

    procedure Schedule(Index:FileIndex);
       {continue a reader or writer waiting to use the given file}

    procedure export Enter(Findex:FileIndex; AccMode:Access;
                             var Status:CallStatus);
       {if the calling process is a reader, it is delayed
        if a writer is using the file; if it is a writer,
        it is delayed if a reader or writer is using the file}

    procedure export Mark(Owner:DirAdr; Fname:Name);
       {the calling process is the deleter; if the file is
        active, the caller is delayed in ShrdFiles[Findex].DeleteQ}

    procedure export Close(Findex:FileIndex);
       {deactivate the file and if the file becomes inactive
        continue the deleter, if waiting; otherwise, if the
        caller is a writer or the last reader (i.e., ReadCount=0)
        invoke Schedule to continue a waiting
        reader or writer}

  end Arbiter;



    {***                   ***}
    {***      Arbiter      ***}
    {*** –Implementation ***}

var
    Arbiter: monitor
                import
                    var : ActFiles
                end;
      type
        Request = (Reader, Writer);

      var
        ShrdFiles: array [FileIndex] of
                      record
                         ReadCount: integer;
                         WriteFlag: Boolean; DeleteQ: queue
                      end ShrdFiles;
```

```
RWq: array [ProcIndex] of
        record
            Q: queue;
            Findex: FileIndex; Req: Request
        end RWq;


procedure Suspend(Index:FileIndex; CurrReq:Request);
    begin
        with RWq[ProcId] do
        begin
            Findex := Index; Req := CurrReq;
            delay(Q)
        end;
        if CurrReq = Reader then
        begin
            with ShrdFiles[Index]
                do ReadCount := ReadCount + 1;
            for I in 1 to ProcMax do
                with RWq[I] do
                    if delayed(Q) then
                        if (Findex = Index) and (Req = Reader) then
                        begin
                            continue(Q); exit
                        end
        end
        else ShrdFiles[Index].WriteFlag := true
    end Suspend;


procedure export Enter(Findex:FileIndex; AccMode:Access;
                        var Status:CallStatus);
    var
        CurrReq: Request;
    begin
        Status := Success;
        if AccMode = Read
            then CurrReq := Reader
        else CurrReq := Writer;
        with ShrdFiles[Findex] do
            if WriteFlag or (ReadCount ≠ 0) then
                if WriteFlag then
                    if AccMode = Write
                        then Status := DuplicateName
                    else Suspend(Findex, CurrReq)
                else
                    if CurrReq ≠ Reader
                        then Suspend(Findex, CurrReq)
                    else
                    begin
                        ReadCount := ReadCount + 1;
                        RWq[ProcId].Req := Reader
                    end
```

```
        else
        begin
          if CurrReq = Reader
            then ReadCount := 1
          else WriteFlag := true;
          RWq[ProcId].Req := CurrReq
        end
  end Enter;

procedure export Mark(Owner:DirAdr; Fname:Name);
  var
    Findex: FileIndex; Active: Boolean;
  begin
    ActFiles.IsActive(Owner, Fname, Findex, Active);
    if Active
      then delay(ShrdFiles[Findex].DeleteQ)
  end Mark;

procedure Schedule(Index:FileIndex);
  begin
    for I in 1 to ProcMax do
      with RWq[I] do
        if delayed(Q) and (Findex = Index) then
        begin
          continue(Q); exit
        end
  end Schedule;

procedure export Close(Findex:FileIndex);
  var
    Inactive: Boolean;
  begin
    with ShrdFiles[Findex] do
    begin
      ActFiles.Deactivate(Findex, Inactive);
      if Inactive and delayed(DeleteQ)
        then continue(DeleteQ);
      if not Inactive then
        if RWq[ProcId].Req = Reader then
        begin
          ReadCount := ReadCount – 1;
          if ReadCount = 0
            then Schedule(Findex)
        end
        else
        begin
          WriteFlag := false;
          Schedule(Findex)
        end
    end
  end Close;
```

```
begin
  for I in 1 to ActFileMax do
    with ShrdFiles[I] do
    begin
      ReadCount := 0; WriteFlag := false
    end
end Arbiter;
```

```
{***                    ***}
{*** Job Directories ***}
{***      -Outline      ***}
```

```
var
  JobDir: monitor;
    type export
      DirCap =
        record
          Adr: DirAdr; DirPtr: DiskAdr;
          Rights: AccessRights
        end DirCap;
    type
      DirIndex = 1 .. ActDirMax;
      JobRec =
        record
          ...
        end JobRec;
      DirRec =
        record
          ...
        end DirRec;

    var
      DirArr: array [DirIndex] of DirRec;
      JobArr: array [ProcIndex] of JobRec;
      MFDDesc: DirCap;

    procedure ChkActive(AdrDir:DirAdr; var Index:DirIndex;
                        var Active:Boolean);
    procedure MakeActive(AdrDir:DirAdr; Quota:integer;
                         var Index:DirIndex; var Done:Boolean);
    procedure MakeInactive(Adr:DirAdr);
      {a directory is made active by making an entry for it
       in DirArr, if not already there; otherwise, the UseCount
       of the entry is incremented; the UseCount is decremented
       when the directory is deactivated}

    procedure export Activate(Adr:DirAdr; Credit:integer;
                              var Done:Boolean);
```

```
      procedure export DeActivate(Adr:DirAdr);
      function export IsActive(Adr:DirAdr) return Boolean;

      function GetIndex(Adr:DirAdr) return DirIndex;
      procedure export NewJob(ProcNum:ProcIndex;
                              DirDesc,ShrDesc:DirCap;
                              Credit:integer; var Done:Boolean);
      procedure export SetCurrent(DirDesc:DirCap; Credit:integer;
                              var Done:Boolean);
      procedure export SetRoot;
      procedure export SetShrDir;
         {when a directory is set current, the previous directory
          is deactivated and the chosen directory is activated}

      procedure export GetDir(var DirDesc:DirCap);
      procedure export GetShrDir(var ShrDesc:DirCap);
      procedure export DecQuota(DirDesc:DirCap; Amount:integer;
                              var Done:Boolean);
      procedure export IncQuota(DirDesc:DirCap; Amount:integer);
      function export GetQuota(DirDesc:DirCap) return integer;
      procedure export GetStatus(Adr:DirAdr; var Credit:integer;
                              var Active:Boolean);
      procedure export GetMFD(var MFDCap:DirCap);
      procedure export SetMFD(MFDCap:DirCap);

   end JobDir;




   {***                   ***}
   {***   Job directories  ***}
   {*** –Implementation ***}

var
   JobDir: monitor;
      type export
         DirCap =
            record
               Adr: DirAdr; DirPtr: DiskAdr;
               Rights: AccessRights
            end DirCap;
      type
         DirIndex = 1 .. ActDirMax;
         JobRec =
            record
               Root, ShrDir, Current: DirCap;
               CurInd: DirIndex
            end JobRec;
```

```
DirRec =
  record
    Adr: DirAdr; UseCount, Credit: integer
  end DirRec;

var
  DirArr: array [DirIndex] of DirRec;
  JobArr: array [ProcIndex] of JobRec;
  MFDDesc: DirCap;

procedure ChkActive(AdrDir:DirAdr; var Index:DirIndex;
                    var Active:Boolean);
  begin
    Active := false;
    for I in 1 to ActDirMax do
      with DirArr[I] do
        if (UseCount ≠ 0) and (Adr = AdrDir) then
        begin
          Active := true; Index := I; exit
        end
  end ChkActive;

procedure MakeActive(AdrDir:DirAdr; Quota:integer;
                     var Index:DirIndex;
                     var Done:Boolean);
  begin
    Done := false;
    ChkActive(AdrDir, Index, Done);
    if Done then
      with DirArr[Index]
        do UseCount := UseCount + 1
    else
      for I in 1 to ActDirMax do
        with DirArr[I] do
          if UseCount = 0 then
          begin
            Done := true; Index := I;
            UseCount := 1; Credit := Quota; Adr := AdrDir;
            exit
          end
  end MakeActive;

procedure MakeInactive(Address:DirAdr);
  begin
    for I in 1 to ActDirMax do
      with DirArr[I] do
        if (UseCount ≠ 0) and (Adr = Address) then
        begin
          UseCount := UseCount - 1; exit
        end
  end MakeInactive;
```

```
procedure export Activate(Adr:DirAdr; Credit:integer;
                              var Done:Boolean);
  var
    Index: DirIndex;
  begin
    MakeActive(Adr, Credit, Index, Done)
  end Activate;

procedure export DeActivate(Adr:DirAdr);
  begin
    MakeInactive(Adr)
  end DeActivate;

function export IsActive(Adr:DirAdr) return Boolean;
  var
    Index: DirIndex; Active: Boolean;
  begin
    ChkActive(Adr, Index, Active); return Active
  end IsActive;

procedure export NewJob(ProcNum:ProcIndex;
                        DirDesc,ShrDesc:DirCap;
                        Credit:integer; var Done:Boolean);
  begin
    with JobArr[ProcNum] do
    begin
      Root := DirDesc; Current := Root;
      ShrDir := ShrDesc;
      MakeActive(DirDesc.Adr, Credit, CurInd, Done)
    end
  end NewJob;

procedure export SetCurrent(DirDesc:DirCap; Credit:integer;
                            var Done:Boolean);
  begin
    with JobArr[ProcId] do
    begin
      if Current.Adr ≠ Root.Adr
        then MakeInactive(Current.Adr);
      MakeActive(DirDesc.Adr, Credit, CurInd, Done);
      if Done
        then Current := DirDesc
    end
  end SetCurrent;

function GetIndex(AdrDir:DirAdr) return DirIndex;
  var
    Index: DirIndex;
  begin
    with JobArr[ProcId] do
      if Current.Adr = AdrDir
```

```
                then Index := CurInd
             else
               for I in 1 to ActDirMax do
                 with DirArr[I] do
                   if (UseCount ≠ 0) and (Adr = AdrDir) then
                   begin
                     Index := I; exit
                   end;
          return Index
       end GetIndex;


    procedure export SetRoot;
      begin
        with JobArr[ProcId] do
        begin
          CurInd := GetIndex(Root.Adr);
          Current := Root
        end
      end SetRoot;


    procedure export SetShrDir(var Done:Boolean);
      begin
        with JobArr[ProcId] do
        begin
          MakeActive(ShrDir.Adr, 0, CurInd, Done);
          if Done
            then Current := ShrDir
        end
      end SetShrDir;


    procedure export GetDir(var DirDesc:DirCap);
      begin
        DirDesc := JobArr[ProcId].Current
      end GetDir;


    procedure export GetShrDir(var ShrDesc:DirCap);
      begin
        ShrDesc := JobArr[ProcId].ShrDir
      end GetShrDir;


    procedure export DecQuota(DirDesc:DirCap; Amount:integer;
                                    var Done:Boolean);
      begin
        with DirArr[GetIndex(DirDesc.Adr)] do
          if Credit – Amount < 0
            then Done := false
          else
          begin
            Credit := Credit – Amount; Done := true
          end
      end DecQuota;
```

```
procedure export IncQuota(DirDesc:DirCap; Amount:integer);
  begin
    with DirArr[GetIndex(DirDesc.Adr)]
      do Credit := Credit + Amount
  end IncQuota;

function export GetQuota(DirDesc:DirCap) return integer;
  begin
    with DirArr[GetIndex(DirDesc.Adr)]
      do return Credit
  end GetQuota;

procedure export GetStatus(Adr:DirAdr; var Credit:integer;
                           var Active:Boolean);
  var
    Index: DirIndex;
  begin
    ChkActive(Adr, Index, Active);
    if Active
      then Credit := DirArr[Index].Credit
  end GetStatus;

procedure export GetMFD(var MFDCap:DirCap);
  begin
    MFDCap := MFDDesc
  end GetMFD;

procedure export SetMFD(MFDCap:DirCap);
  begin
    MFDDesc := MFDCap
  end SetMFD;

begin
  for I in 1 to ActDirMax
    do DirArr[I].UseCount := 0
end JobDir;




{***                    ***}
{*** File Error Handling ***}
{***      –Outline       ***}

var
  FileErr: monitor;
    var
      ErrQ: FiFoQ(ErrQMax);
      ErrMsg: array [1 .. ErrQMax] of
```

```
                    record
                        Err: FileSysErr; Posn: DiskAdr
                    end ErrMsg;

    procedure export PutError(Msg:FileSysErr; Posn:DiskAdr);
    function export IsError return Boolean;
    procedure export GetError(var Msg:FileSysErr; var Posn:DiskAdr);

  end FileErr;
```

```
{***                      ***}
{***  File Error Handling ***}
{***   –Implementation    ***}
```

```
var
   FileErr: monitor;

      var
         ErrQ: FiFoQ(ErrQMax);
         ErrMsg: array [1 .. ErrQMax] of
                       record
                           Err: FileSysErr; Posn: DiskAdr
                       end ErrMsg;

      procedure export PutError(Msg:FileSysErr; DiskPosn:DiskAdr);
         begin
            if not ErrQ.Full then
              with ErrMsg[ErrQ.Put] do
              begin
                Err := Msg; Posn := DiskPosn
              end
         end PutError;

      function export IsError return Boolean;
         begin
            return not ErrQ.Empty
         end IsError;

      procedure export GetError(var Msg:FileSysErr;
                                var DiskPosn:DiskAdr);
         begin
            if not ErrQ.Empty then
              with ErrMsg[ErrQ.Get] do
              begin
                Msg := Err; DiskPosn := Posn
              end
         end GetError;

   end FileErr;
```

```
{***                    ***}
{*** Directory Handler ***}
{***      –Outline      ***}
```

var
  DirHandler: **monitor**;

    type export
      FileAttr =
        record
            ...
          end FileAttr;
      Entry = (File, SubDir, Root, Link);
      DirEntry =
        record
            ...
          end DirEntry;

    var
      Dir:
        record
          Quota, Consumed: **integer**;
          FileArr: **array** [1 .. FileIndex] **of** DirEntry
          end Dir;
      Loaded: **Boolean**; PresentDir: DiskAdr;
      Vadr, Vsize: **integer**; {needed for disk input/output}

    procedure LogError(Err:IoErr; Posn:DiskAdr; **var** Msg:FileSysErr);
    procedure LoadDir(DirPtr:DiskAdr)
      error FileSysErr;
      {a directory is read from disk only if it is not already
       loaded; errors encountered during disk transfer are logged
       through LogError}

    procedure CheckEntry(DirPtr:DiskAdr; Fname:Name;
                            var Index:**integer**; **var** Found:**Boolean**);
    procedure export Lookup(DirPtr:DiskAdr; Fname:Name;
                            var Status:CallStatus);
    procedure export GetEntry(DirPtr:DiskAdr; Fname:Name;
                            var Fentry:DirEntry;
                            var Status:CallStatus);
    procedure export ListEntry(DirPtr:DiskAdr; Index:**integer**;
                            var Fentry:DirEntry;
                            var Status:CallStatus);
      {Lookup merely checks for an entry with the given
       name but GetEntry checks further if the view of the entry
       is the same as the view of Fentry; ListEntry returns
       the entry of the indexed element of the directory}

    procedure WriteEntry(DirPtr:DiskAdr; Fentry:DirEntry;
                            var Done:**Boolean**)
      error FileSysErr;
```
```

```
                procedure export NewEntry(DirPtr:DiskAdr; Fentry:DirEntry;
                                    var Status:CallStatus);
                procedure export UpdateEntry(DirPtr:DiskAdr; Fentry:DirEntry;
                                        var Status:CallStatus);
                {if the entry created or updated is an owner capability
                Dir.Consumed is updated suitably}
                procedure export Rename(DirDesc:DirCap;
                                            OldName,NewName:Name;
                                        var Status:CallStatus);
                procedure FetchObj(DirDesc:DirCap; Fname:Name;
                                    var Owner:DirCap;
                                    var Fentry:DirEntry; var Found:Boolean);
                {fetch the owner capability of the specified object
                if access to the object has not been revoked}
                procedure export GetFile(DirDesc:DirCap; Fname:Name;
                                        var Fentry:DirEntry; var Owner:DirCap;
                                        var Findex:FileIndex;
                                        var Status:CallStatus);
                {get the owner capability of the file after activating
                the file and the owner directory}
                function IsEmpty(Adr:DirAdr) return CallStatus;
                procedure export DeleteEntry(DirPtr:DiskAdr; Fname:Name;
                                        var Fentry:DirEntry;
                                        var Status:CallStatus);
                {the owner capability of a directory can be deleted only
                if the directory is not active and empty; when an owner
                capability of a file or directory is deleted, Dir.Consumed
                is to be updated}
                procedure export SetCurDir(DirDesc:DirCap; DirName:Name;
                                        var Status:CallStatus);
                procedure export GetDirData(DirPtr:DiskAdr;
                                            var Qta,Used:integer;
                                            var Status:CallStatus);
                procedure export InitDir(Qta:integer; DirPtr:DiskAdr;
                                        var Status:CallStatus);
            end DirHandler;



        {***                        ***}
        {*** Directory Handler ***}
        {*** –Implementation  ***}


    var
        DirHandler: monitor
                        import
                            var : SysIndir, ActFiles, JobDir, Disk, FileErr
                        end;
```

```
type export
  FileAttr =
    record
      Kind: FileKind; Mode: FileMode;
      BlkAlloc, LastSeg, LastSegsize: integer;
      FileDescAdr: integer
    end FileAttr;
  Entry = (File, SubDir, Root, Link);
  DirEntry =
    record
      Used: Boolean;
      LocalName: Name; Rights: AccessRights;
      CreationDate, CreationTime: integer;
      case Entry of
        File: (Fattr: FileAttr);
        SubDir: (Adr: DirAdr);
        Root: (PassWord: Name; Adr, ShrDirAdr: DirAdr);
        Link: (OwnerCap: Name; OwnerDirAdr: DirAdr)
    end DirEntry;


type
  Directory =
    record
      Quota, Consumed: integer;
      FileArr: array [1 .. FileMax] of DirEntry
    end Directory;


var
  Dir: Directory; Loaded: Boolean; PresentDir: DiskAdr;
  Vadr, Vsize: integer;

procedure LogError(Err:IoErr; Posn:DiskAdr; var Msg:FileSysErr);
  begin
    case Err of
      NotAvail: Msg := PackOffLine;
      Fail: Msg := BadDirectory
    end;
    FileErr.PutError(Msg, Posn)
  end LogError;

procedure LoadDir(DirPtr:DiskAdr)
  error FileSysErr;
  var
    Msg: FileSysErr;
  begin
    if not Loaded or (DirPtr ≠ PresentDir) then
```

```
    begin
      Disk.Read(DirPtr, 0, Vsize, Vadr)
        iferror
          begin
            Loaded := false;
            LogError(errorval, DirPtr, Msg);
            return error Msg
          end;
        Loaded := true; PresentDir := DirPtr
    end
  end LoadDir;


  procedure CheckEntry(DirPtr:DiskAdr; Fname:Name;
                       var Index:integer; var Found:Boolean)
    error FileSysErr;
    begin
      Found := false;
      LoadDir(DirPtr)
        iferror return error errorval;
        for I in 1 to FileMax do
          with Dir.FileArr[I] do
            if Used and (LocalName = Fname) then
              begin
                Found := true; Index := I; exit
              end
    end CheckEntry;


  procedure export Lookup(DirPtr:DiskAdr; Fname:Name;
                          var Status:CallStatus);
    var
      Index: 1 .. FileMax; Found: Boolean;
    begin
      CheckEntry(DirPtr, Fname, Index, Found)
        iferror Status := errorval
        otherwise
          if Found
            then Status := Success
            else Status := ObjNotFound
    end Lookup;


  procedure export GetEntry(DirPtr:DiskAdr; Fname:Name;
                            var Fentry:DirEntry;
                            var Status:CallStatus);
    var
      Index: 1 .. FileMax; Found: Boolean;
    begin
      CheckEntry(DirPtr, Fname, Index, Found)
        iferror
          begin
            Status := errorval; return
          end;
```

```
      if Found
        then copyview(Fentry, Dir.FileArr[Index])
              iferror Found := false;
      if Found
        then Status := Success
        else Status := ObjNotFound
    end GetEntry;

procedure export ListEntry(DirPtr:DiskAdr; Index:integer;
                           var Fentry:DirEntry;
                           var Status:CallStatus);
  begin
    Status := Success;
    if Index > FileMax
      then Status := FileNotFound
      else LoadDir(DirPtr)
            iferror Status := errorval
            otherwise Fentry := Dir.FileArr[Index]
  end ListEntry;

procedure WriteEntry(DirPtr:DiskAdr; Fentry:DirEntry;
                     var Done:Boolean)
  error FileSysErr;
  var
    Msg: FileSysErr;
  begin
    Done := false;
    with Dir do
    begin
      for I in 1 to FileMax do
        if not FileArr[I].Used then
        begin
          copyview(FileArr[I], Fentry);
          FileArr[I].Used := true; Done := true;
          exit
        end;
      if Done then
      begin
        case view(Fentry) of
          File: Consumed := Consumed + Fentry.Fattr.BlkAlloc;
          Root, SubDir: Consumed := Consumed + DirSegSize
        end;
        Disk.Write(DirPtr, 0, Vsize, Vadr)
          iferror
            begin
              LogError(errorval, DirPtr, Msg);
              return error Msg
            end
      end
    end
  end WriteEntry;
```

```
procedure export NewEntry(DirPtr:DiskAdr; Fentry:DirEntry;
                              var Status:CallStatus);
var
   Found, Done: Boolean; Index: 1 .. FileMax;
begin
   Status := Success;
   CheckEntry(DirPtr, Fentry.LocalName, Index, Found)
      iferror Status := errorval
      otherwise
        if Found
           then Status := DuplicateName
        else WriteEntry(DirPtr, Fentry, Done)
                 iferror Status := errorval
                 otherwise
                    if not Done
                       then Status := DirFull
end NewEntry;


procedure export UpdateEntry(DirPtr:DiskAdr; Fentry:DirEntry;
                                var Status:CallStatus);
var
   OldEntry: DirEntry; Index: integer;
   Found: Boolean; Msg: FileSysErr;
begin
   Status := Success;
   CheckEntry(DirPtr, Fentry.LocalName, Index, Found)
      iferror
        begin
           Status := errorval;
           return
        end;
      if not Found
        then Status := ObjNotFound
      else
      begin
        copyview(OldEntry, Dir.FileArr[Index]);
        if view(Fentry, File) then
           if view(OldEntry, File)
              then Dir.Consumed := Dir.Consumed
                                    + Fentry.Fattr.BlkAlloc
                                    - OldEntry.Fattr.BlkAlloc;
        copyview(Dir.FileArr[Index], Fentry);
        Disk.Write(DirPtr, 0, Vsize, Vadr)
           iferror
              begin
                 LogError(errorval, DirPtr, Msg);
                 Status := Msg
              end
      end
end UpdateEntry;
```

```
procedure export Rename(DirDesc:DirCap;
                          OldName,NewName:Name;
                          var Status:CallStatus);
var
   Index: 1 .. FileMax; Found: Boolean;
   Msg: FileSysErr;
begin
   Status := Success;
   CheckEntry(DirDesc.DirPtr, OldName, Index, Found)
      iferror
         begin
            Status := errorval;
            return
         end;
      if not Found
         then Status := ObjNotFound
      else
      begin
         if viewval(Dir.FileArr[Index]) = File
            then ActFiles.Rename(DirDesc.Adr, OldName, NewName,
                                   Found);
         Dir.FileArr[Index].LocalName := NewName;
         Disk.Write(DirDesc.DirPtr, 0, Vsize, Vadr)
            iferror
               begin
                  LogError(errorval, DirDesc.DirPtr, Msg);
                  Status := Msg
               end
      end
end Rename;


procedure FetchObj(DirDesc:DirCap; Fname:Name;
                    var OwnerDir:DirCap;
                    var Fentry:DirEntry; var Found:Boolean)
   error FileSysErr;
var
   Index: 1 .. FileMax; Rts: AccessRights;
begin
   CheckEntry(DirDesc.DirPtr, OwnerCap, Index, Found)
      iferror return error errorval;
   if Found then
   begin
      Rts := Dir.FileArr[Index].Rights;
      if view(Dir.FileArr[Index], Link) then
      begin
         SysIndir.GetDiskAdr(OwnerDirAdr, OwnerDir.DirPtr, Found);
         if Found then
         begin
            OwnerDir.Adr := OwnerDirAdr;
            CheckEntry(OwnerDir.DirPtr, Fname, Index, Found)
               iferror return error errorval
```

```
          end
        end
        else OwnerDir := DirDesc
      end;
      if Found
        then copyview(Fentry, Dir.FileArr[Index])
              iferror Found := false
              otherwise Fentry.Rights := Rts
    end FetchObj;

procedure export GetFile(DirDesc:DirCap; Fname:Name;
                        var Fentry:DirEntry; var OwnerDir:DirCap;
                        var Findex:FileIndex;
                        var Status:CallStatus);
  var
    Credit: integer; Found, Active: Boolean;
  begin
    FetchObj(DirDesc, Fname, OwnerDir, Fentry, Found)
      iferror
        begin
          Status := errorval; return
        end;
    JobDir.GetStatus(OwnerDir.Adr, Credit, Active);
    if not Active
      then Credit := Dir.Quota – Dir.Consumed;
    JobDir.Activate(OwnerDir.Adr, Credit, Active);
    if not Active
      then Status := ActDirTooMany
    else
      if not Found
        then Status := FileNotFound
      else
      begin
        ActFiles.Activate(OwnerDir.Adr, Fentry.LocalName, Findex,
                          Active);
        if not Active
          then Status := ActFilesTooMany
        else Status := Success
      end
  end GetFile;

function IsEmpty(Adr:DirAdr) return CallStatus;
  var
    Found: Boolean; DirPtr: DiskAdr;
  begin
    SysIndir.GetDiskAdr(Adr, DirPtr, Found);
    LoadDir(DirPtr)
      iferror return errorval;
    for I in 1 to FileMax do
      if Dir.FileArr[I].Used
        then return DirNonEmpty;
```

```
      return Success
   end IsEmpty;

procedure export DeleteEntry(DirPtr:DiskAdr; Fname:Name;
                             var Fentry:DirEntry;
                             var Status:CallStatus);
var
   Index, Size: integer; Found: Boolean;
   Msg: FileSysErr;
begin
   Status := Success;
   CheckEntry(DirPtr, Fname, Index, Found)
      iferror
         begin
            Status := errorval; return
         end;
   if not Found
      then Status := ObjNotFound
   else copyview(Fentry, Dir.FileArr[Index])
           iferror Status := ObjNotFound
           otherwise
             case view(Fentry) of
                File: Size := Fentry.Fattr.BlkAlloc;
                SubDir:
                   begin
                     Size := DirSegsize;
                     if JobDir.IsActive(Adr)
                        then Status := DirActive
                        else Status := IsEmpty(Adr)
                   end;
                Root:
                   begin
                     Size := DirSegsize;
                     if JobDir.IsActive(Adr)
                           or JobDir.IsActive(ShrDirAdr)
                        then Status := DirActive
                        else Status := IsEmpty(Adr)
                   end;
                Link: Size := 0
             end;
   if Status = Success then
   begin
      LoadDir(DirPtr)
         iferror
            begin
               Status := errorval; return
            end;
      with Dir do
      begin
         Consumed := Consumed – Size;
         FileArr[Index].Used := false
```

```
        end;
      Disk.Write(DirPtr, 0, Vsize, Vadr)
        iferror
          begin
            LogError(errorval, DirPtr, Msg);
            Status := Msg
          end
    end
  end DeleteEntry;


procedure export SetCurDir(DirDesc:DirCap; DirName:Name;
                           var Status:CallStatus);
  var
    NewDir, OwnerDir: DirCap; Done, Active: Boolean;
    Credit: integer;
    Fentry: DirEntry(SubDir);
  begin
    FetchObj(DirDesc, DirName, OwnerDir, Fentry, Done)
      iferror
        begin
          Status := errorval; return
        end;
      if not Done
        then Status := DirNotFound
      else
      begin
        NewDir.Adr := Fentry.Adr; NewDir.Rights := Fentry.Rights;
        SysIndir.GetDiskAdr(NewDir.Adr, NewDir.DirPtr, Done);
        JobDir.GetStatus(NewDir.Adr, Credit, Active);
        if not Active then
        begin
          LoadDir(NewDir.DirPtr)
            iferror
              begin
                Status := errorval;
                return
              end;
          Credit := Dir.Quota - Dir.Consumed
        end;
        JobDir.SetCurrent(NewDir, Credit, Done);
        if Done
          then Status := Success
        else Status := ActDirTooMany
      end
  end SetCurDir;


procedure export GetDirData(DirPtr:DiskAdr;
                            var Qta,Used:integer;
                            var Status:CallStatus);
  begin
    LoadDir(DirPtr)
```

```
            iferror Status := errorval
            otherwise
              with Dir do
              begin
                Status := Success; Qta := Quota; Used := Consumed
              end
        end GetDirData;

    procedure export InitDir(Qta:integer; DirPtr:DiskAdr;
                             var Status:CallStatus);

      var
        Msg: FileSysErr;
      begin
        Status := Success;
        with Dir do
        begin
          Quota := Qta; Consumed := 0;
          for I in 1 to FileMax
            do FileArr[I].Used := false
        end;
        Disk.Write(DirPtr, 0, Vsize, Vadr)
          iferror
            begin
              LogError(errorval, DirPtr, Msg);
              Status := Msg
            end
      end InitDir;

    begin
      Vadr := varadr(Dir); Vsize := varsize(Dir);
      Loaded := false
    end DirHandler;



    {***                      ***}
    {*** File Descriptor ***}
    {***      –Outline      ***}

var
  FileDesc: monitor;

    type export
      SegAttr =
        record
            ...
          end SegAttr;
    type
      FileDescriptor = array [1 .. SegMax] of SegAttr;
```

```
var
   Desc: FileDescriptor;
   DescAdr, DescSize: integer;
   Loaded: Boolean; CurrentDesc: DiskAdr;

   procedure LogError(Err:IoErr; Posn:DiskAdr; var Msg:FileSysErr);
   procedure LoadDesc(FileAdr:DiskAdr)
      error FileSysErr;
   procedure export InitDesc(FileAdr:DiskAdr; var Status:CallStatus);
   procedure export GetSegAttr(FileAdr:DiskAdr; SegNum:integer;
                              var Attr:SegAttr;
                              var Status:CallStatus);
   procedure export AddSeg(FileAdr:DiskAdr; SegNum:integer;
                          Adr:DiskAdr; var Status:CallStatus);
   procedure export Delete(FileAdr:DiskAdr; var Status:CallStatus);

end FileDesc;
```

```
{***                    ***}
{***   File Descriptor  ***}
{*** –Implementation ***}
```

```
var
   FileDesc: monitor
                import
                   var : FileErr, Disk, DiskSpace
                end;
      type export
         SegAttr =
            record
               Used: Boolean; SegAdr: DiskAdr
            end SegAttr;
      type
         FileDescriptor = array [1 .. SegMax] of SegAttr;
      var
         Desc: FileDescriptor;
         DescAdr, DescSize: integer;
         Loaded: Boolean; CurrentDesc: DiskAdr;

      procedure LogError(Err:IoErr; Posn:DiskAdr; var Msg:FileSysErr);
         begin
            case Err of
               NotAvail: Msg := PackOffLine;
               otherwise: Msg := BadDescriptor
            end;
            FileErr.PutError(Msg, Posn)
         end LogError;
```

```
procedure export InitDesc(FileAdr:DiskAdr; var Status:CallStatus);
  var
    Msg: FileSysErr;
  begin
    Status := Success;
    for I in 1 to SegMax
      do Desc[I].Used := false;
    Disk.Write(FileAdr, 0, DescSize, DescAdr)
      iferror
        begin
          LogError(errorval, FileAdr, Msg);
          Status := Msg
        end
  end InitDesc;

procedure LoadDesc(FileAdr:DiskAdr)
  error FileSysErr;
  var
    Msg: FileSysErr;
  begin
    if not Loaded or (CurrentDesc ≠ FileAdr) then
    begin
      Disk.Read(FileAdr, 0, DescSize, DescAdr)
        iferror
          begin
            Loaded := false;
            LogError(errorval, FileAdr, Msg);
            return error Msg
          end;
      Loaded := true;
      CurrentDesc := FileAdr
    end
  end LoadDesc;

procedure export GetSegAttr(FileAdr:DiskAdr; SegNum:integer;
                           var Attr:SegAttr;
                           var Status:CallStatus);
  begin
    LoadDesc(FileAdr)
      iferror Status := errorval
      otherwise
        begin
          Attr := Desc[SegNum]; Status := Success
        end
  end GetSegAttr;

procedure export AddSeg(FileAdr:DiskAdr; SegNum:integer;
                        Adr:DiskAdr;
                        var Status:CallStatus);
  var
    Msg: FileSysErr;
```

```
begin
  Status := Success;
  LoadDesc(FileAdr)
    iferror
      begin
        Status := errorval; return
      end;
  with Desc[SegNum] do
  begin
    Used := true; SegAdr := Adr
  end;
  Disk.Write(FileAdr, 0, DescSize, DescAdr)
    iferror
      begin
        LogError(errorval, FileAdr, Msg);
        Status := Msg
      end
end AddSeg;

procedure export Delete(FileAdr:DiskAdr; var Status:CallStatus);
  begin
    Status := Success;
    LoadDesc(FileAdr)
      iferror Status := errorval;
    if Status = Success then
    begin
      for I in 1 to SegMax do
        if Desc[I].Used
          then DiskSpace.Release(Desc[I].SegAdr);
      DiskSpace.Release(FileAdr)
    end
  end Delete;

begin
  DescAdr := varadr(Desc); DescSize := varsize(Desc);
  Loaded := false
end FileDesc;

{***              ***}
{*** File Base ***}
{*** -Outline ***}

var
  FileBase: monitor;
    var
      FileArr: array [FileIndex] of
                      record
                        ...
                      end FileArr;
```

```
    procedure export GetFileAttr(Findex:FileIndex; var Owner:DirAdr;
                                 var Ent:DirEntry(File));
    procedure export PutFileAttr(Findex:FileIndex; Owner:DirAdr;
                                 Ent:DirEntry(File));
    procedure export GetCurrentSeg(Findex:FileIndex;
                                   var SegNum:integer;
                                   var Attr:SegAttr);
    procedure export SetCurrentSeg(Findex:FileIndex;
                                   SegNum:integer;
                                   Attr:SegAttr);
  end FileBase;



    {***                    ***}
    {***       File Base     ***}
    {*** –Implementation ***}

var
  FileBase: monitor;
    var
      FileArr: array [FileIndex] of
                      record
                        Owner: DirAdr;
                        Fentry: DirEntry(File);
                        CurrentSeg: integer;
                        CurSegAttr: SegAttr
                      end FileArr;

    procedure export GetFileAttr(Findex:FileIndex;
                                 var OwnerDir:DirAdr;
                                 var Ent:DirEntry(File));
      begin
        with FileArr[Findex] do
        begin
          OwnerDir := Owner;
          Ent := Fentry
        end
      end GetFileAttr;


    procedure export PutFileAttr(Findex:FileIndex; OwnerDir:DirAdr;
                                 Ent:DirEntry(File));
      begin
        with FileArr [Findex] do
        begin
          Owner := OwnerDir;
          Fentry := Ent
        end
      end PutFileAttr;
```

```
procedure export GetCurrentSeg(Findex:FileIndex;
                                    var SegNum:integer;
                                    var Attr:SegAttr);
begin
  with FileArr[Findex] do
  begin
    SegNum := CurrentSeg; Attr := CurSegAttr
  end
end GetCurrentSeg;

procedure export SetCurrentSeg(Findex:FileIndex;
                                    SegNum:integer;
                                    Attr:SegAttr);
begin
  with FileArr[Findex] do
  begin
    CurrentSeg := SegNum; CurSegAttr := Attr
  end
end SetCurrentSeg;

end FileBase;
```

```
{***                    ***}
{*** File Management ***}
{***        –Outline     ***}
```

```
var
  FileMan: pure class;

  procedure CreateFile(DirDesc:DirCap; var FileAdr:DiskAdr;
                          var Status:CallStatus);
  procedure export OpenFile(Fname:Name; Fkind:FileKind;
                          Fmode:FileMode;
                          AccMode:Access; var Status:CallStatus;
                          var Findex:FileIndex;
                          var LastSeg,LastSegsize:integer);
  {check if the attempted access is legal; if AccMode=Write,
  create a descriptor for the file}

  procedure export CloseFile(Findex:FileIndex; AccMode:Access;
                          var Status:CallStatus);
  {update the owner capability of the file, deactivate the owner
  directory and invoke Arbiter.Close}

  procedure export DeleteFile(Owner:DirAdr; Fname:Name;
                          FileAdr:DiskAdr;
                          var Status:CallStatus);
  {invoke Arbiter.Mark to wait till the file becomes inactive
  and then delete the segments and the descriptor}
```

```
        procedure export SetSegCurrent(Findex:FileIndex;
                                SegNum:integer;
                                var SegUsed:Boolean;
                                var Status:CallStatus);
        procedure export CreateSeg(Findex:FileIndex; SegNum:integer;
                                var Status:CallStatus);
          {create a segment if there is enough quota and make the
          segment current for the file}

        procedure export AddSeg(Findex:FileIndex; DataSize:integer;
                                var Status:CallStatus);
          {include the current segment in the descriptor of the file;
          update the entry of the file in FileBase to make
          the current segment the last}

        procedure export Read(Findex:FileIndex;
                                BlkNum,MemAdr,Size:integer;
                                var Status:CallStatus);
        procedure export Write(Findex:FileIndex;
                                BlkNum,MemAdr,Size:integer;
                                var Status:CallStatus);
          {transfer data from or to the current segment of the file
          starting from the given block}


      end FileMan;




    {***                    ***}
    {***  File Management ***}
    {***  –Implementation  ***}

var
    FileMan: pure class
                import
                    var : Arbiter, FileDesc, FileBase, DirHandler,
                            DiskSpace, ActFiles, JobDir, SysIndir, Disk
                end;

    procedure CreateFile(DirDesc:DirCap; var FileAdr:DiskAdr;
                            var Status:CallStatus);
      var
        Done: Boolean;
      begin
        JobDir.DecQuota(DirDesc, FileDescsize, Done);
        if not Done
          then Status := QuotaFull
        else
        begin
          FileAdr.Pack := DirDesc.DirPtr.Pack;
          DiskSpace.AllotNew(FileAdr, FileDescsize)
```

```
                    iferror Status := PackFull
                    otherwise FileDesc.InitDesc(FileAdr, Status)
            end
        end CreateFile;


procedure export OpenFile(Fname:Name; Fkind:FileKind;
                          Fmode:FileMode;
                          AccMode:Access; var Status:CallStatus;
                          var Findex:FileIndex;
                          var Lastseg,LastSegsize:integer);
    var
        Fentry: DirEntry(File); DirDesc, OwnerDir: DirCap;
        Found, Created, Active: Boolean;
    begin
        Status := Success;
        Created := false; Active := false;
        JobDir.GetDir(DirDesc);
        DirHandler.GetFile(DirDesc, Fname, Fentry, OwnerDir,
                           Findex, Status);
        if Status = FileNotFound then
        begin
            if AccMode = Write then
                if not (Write in DirDesc.Rights)
                    then Status := RightsCheck
                else
                begin
                    with Fentry do
                    begin
                        LocalName := Fname;
                        if Fmode = Sequential
                            then Rights := AccessRights[Read, Write, Append,
                                                        Execute]
                            else Rights := AccessRights[Read, Write, Update,
                                                        Execute];
                        with Fattr do
                        begin
                            Kind := FKind; Mode := Fmode; BlkAlloc := 0;
                            LastSeg := 0; LastSegsize := 0
                        end
                    end;
                    Createfile(DirDesc, Fentry.Fattr.FileDescAdr, Status);
                    if Status = Success then
                    begin
                        Created := true;
                        ActFiles.Activate(DirDesc.Adr, Fname, Findex, Active);
                        if not Active
                            then Status := ActFilesTooMany
                    end
                end
        end
        else
```

```
          if Status = Success then
          begin
            Active := true;
            if AccMode = Write
              then Status := DuplicateName
            else
              with Fentry do
              begin
                if Fkind ≠ Fattr.Kind
                  then Status := IllegalKind
                else
                  if Fmode ≠ Fattr.Mode
                    then Status := IllegalMode
                  else
                    if not (AccMode in Rights)
                    then Status := RightsCheck
              end
          end;
          if Status = Success
            then Arbiter.Enter(Findex, AccMode, Status);
          if Status ≠ Success then
          begin
            if Created then
            begin
              DiskSpace.Release(Fentry.Fattr.FileDescAdr);
              JobDir.IncQuota(DirDesc, FileDescsize)
            end;
            if Active
              then ActFiles.DeActivate(Findex, Active);
            JobDir.DeActivate(OwnerDir.Adr)
          end
          else
          begin
            FileBase.PutFileAttr(Findex, OwnerDir.Adr, Fentry);
            with Fentry do
            begin
              LastSeg := Fattr.LastSeg; LastSegsize := Fattr.LastSegsize
            end
          end
        end OpenFile;


      procedure export CloseFile(Findex:FileIndex; AccMode:Access;
                                var Status:CallStatus);
        var
          Fentry: DirEntry(File); OwnerDir: DirCap; Found: Boolean;
        begin
          if AccMode ≠ Read then
          begin
            FileBase.GetFileAttr(Findex, OwnerDir.Adr, Fentry);
            SysIndir.GetDiskAdr(OwnerDir.Adr, OwnerDir.DirPtr, Found);
            if AccMode = Write
```

```
        then DirHandler.NewEntry(OwnerDir.DirPtr, Fentry, Status)
        else DirHandler.UpdateEntry(OwnerDir.DirPtr, Fentry, Status)
      end;
      JobDir.DeActivate(OwnerDir.Adr);
      Arbiter.Close(Findex)
    end CloseFile;

  procedure export DeleteFile(Owner:DirAdr; Fname:Name;
                              FileAdr:DiskAdr;
                              var Status:CallStatus);
    begin
      Arbiter.Mark(Owner, Fname);
      FileDesc.Delete(FileAdr, Status)
    end DeleteFile;

  procedure export SetSegCurrent(Findex:FileIndex;
                              SegNum:integer;
                              var SegUsed:Boolean;
                              var Status:CallStatus);
    var
      Fentry: DirEntry(File); Owner: DirAdr;
      Attr: SegAttr;
    begin
      Status := Success;
      FileBase.GetFileAttr(Findex, Owner, Fentry);
      FileDesc.GetSegAttr(Fentry.Fattr. FileDescAdr,SegNum,
                              Attr, Status);
      if Status = Success then
      begin
        if Attr.Used
          then Filebase.SetCurrentSeg(Findex,SegNum,
                              Attr);
        SegUsed := Attr.Used
      end
    end SetSegCurrent;

  procedure export CreateSeg(Findex:FileIndex; SegNum:integer;
                              var Status:CallStatus);
    var
      Owner: DirCap; Fentry: DirEntry(File);
      Attr: SegAttr; Done: Boolean;
    begin
      Status := Success;
      FileBase.GetFileAttr(Findex, Owner.Adr, Fentry);
      SysIndir.GetDiskAdr(Owner.Adr, Owner.DirPtr, Done);
      JobDir.DecQuota(Owner, Segsize, Done);
      if not Done
        then Status := QuotaFull
```

```
        else
        begin
           DiskSpace.AllotNext(Fentry.Fattr.FileDescAdr,
                               Attr.SegAdr, Segsize)
              iferror Status := PackFull
              otherwise
                begin
                   Attr.Used := true;
                   FileBase.SetCurrentSeg(Findex, SegNum, Attr)
                end
        end
      end CreateSeg;


procedure export AddSeg(Findex:FileIndex; DataSize:integer;
                        var Status:CallStatus);
   var
      Owner: DirAdr; Fentry: DirEntry(File); SegNum: integer;
      Attr: SegAttr;
   begin           '
      FileBase.GetFileAttr(Findex, Owner, Fentry);
      FileBase.GetCurrentSeg(Findex, SegNum, Attr);
      FileDesc.AddSeg(Fentry.Fattr.FileDescAdr, SegNum, Attr.SegAdr,
                      Status);
      if Status = Success then
      begin
        with Fentry.FAttr do
        begin
           LastSeg := SegNum; LastSegsize := DataSize
        end;
        FileBase.PutFileAttr(Findex, Owner, Fentry)
      end
   end AddSeg;


procedure export Read(Findex:FileIndex;
                      BlkNum,MemAdr,Size:integer;
                      var Status:CallStatus);
   var
      SegNum: integer; Attr: SegAttr;
   begin
      Status := Success;
      FileBase.GetCurrentSeg(Findex, SegNum, Attr);
      Disk.Read(Attr.SegAdr, BlkNum, Size, MemAdr)
         iferror
           if errorval = NotAvail
             then Status := PackOffLine
           else Status := BadSegment
   end Read;
```

```
procedure export Write(Findex:FileIndex;
                       BlkNum,MemAdr,Size:integer;
                       var Status:CallStatus);
  var
    SegNum: integer; Attr: SegAttr;
  begin
    Status := Success;
    FileBase.GetCurrentSeg(Findex, SegNum, Attr);
    Disk.Write(Attr.SegAdr, BlkNum, Size, MemAdr)
      iferror
        if errorval = NotAvail
          then Status := PackOffLine
          else Status := BadSegment
  end Write;

end FileMan;
```

```
{***                              ***}
{*** Other File System Operations ***}
{***            –Outline          ***}
```
                                                        •

```
var
  FileSys: pure class;

    procedure export SetCurDir(DirName:Name; var Status:CallStatus);
    procedure export SetRoot;
    procedure export SetShrDir(var Status:CallStatus);
    procedure export Dirgen(DirName:Name; Quota:integer;
                            var Status:CallStatus);
      {create a directory if there is enough quota; to perform
       this operation the caller should have Write rights for
       the current directory}

    procedure export Lookup(Fname:Name; var Status:CallStatus);
    procedure export ListEntry(Index:integer; var Ent:DirEntry;
                               var Status:CallStatus);
      {the above two require Read rights}

    procedure export Rename(OldName,NewName:Name;
                            var Status:CallStatus);
    procedure export Delete(Fname:Name; var Status:CallStatus);
      {the above two require Update rights; delete the capability
       by calling DirHandler.DeleteEntry; if the capability is
       an owner capability for a file, invoke FileMan.DeleteFile;
       for an owner capability for a directory, release the disk
       segment allocated for the directory}
    procedure GetShrDir(DirName:Name; var ShrDesc:DirCap;
                        var Status:CallStatus);
```

```
        procedure export Share(ShrdObj,DestDir,DestLink:Name;
                                Rts:AccessRights; var Status:CallStatus);
          {to enter a link in the shared directory of a user, check
           if the pack containing the directory is mounted and
           create a link in that directory}

        procedure export GetLink(OldLink,NewLink:Name;
                                 var Status:CallStatus);
        procedure export CopyLink(ShrdObj,DestDir,NewLink:Name;
                                  Rts:AccessRights;
                                  var Status:CallStatus);


     end FileSys;




  {***                      ***}
  {*** Other File System Operations ***}
  {***      –Implementation       ***}

var
   FileSys: pure class
              import
                 var : Disk, SysIndir, DirHandler, DiskSpace, FileMan,
                       JobDir, FileErr
              end;

     procedure export SetCurDir(DirName:Name; var Status:CallStatus);
        var
          DirDesc: DirCap;
        begin
          JobDir.GetDir(DirDesc);
          DirHandler.SetCurDir(DirDesc, Dirname, Status)
        end SetCurDir;

     procedure export SetRoot;
        begin
          JobDir.Setroot
        end SetRoot;

     procedure export SetShrDir(var Status:CallStatus);
        var
          Done: Boolean;
        begin
          JobDir.SetShrDir(Done);
          if not Done
            then Status := ActDirTooMany
            else Status := Success
        end SetShrDir;
```

```
procedure export Dirgen(DirName:Name; Quota:integer;
                        var Status:CallStatus);
  var
    DirDesc: DirCap; Fentry: DirEntry(SubDir); Done: Boolean;
    DirPtr: DiskAdr;
  begin
    JobDir.GetDir(DirDesc); Status := Success;
    JobDir.DecQuota(DirDesc, Quota + DirSegsize, Done);
    if not Done then
    begin
      Status := QuotaFull; return
    end;
    if not (Write in DirDesc.Rights)
      then Status := RightsCheck
    else
    begin
      DirPtr.Pack := DirDesc.DirPtr.Pack;
      DiskSpace.AllotNew(DirPtr, DirSegsize)
        iferror Status := PackFull
        otherwise DirHandler.InitDir(Quota, DirPtr, Status);
      if Status = Success then
        with Fentry do
        begin
          LocalName := DirName;
          Rights := AccessRights[Read, Write, Update];
          SysIndir.NewDir(DirPtr, Adr, Done);
          if not Done
            then Status := DirTooMany
          else
          begin
            DirHandler.NewEntry(DirDesc.DirPtr, Fentry,
                                Status);
            if Status ≠ Success
              then SysIndir. RemoveDir(Adr)
          end
        end;
      if (Status ≠ Success) and (Status ≠ PackFull)
        then DiskSpace. Release(DirPtr)
    end;
    if Status ≠ Success
      then JobDir.IncQuota(DirDesc, Quota + DirSegsize)
  end Dirgen;

procedure export Lookup(Fname:Name; var Status:CallStatus);
  var
    DirDesc: DirCap;
  begin
    Status := Success; JobDir.GetDir(DirDesc);
    if not (Read in DirDesc.Rights)
      then Status := RightsCheck
    else DirHandler.Lookup(DirDesc.DirPtr, Fname, Status)
  end Lookup;
```

```
procedure export Rename(OldName,NewName:Name;
                        var Status:CallStatus);
var
  DirDesc: DirCap;
begin
  Status := Success;
  JobDir.GetDir(DirDesc);
  if not (Update in DirDesc.Rights)
    then Status := RightsCheck
  else DirHandler.Rename(DirDesc, OldName, NewName, Status)
end Rename;

procedure export ListEntry(Index:integer; var Ent:DirEntry;
                           var Status:CallStatus);
var
  DirDesc: DirCap;
begin
  Status := Success;
  JobDir.GetDir(DirDesc);
  if not (Read in DirDesc.Rights)
    then Status := RightsCheck
  else DirHandler.ListEntry(DirDesc.DirPtr, Index, Ent, Status)
end ListEntry;

procedure export Delete(Fname:Name; var Status:CallStatus);
var
  DirDesc: DirCap; Fentry: DirEntry; DirPtr: DiskAdr;
  Found: Boolean;
begin
  Status := Success;
  JobDir.GetDir(DirDesc);
  if not (Update in DirDesc.Rights)
    then Status := RightsCheck
  else
  begin
    DirHandler.DeleteEntry(DirDesc.DirPtr, Fname, Fentry,
                           Status);
    if Status = Success then
      case view(Fentry) of
        File: FileMan.DeleteFile(DirDesc.Adr, Fname,
                                 Fentry.Fattr.FileDescAdr,
                                 Status);
        SubDir:
          begin
            SysIndir.GetDiskAdr(Fentry.Adr, DirPtr, Found);
            SysIndir.RemoveDir(Fentry.Adr);
            DiskSpace.Release(DirPtr)
          end
      end
  end
end Delete;
```

```
procedure GetShrDir(DirName:Name; var ShrDesc:DirCap;
                        var Status:CallStatus);
  var
    MFDDesc: DirCap; Fentry: DirEntry(Root);
    Found: Boolean;
  begin
    Status := Success;
    JobDir.GetMFD(MFDDesc);
    DirHandler.GetEntry(MFDDesc.DirPtr, DirName, Fentry, Status);
    if Status = BadDirectory then
    begin
      FileErr.PutError(BadMFD, MFDDesc.DirPtr);
      Status := BadMFD
    end;
    if Status = Success then
    begin
      SysIndir.GetDiskAdr(Fentry.ShrDirAdr, ShrDesc.DirPtr, Found);
      if not Found
        then Status := DirNotFound
    end;
    if Status = Success then
      if Disk.IsMounted(ShrDesc.DirPtr,Pack)
        then ShrDesc.Adr := Fentry.ShrDirAdr
      else Status := PackOffLine
  end GetShrDir;


procedure export Share(ShrdObj,DestDir,DestLink:Name;
                         Rts:AccessRights; var Status:CallStatus);
  var
    SdirDesc, DdirDesc: DirCap; Fentry: DirEntry(Link);
    Obj: DirEntry;
  begin
    JobDir.GetDir(SdirDesc);
    DirHandler.GetEntry(SdirDesc.DirPtr, ShrdObj, Obj, Status);
    if Status = Success then
    begin
      GetShrDir(DestDir, DdirDesc, Status);
      if Status = Success then
      begin
        with Fentry do
        begin
          LocalName := DestLink; Rights := Rts;
          case view(Obj) of
            Link:
              with Fentry do
              begin
                OwnerDirAdr := Obj.OwnerDirAdr;
                OwnerCap := Obj.OwnerCap
              end;
            otherwise:
```

```
                    begin
                       OwnerDirAdr := SdirDesc.Adr;
                       OwnerCap := ShrdObj
                    end
                end
             end;
             DirHandler.NewEntry(DdirDesc.DirPtr, Fentry, Status);
          end
       end
    end Share;

  procedure export GetLink(OldLink,NewLink:Name;
                              var Status:CallStatus);
     var
        DirDesc, ShrDirDesc: DirCap; Fentry: DirEntry(Link);
     begin
        Status := Success;
        JobDir.GetDir(DirDesc);
        if not (Write in DirDesc.Rights)
           then Status := RightsCheck
        else
        begin
           JobDir.GetShrDir(ShrDirDesc);
           DirHandler.GetEntry(ShrDirDesc.DirPtr, OldLink, Fentry,
                                 Status);
           if Status = Success then
           begin
              Fentry.LocalName := NewLink;
              DirHandler.NewEntry(DirDesc.DirPtr, Fentry, Status);
           end
        end
     end GetLink;

  procedure export CopyLink(ShrdObj,DestDir,NewLink:Name;
                               Rts:AccessRights;
                               var Status:CallStatus);
     var
        Obj: DirEntry; NewEntry: DirEntry(Link);
        DirDesc, DestDirDesc: DirCap; Credit: integer;
        Done: Boolean;
     begin
        Status := Success;
        JobDir.GetDir(DirDesc);
        Credit := JobDir.GetQuota(DirDesc);
        DirHandler.GetEntry(DirDesc.DirPtr, ShrdObj, Obj, Status);
        if Status = Success then
        begin
           DirHandler.SetCurDir(DirDesc, DestDir, Status);
           if Status = Success then
           begin
              JobDir.GetDir(DestDirDesc);
```

```
                if not (Write in DestDirDesc.Rights)
                   then Status := RightsCheck
                else
                begin
                   NewEntry.LocalName := NewLink; NewEntry.Rights := Rts;
                   case view(Obj) of
                      Link:
                         with NewEntry do
                         begin
                            OwnerDirAdr := Obj.OwnerDirAdr;
                            OwnerCap := Obj.OwnerCap
                         end;
                      otherwise:
                         with NewEntry do
                         begin
                            OwnerDirAdr := DirDesc.Adr;
                            OwnerCap := ShrdObj
                         end
                      end;
                      DirHandler.NewEntry(DestDirDesc.DirPtr, New Entry,
                                          Status);
                end
             end;
             JobDir.SetCurrent(DirDesc, Credit, Done)
          end
       end CopyLink;

   end FileSys;


   {***                             ***}
   {*** File System Administration ***}
   {***          –Outline           ***}

var
   FileAdmn: pure class;

   procedure export NewUser(PackName:PackId;
                            DirName,Pswrd:Name;
                            Quota:integer; var Status:CallStatus);
      {create a root directory with the given name and quota}
   procedure export Authenticate(DirName,Pswrd:Name;
                                 ProcNum:ProcIndex;
                                 var Status:CallStatus);
      {check if the given password matches with that contained in
       the MFD for that directory; further, check if the pack
       containing the directory is mounted; if successful,
       make that directory the root for the given job}

   procedure export CreatePack(PackName:PackId;
                               var Status:CallStatus);
```

```
      procedure export CreateMFD(PackName:PackId;
                                   var Status:CallStatus)

  end FileAdmn;




  {***                        ***}
  {*** File System Administration ***}
  {***     –Implementation      ***}

var
  FileAdmn: pure class
            import
                var : SysIndir, JobDir, DirHandler, Disk, DiskSpace,
                      FileErr
            end;

  procedure export NewUser(PackName:PackId;
                           DirName,Pswrd:Name;
                           Quota:integer; var Status:CallStatus);
    var
      MFDDesc, DirDesc, ShrDesc: DirCap; Fentry: DirEntry(Root);
      Done: Boolean;
    begin
      if not Disk.IsMounted(PackName) then
      begin
        Status := PackOffLine;
        return
      end;
      Status := Success;
      JobDir.GetMFD(MFDDesc);
      DirDesc.DirPtr.Pack := PackName;
      ShrDesc.DirPtr.Pack := PackName;
      DiskSpace.AllotNew(DirDesc.DirPtr, DirSegsize)
        iferror Status := PackFull
        otherwise DiskSpace.AllotNew(ShrDesc.DirPtr, DirSegsize)
            iferror
              begin
                DiskSpace.Release(DirDesc.DirPtr);
                Status := PackFull
              end;
      if Status = Success then
      begin
        SysIndir.NewDir(DirDesc.DirPtr, DirDesc.Adr, Done);
        if Done then
        begin
          SysIndir.NewDir(ShrDesc.DirPtr, ShrDesc.Adr, Done);
          if not Done
            then SysIndir.RemoveDir(DirDesc.Adr)
```

```
        end;
        if not Done then
        begin
          DiskSpace.Release(DirDesc.DirPtr);
          DiskSpace.Release(ShrDesc.DirPtr);
          Status := DirTooMany
        end
        else
        begin
          DirHandler.InitDir(Quota, DirDesc.DirPtr, Status);
          if Status = Success
            then DirHandler.InitDir(0, ShrDesc.DirPtr, Status);
          if Status = Success then
          begin
            with Fentry do
            begin
              LocalName := DirName;
              Rights := AccessRights[Read, Write, Update];
              Password := Pswrd;
              Adr := DirDesc.Adr; ShrDirAdr := ShrDesc.Adr
            end;
            DirHandler.NewEntry(MFDDesc.DirPtr, Fentry, Status);
            if Status = BadDirectory then
            begin
              FileErr.PutError(BadMFDDesc.DirPtr);
              Status := BadMFD
            end
          end;
          if Status ≠ Success then
          begin
            DiskSpace.Release(DirDesc.DirPtr);
            DiskSpace.Release(ShrDesc.DirPtr);
            SysIndir.RemoveDir(DirDesc.Adr);
            SysIndir.RemoveDir(ShrDesc.Adr)
          end
        end
      end
    end
  end NewUser;

procedure export Authenticate(DirName,Pswrd:Name;
                              ProcNum:ProcIndex;
                              var Status:CallStatus);
var
  MFDDesc: DirCap; Fentry: DirEntry(Root);
  Found, Done: Boolean;
  DirDesc, ShrDesc: DirCap; Qta, Used: integer;
begin
  Status := Success;
  JobDir.GetMFD(MFDDesc);
```

```
      DirHandler.GetEntry(MFDDesc.DirPtr, DirName, Fentry, Status);
      if Status = BadDirectory then
      begin
        FileErr.PutError(BadMFD, MFDDesc.DirPtr);
        Status := BadMFD
      end
      else
        if Status = DirNotFound
          then Status := NoSuchUser;
      if Status = Success then
        if Fentry.Password ≠ Pswrd
          then Status := IncorrectPassword
        else
        begin
          DirDesc.Adr := Fentry.Adr;
          DirDesc.Rights := Fentry.Rights;
          ShrDesc.Adr := Fentry.ShrDirAdr;
          ShrDesc.Rights := AccessRights[Read, Update];
          SysIndir.GetDiskAdr(DirDesc.Adr, DirDesc.DirPtr, Found);
          if Found
            then SysIndir.GetDiskAdr(ShrDesc.Adr, ShrDesc.DirPtr,
                                     Found);
          if not Found
            then Status := DirNotFound
          else
            if not Disk.IsMounted(DirDesc.DirPtr.Pack)
              then Status := PackOffLine
            else
            begin
              DirHandler.GetDirData(DirDesc.DirPtr, Qta, Used,
                                    Status);
              if Status = Success then
              begin
                JobDir.NewJob(ProcNum, DirDesc, ShrDesc,
                              Qta – Used, Done);
                if not Done
                  then Status := ActDirTooMany
              end
            end
        end
  end Authenticate;


  procedure export CreatePack(PackName:PackId;
                              var Status:CallStatus);
  begin
    Status := Success;
    DiskSpace.InitPack(PackName)
      iferror Status := BadPack
  end CreatePack;
```

```
procedure export CreateMFD(PackName:PackId;
                              var Status:CallStatus);
  var
    MFDDesc: DirCap; Done: Boolean;
  begin
    with MFDDesc do
    begin
      DirPtr.Pack := PackName;
      DiskSpace.AllotNew(DirPtr, DirSegsize);
      DirHandler.InitDir(0, DirPtr, Status);
      if Status = BadDirectory then
      begin
        Status := BadMFD;
        FileErr.PutError(BadMFD, DirPtr);
        DiskSpace.Release(DirPtr)
      end
      else
      begin
        SysIndir.NewDir(DirPtr, Adr, Done);
        JobDir.SetMFD(MFDDesc)
      end
    end
  end CreateMFD;

end FileAdmn;
```

```
{***                    ***}
{*** User File Class ***}
{*** Sequential File ***}
{***     –Outline     ***}
```

```
type export
  SeqFile(Kind: FileKind) = class;
    var
      FilBuf: Buffer(BlkSize, Kind);
      FileOpened: Boolean; AccMode: Access;
      CurrSeg: 0 .. SegMax;
      CurrBlk, CurrPtr, LastSeg, LastBlk, LastSegsize, CurrBlksize,
      Lastblksize, CurrSegsize: integer;
      Findex: FileIndex;

    procedure MakeCurrent(SegNum:integer; var Status:CallStatus);
      {make the segment current for the file; compute
       LastBlk and LastBlksize based on the size of the segment}

    procedure export Open(Fname:Name; Facc:Access;
                            var Status:CallStatus);
      {invoke FileMan.OpenFile to open the file and if successful
       set the current position of the file to be at the end
       of the hypothetical zeroth segment for Read and Write accesses;
```

for Append access, the current position is at the end of the
last segment and the last block is read in if not full}

procedure export Get(**var** UsrBuf:Buffer(?N,Kind);
                              var Size:**integer**;
                              var Status:CallStatus);
{transfer data from the current position of the file
into UsrBuf}

procedure export Put(UsrBuf:Buffer(?N,Kind); **var** Size:**integer**;
                              var Status:CallStatus);
{transfer data from UsrBuf to the file starting from the
current position creating segments when necessary;}

procedure export Close(**var** Status:CallStatus);
{for Write or Append accesses, flush out the data in UsrBuf
to the file and add the segment to the file; invoke
FileMan.CloseFile to close the file}

end SeqFile;

```
{***                    ***}
{***   User File Class   ***}
{***   Sequential File   ***}
{*** –Implementation  ***}
```

type export
   SeqFile(Kind: FileKind) = **class**
                             import
                              var : FileMan
                             end;
     var
       FilBuf: Buffer(BlkSize, Kind);
       FileOpened: **Boolean**; AccMode: Access;
       CurrSeg: 0 .. SegMax;
       CurrBlk, CurrPtr, LastSeg, LastBlk, LastSegsize, CurrBlksize,
       LastBlksize, CurrSegsize: **integer**;
       Findex: FileIndex;

     procedure MakeCurrent(SegNum:**integer**; **var** Status:CallStatus);
       var
         SegUsed: **Boolean**;
       begin
         if SegNum ≠ 0
           then FileMan.SetSegCurrent(Findex, SegNum, SegUsed,
                                       Status);
         if Status = Success
           then

```
    begin
      CurrSeg := SegNum;
      if (SegNum ≠ 0) and (SegNum = LastSeg) then
      begin
        LastBlk := (LastSegsize – 1) div Blksize + 1;
        LastBlksize := LastSegsize mod (Blksize + 1)
      end
      else
      begin
        LastBlk := BlkMax; LastBlksize := BlkSize
      end
    end
  end MakeCurrent;

  procedure export Open(Fname:Name; Facc:Access;
                        var Status:CallStatus);
    begin
      if FileOpened
        then Status := DuplicateOpen
      else
      begin
        FileMan.OpenFile(Fname, Kind, Sequential, Facc, Status,
                         Findex, LastSeg, LastSegSize);
        if Status = Success then
        begin
          AccMode := Facc;
          if AccMode = Append
            then MakeCurrent(LastSeg, Status)
          else MakeCurrent(0, Status);
          if Status = Success then
          begin
            CurrBlk := LastBlk; CurrBlkSize := LastBlkSize;
            CurrPtr := CurrBlkSize;
            if AccMode = Append then
          begin
            if CurrPtr ≠ BlkSize
              then FileMan.Read(Findex, CurrBlk – 1,
                                varadr(FilBuf),
                                varsize(FilBuf), Status);
            if Status = Success then
            begin
              FileOpened := true;
              CurrSegsize := LastSegsize
            end
          end
          else
          begin
            FileOpened := true;
            CurrSegsize := 0
          end
        end
```

```
            end
          end
        end Open;

    function Min(X,Y:integer) return integer;
      begin
        if X < Y
          then return X
        else return Y
      end Min;

    procedure export Get(var UsrBuf:Buffer(?N,Kind);
                         var Size:integer;
                         var Status:CallStatus);
      var
        ReqSize, DataInBuf, Tsize: integer;
      begin
        if not FileOpened
          then Status := FileNotOpened
        else
          if AccMode ≠ Read
            then Status := NotOpenedForRead
          else
          begin
            Status := Success;
            ReqSize := Min(N, Size); Size := 0;
            repeat
              DataInBuf := CurrBlkSize − CurrPtr;
              if (ReqSize ≠ Size) and (DataInBuf ≠ 0) then
              begin
                Tsize := Min(DataInBuf, ReqSize − Size);
                case view(UsrBuf) of
                  Text:
                    if view(FilBuf, Text) then
                      for I in 1 to Tsize
                        do UsrBuf.TextBuf[Size + I]
                           := TextBuf[CurrPtr + I];
                  Binary:
                    if view(FilBuf, Binary) then
                      for I in 1 to Tsize
                        do UsrBuf.BinaryBuf[Size + I]
                           := BinaryBuf[CurrPtr + I]
                end;
                Size := Size + Tsize; CurrPtr := CurrPtr + Tsize
              end;
              if (ReqSize ≠ Size) and (Status = Success) then
              begin
                if CurrBlk ≠ LastBlk
                  then CurrBlk := CurrBlk + 1
                else
                begin
```

```
                        if CurrSeg ≠ LastSeg then
                        begin
                           MakeCurrent(CurrSeg + 1, Status); CurrBlk := 1
                        end
                        else Status := Eof
                     end;
                     if Status = Success then
                     begin
                        FileMan.Read(Findex, CurrBlk – 1, varadr(FilBuf),
                                    varsize(FilBuf), Status);
                        if CurrBlk = LastBlk
                           then CurrBlksize := LastBlksize
                        else CurrBlksize := Blksize;
                        CurrPtr := 0
                     end
                  end
               until (ReqSize = Size) or (Status = Eof)
                     or (Status ≠ Success)
            end
         end Get;

      procedure export Put(var UsrBuf:Buffer(?N,Kind);
                           var Size:integer;  var Status:CallStatus);
         var
            ReqSize, EmptyBufSize, Tsize: integer;
         begin
            if not FileOpened
               then Status := FileNotOpened
            else
               if AccMode = Read
                  then Status := OpenedForRead
               else
               begin
                  Status := Success;
                  ReqSize := Min(Size, N); Size := 0;
                  repeat
                     EmptyBufSize := Blksize – CurrPtr;
                     if (ReqSize ≠ Size) and (EmptyBufSize ≠ 0) then
                     begin
                        Tsize := Min(EmptyBufSize, ReqSize – Size);
                        case view(UsrBuf) of
                           Text:
                              if view(FilBuf, Text) then
                                 for I in 1 to Tsize
                                    do TextBuf[CurrPtr + I]
                                       := UsrBuf.TextBuf[Size + I];
                           Binary:
                              if view(FilBuf, Binary) then
                                 for I in 1 to Tsize
                                    do BinaryBuf[CurrPtr + I]
                                       := UsrBuf.BinaryBuf[Size + I]
                        end;
```

```
                    Size := Size + Tsize;
                    CurrSegsize := CurrSegsize + Tsize;
                    CurrPtr := CurrPtr + Tsize;
                    if CurrPtr = Blksize
                      then FileMan.Write(Findex, CurrBlk – 1,
                                            varadr(FilBuf),
                                            varsize(FilBuf), Status)
                  end;
                  if (ReqSize ≠ Size) or (Status = Success) then
                  begin
                    if CurrBlk ≠ BlkMax then
                    begin
                      CurrBlk := CurrBlk + 1; CurrPtr := 0
                    end
                    else
                    begin
                      if CurrSegsize ≠ 0
                        then FileMan.AddSeg(Findex, CurrSegsize, Status);
                      if Status = Success then
                        if CurrSeg ≠ SegMax then
                        begin
                          CurrSeg := CurrSeg + 1;
                          FileMan.CreateSeg(Findex, CurrSeg, Status);
                          CurrSegsize := 0;
                          CurrPtr := 0; CurrBlk := 1
                        end
                        else Status := FileFull
                    end
                  end
                until (ReqSize = Size) or (Status = FileFull)
                        or (Status ≠ Success)
          end
        end Put;


        procedure export Close(var Status:CallStatus);
          begin
            Status := Success;
            if FileOpened then
            begin
              if (AccMode = Write) or (AccMode = Append) then
              begin
                if CurrPtr ≠ BlkSize
                  then FileMan.Write(Findex, CurrBlk – 1, varadr(FilBuf),
                                        varsize(FilBuf), Status);
                if Status = Success
                  then FileMan.AddSeq(Findex, CurrSegSize, Status)
              end;
              if Status = Success
                then FileMan.CloseFile(Findex, AccMode, Status);
              if Status = Success
```

```
                then FileOpened := false
            end
        end Close;

    end SeqFile;
```

```
{***                    ***}
{*** User File Class ***}
{***   Random File   ***}
{***     –Outline     ***}
```

type
    RandFile = **class**;

        var
            AccMode: Access; FileOpened, SegUsed: **Boolean**;
            Findex: FileIndex; Kind: FileKind;

        procedure export Open(Fname:Name; Facc:Access;
                            var Status:CallStatus);

        procedure export Get(**var** UsrSeg:Segment(Kind); SegNum:**integer**;
                            var Status:CallStatus);
            {if the specified segment exists in the file, it is read into UsrSeg}

        procedure export Put(**var** UsrSeg:Segment(Kind); SegNum:**integer**;
                            var Status:CallStatus);
            {if the specified segment already exists, overwrite that segment;
            otherwise create a segment and copy data from UsrSeg}

        procedure export Close(**var** Status:CallStatus)

    end RandFile;

```
{***                      ***}
{***   User File Class   ***}
{***     Random File     ***}
{*** –Implementation     ***}
```

type export
    RandFile = **class**
                        import
                            var : Fileman
                        end;

```
var
  AccMode: Access; SegUsed: Boolean;
  FileOpened: Boolean;
  Findex: FileIndex; Kind: FileKind;

procedure export Open(Fname:Name; Facc:Access;
                           var Status:CallStatus);
  var
    LastSeg, LastSegSize: integer;
  begin
    if FileOpened
      then Status := DuplicateOpen
    else
    begin
      FileMan.OpenFile(Fname, Kind, Random, Facc, Status, Findex,
                       LastSeg, LastSegSize);
      if Status = Success then
      begin
        FileOpened := true;
        AccMode := Facc
      end
    end
  end Open;

procedure export Get(var UsrSeg:Segment(Kind); SegNum:integer;
                          var Status:CallStatus);
  begin
    if not FileOpened
      then Status := FileNotOpened
    else
      if AccMode ≠ Read
        then Status := NotOpenedForRead
      else
      begin
        FileMan.SetSegCurrent(Findex, SegNum, SegUsed, Status);
        if Status = Success then
          if SegUsed
            then FileMan.Read(Findex, 0, varadr(UsrSeg),
                                varsize(UsrSeg), Status)
          else Status := SegmentNotFound
      end
  end Get;

procedure export Put(var UsrSeg:Segment(Kind); SegNum:integer;
                          var Status:CallStatus);
  begin
    if not FileOpened
      then Status := FileNotOpened
    else
      if AccMode = Read
        then Status := OpenedForRead
```

```
      else
      begin
        FileMan.SetSegCurrent(Findex, SegNum, SegUsed, Status);
        if Status = Success then
          if not SegUsed then
          begin
            FileMan.CreateSeg(Findex, SegNum, Status);
            if Status = Success
              then FileMan.AddSeg(Findex, SegSize, Status)
          end;
          if Status = Success
            then FileMan.Write(Findex, 0, varadr(UsrSeg),
                                      varsize(UsrSeg), Status)
      end
  end Put;

  procedure export Close(var Status:CallStatus);
  begin
    if FileOpened then
    begin
      FileMan.CloseFile(Findex, AccMode, Status);
      if Status = Success
        then FileOpened := false
    end
  end Close;

end RandFile;
```

10 INPUT/OUTPUT HANDLING

Introduction

The file system allows a user to read and write information using a file, i.e. to perform input and output operations with files. A file can be treated as a *logical* input/output device which has its representation on a physical (disk) device. In this chapter, we shall consider the ways in which *physical* input/output devices can be programmed for use, within the operating system and by user programs.

A disk is an example of a physical device that is shared between different user programs. Any device for which the operations of different user programs can be interleaved is called *shareable*. In contrast to this, there are devices such as card readers, line printers and terminals that must be allocated to one program at a time: such devices are called *assigned* devices. At one level, the distinction between the two kinds of device may appear to be arbitrary, as no device can be shared for a single operation and all devices can ultimately be used by any process. But we can distinguish between them on one criterion:

> a shareable device performs just *one* transfer at a time for each waiting user process, while an assigned device is allotted to a process for a transaction (i.e. possibly several transfers) and must be released by that process before it can be reassigned to another process.

The sequence of operations for using an assigned device would thus be:

```
begin
    "Acquire Device";
```

```
repeat
   "Perform Transfer Operation"
until Over;
   "Release Device";
end;
```

which has striking similarity with the operations used to manipulate files (notice, though, that 'acquiring' a file is a more elaborate operation which depends on the rules for concurrent access to files). With similarity of this extent, we should obviously go further and see if we can make input and output devices appear like files for all operations. This will take us one step towards making the statements of a user program (relatively) independent of the actual devices and files with which they may be operating. Providing *device independence* will simplify the task of programming and will give user programs some desirable flexibility.

Device Handling in the Kernel

Before we discuss the input/output mechanisms of the operating system, let us take a brief look at the mechanisms provided for that purpose by the Kernel. Within the Kernel, a device is identified by its kind and its unique number within that kind. For each device, the Kernel provides operations to read or write a *sequence* of characters or bytes.

The read operation can be performed on any input device. The simplest input devices are those that read single characters (or bytes) of data. Keyboards, paper-tape readers and some card readers read data in this way. They can vary in reading speed from 10 to 1000 units of data a second, and some of them may use symbolic codes other than ASCII. The Kernel will undertake all the necessary conversion of codes so that, within the operating system, we can assume all symbolic information is in ASCII.

The write operation can be performed on output devices, such as displays, paper-tape punches and printers, which function at speeds comparable to the corresponding input devices. Once again, the Kernel can be left with the task of code conversion—from ASCII to the appropriate device code.

One special case we must consider is the interactive terminal. A terminal has a keyboard for input to a program, and a display or printer for output. A terminal is said to operate in half-duplex mode if, at any given time, it acts either as a keyboard, or as a printer, but not both. In full-duplex mode, the terminal can act simultaneously as both a keyboard and a printer. The Kernel operates all terminals in full duplex mode. A number of additional operations are provided. For example,

1. The display of characters typed on the keyboard (i.e., echoing) can be selective. Many interactive programs are designed to read

a single-character command without echoing the character, and most operating systems do not echo passwords typed by users;

2. Characters typed on the keyboard can be read into a buffer even before the program makes a request to read data from the terminal. This 'type-ahead' feature allows the relatively slow input from a keyboard to be accumulated, so that the program is not delayed when it is ready to read more data.

3. Input from a keyboard can be read in either 'formatted' or 'unformatted' mode. In formatted mode, the keystroke, Delete, can be used to delete the last character in the buffer; used repeatedly, characters up to the start of the buffer can be deleted. Further, the input buffer can be displayed: this is useful if there have been mistakes and corrections in typing.

4. Output from a program can be ignored if a special character is typed on input; typing the character a second time will resume the display of program output. This allows the user to reduce the amount of data that is displayed, without altering the program.

5. By typing a special character on the terminal, it is possible to abnormally terminate the execution of a program and to return control to a standard program (see Chapter 11).

The input/output operations provided by the Kernel have the following outline:

```
type
    DevKind = (DiskDev, CRDev, LPDev, TTYDev);
    TTYop = (Echo, NoEcho, Format, NoFormat);
    IOStatus = (Done, OffLine, TransferErr, EndOfFile);

procedure Read(Kind:DevKind; DevNum:integer;
               MemAdr:Address; Size:integer;
               var Status:IOStatus; var Count:integer);

procedure Write(Kind:DevKind; DevNum:integer;
                MemAdr:Address; Size:integer;
                var Status:IOStatus; var Count:integer);

procedure DiskRead(DriveNum,Cylinder,Sector:integer;
                   MemAdr:Address; Size:integer; var Status:IOStatus);

procedure DiskWrite(DriveNum,Cylinder,Sector:integer;
                    MemAdr:Address; Size:integer;
                    var Status:IOStatus);

procedure SetTTY(TTYNum:integer; Op:TTYop);
```

The operating system builds all its input/output structures using these operations.

Disk Input/Output

In the disk space allocator and the file system, disk storage is viewed as a collection of packs, each pack being uniquely identified by a PackId. A pack is a virtual disk and must be mounted (i.e. 'made on-line') on a physical disk drive unit before it can be used. Since the number of disk drives is limited, not all packs may be on-line at the same time.

We define a simple monitor to provide the mapping between a pack and a drive.

```
    var
      DiskMount: monitor;

        var
          Drives: array [1 .. DiskMax] of
                        record
                            Free: Boolean; Pack: PackId
                        end Drives;

        function export IsMounted(Id:PackId) return integer;
          begin
            for I in 1 to DiskMax do
              with Drives[I] do
                if not Free and (Pack = Id)
                  then return I;
            return 0
          end IsMounted;

        procedure export Mount(Id:PackId; var DriveNum:integer);
          begin
            DriveNum := 0;
            for I in 1 to DiskMax do
              with Drives[I] do
                if Free then
                begin
                  Free := false; Pack := Id; DriveNum := I;
                  exit
                end
          end Mount;

        procedure export Dismount(Id:PackId);
          begin
            for I in 1 to DiskMax do
              with Drives[I] do
                if not Free and (Pack = Id) then
                begin
                  Free := true; exit
                end
          end Dismount;
```

```
      begin
        for I in 1 to DiskMax
          do Drives[I].Free := true
      end DiskMount;
```

Before information can be read from or written to a disk pack, we must ensure that the pack is mounted and find the number of the drive on which it is mounted. When this has been done, the request can be handed over to the Kernel for the operation to be performed. To mount a pack which is currently off-line, a free drive has to be acquired by calling DiskMount.Mount and then requesting the operator to mount the pack on that drive. Similarly, the procedure Dismount must be called when a pack is removed from a drive. The pure class, Disk, performs these operations.

```
    var
      Disk: pure class;
        type
          IoErr = (NotAvail, Fail);

        procedure GetDiskAdr(Adr:DiskAdr; BlkOffset:integer;
                                    var Cylinder,Block:integer);
          begin
            "Add BlkOffset to Adr and compute
            Cylinder and Block ";
          end GetDiskAdr;

        procedure export Read(Adr:DiskAdr; BlkOffset,Size:integer;
                                    MemAdr:Address)
          error IoErr;
          var
            Drive, Cylinder, Block: integer; Status: IOStatus;
          begin
            Drive := DiskMount.IsMounted(Adr.Pack);
            if Drive = 0
              then return error NotAvail;
            GetDiskAdr(Adr, BlkOffset, Cylinder, Block);
            Kernel.DiskRead(Drive, Cylinder, Block, MemAdr, Size,
                                    Status);
            if Status = TransferErr
              then return error Fail
          end Read;

        procedure export Write(Adr:DiskAdr; BlkOffset,Size:integer;
                                    MemAdr:Address)
          error IoErr;
          var
            Drive, Cylinder, Block: integer; Status: IOStatus;
```

```
begin
  Drive := DiskMount.IsMounted(Adr.Pack);
  if Drive = 0
    then return error NotAvail;
  GetDiskAdr(Adr, BlkOffset, Cylinder, Block);
  Kernel.DiskWrite(Drive, Cylinder, Block, MemAdr, Size,
                          Status);
  if Status = TransferErr
    then return error Fail
  end Write;

function export IsMounted(Id:PackId) return Boolean;
  begin
    return DiskMount.IsMounted(Id) ≠ 0
  end IsMounted;

procedure export Mount(Id:PackId)
  error IoErr;
  var
    Drive: integer;
  begin
    DiskMount.Mount(Adr.Pack, Drive);
    if Drive = 0
      then return error NotAvail;
    "Request the operator to mount the pack on Drive
    and wait till it is mounted";
  end Mount;

procedure export Dismount(Id:PackId);
  begin
    DiskMount.Dismount(Id);
    "Request the operator to dismount the pack
    and wait till it is completed";
  end Dismount;

end Disk;
```

Assigned Devices

As for files, it should be possible to use an input or output device in a program by instantiating an abstract data type. We will treat such devices as having only a sequential mode of transfer and, depending on the kind of device, they can be used either to read or write information in text or binary form. The outline of a general abstraction, AsgnDevice, will have the following form:

```
type
  AsgnDevice(Kind: FileKind) = class;
```

```
var
   DevNum: integer; Device: DevKind;
   Opened: Boolean;

procedure export Open(Dev:DevKind; Acc:Access;
                              var Status:CallStatus);
   begin
      if "device kind and access do not match"
         then Status := IllegalAccess
      else
      begin
         "Acquire device and get its index in DevNum";
         Device := Dev;
         Opened := true;
      end

   end Open;

procedure export Get(var UsrBuf:Buffer(?N,Kind);
                             var Size:integer;
                             var Status:CallStatus);
   begin
      if Opened then
      begin
         "Transfer up to Size units of data into UsrBuf";
         "Set Size to the number actually transferred";
      end;
   end Get;

procedure export Put(UsrBuf:Buffer(?N,Kind); Size:integer;
                             var Status:CallStatus);
   begin
      if Opened
         then "Transfer Size units of data from UsrBuf to device";
   end Put;

procedure export Close(var Status:CallStatus);
   begin
      "Release device";
      Opened := false;
   end Close;

procedure export SetTTY(Op:TTYop);
   begin
      Kernel.SetTTY(DevNum, Op)
   end SetTTY;

   ...

begin
   Opened := false;
end AsgnDevice;
```

A device can then be instantiated in a program and used in a very similar way to a file. A simple program to print the information on a deck of cards would have the form:

```
var
    Input, Output: AsgnDevice(Text); MyBuf: Buffer(100, Text);
    Status: CallStatus; Size: integer;
begin
    Input.Open(CRDev, Read, Status);
    Output.Open(LPDev, Write, Status);
    Input.Get(MyBuf, Size, Status);
    repeat
        Output.Put(MyBuf, Size, Status);
        Input.Get(MyBuf, Size, Status);
    until Status = EOF;
end;
```

Device Independence

The abstraction of an assigned device, AsgnDevice, is quite similar to SeqFile, the abstraction of a sequential file. It would be very useful to provide a single abstraction which can be used for *either* a sequential file or an assigned device. It would then be possible to use a single instance of this abstraction to access a sequential file or an assigned device, with the choice being determined dynamically. Writing utility programs, like a general program to copy data from one device to another, would be greatly simplified with such device independence.

Let us call this combined abstraction, SeqIO, and give it the following outline:

```
type
    SeqIO(Kind: FileKind) = class;
        var
            AsgnDev: AsgnDevice(Kind);
            FileDev: SeqFile(Kind);
            Device: DevKind;
            Opened: Boolean;

        procedure export Open(Dev:DevKind; Fname:Name; Acc:Access;
                                var Status:CallStatus);
        begin
            if Dev = DiskDev
                then FileDev.Open(Fname, Acc, Status)
            else AsgnDev.Open(Dev, Acc, Status);
            if Status = Success then
```

```
    begin
      Opened := true; Device := Dev
    end
  end Open;

procedure export Close(var Status:CallStatus);
  begin
    if Opened then
    begin
      if Device = DiskDev
        then FileDev.Close(Status)
      else AsgnDev.Close(Status);
      if Status = Success
        then Opened := false
    end
  end Close;


    ...


  end SeqIO;
```

The class, SeqIO, is made 'device independent' by providing it with instantiations of *both* SeqFile and AsgnDevice. Each operation of SeqIO is performed by invoking the corresponding operation of the appropriate instance. This is functionally adequate, but not very imaginative. It would be preferable to provide more convenient primitives for sequential input/output than are available, for example, through the operations Get and Put of AsgnDevice and SeqFile.

Symbolic input from devices can be conveniently read in units called 'records' (which should be distinguished from the language feature, record). Typically, an input record is a line of text terminated by a carriage return or line feed character. But there are many programming require-ments for reading either single characters (e.g., for commands to an editor) or for choosing different terminating characters for input.

Let

```
type
  CharSet = set of char;
```

We can then provide a procedure, SetEndChars, by which the set of terminating characters can be chosen by a program and then used in the Read operation. (If the device is an assigned device, the terminating characters are set at the Kernel level, so that an input record from the device can be read using a single Kernel.Read operation.)

The complete listing of SeqIO is given at the end of the chapter. SeqIO is a

little more general than required for any single type of device but this is
necessary if it is to be used for any sequential input/output device.

Device Allocation

To perform input/output through an assigned device, an instance of
AsgnDevice is first made and the device is then acquired through the
procedure Open. Different user programs may concurrently try to acquire a
device but the device can be allocated only serially. The device allocation is
performed by the monitor DevAlloc.

```
var
  DevAlloc: monitor;
    type
      DevIndex = 1 .. DevMax;
      ProcIndex = 1 .. ProcMax;
    var
      DevTable: array [DevIndex] of
                      record
                        Allocated: Boolean;
                        Kind: DevKind; DevNum: DevIndex
                      end DevTable;
      DevQ: array [ProcIndex] of
                   record
                     Device: DevKind;
                     Q: queue
                   end DevQ;

    procedure export Acquire(Dev:DevKind; var Num:DevIndex);
      begin
        loop
          for I in 1 to DevMax do
            with DevTable[I] do
              if (Kind = Dev) and not Allocated then
              begin
                Allocated := true; Num := DevNum;
                return
              end;
          with DevQ[ProcId] do
          begin
            Device := Dev; delay(Q)
          end
        end
      end Acquire;

    procedure export Release(Dev:DevKind; Num:DevIndex);
      begin
        for I in 1 to DevMax do
          with DevTable[I] do
```

```
            if (Kind = Dev) and (DevNum = Num) then
            begin
               Allocated := false; exit
            end;
         for I in 1 to ProcMax do
            with DevQ[I] do
               if delayed(Q) and (Device = Dev) then
               begin
                  continue(Q); exit
               end
      end Release;

   function export Assigned(Dev:DevKind; Num:DevIndex)
                                 return Boolean;
      begin
         for I in 1 to DevMax do
            with DevTable[I] do
               if (Kind = Dev) and (DevNum = Num)
                  then return Allocated
      end Assigned;

   begin {DevAlloc}
      for I in 1 to DevMax do
         with DevTable[I] do
         begin
            Allocated := false;
            Kind := "the kind of the device";
            DevNum := "its unique number within its kind"
         end
   end DevAlloc;
```

DISCUSSION

Device Spooling

An assigned device is allocated to a job for the duration of a transaction and, during this period, no other job can make use of the device. Exclusive allocation, in this manner, is well suited for devices that are not in great demand by different user jobs. But there are other devices, like card readers and line printers, which are used by many user jobs. For such devices, it is undesirable, and inefficient, for allocation to be exclusive. For example, if a card reader is allotted to a user job, no other job can use this device until it is released. If batch jobs are read in from this card reader, at most one batch job can then be executed at a time. Similarly, if the sole printer in the system is allotted to a user job, requests for printing from all other jobs will be delayed until the printer is released.

It is obviously not possible to allocate a single device to more than one job. But we can allow multiple access to abstractions of these devices if we simulate these abstractions using devices that *are* shareable (e.g. the disk). A spooler is a program which provides abstractions of some input or output device by creating files on the disk. Thus, if a user program needs a printer, instead of allocating the printer device to the job, a sequential file (called a spooled file) is created and all requests by the program for printing information are directed to the file. When the job releases the printer, the spooled file is closed. The real printer is assigned to the printer spooler, and this program sequentially prints spooled files.

Input Spooling

Among the spooled devices, the card reader requires particular attention, if it is to be used to submit batch jobs. These batch jobs may themselves need to read input from the card reader and the spooler must take both kinds of input into account.

Let us assume that batch jobs are separated from each other by control cards. The input spooler will read all the cards for one job and create three kinds of files:

1. A file for each *program* submitted as part of the job.
2. A file for each set of *data*.
3. A control file which contains the commands that direct the execution of the job.

Once these files are created, the input spooler will register the arrival of a batch job in standard file, called BatchQ. This file will be periodically examined by the operating system when batch jobs are to be selected for execution. (Job management is discussed in detail in Chapter 11.)

The class SeqIO will need to be modified to allow use of spooled devices. Input from a spooled device must be read from the file into which the input has been stored by the spooler, and output to a spooled device must be directed to a spooler file. We leave these modifications to SeqIO as an exercise.

Summary

Descriptions of input and output device handling are available for several operating systems (e.g., Stoy and Strachey, 1972; Welsh and McKeag,

1980) and we have little to add to these. The abstractions described here differ from the earlier descriptions primarily in the way functions are divided between the Kernel and the operating system. We have chosen to leave several mechanisms for implementation in the Kernel, not because they cannot be done in the operating system, but because they must be performed frequently and quickly. For example, the Kernel keeps buffers of characters read from keyboards, and reads characters into these buffers ahead of actual requests from programs. These characters can be deleted and replaced without special attention from the operating system. By providing these features in the Kernel, we can be sure that terminal input, at the level of single records, will receive quick attention. There is little to be gained by performing these functions in the operating system, as they are simple and repetitive.

The use of standardized input/output operations is common in several operating systems and has much to commend it: for example, it makes it possible for the input/output operations of utility programs to be applicable for a wide class of devices (including files), rather than only for specific input and output devices. If the choice of device can be made at compile time, a utility can be 'tailored' for particular uses. But much flexibility is lost if only compile time choice is available. In most practical cases, the selection of devices is most conveniently done by the interactive or batch user, at run time. There is a price to be paid for this flexibility: the abstraction that handles devices must be capable of performing its operations on any of a set of devices. The inelegance that this introduces is particularly evident when all operations on devices are performed in one abstraction. But it is no less present in operating systems where operations on devices are independently performed.

EXERCISES

1. Introduce a new abstraction, MagTape, for handling input/output operations on magnetic tapes. MagTape should have the following outline:

type
    MagTape(Kind: FileKind) = **class**;
      type
        TapeOp = (SkipFile, SkipRecord);

      procedure Open(TapeId:Name; Acc:Access;
                 var Status:CallStatus);
        {Acquire a tape drive and request the operator to mount
        the specified tape on that drive}

```
procedure Read(var UsrBuf:Buffer(?N,Kind); var Size:integer;
                var Status:CallStatus);
procedure Write(UsrBuf:Buffer(?N,Kind); var Size:integer;
                var Status:CallStatus);
   {Implement the data transfer operations using SeqIO}
procedure Position(Op:TapeOp; Count:integer;
                var Status:CallStatus);
   {Skip the specified number of files or records forward
    if Count is positive or backward if Count is negative}
end MagTape;
```

2. Assume the job manager (Chapter 11) provides the following two procedures:

```
procedure CRSpool(var Spooled:Boolean; var FileName:Name);
procedure LPSpool(var Spooled:Boolean; var FileName:Name);
```

These two procedures can be called to find out if, for the calling job, files have been designated for spooled input from card reader and spooled output to line printer. Use these procedures to extend SeqIO to read from and write to spooled devices.

3. (Group Exercise.) Assume the following control cards are used for batch jobs:

   (a) $JOB JOBNAME USER PASSWORD TIMELIMIT
       marks the beginning of a batch job.
   (b) $DECK FileName
       marks the beginning of program or data cards.
   (c) $COMMANDS
       indicates that the cards that follow contain commands that
       direct the execution of the job.
   (d) $EOJ
       marks the end of a batch job.

A *control* file and a *log* file are associated with each batch job. These two files simulate the controlling terminal for the batch job: the control file simulates the 'keyboard' and the log file simulates the 'printer'.

Design a card input spooler process that

   (a) on reading a $JOB card performs authentication checks and, if successful, creates a control file and a log file for that batch job,
   (b) reads all cards between a $DECK card and the next control card into a file with the name specified in the $DECK card,
   (c) reads all cards between a $COMMANDS card and the next control card into the control file of the batch job, and
   (d) on reading a $EOJ card, records the arrival of the batch job in a standard file, called BatchQ. BatchQ contains an entry for each batch job indicating the name of the user, and the names of the control and log files.
       How will you organize BatchQ? (Note that the entry for a batch job can be deleted after the job completes execution.)

THE INPUT/OUTPUT PROGRAM

```
{***                ***}
{*** DiskMount ***}
{***   –Outline   ***}

var
  DiskMount: monitor;
    var
      Drives: array [1 .. DiskMax] of
                    record
                      Free: Boolean; Pack: PackId
                    end Drives;
    function export IsMounted(Id:PackId) return integer;
        { return 0 if the pack is not mounted}
    procedure export Mount(Id:PackId; var DriveNum:integer);
        {return 0 if no free drive available}
    procedure export Dismount(Id:PackId)
  end DiskMount;



{***                    ***}
{***      DiskMount      ***}
{*** –Implementation ***}

var
  DiskMount: monitor;

    var
      Drives: array [1 .. DiskMax] of
                    record
                      Free: Boolean; Pack: PackId
                    end Drives;

    function export IsMounted(Id:PackId) return integer;
      begin
        for I in 1 to DiskMax do
          with Drives[I] do
            if not Free and (Pack = Id)
              then return I;
        return 0
      end IsMounted;

    procedure export Mount(Id:PackId; var DriveNum:integer);
      begin
        DriveNum := 0;
        for I in 1 to DiskMax do
          with Drives[I] do
```

```
                    if Free then
                    begin
                       Free := false; Pack := Id; DriveNum := I;
                       exit
                    end
              end Mount;

       procedure export Dismount(Id:PackId);
          begin
             for I in 1 to DiskMax do
                with Drives[I] do
                   if not Free and (Pack = Id) then
                   begin
                      Free := true; exit
                   end
             end Dismount;

       begin
          for I in 1 to DiskMax
             do Drives[I].Free := true
          end DiskMount;




    {***              ***}
    {***    Disk      ***}
    {*** –Outline     ***}

var
   Disk: pure class;
      type export
         IoErr = (NotAvail, Fail);

      procedure GetDiskAdr(Adr:DiskAdr; BlkOffset:integer;
                              var Cylinder,Block:integer);
         {compute the cylinder and sector address of the
          specified block of the given segment}

      procedure export Read(Adr:DiskAdr; BlkOffset,Size:integer;
                              MemAdr:Address)
         error IoErr;
      procedure export Write(Adr:DiskAdr; BlkOffset,Size:integer;
                              MemAdr:Address)
         error IoErr;
         {compute the cylinder and sector address of the
          given block and transfer data from or to memory}

      function export IsMounted(Id:PackId) return Boolean;
      procedure export Mount(Id:PackId)
         error IoErr;
```

{find a free drive and request the operator to
mount the pack; if no drive available return
error NotAvail}

procedure export Dismount(Id:PackId)

end Disk;

```
{***                   ***}
{***      Disk         ***}
{*** –Implementatioɴ ***}
```

var
   Disk: **pure class**
            import
                var : DiskMount
            end;
        type export
      IoErr = (NotAvail, Fail);

   procedure GetDiskAdr(Adr:DiskAdr; BlkOffset:**integer**;
                           var Cylinder,Block:**integer**);
      begin
        "Add BlkOffset to Adr and compute
         Cylinder and Block";
      end GetDiskAdr;

   procedure export Read(Adr:DiskAdr; BlkOffset,Size:**integer**;
                           MemAdr:Address)
      error IoErr;
      var
        Drive, Cylinder, Block: **integer**; Status: IOStatus;
      begin
        Drive := DiskMount.IsMounted(Adr.Pack);
        if Drive = 0
           then return error NotAvail;
        GetDiskAdr(Adr, BlkOffset, Cylinder, Block);
        Kernel.DiskRead(Drive, Cylinder, Block, MemAdr, Size, Status);
        if Status = TransferErr
           then return error Fail
      end Read;

   procedure export Write(Adr:DiskAdr; BlkOffset,Size:**integer**;
                            MemAdr:Address)
      error IoErr;
      var
        Drive, Cylinder, Block: **integer**; Status: IOStatus;
```
```

```
      begin
        Drive := DiskMount.IsMounted(Adr.Pack);
        if Drive = 0
          then return error NotAvail;
        GetDiskAdr(Adr, BlkOffset, Cylinder, Block);
        Kernel.DiskWrite(Drive, Cylinder, Block, MemAdr, Size, Status);
        if Status = TransferErr
          then return error Fail
      end Write;

    function export IsMounted(Id:PackId) return Boolean;
      begin
        return DiskMount.IsMounted(Id) ≠ 0
      end IsMounted;

    procedure export Mount(Id:PackId)
      error IoErr;
      var
        Drive: integer;
      begin
        DiskMount.Mount(Adr.Pack, Drive);
        if Drive = 0
          then return error NotAvail;
        "Request the operator to mount the pack on Drive
         and wait till it is mounted";
      end Mount;

    procedure export Dismount(Id:PackId);
      begin
        DiskMount.Dismount(Id);
        "Request the operator to dismount the pack
         and wait till it is completed";
      end Dismount;

  end Disk;



{***              ***}
{*** DevAlloc ***}
{*** –Outline  ***}

var
  DevAlloc: monitor;
    type
      DevIndex = 1 .. DevMax;
      ProcIndex = 1 .. ProcMax;
    var
      DevTable: array [DevIndex] of
                    record
                        ...
                    end DevTable;
```

```
          DevQ: array [ProcIndex] of
                record
                      ...
                end DevQ;

     procedure export Acquire(Dev:DevKind; var Num:DevIndex);
          {allocate a device of the specified kind
           to the calling process, if the device
           is free; otherwise delay the caller}

     procedure export Release(Dev:DevKind; Num:DevIndex);
          {deallocate the device for the caller and continue
           a process waiting for the device}

     function export Assigned(Dev:DevKind; Num:DevIndex)
                              return Boolean;

     end DevAlloc;



     {***                    ***}
     {***      DevAlloc      ***}
     {*** –Implementation ***}

var
   DevAlloc: monitor;
      type
         DevIndex = 1 .. DevMax;
         ProcIndex = 1 .. ProcMax;
      var
         DevTable: array [DevIndex] of
                     record
                        Allocated: Boolean;
                        Kind: DevKind; DevNum: DevIndex
                     end DevTable;
         DevQ: array [ProcIndex] of
                  record
                     Device: DevKind;
                     Q: queue
                  end DevQ;

     procedure export Acquire(Dev:DevKind; var Num:DevIndex);
        begin
          loop
            for I in 1 to DevMax do
               with DevTable[I] do
                  if (Kind = Dev) and not Allocated then
                  begin
                     Allocated := true; Num := DevNum;
```

```
              return
            end;
        with DevQ[ProcId] do
        begin
          Device := Dev; delay(Q)
        end
      end
    end Acquire;

  procedure export Release(Dev:DevKind; Num:DevIndex);
    begin
      for I in 1 to DevMax do
        with DevTable[I] do
          if (Kind = Dev) and (DevNum = Num) then
          begin
            Allocated := false; exit
          end;
      for I in 1 to ProcMax do
        with DevQ[I] do
          if delayed(Q) and (Device = Dev) then
          begin
            continue(Q); exit
          end
    end Release;

  function export Assigned(Dev:DevKind; Num:DevIndex)
                            return Boolean;
    begin
      for I in 1 to DevMax do
        with DevTable[I] do
          if (Kind = Dev) and (DevNum = Num)
            then return Allocated
    end Assigned;

begin
  for I in 1 to DevMax do
    with DevTable[I] do
    begin
      Allocated := false;
      Kind := "the kind of the device";
      DevNum := "its unique number within its kind"
    end
end DevAlloc;


{***                 ***}
{*** AsgnDevice ***}
{***  –Outline   ***}

type
  AsgnDevice(Kind: FileKind) = class;
```

```
var
   DevNum: integer; Device: DevKind;
   Opened: Boolean;
procedure export Open(Dev:DevKind; Acc:Access;
                              var Status:CallStatus);
   {acquire a device of the specified kind if the kind
    and attempted access match}

procedure export Get(var UsrBuf:Buffer(?N,Kind);
                           var Size:integer;
                           var Status:CallStatus);
procedure export Put(UsrBuf:Buffer(?N,Kind); var Size:integer;
                           var Status:CallStatus);
   {call the corresponding kernel operation to perform
    the data transfer}

procedure export Close(var Status:CallStatus);
procedure export SetEndChars(Tset:CharSet);
procedure export SetTTY(Op:TTYop)

end AsgnDevice;




{***                    ***}
{***    AsgnDevice    ***}
{*** –Implementation ***}

type
   AsgnDevice(Kind: FileKind) = class
                                    import
                                       var : DevAlloc
                                    end;
   var
      DevNum: integer; Device: DevKind;
      Opened: Boolean;

   procedure export Open(Dev:DevKind; Acc:Access;
                             var Status:CallStatus);
      begin
         if "device kind and access do not match"
            then Status := IllegalAccess
         else
         begin
            DevAlloc.Acquire(DevKind, DevNum);
            Device := Dev;
            Opened := true;
            Status := Success
         end
      end Open;
```

```
procedure export Get(var UsrBuf:Buffer(?N,Kind);
                     var Size:integer;
                     var Status:CallStatus);
   begin
     if Opened
        then Kernel.Read(Device, DevNum, varadr(UsrBuf), Size,
                         Status, Size)
        else Status := FileNotOpened
   end Get;

procedure export Put(UsrBuf:Buffer(?N,Kind); Size:integer;
                     var Status:CallStatus);
   begin
     if Opened
        then Kernel.Write(Device, DevNum, varadr(UsrBuf), Size,
                          Status, Size)
        else Status := FileNotOpened
   end Put;

procedure export Close(var Status:CallStatus);
   begin
     if Opened then
     begin
        DevAlloc.Release(Device, DevNum);
        Opened := false
     end
   end Close;

procedure export SetTTY(Op:TTYop);
   begin
     if Opened and (Device = TTYDev)
        then Kernel.SetTTY(DevNum, Op)
   end SetTTY;

procedure export SetEndChars(TSet:CharSet);
   begin
     if Opened
        then "set the terminating characters at the kernel level
              by calling the appropriate kernel operation"
   end SetEndChars;
begin
   Opened := false;
end AsgnDevice;



{***              ***}
{*** SeqIO ***}
{*** –Outline ***}


type
   SeqIO(Kind: FileKind) = class;
```

```
var
  AsgnDev: AsgnDevice(Kind);
  FileDev: SeqFile(Kind);
  Device: DevKind;
  Opened: Boolean; TermSet: CharSet;

procedure export Open(Dev:DevKind; Fname:Name; Acc:Access;
                          var Status:CallStatus);
  {if Dev=DiskDev, open the file Fname; otherwise
   acquire a device of the specified kind}

procedure export Read(var Buf:Buffer(?N,Kind);
                          var Size:integer;
                          var Status:CallStatus);
procedure export Write(Buf:Buffer(?N,Kind); var Size:integer;
                          var Status:CallStatus);
procedure export SetEndChars(TSet:CharSet);
procedure export SetTTY(Op:TTYop);
procedure export Close(var Status:CallStatus);

end SeqIO;
```

```
{***                      ***}
{***        SeqIO         ***}
{*** –Implementation ***}
```

```
type
  SeqIO(Kind: FileKind) = class;

    var
      AsgnDev: AsgnDevice(Kind);
      FileDev: SeqFile(Kind);
      Device: DevKind;
      Opened: Boolean;
      TermSet: CharSet;

    procedure export Open(Dev:DevKind; Fname:Name; Acc:Access;
                              var Status:CallStatus);
      begin
        if Dev = DiskDev
          then FileDev.Open(Fname, Acc, Status)
          else AsgnDev.Open(Dev, Acc, Status);
        if Status = Success then
        begin
          Opened:= true; Device := Dev
        end
      end Open;
```

```
procedure export Close(var Status:CallStatus);
  begin
    if Opened then
    begin
      if Device = DiskDev
        then FileDev.Close(Status)
        else AsgnDev.Close(Status);
      if Status = Success
        then Opened := false
    end
  end Close;

procedure export SetEndChars(TSet:CharSet; var Status:CallStatus);
  begin
    Status := Success;
    if Opened then
      if Device = DiskDev
        then TermSet := TSet
        else AsgnDev.SetEndChars(TSet)
    else Status := FileNotOpened
  end SetEndChars;

procedure export Read(var Buf:Buffer(?N,Kind); var Size:integer;
                      var Status:CallStatus);
  var
    Ch: Buffer(1, Text);
    Count, Tsize: integer; Over: Boolean;
  begin
    if not Opened
      then Status := FileNotOpened
    else
      if Device ≠ DiskDev
        then AsgnDev.Get(Buf, Size, Status)
      else
      begin
        case view(Buf) of
          Text:
            begin
              Count := 0;
              repeat
                Tsize := 1;
                FileDev.Get(Ch, Tsize, Status);
                if Status = Success then
                begin
                  Count := Count + 1;
                  Buf[Count] := Ch[1];
                  Over := Ch[1] in Termset
                end
              until Over or (Count = Size) or (Status ≠ Success);
              Size := Count
            end;
```

```
                  Binary: FileDev.Get(Buf, Size, Status)
            end
          end;
      end Read;

  procedure export Write(Buf:Buffer(?N,Kind); var Size:integer;
                          var Status:CallStatus);
      begin
        if not Opened
          then Status := FileNotOpened
        else
          if Device = DiskDev
            then FileDev.Put(Buf, Size, Status)
          else AsgnDev.Put(Buf, Size, Status)
      end Write;

  procedure export SetTTY(Op:TTYop);
      begin
        if Opened and (Device = TTYDev)
          then AsgnDev.SetTTY(Op)
      end SetTTY;

begin
    Opened := false;
    {Carriage-return and Line-feed are the initial
     terminating characters}
    TermSet := CharSet[Cret, Lfeed]
end SeqIO;
```

11 JOB MANAGEMENT

Introduction

The previous chapters have described how the complexities of resource management for main memory space, disk space and input/output devices can be handled within abstractions that have a fairly simple external appearance. We have already made use of some of these abstractions to build *logical* resources—directories and files—that have more convenient properties than those of the basic resources of which they are composed. We are yet to consider the management of a critical resource, the processor, and we must describe how user programs can be executed on the system. Processor management and user job management are closely related. The problems of job management are really those of resource allocation—to decide how limited physical resources, including processors, are to be shared between competing user jobs. But, compared to other resources, processors have a more commanding influence as the resource requirements of a job can vary only if it is executed, i.e. if it is given some share of a processor resource. As a first approximation, we can say that the management of a job consists in controlling the use of other physical resources by regulating the allocation of a processor to the job.

User Job Execution

So far, we have casually referred to a 'user program' and a 'user job' without explaining how these terms relate to a program submitted for execution by a user. We can now make this association more explicit. To execute a program, a user must initiate a *job*. This can be done in two ways: through a terminal, or by submitting a deck of cards. Jobs initiated through terminals are called interactive jobs. An interactive job is initiated by a user 'logging-in' at a terminal. A batch job has a deck of cards prefixed with job control cards (which we shall not describe in detail). As we saw in Chapter 4, each job has an authentication check to ensure that the user is authorized to use the system. After authentication, the job begins execution of a user's commands. A skeleton interactive job will have the form:

```
LOGIN <User Identification>     – User types identification
PASSWORD <User Password> – User types password
                                – User job to be authenticated now
logged in at <time> on <date>

<User commands>                 – Each command to be executed

LOGOUT                          – End of job
logged out at <time> on <date>
```

User commands are interpreted by a Command Program. The most commonly used command is one asking for the execution of a program that has earlier been compiled and stored as a file; e.g. to execute the Pascal compiler, the command could be

```
*RUN PASCAL(SourceFile, ListFile, CodeFile)
                    —execute the Pascal compiler with
                    —input from SourceFile; send output to
                    —ListFile and compiled program to CodeFile
```

Through a single job, a user can successfully execute several programs that have been compiled and stored in files. The Command program causes a program to be executed by calling a system procedure, Enter, with the name of the program file as the argument. The Enter procedure will collect the parameters for a program call into a *parameter block* which is passed to the called program. Most jobs will just consist of a sequence of such commands. But it is possible for a job to have a more complicated structure: a program that is executed by one command may itself call the procedure Enter to ask for the execution of another program. So, programs may 'call' each other in procedure-like fashion, returning control to the previous program using the system procedure Depart.

When a program is called for execution through the procedure Enter, the program file must be loaded into main memory. From Chapter 2, we know a program file can either be 'mixed', i.e. consist of instructions and data, or 'separated', in which case it will consist of an instruction part and a data part. When a separated program is called, both parts must be loaded into memory. A separated program has the advantage that when it is called by different jobs, a single storage segment can be used for instructions while separate data segments are used for each calling job (i.e., a separated program is 're-entrant'). This can result in considerable saving of space for often-used programs, such as system utilities.

```
procedure Enter(NewProg:Name; "Parameter information");
  begin
    "Collect parameters in ParBlock";
    if "NewProg is mixed"
      then "register new entry for NewProg"
    else {NewProg is separated}
    begin
      if "NewProg not loaded"
        then "register entry for instruction part of NewProg";
      "Register entry for data part of NewProg";
    end;
    "Wait until program segments are loaded";
    "Call NewProg with parameters in ParBlock";
  end Enter;

procedure Depart("Parameter information");
  begin
    "Release program segments if no other users";
    "Copy parameters returned by called program";
    "Return to previous program";
  end Depart;
```

Programs are often developed through interactive jobs. During testing, it sometimes becomes necessary to terminate the execution of a program (for example, because it is in a loop). A program executed from an interactive job can be unconditionally terminated by typing a special character on the terminal. The Kernel recognizes this character and causes the program to return control with an error. Naturally, this flexibility cannot be provided for batch jobs. But the control cards for a batch job may specify a limit to the time that can be used by a job and this will eventually cause even a looping program to be stopped. Control cards can specify other limits, such as the maximum memory to be used for the job, and conditions, such as the time when the job should be taken for execution.

Job Representation

From the viewpoint of the operating system, a user job is a **process** which can be scheduled for execution on a processor. Every process must be represented by some data that characterizes it (e.g., a process identifier), limits the resources that can be used (e.g., an execution time limit), and defines its *state* so that it can be executed on a physical processor (e.g., the state could consist of the storage segments occupied by instructions and data for the process, and the value of the instruction counter). Process data occupies memory space, so it would normally be advisable to reduce this requirement to the minimum. For example, if an operating system is executing only ten jobs at some time, in principle there need be only ten sets of process data, even if there are other times when more than this number of jobs is executed.

But user jobs make their appearance fairly unpredictably. The operating system has no means of knowing how many terminal users there will be, or how many batch jobs will be submitted, at any time in the future. Every user job is executed as a *job process*, so one way to deal with this situation is to dynamically *create* a new process whenever a new user job is encountered. This will require some memory to be dynamically allocated for each new process. We can avoid this if the system initially creates a fixed number of job processes that are idle, or free, until they are allocated to execute user jobs. When a new user job appears, a free job process is found and allocated to the user job. Many operating systems follow a similar practice: those that do not have job processes in the form we have described them here, have limits to the number of jobs that can be created at any time. Having a fixed number of jobs, or job processes, allows the operating system tables to have a simple structure.

Let us therefore start with the assumption that the operating system has a fixed number of job processes, as it has the advantage of simplicity.

The basic structure of each job process will be

```
type
  JobProcess = process;
    begin
      loop
        "Initialize local variables";
        "Wait for user job";
        if "job is interactive"
          then "set control device for Job";
        "Execute user job";
        { authenticate user
          and execute user commands}
        "Do finalization work – close files etc."
        "Update accounting file for user";
      end;
    end JobProcess;
```

The fixed number of processes can be declared as an array:

```
var
    Jobs: array [JobMin .. JobMax] of JobProcess;
```

and we can use the array index of a job process as its identifier. A user job is 'created' when it is associated with a waiting job process. For an interactive job, the job process calls the Kernel to register the terminal as the control device which can be used to unconditionally terminate execution of user programs. After this, the job process executes as the user job, by performing all its commands and printing a log giving the execution history of the job. The job process is then freed from this particular job and waits for another user job to appear.

All job processes in the system are represented in a data structure called the Job Table. An entry in this table stores the identification of each process, and its status (e.g., whether it is free, and whether its program has been swapped out of memory). JobTable is a monitor whose operations are used by job processes and by other processes in the operating system.

Levels of Scheduling

The number of user jobs that can be created at one time may be limited by administrative policy, e.g., according to the time of the day. The first step in job management is to determine *when* a user job can be run. A standard operating system process, the Job Initiator, performs this function. The appearance of a new interactive user job is signalled by input from a terminal that has not already been assigned to a job. Batch jobs are chosen for execution from the entries in the batch queue. As described in Chapter 10, the input spooler reads cards, creates program and data files and records the arrival of a batch job request in the batch queue. The batch queue is maintained as a file to which both the input spooler and the Job Initiator have access. The Job Initiator periodically looks through the batch queue and checks the entries to decide if a job is to be created.

Let MaxTerminals and MaxBatch be the limits to the number of terminal and batch jobs that can be created at one time, and let TerminalJobs and BatchJobs be the number actually created. Then the process JobInitiator has the following outline:

```
var
    JobInitiator: process;
    begin
        loop
            while ((TerminalJobs < MaxTerminals) and "new job waiting")
                    or (BatchJobs < MaxBatchJobs)
                    and "batch queue not empty") do
```

```
        begin
          "Find a free job process in the Job Table";
          if "job is batch job" then
          begin
            "Set up standard input and output files";
            BatchJobs := BatchJobs + 1;
          end
          else TerminalJobs := TerminalJobs + 1;
          "Associate a job process with the user job";
          "Continue the job process";
        end;
          "Suspend execution";
        end
      end JobInitiator;
```

JobInitiator binds a user job to a waiting job process and then performs a **continue** operation on the job process. When it resumes execution, the job process will authenticate the user and execute its commands. For a batch job, standard input and output files take the place of terminal input and output. The input file contains the commands for the execution of programs, and responses from the programs are recorded in the output file. JobInitiator does a cycle of job creation and then 'suspends' its execution so that it will be free to resume execution when it is next scheduled. Note that it does not simply delay itself on a queue variable, as it must be ready for execution either when a new job is waiting at a terminal, or when a batch job is to be created. We have chosen this unusual way of suspending execution because JobInitiator must repeat its loop irrespective of whether or not other processes are delayed. The Kernel provides a special operation, Suspend, for this purpose.

The next level of scheduling consists in determining when user jobs that have been created can be scheduled for execution on various processors. Policy decisions to be made at this level are:

1. What is the execution 'mix' of batch and interactive jobs? One policy may be to ensure that terminal users have rapid response to their commands, another to maximize the throughput by executing as many jobs as possible, irrespective of the effect this may have on any particular user.
2. What is the degree of multiprogramming? Which programs are to be in primary memory and which should be swapped out on secondary storage?
3. How large a processor time slice should be given to each job when it is scheduled to run on a processor?

An important system process, called the Job Manager, has the task of implementing these decisions. Every process to be executed on a processor must have its identification (and other information) entered into a table that can be accessed by a processor scheduler. This is done by an operation, EnterProc, performed in one of an array of monitors called CPUQs. Apart from user jobs, the Job Manager must schedule the operating systems processes, *including itself*. The Job Manager must also decide which programs should be swapped into or out of memory. The outline for the process, JobManager, is given below:

```
var
    JobManager: process;
        begin
        loop
            while "there is an active operating system process" do
                for P in 1 to CPUMax do
                    if "CPUQs[P] can accommodate process" then
                    begin
                        CPUQs[P].EnterProc("chosen process", "time slice",
                                            "other parameters");
                        exit;
                    end;
            while "there is an active user job process"
            and "all CPUQs are not full" do
                for P in 1 to CPUMax do
                    if "CPUQs[P] can accommodate process" then
                    begin
                        CPUQs[P].EnterProc("chosen process", "time slice",
                                            "other parameters");
                        exit;
                    end;
            "Suspend execution";
            "Retrieve executed processes from CPUQs";
            "Decide if any programs should be swapped";
        end
    end JobManager;
```

Like JobInitiator, JobManager suspends its execution after performing its main tasks (scheduling jobs, and choosing programs to be swapped in or out) so that it is free to resume work when it is next scheduled. A separate Swapper process swaps programs according to information left for it by JobManager.

```
type
    CPUQ = monitor;
        var
        RunQ: array [1 .. RunMax] of
                    record
                        "process information";
                        "time slice";
                        "other parameters"
                    end RunQ;
        RunQPtr: FiFoQ(RunMax);
            ...
```

```
    procedure export EnterProc(Pr:"process information";
                              Tm:"time slice"; "other parameters");
      begin
        "Put Pr, Tm and other parameters at the end of RunQ";
      end EnterProc;

    procedure export Next(var Pr:"process information";
                          var Tm:"time slice"; "other parameters");
      begin
        with "next process in RunQ" do
        begin
          Pr := "information on process";
          Tm := "value of time slice";
          "Copy other parameters";
        end;
      end Next;
      ...
  end CPUQ;

var
  CPUQs: array [1 .. CPUMax] of CPUQ;
```

At the lowest level of scheduling, a scheduler process on every processor selects processes for execution from the associated element of CPUQs.

```
type
  Scheduler(CPUNum: integer) = process;
    ...
    begin
      loop
        if "there is a process to be run in CPUQs[CPUNum]" then
        begin
          CPUQs[CPUNum].Next(Pr, Tm, "other parameters");
          Kernel.Run(Pr, Tm, "other parameters");
        end
      end
    end Schedulers;
```

The Kernel call, Run, transfers control from the scheduler to the chosen process so that it will then begin execution. This call is like a procedure call: control will be returned to the scheduler

(a) if the time slice allotted to the process has been fully used, or
(b) if the process is blocked on entry to a monitor or on a queue variable.

On resuming control, the scheduler will resume its search in CPUQs for the next process to be executed.

MANAGEMENT OF JOBS AND PROGRAMS

Having sketched the general structure we shall use for job management, we must now fill in details and look closely at some of the problems that have been identified. The major functions of job management are carried out, appropriately, by the Job Manager process. Supporting functions, like job initiation and swapping, are performed by other processes. There are two central data structures, both monitors, that are shared by JobManager and the supporting processes. These data structures are JobTable, which we have mentioned earlier, and ProgTable.

The Job Table

There are two kinds of data that are used to represent a job: its low-level representation, in terms of storage segment addresses, the contents of machine registers, and the instruction counter, and a higher-level description of the job characteristics. The low-level data for each process is stored in a *frame* by the Kernel. The job characteristics consist of:

1. The unique identifier for the user, which is required to 'authenticate' the user when he logs in, and to lead to the root directory for his files.
2. The type of job, i.e. whether it is a terminal or a batch job. A terminal job has a controlling device, i.e. the terminal, which can be used to unconditionally return control from a program.
3. The program it is executing (this will be described more fully in ProgTable), and the processors on which the process can be executed.
4. Limits to the resources that can be used by the job. Such limits are usually set by policies of the System Administrator, and can control the execution time, the memory used and the use of any of the other resources in the system.
5. An account of the resources that have already been used by the job. Together with the limits listed in (4), this data can be used to decide when user jobs are to be scheduled.
6. The status of the job—whether it has been scheduled to execute its program, or whether it is waiting to be run on a processor.

An entry in JobTable will consist of a record of information defined as follows:

```
type
    JobType = (BatchProc, TerminalProc);
    TerminalDev = (None, Terminal1, ... , TerminalN);
    CPU = 1 .. CPUMax;
    CPUSet = set of CPU;
    ProcIndex = 1 .. ProcessMax;
```

```
ProgIndex = 1 .. ProgMax;
JobData =
  record
    UserId: Name;
    JobKind: JobType;
    ControlDev: TerminalDev;
    CurrentProg, CurrentData: ProgIndex;
    CPUs: CPUSet;
    MemLimit, TimeLimit,
    SpaceTime, ProgSize, TimeUsed: integer;
    NewProgram, OnCPU: Boolean
  end JobData;
```

JobTable is a monitor with an array, JobArr, containing one entry for each job process. (A separate table stores entries for the operating system processes.) If ProcessMax is the maximum number of processes in the system, let processes from 1 to SystProcMax be system processes, and processes from JobMin to JobMax be user job processes, where

```
JobMin = SystProcMax + 1
JobMax = ProcessMax
Maximum number of user jobs, MaxJobs = JobMax – JobMin + 1
```

The array, JobArr, therefore has the bounds JobMin .. JobMax.

The monitor has a number of procedures and functions that are used by job processes, and the system processes JobInitiator and JobManager. The procedure WaitForJob is called by job processes when they have completed execution of a user job. The procedure ResumeJob is called by JobInitiator to associate a free job process with a user job. After authentication, the job process enters the user identification into JobTable entry by calling the procedure SetId.

The information in an entry of JobArr must be updated whenever a job process calls a new program, and when it returns from one program to a previous program. This is done in the procedure NextProg. This procedure also computes the 'space-time' product for the program call, obtained by multiplying the size of allocated memory by the processor time used, and stores this for accounting purposes.

An entry in JobArr can be examined by calling the function, GetData. JobManager uses the procedure SetCPUs to record the set of processors on which the process can be executed. The procedure SetTime alters the field, TimeUsed, by adding the execution time of the last slice used by the job process. The procedure MarkRun sets the field, OnCPU, to be **true**. Notice the use of the field, NewProgram: this Boolean is set to **true** when a new program is first called and when it is swapped into memory, and to **false** after the job has had one execution slice of a processor. The value of NewProgram can be used to ensure that a newly loaded program is not swapped out before the job process has had at least one execution slice.

```
var
  JobTable: monitor;
    type export
      JobIndex = JobMin .. JobMax;
    var
      JobArr: array [JobIndex] of JobData;
      JobWaitQ: array [JobIndex] of queue;

    procedure export WaitForJob;
      begin
        delay(JobWaitQ[ProcId]);
        {Function ProcId returns the process number }
      end WaitForJob;

    procedure export ResumeJob(Kind:JobType; MLim,TLim:integer;
                                        CntrlDev:TerminalDev);
      begin
        for I in JobMin to JobMax do
          if delayed(JobWaitQ[I]) then
          begin
            with JobArr[I] do
            begin
              JobKind := Kind;
              UserId := 'SYSTEM'; {Start as System process}
              ControlDev := CntrlDev;
              NewProgram := true;
              MemLimit := MLim; TimeLimit := TLim;
              SpaceTime := 0; ProgSize := 0; ProgTime := 0;
              TimeUsed := 0;
            end;
            continue(JobWaitQ[I]);
            exit;
          end;
      end ResumeJob;

    procedure export SetId(UserName:Name);
      begin
        JobArr[ProcId].UserId := UserName;
      end SetId;

    procedure export NextProg(PIndex,DIndex:ProgIndex;
                                        MemSize:integer);
      begin
        with JobArr[ProcId] do
        begin
          CurrentProg := PIndex; CurrentData := DIndex;
          NewProgram := true;
          SpaceTime := SpaceTime + ProgSize * TimeUsed;
          ProgSize := MemSize;
        end;
      end NextProg;
```

```
function export GetData(JobNum:ProcIndex) return JobData;
begin
  return JobArr[JobNum];
end GetData;

procedure export SetCPUs(JobNum:ProcIndex;
                                  CPUChoice:CPUSet);
begin
  with JobArr[JobNum]
    do CPUs := CPUChoice;
end SetCPUs;

procedure export SetTime(JobNum:ProcIndex; UsedTime:integer);
begin
  with JobArr[JobNum] do
  begin
    TimeUsed := TimeUsed + UsedTime;
    NewProgram := false; OnCPU := false;
  end;
end SetTime;

procedure export MarkRun(JobNum:ProcIndex);
begin
  JobArr[JobNum].OnCPU := true;
end MarkRun;

begin {JobTable}
  for I in JobMin to JobMax do
    with JobArr[I] do
    begin
      UserId := 'SYSTEM';
      {All job processes start as system processes with batch mode as
      the default}
      JobKind := BatchProc;
      ControlDev := None;
      "Set initial values for MemLimit and TimeLimit";
      "Set CurrentProg and CurrentData for LOGIN program";
      OnCPU := false; NewProgram := true;
    end;
end JobTable;
```

The Program Table

As long as it is associated with a user job, a job process executes some program that has been stored as a file. When a job is first initiated, it executes the Login program. After that, it executes the Command program, which accepts commands to execute any program in a file that is accessible to the user: i.e., a file that can be accessed through the user's directories, or a file in the directory, System, which is accessible to all users. For our purposes, a program is represented by the unique identifier of a directory and the name of the file in which the program is stored.

There are two important factors we must consider in the design of ProgTable. First, one program may 'call' another, like a procedure. Implementation of a procedure call in a programming language uses a stack for such calls, so that return from one procedure will resume the execution of the previous procedure. We must have a similar stack for program calls. An entry in this stack will contain the identification of the program and data segments in use. Second, a program call requires a number of actions to be taken; the skeleton of the Enter procedure shows what operations must be performed to record the association of program and data segments with a process. Since separated programs can be shared, we should keep a count of the number of user jobs using the same program segment.

When a program call is made, one or two new segments of information will always need to be loaded into memory. Irrespective of whether a segment is being loaded for the first time (as for a program call) or being swapped in, the transfer of the segment from the disk is performed by the Swapper process. Until this transfer is over, the program call will be delayed. As there may be several requests for loading new segments, JobManager must decide which program and data segments should be loaded, depending on the availability of memory. Segments can be loaded either in shared memory or in the local memory of some processor.

```
type
    MemKind = (Share, Loc1, Loc2, ... , LocN);
    MemSet = set of MemKind;
```

There is a constraint in choosing where program and data segments will be allocated space: they can both be in shared memory but, if one of them is in a local memory the other can only be either in shared memory or in the same local memory. A process which uses the local memory of a processor can only be scheduled for allocation on that processor. If memory space is not available, it must be found by releasing space allocated to some other program or data segment.

The Program Table is implemented as a monitor, ProgTable. It has two arrays, ProgArr and DataArr, which contain entries with information on each program and data segment used by job processes.

var
    ProgArr: **array** [ProgIndex] **of** ProgInf;
    DataArr: **array** [ProgIndex] **of** DataInf;

Every program segment being used by a job process has an entry in the array, ProgArr. In each such entry, of type ProgInf, the number of jobs that have called the program is stored in a field called EnterCount. A similar field, LeaveCount, records the number of jobs that have made calls from that program to another. For any program,

    JobMax ⩾ EnterCount ⩾ LeaveCount
and
    Number of jobs currently using program = EnterCount − LeaveCount

Values of EnterCount and LeaveCount can be used by JobManager to decide when a segment should be swapped out to release space.

type
    ProgType = (Mixed, Separated);
    SwapState = (InMemory, SwapThisOut, SwappedOut, SwapThisIn);
    ProgInf =
      record
        Used: **Boolean**;
        ProgDirectory: DirAdr;
        ProgName: Name;
        Ptype: ProgType;
        InstrSeg: Seg;
        PSegPosn: MemKind;
        EntryPoint: Address;
        EnterCount, LeaveCount: **integer**;
        ProgState: SwapState;
        InstrSwapAdr: DiskAdr
      end ProgInf;

The fields, ProgDirectory and ProgName, uniquely identify the program file and Ptype indicates whether the program is mixed or separated. EntryPoint is the address at which execution of the program will start. The value of ProgState shows whether the program is in memory, if it has been swapped out, or whether the program is *to be* swapped into or out of memory. InstrSwapAdr has the disk address of a program that has been swapped out. Before a program is loaded, InstrSwapAdr will have the disk address of the program file. ProgIndex is used to determine the size of the Program Table.

Each data segment being used by a job process has an entry of type DataInf in the array, DataArr. A data segment will be used by only one job at a time. Its status can simply be represented by a Boolean, Left, which is **true** when the job has called another program (i.e., when the data segment must still be preserved but is not currently in use).

```
type
  DataInf =
    record
      Used: Boolean;
      DataSeg: Seg;
      DSegPosn: MemKind;
      Left: Boolean;
      DataState: SwapState;
      DataSwapAdr: DiskAdr
    end DataInf;
```

The fields, DataState and DataSwapAdr, have the same functions as their counterparts in the record type ProgInf.

Every job process has a stack, JobStack, with entries for each program and data segment used by the process in nested program calls. Each entry contains

1. the indices of the entries in ProgArr and DataArr of the instruction and data segments of a program;
2. the low-level description of the program and data state, called a *frame*; this is an instance of the Kernel class type, Frame.

A new entry is 'pushed' onto JobStack when the job process calls a program; the topmost entry is 'popped' off when the job process returns from a called program.

```
type
  StackEntry =
    record
      ProgInd, DataInd: ProgIndex;
      CurrFrame: Kernel.Frame
    end StackEntry;
```

The field, CurrFrame, contains the frame for the process when it is executing the program referred to by the field, ProgInd. When the process calls a new program, the frame storing its state in the old program is saved and execution of the new program starts with a new frame. On return from a program, the previous frame is retrieved and execution of the previous program is resumed from the instruction following the program call. Thus, corresponding to each program and data entry in JobStack, there is one frame.

In addition to the frames stored in JobStack, one frame is needed for each process to make operating system calls. When a job process is executing a program, its state is preserved in the field, CurrFrame, of the topmost entry in its JobStack. But when it makes a call to the operating system, a separate frame is needed to preserve its status during the call. This frame, OSFrame, is needed because

1. a process may be delayed in the operating system: when this happens, its state must be saved so that its execution can resume when it is continued,
2. job processes start their execution in the operating system.

```
var
  ProgTable: monitor;
    var
      ProgArr: array [ProgIndex] of ProgInf;
      DataArr: array [ProgIndex] of DataInf;
      JobProgs: array [JobMin .. JobMax] of
                    record
                        JobStack: array [ProgLevel] of StackEntry;
                        CurrProg: ProgLevel; {Stack pointer}
                        OSFrame: Kernel.Frame;
                    end JobProgs;

    procedure export FindNewProg(...);
      begin
        "Check if the program is already loaded";
      end FindNewProg;

    procedure export NewProgram(...);
      begin
        "Enter new program information in ProgArr";
      end NewProgram;

    procedure export NewData(...);
      begin
        "Enter new data information in DataArr";
      end NewData;

    procedure export EnterProgram(...);
      begin
        "Wait for Job Manager to check if new program
          and data segments are in memory";
      end EnterProgram;

    procedure export LeaveProgram(...);
      begin
        if "program segment has no other user"
          then "remove entry in ProgArr";
        if "a data segment was used"
          then "remove entry in DataArr";
      end LeaveProgram;

    procedure export ReturnToProg;
      begin
        "Wait for Job Manager to check if old program
          and data segments are in memory";
      end ReturnToProg;
```

```
procedure export GetFrames(...);
  begin
    "Supply current frame and OSFrame for process";
  end GetFrames;

function export GetProgEnt(...) return ProgInf;
  begin
    return "values of entry in ProgArr";
  end GetProgEnt;

procedure export SetProgEnt(...);
  begin
    "Put new values into entry in ProgArr";
  end SetProgEnt;

function export GetDataEnt(...) return "DataArr entry";
  begin
    return "values of entry in DataArr";
  end GetDataEnt;

procedure export SetDataEnt(...);
  begin
    "Put new values into entry in DataArr";
  end SetDataEnt;

{Other procedures and functions}

end ProgTable;
```

The procedures FindNewProg, NewProg, NewData and EnterProgram are used by a job process before it makes a program call. On return from a program call, the job process calls the procedure LeaveProgram. The procedure GetFrames supplies the current execution frame, and the OSFrame, for the process. The Kernel uses these frames to retrieve the low-level state information for a process that is to be run and to store such information when it ceases execution on a processor. JobManager calls the functions GetProgEnt and GetDataEnt to read information about a job process's program and data segments (e.g., whether they are in memory); the procedures SetProgEnt and SetDataEnt are used to alter values in these entries.

The detailed structure of ProgTable is given in a later section.

The CPU Queues

For each processor there is a queue of processes to be executed on the processor; this queue is managed by an instance of a monitor type, CPUQ. The CPUQ monitors of all processors are organized as an array, CPUQs.

The scheduler for processor I picks a process from CPUQs[I] and executes it on its processor.

Each CPUQs[I] contains a FiFo queue, RunQ, of processes waiting to be run on the processor, and a second FiFo queue, OverQ, of processes that have been executed. (The class type, FiFoQ, is described in Chapter 2). JobManager calls the procedure EnterProc to put a process in RunQ, and the procedure RemoveProc to retrieve an executed process from OverQ. A scheduler calls the procedure Next to find the process which is to be scheduled on that processor. Boolean functions, ProcReady and ProcOver, indicate when a process is ready for the scheduler, and when a process can be removed, and RunQFull and OverQFull indicate when RunQ and OverQ are full. If RunQ is empty, or if OverQ is full, the scheduler must repeat its call.

```
type
  CPUQ(RunMax: integer) = monitor;
    type export
      RunEntry =
        record
          Id: ProcIndex;
          PFrameAdr, OFrameAdr: Address;
          Slice: integer
        end RunEntry;
      OverEntry =
        record
          Id: ProcIndex;
          TimeUsed: integer
        end OverEntry;
    var
      RunQ: array [1 .. RunMax] of RunEntry;
      OverQ: array [1 .. RunMax] of OverEntry;
      RunQPtr, OverQPtr: FiFoQ(RunMax);

    function export ProcReady return Boolean;
      begin
        return not RunQPtr.Empty;
      end ProcReady;

    function export RunQFull return Boolean;
      begin
        return RunQPtr.Full;
      end RunQFull;

    function export ProcOver return Boolean;
      begin
        return not OverQPtr.Empty;
      end ProcOver;
```

```
function export OverQFull return Boolean;
  begin
    return OverQPtr.Full;
  end OverQFull;

procedure export EnterProc(NewEntry:RunEntry);
  begin
    RunQ[RunQPtr.Put] := NewEntry;
  end EnterProc;

procedure export RemoveProc(var OldEntry:OverEntry);
  begin
    OldEntry := OverQ[OverQPtr.Next];
  end RemoveProc;

procedure export Next(var RunProc:RunEntry);
  begin
    RunProc := RunQ[RunQPtr.Next];
  end Next;

procedure export Over(OverProc:OverEntry);
  begin
    OverQ[OverQPtr.Put] := OverProc;
  end Over;

end CPUQ;

var
  CPUQs: array [1 .. CPUMax] of CPUQ;
```

A scheduler process invokes operations in the monitor CPUQs[I]. But what will it do if JobManager, running on some other processor, is already executing an operation of CPUQs[I]? Normally, a process is blocked if it attempts to enter a monitor when some other process is already executing a monitor operation. But if this technique is used for a scheduler, it will be blocked and there will be no process to execute on that processor. This can happen to any scheduler, so it is possible that many schedulers are blocked and no process will be executed on any of those processors.

The procedures and functions of each monitor in CPUQs need monitor-like mutual exclusion over their execution but the available mechanisms for implementing monitors are not adequate for this purpose. There is no alternative but to use a different mechanism that will accomplish the same results, *without* blocking processes. A solution is to have a 'busy- waiting' operation for entry to this monitor. This operation acts on a Boolean 'lock' and loops repeatedly until the Boolean has the value **true**. If the initial value of the Boolean is **true**, the first process to execute this operation will proceed while the others will busy-wait. When the first process is ready to leave the monitor, it will use an operation to reset the Boolean. After this, one waiting process will be able to proceed past the lock. As we shall see in Chapter 12, the Kernel must make use of a system-wide indivisible operation to implement these two operations. When written in CCNPascal, the type CPUQ is defined as a *low-level* monitor, using the special notation

```
type
    CPUQ(RunMax: integer) = monitor*;
        ...
    end CPUQ;
```

A little reflection on the way JobManager shares other monitors with operating system and job processes will show that a similar problem exists in each such case. If JobManager is blocked, it will be returned to its scheduler by the Kernel. However, JobManager is the process that schedules all processes, including itself. So, when JobManager is blocked, there is no means for it to be scheduled again even when it is ready to proceed. There is a simple solution. *Every* monitor that is entered by the JobManager can have busy-waiting at its entries. But this is an implementation issue: none of the assumptions we make about JobTable and other such monitors is invalidated by the use of busy-waiting for entries. Busy-waiting is a sound implementation technique for this purpose, but it is expensive in terms of wasted processor time and it must be used as infrequently as possible.

The Processor Scheduler

The actions of the scheduler for each processor have already been described in the previous section. The scheduler process has the following structure:

```
type
    Scheduler(CPUNum: integer) = process;
        var
            ProcNum, Elapsed: integer;
            RunProc: RunEntry; OverProc: OverEntry;
        begin
            with CPUQS[CPUNum] do
                loop
                    if ProcReady then
                    begin
                        Next(RunProc);
                        Elapsed := Kernel.Time;
                        with RunProc
                            do Kernel.Run(Id, PFrameAdr, OFrameAdr, Slice);
```

```
          Elapsed := Kernel.Time – Elapsed;
          with OverProc do
          begin
            Id := RunProc.Id; TimeUsed := Elapsed;
          end;
          loop
            if not OverQFull then
            begin
              Over(OverProc);
                exit;
              end;
            end;
          end;
        end;
    end Scheduler;

  var
    Scheduler1: Scheduler(1);
    Scheduler2: Scheduler(2);
      ...
    SchedulerN: Scheduler(CPUMax);
```

Each scheduler instance has a parameter identifying the processor that it is to serve. Separate variable declarations are used so that each instance of Scheduler can be supplied a different processor number. The same effect cannot, unfortunately, be accomplished as conveniently if an array of Scheduler is declared (this illustrates a minor deficiency in CCNPascal).

A scheduler loops until it finds a process to be executed; it then records the time in the variable, Elapsed, and calls the Kernel to run the process. On return, the difference between the time and the value stored in Elapsed is a good estimate of the time used by the process. Following this, the scheduler loops until it is able to return the process through the procedure, Over.

Scheduling Processes

Let us now return to the steps that the Job Manager must take to schedule processes. The Job Manager must choose processes from JobTable for execution. The limits, MaxTerminals and MaxBatchJobs, determine how many user jobs may be initiated at any time. These jobs will be in various states—executing commands or competing for resources—and an important scheduling function will be to choose that subset of these jobs for which it is most profitable to allocate resources at that time. Preferences can be exercised in choosing one job over another, according to different objectives:

1. To reduce the terminal response time, terminal jobs can be chosen for execution whenever they are not blocked. Batch jobs will be executed only when there is no terminal job that can be run.

2. To increase batch throughput, batch jobs can be executed in a regular cycle and terminal jobs will be scheduled only when there is no batch job that can be run.

Both these choices are somewhat extreme. Most practical policies are less rigid in their choices but they will usually ensure that either terminal jobs, or batch jobs, get preference in scheduling. In fact, it would seem pointless to allow terminal use at all unless some minimum response time will be assured. Thus, it would be simpler just to reduce the number of terminal or batch jobs, than to delay their scheduling. This can be done when the limits, MaxTerminals and MaxBatchJobs, are set. The Job Manager can still differentiate between these jobs by allocating the processor resource for different time slices. We discuss the issue of choosing the length of a time slice in a separate section.

All the information needed to schedule job processes is held in JobTable and ProgTable. System processes have information stored in a separate monitor, SystemTable.

```
var
   SystemTable(SystProcMax: ProcIndex): monitor;
      type export
         SystInf =
            record
               SystId: Name;
               Procs: CPUSet;
               ProcFrame: Kernel.Frame;
               OnCPU: Boolean
            end SystInf;

      var
         SystArr: array [1 .. SystProcMax] of SystInf;

      function export GetData(SystNum:ProcIndex) return SystInf;
         begin
            return SystArr[SystNum];
         end GetData;

      procedure export SetData(SystNum:ProcIndex; Inf:SystInf);
         begin
            SystArr[SystNum] := Inf;
         end SetData;
```

```
procedure export SetOnCPU(SystNum:ProcIndex);
   begin
      SystArr[SystNum].OnCPU := true;
   end SetOnCPU;

procedure export SetOffCPU(SystNum:ProcIndex);
   begin
      SystArr[SystNum].OnCPU := false;
   end SetOffCPU;

end SystemTable;
```

As trusted processes, it can be assumed that system processes will only
need to be executed when they have important work to do. So any system
process that is not blocked can be chosen for scheduling with an arbitrarily
large time slice, MaxSlice. The procedure ScheduleProcs first begins by
allocating processors to system processes that are not blocked; after this,
job processes that are not blocked are scheduled. The procedure
ChooseCPU allocates processors to processes in a manner that spreads the
load relatively evenly. Processes that have been executed are retrieved by
the procedure GetProcs.

```
var
   JobManager: process;
      var
         CPULoad: array [CPU] of integer;
         JobSlice: integer;
         { Other declarations }

      procedure ChooseCPU(ProcData:RunEntry; CPUs:CPUSet;
                              var CPUNum:CPU);
         var
            MinLoad: integer;
         begin
            CPUNum := 0; MinLoad := "largest integer value";
            for I in 1 to CPUMax do
               if I in CPUs then
                  if not CPUQs[I].RunQFull and (CPULoad[I] < MinLoad)
                     then
                     begin
                        CPUNum := I; MinLoad := CPULoad[I];
                     end;
            if CPUNum ≠ 0 then
            begin
               CPUQs[CPUNum].EnterProc(ProcData);
               CPULoad[CPUNum] := CPULoad[CPUNum] + 1;
            end;
         end ChooseCPU;
```

```
procedure ScheduleProcs;
  var
    CPUNum: integer; ProcData: RunEntry;
    JobSpecs: JobInf; SystSpecs: SystInf;
    ProgSpecs: ProgInf; DataSpecs: DataInf;
  begin
    {first schedule all active system processes}
    for I in 1 to SystProcMax do
    begin
      SystSpecs := SystemTable.GetData(I);
      with SystSpecs do
      begin
        if not (Kernel.IsBlocked(I) or Kernel.WaitingForIO(I)
            or OnCPU) then
          with ProcData do
          begin
            Id := I; OFrameAdr := varadr(ProcFrame);
            PFrameAdr := OFrameAdr; Slice := MaxSlice;
            repeat
              ChooseCPU(ProcData, Procs, CPUNum);
            until CPUNum ≠ 0;
            SystemTable.SetOnCPU(I);
          end
      end;
    end;

    {schedule user job processes}
    for I in JobMin to JobMax do
    begin
      JobSpecs := JobTable.GetData(I);
      with JobSpecs do
        if not (Kernel.IsBlocked(I) or Kernel.WaitingForIO(I)
            or OnCPU) then
          with ProgTable do
          begin
            ProgSpecs := GetProgEnt(CurrentProg);
            DataSpecs := GetDataEnt(CurrentData);
            with ProcData do
            begin
              GetFrames(I, PFrameAdr, OFrameAdr);
              Id := I; Slice := "Time slice for Job";
            end;
            if (ProgSpecs.ProgState = InMemory) and
               (DataSpecs.DataState = InMemory) then
            begin
              ChooseCPU(ProcData, CPUs, CPUNUM);
              if CPUNum ≠ 0
                then JobTable.MarkRun(I);
            end
          end
    end
  end ScheduleProcs;
```

```
procedure GetProcs;
  var
    ProcNum: ProcIndex; UsedTime: integer;
  begin
    for I in 1 to CPUMax do
      with CPUQs[I] do
        while ProcOver do
        begin
          Remove(ProcNum, UsedTime);
          CPULoad[I] := CPULoad[I] - 1;
          if ProcNum ≤ SystProcMax
            then SystemTable.SetOffCPU(ProcNum)
            else JobTable.SetTime(ProcNum, UsedTime)
        end
  end GetProcs;

  {.. Other procedures and functions of JobManager ..}

end JobManager;
```

The Procedures Enter and Depart

A job process calls the procedure Enter when a new program is to be called. This procedure takes a number of actions before the program call takes place. Control is returned from a program to the previous program by calling the procedure Depart; at this point, too, there are several housekeeping tasks to be done before control actually returns to the previous program. Let us start by describing the actions done in the procedure Enter.

The first action is to get the parameters for the program call and to store these in a block called ParBlock. This block will be forwarded to the next program when the call is made. The next step is to read the first record of the file containing the program to be called. This record has information on the size and type of the program. The function JobTable.GetData is used to read the memory limit set for the process, to ensure that the new program size is within the limit. The procedure FindNewProg in ProgTable is used to see if the program is already in use. If it is not in use, or if the program is not separated, a new entry must be made in the array, ProgArr. This is done through the procedure NewProgram. If there is a separate data part, an entry must also be made in the array, DataArr, by calling the procedure NewData.

Finally, two more actions must be done. NewProgram and NewData return the indices of the program and data segment entries in ProgArr and DataArr. First, the procedure JobTable.NextProg must be called to record these indices. Then, the procedure EnterProgram of ProgTable is called for the program call entry to be pushed on top of the process' JobStack and for the process to wait until its program segment (and data segment, if needed) is swapped into memory. After the call to EnterProgram is over, the process calls the Kernel to transfer control to the new program. This call takes as parameter the address at which execution of the new program is to start. This is available from the program file.

The procedure Depart is called by a program when control is to be returned to the previous program. But this procedure also serves as the 'error handler' for programs so it may also be called if the Kernel encounters an error while executing a program (i.e., either due to program error, or because a 'terminate' character was typed on the control terminal). To distinguish between these two reasons for entry, the procedure first calls the Kernel function, GetError, to check if execution of the called program was abnormally terminated. It then calls the procedure LeaveProgram to pop the topmost entry off the JobStack for the process and to update the entries in ProgArr and DataArr for the program and data segments. If there are no other users of one of these segments, it must be released to the memory allocator. The procedure JobTable.NextProg is called to reset the indices of the program and data segments of the process to their previous values. The last action is to call the procedure ProgTable.ReturnToProg where the job process will wait on a queue variable until continued by the Job Manager.

```
procedure Enter(Dir:Name; NewProg:Name;
                        "Parameters for program call");
    {...declarations ...}
    begin
        "Collect parameters in the variable, ParBlock";
        "Call File System to read file NewProg in directory, Dir";
        if "file cannot be accessed"
            then return error FileNotFound;
        "Read first record of file NewProg";

        {Set the following variables from data in this record}
        EntryAddress := "starting address for program";
        ProgMem := "memory needed for program part";
        DataMem := "memory needed for data part";
        ProgSeparate := "program is separated";
        MemoryReq := ProgMem + DataMem;

        {Get the job process entry from JobTable}
        JobSpecs := JobTable.GetData(ProcId);
        if JobSpecs.MemLimit < MemoryReq
            then return error ProgramTooLarge;
```

```
{Check if the program is already in use}
ProgTable.FindNewProg(Dir, NewProg, PIndex)
   iferror return error TooManyProgCalls;
if PIndex = 0
   then NewProgEntry := true;
if NewProgEntry or not ProgSeparate
   {New entry must be made for data segment)
   then ProgTable.NewData(Dindex, DDiskPosn)
else Dindex := 0; {There is no data part}

{Put program and data entry indices in Job Table}
JobTable.NextProg(PIndex, DIndex, MemoryReq);

{Wait for program and/or data segments to be swapped in}
ProgTable.EnterProgram(PIndex, DIndex, ProgMem, DataMem);

"Call File System to close file NewProg in directory Dir";

{Make Kernel call to transfer control to entry address in NewProg}
Kernel.ProgramCall(EntryAddress, varadr(ParBlock));
end Enter;

procedure Depart("Parameters to be returned");
  var
    UserError: Kernel.ErrorKind;
    {... declarations ...}
  begin
    UserError := Kernel.GetError;
    if UserError = NoError
       then "Collect parameters to be returned in ParBlock";
    {Update entries in Program and Job tables}
    ProgTable.LeaveProgram(FreeISeg, FreeDSeg, ProgLev,
                           PSegPosn, DSegPosn, PSeg, DSeg,
                           PrevMem, PrevPIndex, PrevDIndex);
    JobTable.NextProg(PrevPIndex, PrevDIndex, PrevMem);

    {Return space to memory allocator if no other users of segments}
    if FreeISeg
       then MemorySpace.Release(PSegPosn, PSeg);
    if FreeDSeg
       then MemorySpace.Release(DSegPosn, DSeg);
    {Return to previous program}
    ProgTable.ReturnToProg; {Wait until continued by Job Manager}

    {Call Kernel to return to previous program}
    Kernel.ProgramReturn(varadr(ParBlock), UserError);
  end Depart;
```

Notice that parameters that would normally be **var** parameters in calls to procedures are transformed into addresses when a Kernel call is to be made. The reasons for this will be discussed in the section on call mechanisms.

Program Table—Detailed Structure

We can now describe the detailed structure of the monitor, ProgTable. The types, ProgInf, DataInf and StackEntry have been described earlier. Apart from the arrays, ProgArr, DataArr and JobProgs, two more arrays must be defined. The array, JobWaiting, has one queue element for each job process to delay itself when it is waiting either for space in ProgArr or DataArr, or for its program and data segments to be loaded into memory. The array, MemAvailable, stores the sizes of memory that are still available for allocation in shared and local memory.

```
var
   ProgTable: monitor;
      type
         ProgLevel = 1 .. MaxProgLevel;
      var
         ProgArr: array [ProgIndex] of ProgInf;
         DataArr: array [ProgIndex] of DataInf;
         JobProgs: array [JobMin .. JobMax] of
                        record
                            JobStack: array [ProgLevel] of StackEntry;
                            CurrProg: ProgLevel;
                            OSFrame: Kernel.Frame
                        end JobProgs;
         JobWaiting: array [JobMin .. JobMax] of
                        record
                            Reason: (ProgArrFull, DataArrFull, SwapWait,
                                        ReturnWait);
                            ISize, DSize: integer;
                            JobQ: queue
                        end JobWaiting;
         MemAvailable: array [MemKind] of integer;
         SwapperQ: queue;
```

The first operation, FindNewProg, is simple. This procedure is called from the procedure Enter to determine whether a program has already been loaded. The procedure first checks that there is space on the JobStack for the process to load one more program and updates the entries in ProgArr and DataArr to indicate that the process is about to call a new program.

```
procedure export FindNewProg(Dir:DirAdr; NewProg:Name;
                               var PIndex:ProgIndex);

   begin
      with JobProgs[ProcId] do
```

```
begin
  if CurrProg = MaxProgLevel {Job stack full}
    then return error;
  with JobStack[CurrProg] do
  begin
    with ProgArr[ProgInd]
      do LeaveCount := LeaveCount + 1;
      {For program segment}
    if DataInd > 0
      then {There is a data seg}
      DataArr[DataInd].Left := true;
  end;
end;
for I in 1 to ProgMax do
  with ProgArr[I] do
    if (ProgDirectory = Dir) and (ProgName = NewProg) then
    begin {Program entry "not" found}
      PIndex := I; return ;
    end;
  PIndex := 0; {Program entry not found}
end FindNewProg;
```

If a program is not in use, an entry must be made in the table, ProgArr. This is done in a procedure, NewProgram. First, a free entry in ProgArr must be found (i.e., one for which Used = **false**). For separated programs, another procedure, NewData, searches for a free entry in DataArr.

```
procedure export NewProgram(Dir:DirAdr; NewProg:Name;
                            DiskPosn:DiskAdr;
                            InitialEntry:Address;
                            PKind:ProgType;
                            var PIndex:ProgIndex);
var
  PEntryFound: Boolean;
begin
  PEntryFound := false;
  while not PEntryFound do
  begin
    for I in 1 to ProgMax do
      with ProgArr[I] do
        if not Used then
        begin
          Used := true; ProgDirectory := Dir;
          Progname := NewProg; InstrSwapAdr := DiskPosn;
          EntryPoint := InitialEntry; PType := PKind;
          ProgState := SwappedOut;
          EnterCount := 0; LeaveCount := 0;
          PEntryFound := true; PIndex := I;
          exit;
        end;
```

```
          if not PEntryFound then
            with JobWaiting[ProcId] do
            begin
              Reason := ProgArrFull;
              delay(JobQ);
            end;
        end;
      end NewProgram;

  procedure export NewData(var DIndex:ProgIndex;
                               DataPosn:DiskAdr);
    var
      DEntryFound: Boolean;
    begin
      DEntryFound := false;
      while not DEntryFound do
      begin
        for I in 1 to ProgMax do
          with DataArr[I] do
            if not Used then
            begin
              Used := true;
              DataState := SwappedOut; Left := false;
              DEntryFound := true; DIndex := I;
              DataSwapAdr := DataPosn;
              exit;
            end;
        if not DEntryFound then
          with JobWaiting[ProcId] do
          begin
            Reason := DataArrFull;
            delay(JobQ);
          end;
      end;
    end NewData;
```

On return from the procedures NewProg and NewData, entries will have
been made in the arrays, ProgArr and DataArr. The indices of these entries
must be recorded in JobTable. The job process must then call the
procedure, EnterProgram, to wait for its segments to be swapped into
memory and for its new frame to be set appropriately by the Job Manager.

```
  procedure export EnterProgram(PIndex,DIndex:ProgIndex;
                                ProgMem,DataMem:integer);
    begin
      with JobProgs[ProcId]
        do CurrProg := CurrProg + 1;
      {Allocate a new frame}
      with JobStack[CurrProg] do
```

```
begin
  ProgInd := PIndex;
  DataInd := DIndex;
  with ProgArr[ProgInd]
    do EnterCount := EnterCount + 1;
  with JobWaiting[ProcId] do
  begin
    ISize := ProgMem; DSize := DataMem;
    Reason := SwapWait;
    delay(JobQ); {Wait until segments are swapped in
                  and JobStack[CurrProg].CurrFrame
                  is set by the Job Manager}
  end;
  end;
end EnterProgram;
```

When a process returns from a called program, it must update the entries for the program and data segments it was using and pop the top entry off its JobStack. This is done in the procedure LeaveProgram. If entries in ProgArr or DataArr can be freed, a process waiting for such a free entry is continued. On return from this procedure, two Booleans, FreeISeg and FreeDSeg, indicate whether the parameters, ISeg and DSeg represent segments of memory that can be released. The indices of the previous program and data entries, and the total memory size of the segments, are also returned.

```
procedure export LeaveProgram(var FreeISeg,FreeDseg:Boolean;
                              var ProgLev:ProgLevel;
                              var PSegKind,DSegKind:MemKind;
                              var ISeg,DSeg:Seg;
                              var PrevMemory:integer;
                              var
                              PrevPSeg,PrevDSeg:ProgIndex);
begin
  FreeISeg := false; FreeDSeg := false;
  with JobProgs[ProcId], JobStack[CurrProg] do
  begin
    with ProgArr[ProgInd] do
    begin
      EnterCount := EnterCount - 1;
      if EnterCount = 0
        then {There are no users}
        begin {so free program segment}
          FreeISeg := true; Used := false;
          MemAvailable[PSegPosn] := MemAvailable[PSegPosn]
                                    +InstrSeg.SegSize;
          PSegKind := PSegPosn;
          ISeg := InstrSeg;
          for I in JobMin to JobMax do
            with JobWaiting[I] do
              if delayed(JobQ) and (Reason = ProgArrFull)
              then
```

```
                            begin
                               continue(JobQ);
                               exit;
                            end;
                   end;
               end;
               if DataInd > 0
                  then {Data segment }
                     with DataArr[DataInd]
                        do {can now be freed}
                        begin
                           FreeDSeg := true; InUse := false;
                           DSegKind := DSegPosn;
                           DSeg := DataSeg;
                           for I in JobMin to JobMax do
                              with JobWaiting[I] do
                                 if delayed(JobQ)
                                    and (Reason = DataArrFull) then
                                 begin
                                    continue(JobQ);
                                    exit;
                                 end;
                        end;
               CurrProg := CurrProg – 1;
               with JobStack[CurrProg] do
               begin
                  with ProgArr[ProgInd] do
                  begin
                     LeaveCount := LeaveCount – 1;
                     PrevMemory := InstrSeg.MemSize;
                  end;
                  PrevPSeg := ProgInd;
                  if DataInd > 0 then
                     with DataArr[DataInd] do
                     begin
                        Left := false;
                        PrevMemory := PrevMemory + DataSeg.MemSize;
                     end;
                  PrevDSeg := DataInd;
               end;
               ProgLev := CurrProg;
            end;
         end LeaveProgram;
```

The last procedure concerned with program calls is ReturnToProg, which is called to delay a job process until the Job Manager checks whether the previous program and data segment are in memory. In this procedure, it would appear quite possible for the job process to check for itself if the segments it requires are in memory. But there is a subtle point here (and in the procedure EnterProgram): even when the segments are in memory, the process may not be able to access them from the processor on which it is executing. For example, the segments for one program may be in a particular local memory while the segments for the previous program are in another local memory. The process must therefore wait, in both procedures, until the Job Manager determines the processors on which it may be executed (the Job Manager will call the procedure JobTable.SetCPUs to record this information, before it schedules the process for execution).

```
procedure export ReturnToProg;
  begin
    with JobWaiting[ProcId] do
    begin
      Reason := ReturnWait;
      with JobProgs[ProcId], JobStack[CurrProg] do
      begin
        {Set sizes of program and data segments in ISize,DSize}
        ISize := ProgArr[ProgInd].InstrSeg.SegSize;
        DSize := DataArr[DataInd].DataSeg.SegSize;
      end;
      delay(JobQ);
    end;
  end ReturnToProg;
```

Let us move on to consider the operations that must be performed by the Swapper. Program and data segments require the attention of the Swapper when the fields, ProgState and DataState, have the value SwapThisOut or SwapThisIn. The Swapper finds a segment to be swapped into or out of memory by calling the procedure FindSwapSeg with a Boolean parameter, ToDisk, set to **false** or **true**, respectively. The Boolean parameter, Found, is set to **true** if a segment to be swapped has been found.

```
procedure export FindSwapSeg(ToDisk:Boolean; var MemSeg:Seg;
                             var SwapLoc:DiskAdr;
                             var SegInd:ProgIndex;
                             var
                             ProgFound,DataFound:Boolean);
  begin
    ProgFound := false; DataFound := false;
    for I in 1 to ProgMax do
      with ProgArr[I] do
      begin
        if ((ProgState = SwapThisOut) and ToDisk)
          or ((ProgState = SwapThisIn) and not ToDisk) then
        begin
          MemSeg := ProgSeg; SegInd := I;
          if not ToDisk
            then SwapLoc := InstrSwapAdr;
```

```
                    ProgFound := true;
                    return ;
                  end;
                end;
              for I in 1 to ProgMax do
                with DataArr[I] do
                begin
                  if ((DataState = SwapThisOut) and ToDisk)
                      or ((DataState = SwapThisIn) and not ToDisk) then
                  begin
                    MemSeg := DataSeg; SegInd := I;
                    if not ToDisk
                      then SwapLoc := DataSwapAdr;
                    DataFound := true;
                    return ;
                  end;
                end;
              end FindSwapSeg;

          procedure export SwapperWait;
            begin
              delay(SwapperQ);
            end SwapperWait;
```

When Found is set to **true**, the Swapper will either swap a segment into memory or to the disk. Once this is completed, it calls the procedure MarkSwapped to mark the appropriate entry as swapped. If no segment can be found for swapping, the Swapper calls SwapperWait to delay itself until the Job Manager finds more swapping work to be done.

```
          procedure export MarkSwapped(SegInd:ProgIndex; MemSeg:Seg;
                                       Posn:MemKind; SwapLoc:DiskAdr;
                                       MemReleased:integer;
                                       ToDisk,Prog:Boolean);
        begin
          if Prog
            then {Program segment}
              with ProgArr[SegInd] do
                if ToDisk
                  then {Swapped out}
                  begin
                    ProgState := SwappedOut;
                    InstrSwapAdr := SwapLoc;
                    MemAvailable[Posn] := MemAvailable[Posn]
                                        + MemReleased;
                  end
                else {Swapped In}
                begin
                  ProgState := InMemory;
                  InstrSeg := MemSeg;
                end
```

```
        else {Data segment}
          with DataArr[SegInd] do
            if ToDisk
              then {Swapped out}
              begin
                DataState := SwappedOut;
                DataSwapAdr := SwapLoc;
                MemAvailable[Posn] := MemAvailable[Posn]
                                        + MemReleased;
              end
            else {Swapped in}
            begin
              DataState := InMemory;
              DataSeg := MemSeg;
            end;
      end MarkSwapped;

  procedure export GetCPUs(JobNum:ProcIndex; var CPUs:CPUSet);
    var
      CPUx: CPU;
    begin
      CPUs := CPUSet[];
      with JobProgs[JobNum], JobStack[CurrProg] do
        with ProgArr[ProgInd], DataArr[DataInd] do
          if (ProgState = InMemory) and (DataState = InMemory)
            then
            begin
              if (PSegPosn = DSegPosn) and (PSegPosn = Share)
                then CPUs := CPUSet[1 .. CPUMax]
              else
              begin
                CPUx := 1;
                for M in Loc1 to LocN do
                  if (PSegPosn = M) or (DSegPosn = M) then
                  begin
                    CPUs := CPUSet[CPUx];
                    exit;
                  end
                  else CPUx := succ(CPUx);
              end;
              with JobWaiting[JobNum] do
                if delayed(JobQ) and ((Reason = SwapWait)
                    or (Reason = ReturnWait)) then
                begin
                  CurrFrame.SetUserSegs(InstrSeg, DataSeg);
                  continue(JobQ);
                end;
            end;
      end GetCPUs;
```

The procedure GetCPUs is used to continue a job process after its instruction and data segments are loaded in memory. Based on the positions of these segments, the procedure returns the set of processors on which the job can be executed.

The procedure FindMemory is used by the Job Manager when memory has to be allotted to a waiting job process. FindMemory bases its search for memory on the values in the array, MemAvailable. Note that even when the value of an element of MemAvailable is larger than needed for a segment, the memory actually available may be so fragmented that there is no single segment of adequate size. At this level of job management, the estimates provided by the elements of MemAvailable are sufficient for planning the allocation of memory, and we can leave the actual details of segment allocation to the Memory Allocator.

```
procedure export FindMemory(MemNeeded:integer;
                            MemPosns:MemSet;
                            var Posn:MemKind;
                            var Found:Boolean);
    begin
      Found := false;
      for M in Shared to LocN do
      begin
        if (M in MemPosns) and
            (MemNeeded ≤ MemAvailable[M]) then
        begin
          Posn := M;
          MemAvailable[Posn] := MemAvailable[Posn]
                               - MemNeeded;
          Found := true;
          return ;
        end;
      end;
    end FindMemory;
```

Some miscellaneous procedures and functions follow. The procedure GetFrames is used by the Job Manager to get the addresses of the current program frame and the operating system frame for a process. The functions GetProgEnt and GetDataEnt can be used by the Job Manager to read entries, and the procedures SetProgEnt and SetDataEnt to update entries, in the arrays ProgArr and DataArr. The procedures SetProgEnt and SetDataEnt are also used to continue the Swapper if it has been delayed. The procedure FindMemory is used by the Job Manager when memory has to be allotted to a waiting job process. The procedure MemState returns the sizes of memory presently available for allocation.

```
procedure export GetFrames(JobNum:ProcIndex;
                           var PFrameAdr,OFrameAdr:Address);
  begin
    with JobProgs[JobNum], JobStack[CurrProg] do
    begin
      PFrameAdr := varadr(CurrFrame);
      OFrameAdr := varadr(OSFrame);
    end;
  end GetFrames;

function export GetProgEnt(ProgNum:ProgIndex) return ProgInf;
  begin
    return ProgArr[ProgNum];
  end GetProgData;

function export GetDataEnt(DataNum:ProgIndex) return DataInf;
  begin
    return DataArr[DataNum];
  end GetDataEnt;

procedure export SetProgEnt(ProgNum:ProgIndex; Ent:ProgInf;
                           WakeUpSwapper:Boolean);
  begin
    ProgArr[ProgNum] := Ent;
    if WakeUpSwapper and delayed(SwapperQ)
      then continue(SwapperQ);
  end SetProgEnt;

procedure export SetDataEnt(DataNum:ProgIndex; Ent:DataInf;
                           WakeUpSwapper:Boolean);
  begin
    DataArr[DataNum] := Ent;
    if WakeUpSwapper and delayed(SwapperQ)
      then continue(SwapperQ);
  end SetDataEnt;

procedure export MemState(var ShareSize,Loc1Size ... :integer);
  begin
    ShareSize := MemAvailable[Share];
    Loc1Size := MemAvailable[Loc1];
      ...
    LocNSize := MemAvailable[LocN];
  end MemState;

procedure export InitMem(ShareSize,Loc1Size ... :integer);
  begin
    MemAvailable[Share] := ShareSize;
    MemAvailable[Loc1] := Loc1Size;
      ...
    MemAvailable[LocN] := LocNSize;
  end InitMem;
```

```
begin {ProgTable}
  for I in 1 to ProgMax do
  begin
    ProgArr[I].Used := false;
    DataArr[I].Used := false;
  end;
  for I in JobMin to JobMax
    do JobProgs[I].CurrProg := 0;
end ProgTable; .
```

Choosing Segments to be Swapped

ProgTable has all the information necessary to decide which segments can be swapped out from memory with the fewest processes being suspended. When used together with the information in JobTable, this allows decisions about swapping to be combined with scheduling decisions.

Swapping segments between memory and disk becomes necessary under three conditions:

1. When jobs are waiting for memory to load new program or data segments, or
2. When jobs whose segments have been swapped out have been waiting for execution, or
3. When too many jobs are blocked and processors are idle.

All the conditions may not be independent of each other (e.g., a job waiting for memory is also a blocked job) but they must still be examined separately before deciding if segments are to be swapped out. Condition (2) arises most often in time-sharing systems where there are many terminal jobs of which only a few require service at any time.

The prime candidates for segments to be released are instruction segments, because copies of such segments already exist on disk and the segments themselves cannot be modified in memory. In choosing instruction segments for release, the following criteria appear in order of importance:

1. First choose segments for which EnterCount = LeaveCount, as there are no current users of these segments.
2. Next choose segments for which EnterCount − LeaveCount has small value: few processes will be immediately affected by this.
3. Finally, choose segments for which the value of EnterCount is small as, once again, few processes will be affected.

Data segments can only be released if they are copied to disk. A data segment is used by only one process so it would appear possible to swap a data segment being used by a blocked process. However, this is not always so, because a data segment that is being used for input or output cannot be swapped out. So, before a data segment is chosen for swapping out, the Job Manager must examine the status (by the call, Kernel.WaitingFor-IO("Process number")) of the process using this segment and check that it is not blocked for input or output.

Program and data segments require to be swapped into memory for two reasons: because some process has made a program call which needs these segments, or because the segments were earlier swapped out. A segment can only be swapped in if memory is available. Note that swapping takes an appreciable amount of time, both for disk transfer and for memory allocation or release. The residence time, on disk or in memory, of a swapped segment must be relatively high compared to the swapping time if the well-known phenomenon of 'thrashing' is to be avoided. On the other hand, an interactive job will have poorer response time if its program or data segments are swapped out for long periods.

No mention has yet been made of the fact that segments used by a process that is executing within the operating system should not be swapped out. Unless this precaution is taken, there is the danger that segments for a process executing within a monitor are swapped out, the process is unable to continue execution and no other process is able to enter the monitor. This situation is, in fact, avoided in our system as the Kernel will continue to execute a process when it is in the operating system, even if its time slice is over. For the same reason, care must also be exercised in ensuring that processes that are ready to run after being blocked or delayed within the operating system, are executed as soon as possible.

Very many considerations can be used when choosing segments to be swapped into or out of memory. But there is a limit beyond which it serves little purpose to make complicated choices. Simple and effective steps that avoid 'starvation' of any process are more likely to be useful in an operating system than elaborate procedures that consume a lot of time. When simple steps fail to find a good solution to swapping problems, one possibility remains: to swap *all* program segments, and those data segments not being used for input or output, out of memory and then to allow them to be brought back in a controlled manner. This seemingly drastic solution has been used very successfully in at least one operating system, the Cambridge Titan multi-access operating system (cf. comments by Hartley and Needham, in Hoare and Perrott(1972), p.210).

The procedure MemState, in ProgTable, provides the amount of memory of each kind that is available for allocation. From this information, the Job Manager can decide whether segments must be swapped out before any swapping-in takes place.

The design of two procedures, ChooseSwapIn and ChooseSwapOut, are left as exercises.

```
procedure ChooseSwapIn(var Chosen:Boolean; var JobNum:ProcIndex;
                       var Kind:MemKind; var MemSize:integer);
   begin
      ...
   end ChooseSwapIn;

procedure ChooseSwapOut(Kind:MemKind; MemNeeded:integer;
                        var Chosen:Boolean; var SegNum:ProgIndex);
   begin
      ...
   end ChooseSwapOut;
```

Swapper Processes

For a segment to be swapped out, space must be allocated on some disk. If the swapper process has to go through the normal procedures for acquiring disk space, there is likely to be some delay. To ensure that swapping can be done rapidly, it is normal to reserve space for swapped segments, on one or more disks. This space may be under-used, but that is usually a small price to pay for ensuring fast swapping.

Space in main memory is invariably far too precious a commodity to be reserved in this way. In general, a swapper process must compete with other processes for the allocation of main memory. A single swapper process can swap segments either into or out of memory. When a segment is to be swapped out, it may need to be copied to a disk segment (this would be required for mixed program segments and data segments), and then the swapper process must call the memory allocator to release space. All segments to be swapped into memory require main memory space to be allocated before they are copied from the disk. Allocation of main memory is subject to delay, as a segment of the right size may not be available. In Chapter 6, we saw that release of memory may also be delayed. So a swapper process may be delayed in the memory allocator either while acquiring or releasing memory.

Now consider what will occur if a swapper process is delayed while acquiring memory. The process will be allowed to continue when some other process releases enough space for the swapper's request to be met. But the swapper is the process that will, most often, release space also. And this cannot take place until it completes its earlier request to acquire space. A single swapper process can therefore get delayed in a manner which can cause a deadlock.

At least for this reason, it is necessary to have *two* swapper processes: SwapperIn, to swap segments into memory, and SwapperOut, to swap segments from memory. But having two swappers also has the significant advantage that two swapping operations can take place simultaneously. Introducing two swapper processes requires a few minor changes in ProgTable: the single variable, SwapperQ, must be replaced by two variables, SwapInQ and SwapOutQ, and the procedure SwapperWait must have a two-valued parameter to indicate which swapper is to be delayed.

Having two swappers still does not guarantee that both of them will not be blocked in the memory allocator: one waiting to acquire space and the other to release space. If the memory allocator needs to delay processes while returning memory, it would be necessary for it to have a 'nondelaying' operation for use by the swapper when it has to release memory. The swapper can then re-try this operation when its first request fails.

The Job Manager's Cycle

The Job Manager has a repetitive cycle of actions to be performed. This process has two variables, SwappingIn and SwappingOut, which are set to **true** when a segment is being swapped into and out of memory, respectively. InJob has the identification of the job process whose segments are being brought to memory, and OutSeg the index of the segment being swapped out. In simple form, the Job Manager would have a skeleton such as:

```
var
    JobManager: process;
        var
            CPULoad: array [CPU] of integer;
            SwappingIn, SwappingOut: Boolean;
            InJob: ProcIndex; OutSeg: ProgIndex;
            Kind: MemKind; MemNeeded: integer;
            CPUs: CPUSet;

        procedure ChooseCPU(ProcNum:ProcIndex; Slice:integer;
                            CPUs:CPUSet; var CPUNum:CPU);
        begin
            ...
        end ChooseCPU;

        procedure ScheduleProcs;
        begin
            ...
        end ScheduleProcs;
```

```
procedure GetProcs;
  begin
    ...
  end GetProcs;

procedure ChooseSwapIn(var Chosen:Boolean;
                       var JobNum:ProcIndex;
                       var Kind:MemKind; var MemSize:integer);
  begin
    ...
  end ChooseSwapIn;

procedure ChooseSwapOut(Kind:MemKind; MemNeeded:integer;
                        var Chosen:Boolean;
                        var SegNum:ProgIndex);
  begin
    ...
  end ChooseSwapOut;

begin {JobManager}
  for I in 1 to CPUMax
    do CPULoad[I] := 0;
  SwappingIn := false; SwappingOut := false;

  {Job Management Cycle}
  loop
    ScheduleProcs;
    Kernel.Suspend;
    GetProcs;
    for I in JobMin to JobMax do
    begin
      ProgTable.GetCPUs(I, CPUs);
      JobTable.SetCPUs(I, CPUs)
    end;
    if SwappingIn and not Kernel.IsBlocked(InJob)
      then SwappingIn := false;
    if SwappingOut and "segment has been swapped out"
      then SwappingOut := false;
    if not SwappingIn
      then ChooseSwapIn(SwappingIn, InJob, Kind, MemNeeded);
    if SwappingIn and not SwappingOut
        and "InSwapper is blocked for Memory" then
    begin
      ChooseSwapOut(Kind, MemNeeded, SwappingOut, OutSeg);
      MemNeeded := MemNeeded − "size of OutSeg";
    end
  end
end JobManager;
```

We have not described how accounts are rendered for the resources used by a user job process. JobTable keeps some accounting figures (i.e., the fields, TimeUsed and SpaceTime, of a job's entry) and we can visualize other such figures being maintained. For example, the value of SpaceTime in JobTable is calculated by multiplying the memory size for the program by the processor time used when executing that program but, if necessary, the job 'residence' time could also be recorded, by storing the time at which the job was created. Accounting information is usually just written out to a file, for later processing by an accounting program. This information is often useful also for analysing the performance of the system so a number of figures, not necessarily related to the way charges are calculated for a user, can be saved for subsequent use.

Handling Errors Detected by the Kernel

The execution of a program by a job process will be terminated by the Kernel under the conditions mentioned earlier (e.g., when the slice ends, or when the operation Kernel.Suspend is executed), and also when any of the following events occurs:

1. When a special 'terminate' character is typed on the control device for an interactive job, or
2. When the program being executed causes a hardware error to occur (e.g., due to an attempt to access memory outside the limits set for the program and data segments, or because of an attempt to divide a number by zero).

In each of these cases, the Kernel call, GetError will return a value representing the cause of the error. With nested program calls, it is not always certain that it will be of much use if an error value is returned to the previous program. For simplicity, let us assume that, on the occurrence of such an error, control must return to the Command program. From the job process structure, we know that the Command program is the second program to be called (the first is the Login program). To return to this program, the job will have to successively return from programs until the program level is 2. This can be done in a systematic way by altering the procedure Depart.

```
procedure Depart("Parameters to be returned");
   var
      UserError: Kernel.ErrorKind;
      { other declarations }
   begin
      "Collect parameters in ParBlock";
      UserError := Kernel.GetError;
```

```
repeat
   ProgTable.LeaveProgram(FreeISeg, FreeDSeg, ProgLev,
                          PSegPosn,DSegPosn,
                          PSeg, DSeg, PrevMem,
                          PrevPIndex, PrevDIndex);
   if FreeISeg
      then MemorySpace.Release(PSegPosn, PSeg);
   if FreeDSeg
      then MemorySpace.Release(DSegPosn, DSeg);
until (UserError = NoError) or
      ((UserError ≠ NoError) and (ProgLev = 2));
JobTable.NextProg(PrevPIndex, PrevDIndex, PrevMem);
if UserError ≠ NoError
   then "Call File System to close all files";
ProgTable.ReturnToProg; {Wait until continued by Job Manager}
Kernel.ProgramReturn(varadr(ParBlock), UserError);
end Depart;
```

DISCUSSION

The Operator Process

Though we have not referred to it, the system will need an Operator process which can be executed by the system operator, usually from a particular terminal. The process accepts commands from the operator to examine the status of the system (e.g., to print the information in the Job Table in tabular form) and to set system parameters, such as the number of terminal and batch jobs that can be initiated. An important function for this process is to close down the system, by not allowing any further jobs to be created and warning all existing interactive users that they should cease their work within some time period. A fully fledged Operator process is likely to need some additional operations in the monitors JobTable and ProgTable (e.g., to be able to terminate a user job). It would also be of use if the spoolers shared a monitor with the Operator process, for commands to be sent to the spoolers and for them to supply information on the queued requests to the operator.

Determination of Jobmix and Processor Slice

The first level of scheduling available is to accept user jobs upto some limits: e.g.

> MaxTerminals {The maximum number of terminal jobs}
> MaxBatchJobs {The maximum number of batch jobs}
> MaxJobLimit {The maximum number of jobs of any kind}

Usually, we will have

> MaxJobLimit = MaxTerminals + MaxBatchJobs ≤ JobMax

but, if we were to allow the numbers of terminal and batch jobs to be determined dynamically, according to the demand, we could alter this to

> MaxJobLimit ≤ JobMax
> MaxTerminals ≤ JobMax
> MaxBatchJobs ≤ JobMax

From our array of JobMax job processes, we shall then allow up to MaxJobLimit jobs to be associated with user jobs, T of which could be terminal jobs (T ≤ MaxTerminals) and B of which could be batch jobs (B ≤ MaxBatchJobs), so that

> $B + T$ ≤ MaxJob

The Kernel call, Run, takes an integer parameter Slice which is the maximum continuous time which will be allotted to the process before control is returned to the scheduler. If we intend to give each terminal user a slice of processor time every 1 second, or less, we must choose values of the parameter Slice so that

> T * (Terminal Job Slice) + B * (Batch Job Slice) ≤ 1 second

For the rest of this discussion, we shall assume that processes are scheduled in round-robin order, so that every unblocked process will get one slice before any process gets a second. We shall refer to a scheduling 'cycle' as the act of scheduling each process once, and we shall assume that our target is to complete one scheduling cycle in 1 second.

The limit set by this inequality is a conservative estimate because much of the time there may be fewer terminal and batch jobs than the maximum permitted, and many of the jobs which are present may be blocked. If these assumptions are correct, at most times terminal jobs will get better service than estimated here.

Note that this is a simplistic analysis. To be accurate, there are at least two other factors we must take into account: the fraction of time used by the operating system processes (let's assume there are N), and the time it takes to switch the processor from one process to the next. We can write this down as

T * (Terminal Job Slice) + B * (Batch Job Slice) +
N * (Operating System Process time) +
(T + B + N) * (Process Switch Time) ≤ 1 second

Since the process switch time is an overhead, it is important that the size of a slice is large enough for this overhead to be relatively small. The terminal job slice should therefore be set to the average command execution time, or a time which is several times larger than the process switch time. Only the second consideration applies in choosing the size of slice for batch jobs. But what estimates do we use for the operating system process time? Assuming these processes are programmed with care, they will either complete their tasks in as short a time as possible, or be blocked. For such trusted processes, we can use an arbitrarily large slice in the knowledge that they will only use as much of it as is essential. The operating system process time can then be taken as the average time taken by each of these processes to complete an action or to be blocked. This must be found by experiment or measurement.

Scheduling jobs in this way is less rigid than might appear at first examination. When there are fewer than MaxJobLimit jobs, the scheduling cycle is completed in less than one second and, on average, each job can get more than one slice per second. An added sophistication would be to alter the sizes of slices depending on the number of jobs of each kind that are actually present at any time. In doing so, we must be sure that the improvement in the response time, or in the system throughput, is commensurate with the extra time required to calculate the best size of slice.

Call Mechanisms and Protection

Users of any commercial operating system will know that a call to an operating system differs from calls to procedures in a user program. The operating system, and each user program, executes within what is often called an *address space*, which is an area of memory to which access is controlled by the hardware. This hardware protection prevents inadvertent or capricious modification of memory by a user program. But in preventing illegal access of one address space from another, the hardware also makes it more difficult for a program in one address space to call a program in another. Special instructions are provided in most computers for a user program to call the operating system. The hardware 'traps' the execution of these instructions and automatically transfers control to a fixed location in memory, where the parameter of the trap instruction can be examined and control transferred to the appropriate procedure in the operating system.

Our operating system has to execute a variety of user jobs, so it will need to be protected from illegal access. In other words, the operating system must execute in an address space which is separate from any user program. We shall assume that every call to the operating system (e.g., a call to the operations of the file system, or to the procedures Enter and Depart) occurs through a 'trap' instruction generated by the compiler. The parameters for such a call must be retrieved from the user program space; this is possible if the operating system, being a privileged program, executes in a special hardware mode which allows other address spaces to be accessed.

The fixed location to which trap instructions are directed by the hardware is, in fact, part of the Kernel. After saving the state of the user program in the program frame, the Kernel will transfer control to an operating system procedure using the operating system frame. On completion of the call, the Kernel must resume execution of the user program using the status saved in the program frame.

The Kernel forms part of the operating system and, if we can assume that the operating system is written with care, there is no great need to put the Kernel in a separate address space. So, calls from the rest of the operating system to the Kernel can use the normal procedure call mechanisms.

Special mention must be made of the stack required for a job process. When a call is made from one program to another, in general there will be parameters to be transmitted and returned. If each job process is provided with a large enough stack, this can be used across program calls. There is a danger in this, however, as a malfunctioning program can mutilate the stack in a manner which destroys the past 'history' of calls of the process. It is preferable for each program to have a separate stack, and for the operating system to transmit parameters between programs, as we have done here in the procedures Enter and Depart. Calls to the operating system must be treated in a special way with a separate stack being reserved for each process. The area for this stack is defined in the operating system frame for the process. The operating system stack must be large enough to hold the parameters of the program call and the largest number of local variables which are used in any operating system call (this can be statistically determined).

User Program Structure

The operating system allows user job processes to execute programs which have a procedure-like structure, where there may be calls from one program to another. This feature is not commonly available in commercial operating systems, as it has usually been assumed that each program will execute independently of other programs. Any association between them, such as the fact that one program may need to read a file produced by another program, is assumed to be explicitly programmed in the sequence of commands issued by the user. This has the consequence of making programs large and monolithic, even when a better organization can be envisaged. Structuring programs as sets of procedures has become such an indispensable way of dealing with complexity that it seems worthwhile to extend this facility to programs. For example, a compiler could be built as a set of programs which perform the normal functions of syntax analysis, flow analysis, code generation and peephole optimization. A single driver program could then call these subsidiary programs in the right sequence.

```
CCNPascal (SourceFile, ListFile,      – Call the CCNPascal compiler
          CodeFile, Motorola68000) – to compile SourceFile and
                                    – generate code for
                                    – the Motorola 68000
```

The driver program, CCNPascal, would then have the following structure:

```
"Initialize variables and files";
"Call CCNPasSyntax(SourceFile, SyntaxFile)";
"Call CCNFlowAnalyze(SyntaxFile, InterCodeFile)";
"Call CCN68000Code(InterCodeFile, UnoptCodeFile)";
"Call CCN68000Optimize(UnoptCodeFile, CodeFile)";
```

This allows the compiler to be composed of self-contained modules which can be called in sequence. To generate code for some other machine, the last two calls would need to be changed appropriately (assuming, of course, that each program in the compiler has a well-defined and standard format for file input and output). At any time, only one of the programs need be in memory, and this will greatly reduce storage requirements. In terms of current terminology, each program call has a similar effect to a dynamic 'overlay', but a program call is far simpler to understand and to use.

A requirement we have not mentioned is the need for a program to be able to *dynamically* ask the operating system for additional memory in its data segment. For example, a compiler may, by default, only use a restricted amount of memory for its tables but may give the user the option to execute the compiler with a larger data segment. Similarly, an editor may normally use a small buffer for text manipulation and may need to be able to increase the size of the buffer, depending on the editing task. To add a feature to permit this in our operating system is relatively easy: a new procedure must be added to ProgTable to increase the size of the data segment for the process and, if necessary, the data segment must be copied to a larger area if additional space contiguous to the allocated space is not available.

The program call facility, when properly used, allows large tasks to be built of smaller modules (or programs). A similar objective has been met, in the Unix operating system (Ritchie and Thompson, 1974), by providing 'pipes'. In that case, the flexibility is extended still further by allowing individual modules to execute as much in parallel as input and output requirements will permit them.

As programming practices develop, many simple tasks may find need for a program call feature. For example, a Mail program may need to call a standard editor to format messages, and then to have control returned after editing, so that the message can be transmitted. Other utility programs could, similarly, be called from programs. The popularity and success of 'pipes' in Unix leads to the conclusion that many utility programs can be built as relatively small units which can be composed for parallel execution, or called in sequence, to achieve major tasks which are presently being performed by monolithic programs.

Operating System Process Structure

Principles of sound program design enunciate the need to build primitive abstractions, or abstract objects, which have well-defined properties, and which can be used to build other abstractions. We have followed these rules in designing the abstractions of much of the operating system, but it would appear that we have been somewhat more lax in the design of the job management abstractions. For example, the Kernel provides support for creating and executing the processes of CCNPascal but, in our design, the Kernel does not schedule processes. With the exception of the processor schedulers themselves, processes are scheduled explicitly by the Job Manager. This could be avoided if the Kernel treated each process as a virtual processor and scheduled it whenever it was not blocked and a processor was available. This technique was used with great success in the first version of Modula (Wirth, 1977), for a single processor system.

But now consider what we have attempted to accomplish in terms of job management. We have allowed a flexible association between processes and programs. This has advantages for the user, and it is also a means of managing the use of memory. When there is demand for memory, and little memory is available for allocation (a not infrequent occurrence), the Job Manager assumes the reponsibility of deciding which programs may reside in memory. The fact that a process is not blocked is only one of the criteria that can be used to decide whether it should be scheduled. For example, the segments in use by a process may be swapped out of memory because the process has already had a 'fair' share of processor time, and there are more pressing needs for memory. In this case, the process will not be scheduled even though it is not blocked (in the programming sense of the word). The main reason why the Kernel does not completely support virtual processors is that we need to control memory allocation to programs in a flexible manner.

There are other changes that could be contemplated. For example, the CPU queues could, conceivably, be incorporated in the Kernel. This would require only relatively minor changes in the design. But this change would increase the size of the Kernel and would not contribute greatly to simplifying the design of the operating system.

User Level Concurrency

In our discussion so far, we have considered how job processes and operating system processes can be scheduled for concurrent execution. One of the attractions of having a multiprocessor system is that several processes can be executed at the same time. Can this advantage be put to use in user programs, by designing *user* programs with *concurrent processes*?

Use of concurrent processes at any level within a system requires some implementation of synchronization and scheduling operations. For the operating system processes, synchronization is provided by the Kernel. Scheduling for these processes is performed by the Job Manager, the processor schedulers and, at the lowest level, by the Kernel. If user programs are also allowed to contain processes and monitors, primitives for their implementation must be provided at some lower level.

One alternative is to treat user processes and monitors in the same way as those in the operating system. But note that a process executing in an operating system monitor is allowed to continue its execution (irrespective of the time-slice allotted to it) until it gets blocked or leaves the monitor. This action is taken by the Kernel to ensure that processes complete their execution of monitor operations as quickly as possible. If the same Kernel primitives are to be used in user programs and monitors, we shall be giving them an unnecessary privilege, and one liable for misuse. For example, a user program would receive highly preferential service if it were built as one large monitor! A more reasonable solution to this problem is to provide an altogether different set of primitives for use in user programs. These primitives should be provided by the operating system, so that their use can be coordinated with the scheduling of user processes. The compiler should generate calls to these primitives while compiling user level programs with monitors and processes.

To permit user level concurrency, we must reconsider both the original decision to have a fixed number of job processes in the operating system and the way the Job Initiator associates job processes with new user jobs. Two choices present themselves: concurrent processes in a user program could be run as 'subprocesses' of the same user job process, or separate job processes could be provided (perhaps by creating new job processes) to execute each concurrent process. If the subprocesses share the allocation of processor time given to one job process, there will be no true concurrency. Alternatively, the operating system could treat the concurrent processes of a job as parts of a single program so that they are swapped together, and so that the termination of the job can be defined as the point when all its concurrent processes terminate.

User level concurrency has been provided in two (non-commercial) operating systems: StarOS and Medusa, both for Cm* (Jones *et al.*, 1979; Ousterhout *et al.*, 1979). The family of concurrent processes of a program is called a 'task force'. Each concurrent process is allotted a separate processor, so that it can execute independently of other processes. Clearly, there can only be as many concurrent processes as there are processors but this number, on Cm*, is fairly large (50). Many of the problems we have considered here, of sharing resources between independent user jobs, are not of importance in such a system.

Paging, Segmentation and Virtual Memory

The operating system deals with programs at a relatively macroscopic level—mixed programs are treated as single units and separated programs as two units. The use of each unit of this kind can be correlated with program calls and swapping can be done at the level of whole units. The hardware memory protection required to support this kind of program structure is minimal.

In Chapter 3, different memory protection mechanisms were briefly mentioned. Most of these mechanisms are considerably more elaborate than needed for this operating system, at least as it has been described here. Since techniques like paging have been in use for over 20 years, our apparent neglect of these mechanisms needs some explanation.

The simplest use of paging (or equivalent mechanisms) is to allow storage for a program and its data to be divided into units of fixed size which can be scattered over memory (i.e., which need not be stored contiguously). This can greatly reduce the problems of memory fragmentation. When some variation is allowed in the sizes of the units (as, for example, in segments on PDP-11 computers), there is less reduction in fragmentation but the advantages of 'scatter storage' are still substantial. Efficient and highly successful time-sharing operating systems (such as versions of TOPS-10, for the PDP-10 computer) have been built using paging hardware only for scatter storage. Very few alterations would be needed to incorporate scatter storage techniques into our design.

Two reasons make it necessary to consider more elaborate schemes: the storage addressable by a program may differ from what is physically available as main memory, or memory space limitations may make it necessary for only part of a program (or data) to be loaded into memory at any time. In several models of the PDP-11 and PDP-10 family, the storage directly addressable by a program is *smaller* than the maximum size of memory for the system. More commonly though, the address space of a program is larger than the physical memory and programs are said to execute in 'virtual' memory. In either of these cases, the operating system could take the conservative approach of allotting fewer pages of physical memory to a program than it may eventually use. Many different techniques have been proposed and implemented for pages of a program to be brought into memory as required (demand paging) and to be released when they have passed out of use. Such techniques can reduce the 'space-time' product of the memory needed to execute the program. They are used mainly in large operating systems, where the overhead in processing and disk transfer time required for page and segment management can be tolerated in view of the resulting better use of main memory.

Though it is quite conceivable for paging techniques to be added to our operating system, we have attempted to achieve economy in the use of memory by providing the program call feature. This allows a large task to be decomposed into many smaller tasks (or programs) of which only one need be in memory at any time. If each task is genuinely small, there is little additional economy that would be derived from the use of paging.

EXERCISES

1. A skeleton program for the Job Initiator is given in this chapter. The function DevAlloc.Assigned (see Chapter 10) can be used to check if a terminal has been assigned to a job. There is a Kernel function

    function TTYActive ("terminal number":**integer**)
    return Boolean;

    which returns the value **true** if a character has been typed on a terminal. Assuming there are 24 terminals, numbered from 1 to 24, that are connected to the system, use these two functions and the available operations of JobTable to complete the program for JobInitiator.

2. Write a Login program which can be called when the Job Initiator finds input at an unassigned terminal. The program should have a short dialogue with the user to read the user's name and the password (the latter without echoing what is typed in). The function FileAdmn.Authenticate (see Chapter 9) can be used to check that the user name and password have been registered. (*Note*: the Login program is executed by the process assigned to the job by the Job Initiator; when it successfully logs-in a user, it should transfer control to the Command program).

3. Calls from one program to another are stacked like procedure calls. On return from a program, a job must retrace its path through the previous programs. Suppose this organization is to be changed so that, while user programs can call each other as before, a return executed in a user program will always transfer control back to the Command program (the same action must take place when an error is detected by the Kernel). Modify the procedure Depart to act in this way. With this change, can the structure of the Program Table and the Job Stack be simplified? How will you ensure that programs that are not in use are purged from the memory?

4. The important considerations that apply in the design of the Job Manager's procedures, ChooseSwapIn and ChooseSwapOut, have been described in this chapter. Code these two procedures, assuming that there are usually more jobs than there is memory to contain their segments.

5. Write the programs for two swapper processes, SwapIn and SwapOut. Assume disk space has been reserved for storing swapped segments, and that the main memory allocator has two calls, OSGet and OSReturn, which can be used to obtain and release memory, respectively, without delaying the calling process in case the operations cannot be completed.

6. (*Group Exercise*) Write down some hardware resource limits for a hypothetical three-processor system with some local and some shared memory, and a suitable set of peripherals. For this system, sketch out the complete operating system using the components described in Chapters 5–11. You must provide realistic values for all the constants required for generic components.

PROGRAM COMPONENTS FOR JOB MANAGEMENT

```
const
    ProcessMax = ... ; {Maximum number of processes}
    SystProcMax = ... ; {System processes are numbered
                            from 1 to SystProcMax}
    JobMin = SystProcMax + 1; {and job processes}
    JobMax = ProcessMax; {from JobMin to JobMax}
    ProgMax = ... ; {Maximum number of program segments
                            for all job processes}
    MaxProgLevel = ... ; {Stack limit for JobStack}

type
    JobType = (BatchProc, TerminalProc);
    TerminalDev = (None, Terminal1, ... , TerminalN);
    CPU = 1 .. CPUMax;
    CPUSet = set of CPU;
    ProcIndex = 1 .. ProcessMax;
    ProgIndex = 1 .. ProgMax;
    JobData =
      record
        UserId: Name;
        JobKind: JobType;
        ControlDev: TerminalDev;
        CurrentProg, CurrentData: ProgIndex;
        CPUs: CPUSet;
        MemLimit, TimeLimit,
        SpaceTime, ProgSize, TimeUsed: integer;
        NewProgram, OnCPU: Boolean
      end JobData;
    MemKind = (Share, Loc1, Loc2, ... , LocN);
    MemSet = set of MemKind;
    ProgType = (Mixed, Separated);
    SwapState = (InMemory, SwapThisOut, SwappedOut, SwapThisIn);
    ProgInf =
      record
        Used: Boolean;
        ProgDirectory: DirAdr;
        ProgName: Name;
        PType: ProgType;
        InstrSeg: Seg;
        PSegPosn: MemKind;
        EntryPoint: Address;
        EnterCount, LeaveCount: integer;
        ProgState: SwapState;
        InstrSwapAdr: DiskAdr
      end ProgInf;
    DataInf =
      record
        Used: Boolean;
```

```
          DataSeg: Seg;
          DSegPosn: MemKind;
          Left: Boolean;
          DataState: SwapState;
          DataSwapAdr: DiskAdr
        end DataInf;
```

CPUQ is the monitor used to exchange process scheduling information between the Job Manager and the processor schedulers.

```
{****            ****}
{****   CPUQ   ****}
{**** – Outline ****}
```

```
type
   CPUQ(RunMax: integer) = monitor*;
      function export ProcReady return Boolean;
      function export RunQFull return Boolean;
         {Functions to test the RunQ}
      function export ProcOver return Boolean;
      function export OverQFull return Boolean;
         {Functions to test the OverQ}
      procedure export EnterProc(NewEntry:RunEntry);
      procedure export RemoveProc(var OldEntry:OverEntry);
         {Procedures called by the Job Manager to enter processes in the
          RunQ and remove them from the OverQ}
      procedure export Next(var RunProc:RunEntry);
      procedure export Over(OverProc:OverEntry);
         {Procedures called by the scheduler to take processes
          for scheduling and to return them after execution}
   end CPUQ.
```

```
{****              ****}
{****    CPUQ    ****}
{**** –Implementation ****}
```

```
type
   CPUQ(RunMax: integer) = monitor*;
      type export
        RunEntry =
          record
             Id: ProcIndex;
             PFrameAdr, OFrameAdr: Address;
             Slice: integer
          end RunEntry;
        OverEntry =
          record
             Id: ProcIndex;
             TimeUsed: integer
          end OverEntry;
```

```
var
    RunQ: array [1 .. RunMax] of RunEntry;
    OverQ: array [1 .. RunMax] of OverEntry;
    RunQPtr, OverQPtr: FiFoQ(RunMax);

function export ProcReady return Boolean;
    begin
        return not RunQPtr.Empty;
    end ProcReady;

function export RunQFull return Boolean;
    begin
        return RunQPtr.Full;
    end RunQFull;

function export ProcOver return Boolean;
    begin
        return not OverQPtr.Empty;
    end ProcOver;

function export OverQFull return Boolean;
    begin
        return OverQPtr.Full;
    end OverQFull;

procedure export EnterProc(NewEntry:RunEntry);
    begin
        RunQ[RunQPtr.Put] := NewEntry;
    end EnterProc;

procedure export RemoveProc(var OldEntry:OverEntry);
    begin
        OldEntry := OverQ[OverQPtr.Next];
    end RemoveProc;

procedure export Next(var RunProc:RunEntry);
    begin
        RunProc := RunQ[RunQPtr.Next];
    end Next;

procedure export Over(OverProc:OverEntry);
    begin
        OverQ[OverQPtr.Put] := OverProc;
    end Over;

end CPUQ;

var
    CPUQs: array [1 .. CPUMax] of CPUQ;
```

Scheduler is the process which performs low-level scheduling by calling the Kernel to run processes.

```
{****                    ****}
{**** Scheduler ****}
{****   Process    ****}

type
  Scheduler(CPUNum: integer) = process;
    var
      ProcNum, Elapsed: integer;
      RunProc: RunEntry; OverProc: OverEntry;
    begin
      with CPUQS[CPUNum]
        do
        loop
          if ProcReady then
          begin
            Next(RunProc);
            Elapsed := Kernel.Time;
            with RunProc
              do Kernel.Run(Id, PFrameAdr, OFrameAdr, Slice);
            Elapsed := Kernel.Time – Elapsed;
            with OverProc
            do
            begin
              Id := RunProc.Id; TimeUsed := Elapsed;
            end;
            loop
              if not OverQFull then
              begin
                Over(OverProc);
                exit;
              end;
            end;
          end;
        end;
      end;
    end Scheduler;

    {Declarations for one scheduler for each of 1 .. CPUMax processors}

var
  Scheduler1: Scheduler(1);
  Scheduler2: Scheduler(2);
    ...
  SchedulerN: Scheduler(CPUMax);
```

JobTable is the monitor which stores information on each user process.
Operations of this monitor are called by the Job Manager, the Job Initiator
and each job process.

```
{****              ****}
{**** JobTable ****}
{**** –Outline     ****}
```

var
  JobTable: **monitor**;
    procedure export WaitForJob;
      {Called by job processes when idle}
    procedure export ResumeJob(Kind:JobType; MLim,TLim:**integer**;
                                   CntrlDev:TerminalDev);
      {Called by JobInitiator to assign a job process to a new job}
    procedure export SetId(UserName:Name);
      {Called by job processes to set the user's identification
       in JobTable}
    procedure export NextProg(PIndex,DIndex:ProgIndex);
      {Called by job process when it calls a new program and
       when it returns to a previous program}
    function export GetData(JobNum:ProcIndex) **return** JobData;
      {To get the entry for job JobNum}
    procedure export SetCPUs(JobNum:ProcIndex;
                                CPUChoice:CPUSet);
      {Called by JobManager to set the possible CPUs for a job}
    procedure export SetTime(JobNum:ProcIndex; UsedTime:**integer**);
      {Called by JobManager to record the time used by a job}
    procedure export MarkRun(JobNum:ProcIndex);
      {Called by JobManager to record that a job has been scheduled}
  end JobTable;
```

```
{****                    ****}
{****      JobTable      ****}
{**** – Implementation ****}
```

var
  JobTable: **monitor**;
    type export
      JobIndex = JobMin .. JobMax;
    var
      JobArr: **array** [JobIndex] **of** JobData;
      JobWaitQ: **array** [JobIndex] **of queue**;

    procedure export WaitForJob;
      begin
        delay(JobWaitQ[ProcId]);
        {Function ProcId returns the process number }
      end WaitForJob;

    procedure export ResumeJob(Kind:JobType; MLim,TLim:**integer**;
                                   CntrlDev:TerminalDev);
```

```
begin
  for I in JobMin to JobMax do
    if delayed(JobWaitQ[I]) then
    begin
      with JobArr[I] do
      begin
        JobKind := Kind;
        UserId := 'SYSTEM'; {Start as System process}
        ControlDev := CntrlDev; NewProgram := true;
        MemLimit := MLim; TimeLimit := TLim;
        SpaceTime := 0; ProgSize := 0; ProgTime := 0;
        TimeUsed := 0;
      end;
      continue(JobWaitQ[I]); exit;
    end;
  end ResumeJob;

procedure export SetId(UserName:Name);
  begin
  JobArr[ProcId].UserId := UserName;
  end SetId;

procedure export NextProg(PIndex,DIndex:ProgIndex;
                          MemSize: integer);
  begin
    with JobArr[ProcId] do
    begin
        CurrentProg := PIndex; CurrentData := DIndex;
        NewProgram := true;
        SpaceTime := SpaceTime + (ProgSize * TimeUsed);
        ProgSize := MemSize;
    end;
  end NextProg;

function export GetData(JobNum:ProcIndex) return JobData;
  begin
    return JobArr[JobNum];
  end GetData;

procedure export SetCPUs(JobNum:ProcIndex; CPUChoice:CPUSet);
  begin
    with JobArr[JobNum]
      do CPUs := CPUChoice;
  end SetCPUs;

procedure export SetTime(JobNum:ProcIndex; UsedTime:integer);
  begin
    with JobArr[JobNum] do
    begin
      TimeUsed := TimeUsed + UsedTime;
      NewProgram := false; OnCPU := false;
    end;
  end SetTime;
```

```
    procedure export MarkRun(JobNum:ProcIndex);
      begin
        JobArr[JobNum].OnCPU := true;
      end MarkRun;

    begin {JobTable}
      for I in JobMin to JobMax do
        with JobArr[I] do
        begin
          UserId := 'SYSTEM';
          {All job processes start as system processes}
          JobKind := BatchProc; {with batch mode as a default}
          ControlDev := None;
          "Set initial values for MemLimit and TimeLimit";
          "Set CurrentProg and CurrentData for LOGIN program";
          OnCPU := false; NewProgram := true;
        end;
      end JobTable;
```

ProgTable stores information on the programs called by a job process. Its operations are called by the Job Manager, the Swappers and by job processes (through the procedures Enter and Depart).

```
{****                 ****}
{**** ProgTable ****}
{****   –Outline    ****}
```

```
var
  ProgTable: monitor;
    procedure export FindNewProg(Dir:DirAdr; NewProg:Name;
                                    var PIndex:ProgIndex);
      {Called to see if the new program is already loaded;
       if not, and if there is space in JobStack, a new entry
       must be found in ProgTable}
    procedure export NewProgram(Dir:DirAdr; NewProg:Name;
                                  DiskPosn:DiskAdr;
                                  InitialEntry:Address;
                                  PKind:ProgType;
                                  var PIndex:ProgIndex);
      {Called to enter a new program's information in ProgTable}
    procedure export NewData(var DIndx:ProgIndex; DataPosn:DiskAdr);
      {Called to enter details of a new data segment}
    procedure export EnterProgram(PIndex,DIndex:ProgIndex;
                                    ProgMem,DataMem:integer;
      {Called by the job to wait for its segments to be swapped in}
    procedure export LeaveProgram(FreeISeg,FreeDSeg:Boolean;
                                    var ProgLev:ProgLevel;
                                    var PSegKind,DSegKind:MemKind;
                                    var ISeg,DSeg:Seg;
                                    var PrevMemory:integer;
                                    var
                                    PrevPSeg,PrevDSeg:ProgIndex);
```

{Called when a job is to leave a called program}
procedure export ReturnToProg;
  {Called when a job is to return to a previous program}

procedure export FindSwapSeg(ToDisk:**Boolean**; **var** MemSeg:Seg;
                              var SwapLoc:DiskAdr;
                              var SegInd:ProgIndex;
                              var
                              ProgFound,DataFound:**Boolean**);
  {Called by the Swapper to find a segment to be
  swapped in or out}
procedure export SwapperWait;
  {Called by the Swapper to wait for some work}
procedure export MarkSwapped(SegInd:ProgIndex; MemSeg:Seg
                            Posn:MemKind; SwapLoc:DiskAdr;
                            MemReleased:**integer**;
                            ToDisk,Prog:**Boolean**);
  {Called by the Swapper to record that swapping has been done}
procedure export GetCPUs(JobNum:ProcIndex; **var** CPUs:CPUSet);
  {Called by the Job Manager to determine which CPUs can be used
  for the job JobNum}
procedure export FindMemory(MemNeeded:**integer**;
                            MemPosns:MemSet;
                            var Posn:MemKind;
                            var Found:**Boolean**);
  {Called by the Job Manager to see where memory may be found
  for a waiting job process}
procedure export GetFrames(JobNum:ProcIndex;
                            var PFrameAdr,OFrameAdr:Address);
  {Called by the Job Manager to get the frames for a job}
function export GetProgEnt(ProgNum:ProgIndex) **return** ProgInf;
function export GetDataEnt(DataNum:ProgIndex) **return** DataInf;
procedure export SetProgEnt(ProgNum:ProgIndex; Ent:ProgInf;
                            WakeUpSwapper:**Boolean**);
procedure export SetDataEnt(DataNum:ProgIndex; Ent:DataInf;
                            WakeUpSwapper:**Boolean**);
  {Called by the Job Manager to read and set entries for the
  program and data segments for a job; also to wake up the
  Swapper if swapping is needed}
procedure export MemState(**var** ShareSize,Loc1Size ... :**integer**);
procedure export InitMem(ShareSize,Loc1Size ... :**integer**);
  {Called by the Job Manager to find out how much memory
  is available and to set the limits for memory of each kind}
end ProgTable.

```
{****                      ****}
{****    ProgTable         ****}
{**** –Implementation ****}
```

var
  ProgTable: **monitor**;

```
type
  ProgLevel = 1 .. MaxProgLevel;
var
  ProgArr: array [ProgIndex] of ProgInf;
  DataArr: array [ProgIndex] of DataInf;
  JobProgs: array [JobMin .. JobMax] of
                    record
                        JobStack: array [ProgLevel] of StackEntry;
                        CurrProg: ProgLevel;
                        OSFrame: Kernel.Frame
                    end JobProgs;
  JobWaiting: array [JobMin .. JobMax] of
                    record
                        Reason: (ProgArrFull, DataArrFull, SwapWait,
                                 ReturnWait);
                    end JobWaiting;
  MemAvailable: array [MemKind] of integer;
  SwapperQ: queue;

procedure export FindNewProg(Dir:Uname; NewProg:Name;
                             var PIndex:ProgIndex);
  begin
    with JobProgs[ProcId] do
    begin
      if CurrProg = MaxProgLevel {Job stack full}
        then return error;
      with JobStack[CurrProg] do
      begin
        with ProgArr[ProgInd] {For program segment}
          do LeaveCount := LeaveCount + 1;
        if DataInd > 0
          then {There is a data seg}
          DataArr[DataInd].Left := true;
      end;
    end;
    for I in 1 to ProgMax do
      with ProgArr[I] do
        if (ProgDirectory = Dir) and (ProgName = NewProg) then
        begin {Program entry found}
            PIndex := I; return ;
        end;
    PIndex := 0; {Program entry not found}
  end FindNewProg;

procedure export NewProgram(Dir:Uname; NewProg:Name;
                            DiskPosn:DiskAdr;
                            InitialEntry:Address;
                            PKind:ProgType;
                            var PIndex:ProgIndex);
  var
    PEntryFound: Boolean;
```

```
begin
  PEntryFound := false;
  while not PEntryFound do
  begin
    for I in 1 to ProgMax do
      with ProgArr[I] do
        if not Used then
        begin
          Used := true; ProgDirectory := Dir;
          Progname := NewProg; InstrSwapAdr := DiskPosn;
          EntryPoint := InitialEntry; PType := PKind;
          ProgState := SwappedOut;
          EnterCount := 0; LeaveCount := 0;
          PEntryFound := true; PIndex := I;
          exit;
        end;
    if not PEntryFound then
      with JobWaiting[ProcId] do
      begin
        Reason := ProgArrFull;
        delay(JobQ);
      end;
  end;
end NewProgram;


procedure export NewData(PIndex:ProgIndex; DataPosn:DiskAdr);
  var
    DEntryFound: Boolean;
  begin
    DEntryFound := false;
    while not DEntryFound do
    begin
      for I in 1 to ProgMax do
        with DataArr[I] do
          if not Used then
          begin
            Used := true;
            DataState := SwappedOut; Left := false;
            DEntryFound := true; DIndex := I;
            DataSwapAdr := DataPosn;
            exit;
          end;
      if not DEntryFound then
        with JobWaiting[ProcId] do
        begin
          Reason := DataArrFull;
          delay(JobQ);
        end;
    end;
  end NewData;
```

```
procedure export EnterProgram(PIndex,DIndex:ProgIndex;
                              ProgMem,DataMem:integer);
  begin
    with JobProgs[ProcId]
      do CurrProg := CurrProg + 1;
    {Allocate a new frame}
    with JobStack[CurrProg] do
    begin
      ProgInd := PIndex;
      DataInd := DIndex;
      with ProgArr[ProgInd]
        do EnterCount := EnterCount + 1;
      with JobWaiting[ProcId] do
      begin
        ISize := ProgMem; DSize := DataMem;
        Reason := SwapWait;
        delay(JobQ); {Wait until segments are swapped in
                      and JobStack[CurrProg].CurrFrame
                      is set by the Job Manager}
      end;
    end;
  end EnterProgram;


procedure export LeaveProgram(var FreeISeg,FreeDseg:Boolean;
                              var ProgLev:ProgLevel;
                              var PSegKind,DSegKind:MemKind;
                              var ISeg,DSeg:Seg;
                              var PrevMemory:integer;
                              var
                              PrevPSeg,PrevDSeg:ProgIndex);
  begin
    FreeISeg := false; FreeDSeg := false;
    with JobProgs[ProcId], JobStack[CurrProg] do
    begin
      with ProgArr[ProgInd] do
      begin
        EnterCount := EnterCount – 1;
        if EnterCount = 0
          then {There are no users}
          begin {so free program segment}
            FreeISeg := true; Used := false;
            MemAvailable[PSegPosn] := MemAvailable[PSegPosn]
                                     + InstrSeg.SegSize;
            PSegKind := PSegPosn;
            ISeg := InstrSeg;
            for I in JobMin to JobMax do
              with JobWaiting[I] do
                if delayed(JobQ) and (Reason = ProgArrFull) then
                begin
                  continue(JobQ);
                  exit;
```

```
                    end;
                end;
            end;
            if DataInd > 0
              then {Data segment }
                with DataArr[DataInd] do {can now be freed}
                  begin
                    FreeDSeg := true; InUse := false;
                    DSegKind := DSegPosn;
                    DSeg := DataSeg;
                    for I in JobMin to JobMax do
                      with JobWaiting[I] do
                        if delayed(JobQ)
                              and (Reason = DataArrFull) then
                        begin
                          continue(JobQ);
                          exit;
                        end;
                  end;
            CurrProg := CurrProg - 1;
            with JobStack[CurrProg] do
            begin
              with ProgArr[ProgInd] do
              begin
                LeaveCount := LeaveCount - 1;
                PrevMemory := InstrSeg.MemSize;
              end;
              PrevPSeg := ProgInd;
              if DataInd > 0 then
                with DataArr[DataInd] do
                begin
                  Left := false;
                  PrevMemory := PrevMemory + DataSeg.MemSize;
                end;
              PrevDSeg := DataInd;
            end;
            ProgLev := CurrProg;
          end;
        end LeaveProgram;

procedure export ReturnToProg;
  begin
    with JobWaiting[ProcId] do
    begin
      Reason := ReturnWait;
      with JobProgs[ProcId], JobStack[CurrProg] do
      begin
        {Set sizes of program and data segments in ISize,DSize}
        ISize := ProgArr[ProgInd].InstrSeg.SegSize;
        DSize := DataArr[DataInd].DataSeg.SegSize;
      end;
```

```
           delay(JobQ);
         end;
       end ReturnToProg;


   procedure export FindSwapSeg(ToDisk:Boolean; var MemSeg:Seg;
                                var SwapLoc:DiskAdr;
                                var SegInd:ProgIndex;
                                var
                                ProgFound,DataFound:Boolean);
   begin
     ProgFound := false; DataFound := false;
     for I in 1 to ProgMax do
       with ProgArr[I] do
       begin
         if ((ProgState = SwapThisOut) and ToDisk)
             or ((ProgState = SwapThisIn) and not ToDisk) then
         begin
           MemSeg := ProgSeg; SegInd := I;
           if not ToDisk then SwapLoc := InstrSwapAdr;
           ProgFound := true;
           return ;
         end;
       end;
     for I in 1 to ProgMax do
       with DataArr[I] do
       begin
         if ((DataState = SwapThisOut) and ToDisk)
             or ((DataState = SwapThisIn) and not ToDisk) then
         begin
           MemSeg := DataSeg; SegInd := I;
           if not ToDisk
             then SwapLoc := DataSwapAdr;
           DataFound := true;
           return ;
         end;
       end;
   end FindSwapSeg;


procedure export SwapperWait;
  begin
    delay(SwapperQ);
  end SwapperWait;


procedure export MarkSwapped(SegInd:ProgIndex; MemSeg:Seg;
                            Posn:MemKind; SwapLoc:DiskAdr;
                            MemReleased:integer;
                            ToDisk,Prog:Boolean);
  begin
    if Prog
      then {Program segment}
```

```
            with ProgArr[SegInd] do
              if ToDisk then {Swapped out}
                begin
                  ProgState := SwappedOut;
                  InstrSwapAdr := SwapLoc;
                  MemAvailable[Posn] := MemAvailable[Posn]
                                          + MemReleased;
                end
              else {Swapped in}
              begin
                ProgState := InMemory;
                InstrSeg := MemSeg;
              end
          else {Data segment}
            with DataArr[SegInd] do
              if ToDisk
                then {Swapped out}
                begin
                  DataState := SwappedOut;
                  DataSwapAdr := SwapLoc;
                  MemAvailable[Posn] := MemAvailable[Posn]
                                          + MemReleased;
                end
              else {Swapped in}
              begin
                DataState := InMemory;
                DataSeg := MemSeg;
              end;
      end MarkSwapped;

  procedure export GetCPUs(JobNum:ProcIndex; var CPUs:CPUSet);
      var
        CPUx: CPU;
      begin
        CPUs := CPUSet[];
        with JobProgs[JobNum], JobStack[CurrProg] do
          with ProgArr[ProgInd], DataArr[DataInd] do
            if (ProgState = InMemory) and (DataState = InMemory)
              then
              begin
                if (PSegPosn = DSegPosn) and (PSegPosn = Share)
                  then CPUs := CPUSet[1 .. CPUMax]
                else
                begin
                  CPUx := 1;
                  for M in Loc1 to LocN do
                    if (PSegPosn = M) or (DSegPosn = M) then
                    begin
                      CPUs := CPUSet[CPUx];
                      exit;
                    end
```

```
                        else CPUx := succ(CPUx);
                 end;
                 with JobWaiting[JobNum] do
                    if delayed(JobQ) and ((Reason = SwapWait)
                          or (Reason = ReturnWait)) then
                    begin
                       CurrFrame.SetUserSegs(InstrSeg, Dataseg);
                       continue(JobQ);
                    end;
              end;
           end GetCPUs;

procedure export FindMemory(MemNeeded:integer;
                            MemPosns:MemSet;
                            var Posn:MemKind;
                            var Found:Boolean);
   begin
      Found := false;
      for M in Shared to LocN do
      begin
         if (M in MemPosns) and
            (MemNeeded ≤ MemAvailable[M]) then
         begin
            Posn := M;
            MemAvailable[Posn] := MemAvailable[Posn]
                                  – MemNeeded;
            Found := true;
            return ;
         end;
      end;
   end FindMemory;

procedure export GetFrames(JobNum:ProcIndex;
                           var PFrameAdr,OSFrameAdr:Address);
   begin
      with JobProgs[JobNum], JobStack[CurrProg] do
      begin
         PFrameAdr := varadr(CurrFrame);
         OFrameAdr := varadr(OSFrame);
      end;
   end GetFrames;

function export GetProgEnt(ProgNum:ProgIndex) return ProgInf;
   begin
      return ProgArr[ProgNum];
   end GetProgEnt;

function export GetDataEnt(DataNum:ProgIndex) return DataInf;
   begin
      return DataArr[DataNum];
   end GetDataEnt;
```

```
procedure export SetProgEnt(ProgNum:ProgIndex; Ent:ProgInf;
                            WakeUpSwapper :Boolean);
begin
    ProgArr[ProgNum] := Ent;
    if WakeUpSwapper and delayed (SwapperQ)
      then continue (SwapperQ);
end SetProgEnt;

procedure export SetDataEnt(DataNum:ProgIndex; Ent:DataInf;
                            WakeUpSwapper:Boolean);
begin
    DataArr[DataNum] := Ent;
    if WakeUpSwapper and delayed(SwapperQ)
      then continue(SwapperQ);
end SetDataEnt;

procedure export MemState(var ShareSize,Loc1Size ... :integer);
begin
    ShareSize := MemAvailable[Share];
    Loc1Size := MemAvailable[Loc1];
    ...
    LocNSize := MemAvailable[LocN];
end MemState;

procedure export InitMem(ShareSize,Loc1Size ... :integer);
begin
    MemAvailable[Share] := ShareSize;
    MemAvailable[Loc1] := Loc1Size;
    ...
    MemAvailable[LocN] := LocNSize;
end InitMem;

begin {ProgTable}
    for I in 1 to ProgMax do
    begin
        ProgArr[I].Used := false;
        DataArr[I].Used := false;
    end;
    for I in JobMin to JobMax
        do JobProgs[I].CurrProg := 0;
end ProgTable;
```

SystemTable is a monitor used to store information on all system processes.
It is used primarily by the Job Manager, but both SystemTable and JobTable
would need to be accessed by any process which needs to print out the
status of each process in the system: this is often one of the functions of the
Operator process.

```
{****                  ****}
{**** System Table ****}
{****  -Outline       ****}
```

```
var
   SystemTable(SystProcMax: ProcIndex): monitor;
      function export GetData(SystNum:ProcIndex) return SystInf;
      procedure export SetData(SystNum:ProcIndex; Inf:SystInf);
         {Called by the Job Manager to read and set entries
          for system processes}
      procedure export SetOnCPU(SystNum:ProcIndex);
      procedure export SetOffCPU(SystNum:ProcIndex);
         {Called by the Job Manager to mark when a system process
          has been scheduled and when scheduling is over}
   end SystemTable;
```

```
{****                    ****}
{****      System Table  ****}
{**** –Implementation    ****}
```

```
var
   SystemTable(SystProcMax: ProcIndex): monitor;
      type export
         SystInf =
            record
               SystId: Name;
               Procs: CPUSet;
               ProcFrame: Kernel.Frame;
               OnCPU: Boolean
            end SystInf;

      var
         SystArr: array [1 .. SystProcMax] of SystInf;

      function export GetData(SystNum:ProcIndex) return SystInf;
         begin
            return SystArr[SystNum];
         end GetData;

      procedure export SetData(SystNum:ProcIndex; Inf:SystInf);
         begin
            SystArr[SystNum] := Inf;
         end SetData;

      procedure export SetOnCPU(SystNum:ProcIndex);
         begin
            SystArr[SystNum].OnCPU := true;
         end SetOnCPU;

      procedure export SetOffCPU(SystNum:ProcIndex);
         begin
            SystArr[SystNum].OnCPU := false;
         end SetOffCPU;

   end SystemTable;
```

The Job Manager schedules processes for execution and takes decisions about swapping.

```
{****                    ****}
{**** JobManager ****}
{****                    ****}

var
  JobManager: process;
    var
      CPULoad: array [CPU] of integer;
      JobSlice: integer;
      InJob: ProcIndex; OutSeg: ProgIndex;
      Kind: MemKind; MemNeeded: integer;
      CPUs: CPUSet;

    procedure ChooseCPU(ProcData:RunEntry; CPUs:CPUSet;
                        var CPUNum:CPU);
      var
        MinLoad: integer;
      begin
        CPUNum := 0; MinLoad := "largest integer value";
        for I in 1 to CPUMax do
          if I in CPUs then
            if not CPUQs[I].RunQFull and (CPULoad[I] < MinLoad)
            then
            begin
              CPUNum := I; MinLoad := CPULoad[I];
            end;
        if CPUNum ≠ 0 then
        begin
          CPUQs[CPUNum].EnterProc(ProcData);
          CPULoad[CPUNum] := CPULoad[CPUNum] + 1;
        end;
      end ChooseCPU;

    procedure ScheduleProcs;
      var
        CPUNum: integer; ProcData: RunEntry;
        JobSpecs: JobInf; SystSpecs: SystInf;
        ProgSpecs: ProgInf; DataSpecs: DataInf;
      begin
        {first schedule all active system processes}
        for I in 1 to SystProcMax do
        begin
          SystSpecs := SystemTable.GetData(I);
          with SystSpecs do
          begin
            if not (Kernel.IsBlocked(I) or Kernel.WaitingForIO(I)
                or OnCPU) then
              with ProcData do
```

```
              begin
                Id := I; OFrameAdr := varadr(ProcFrame);
                PFrameAdr := OFrameAdr; Slice := MaxSlice;
                repeat
                  ChooseCPU(ProcData, Procs, CPUNum);
                until CPUNum ≠ 0;
                SystemTable.SetOnCPU(I);
              end
          end;
        end;
        {schedule user job processes}
        for I in JobMin to JobMax do
        begin
          JobSpecs := JobTable.GetData(I);
          with JobSpecs do
            if not (Kernel.IsBlocked(I) or Kernel.WaitingForIO(I)
                or OnCPU) then
              with ProgTable do
              begin
                ProgSpecs := GetProgEnt(CurrentProg);
                DataSpecs := GetDataEnt(CurrentData);
                with ProcData do
                begin
                  GetFrames(I, PFrameAdr, OFrameAdr);
                  Id := I; Slice := "Time slice for Job";
                end;
                if (ProgSpecs.ProgState = InMemory) and
                    (DataSpecs.DataState = InMemory) then
                begin
                  ChooseCPU(ProcData, CPUs, CPUNUM);
                  if CPUNum ≠ 0
                      then JobTable.MarkRun(I);
                end
              end
        end
      end ScheduleProcs;

procedure GetProcs;
  var
    ProcNum: ProcIndex; UsedTime: integer;
  begin
    for I in 1 to CPUMax do
      with CPUQs[I] do
        while ProcOver do
        begin
          Remove(ProcNum, UsedTime);
          CPULoad[I] := CPULoad[I] − 1;
          if ProcNum ≤ SystProcMax
            then SystemTable.SetOffCPU(ProcNum)
          else JobTable.SetTime(ProcNum, UsedTime)
        end
  end GetProcs;
```

```
procedure ChooseSwapIn(var Chosen:Boolean;
                       var JobNum:ProcIndex;
                       var Kind:MemKind; var MemSize:integer);
  begin
    ...
  end ChooseSwapIn;

procedure ChooseSwapOut(Kind:MemKind; MemNeeded:integer;
                        var Chosen:Boolean;
                        var SegNum:ProgIndex);
  begin
    ...
  end ChooseSwapOut;
begin {Job Manager}
  for I in 1 to CPUMax
    do CPULoad[I] := 0;
  SwappingIn := false; SwappingOut := false;

  {Job Management Cycle}
  loop
    ScheduleProcs;
    Kernel.Suspend;
    GetProcs;
    for I in JobMin to JobMax do
    begin
      ProgTable.GetCPUs(I, CPUs);
      JobTable.SetCPUs(I, CPUs)
    end;
    if SwappingIn and not Kernel.IsBlocked(InJob)
      then SwappingIn := false;
    if SwappingOut and "segment has been swapped out"
      then SwappingOut := false;
    if not SwappingIn
      then ChooseSwapIn(SwappingIn, InJob, Kind, MemNeeded);
    if SwappingIn and not SwappingOut
        and "InSwapper is blocked for Memory" then
    begin
      ChooseSwapOut(Kind, MemNeeded, SwappingOut, OutSeg);
      MemNeeded := MemNeeded - "size of OutSeg";
    end
  end
end JobManager;
```

The procedures Enter and Depart appear in the pure class, FileSys, which has been described in Chapters 8 and 9. The procedure Enter is called by a job process to make a call to a new program; the procedure Depart is called by a job process to return to the previous program. Depart is 'automatically' called by the Kernel (see Chapter 12) when there is a malfunction during the execution of a program.

```
procedure export Enter(Dir:Name; NewProg:Name;
                              "Parameters for program call");
   {...declarations ...}
   begin
      "Collect parameters in the variable, ParBlock";
      "Call File System to read file NewProg in directory, Dir";
      if "file cannot be accessed"
         then return error FileNotFound;
      "Read first record of file NewProg";


      {Set the following variables from data in this record}
      EntryAddress := "starting address for program";
      ProgMem := "memory needed for program part";
      DataMem := "memory needed for data part";
      ProgSeparate := "program is separated";
      MemoryReq := ProgMem + DataMem;

      {Get the job process entry from JobTable}
      JobSpecs := JobTable.GetData(ProcId);
      if JobSpecs.MemLimit < MemoryReq
         then return error ProgramTooLarge;


      {Check if the program is already in use}
      ProgTable.FindNewProg(Dir, NewProg, PIndex)
         iferror return error TooManyProgCalls;
      if PIndex = 0
         then NewProgEntry := true;
      if NewProgEntry or not ProgSeparate
         {New entry must be made for program segment}
         then ProgTable.NewProgram(Dir, NewProg, PDiskPosn,
                                   InitialAddress, PKind, PIndex);
      if ProgSeparate
         {New entry must be made for data segment}
         then ProgTable.NewData(DIndex, DDiskPosn)
      else DIndex := 0;
        {There is no data part}


      {Put program and data entry indices in Job Table}
      JobTable.NextProg(PIndex, DIndex, MemoryReq);

      {Wait for program and/or data segments to be swapped in}
      ProgTable.EnterProgram(PIndex, DIndex, ProgMem, DataMem);

      "Call File System to close file NewProg in directory Dir";

      {Make Kernel call to transfer control to entry address in NewProg}
      Kernel.ProgramCall(EntryAddress, varadr(ParBlock));
   end Enter;
```

```
procedure export Depart("Parameters to be returned");
  var
    UserError: Kernel.ErrorKind;
    (other declarations }
  begin
    "Collect parameters in ParBlock";
    UserError := Kernel.GetError;
    repeat
      ProgTable.LeaveProgram(FreeISeg, FreeDSeg, ProgLev,
                             PSegPosn, DSegPosn,
                             PSeg, DSeg, PrevMem,
                             PrevPIndex, PrevDIndex);
      if FreeISeg
        then MemorySpace.Release(PSegPosn, PSeg);
      if FreeDSeg
        then MemorySpace.Release(DSegPosn, DSeg);
    until (UserError = NoError) or
          ((UserError ≠ NoError) and (ProgLev = 2));
    JobTable.NextProg(PrevPIndex, PrevDIndex, PrevMem);
    if UserError ≠ NoError
      then "Call File System to close all files";
    ProgTable.ReturnToProg; {Wait until continued by Job Manager}
    Kernel.ProgramReturn(varadr(ParBlock), UserError);
  end Depart;
```

12 THE KERNEL

The operating system described in the preceding chapters requires low-level support to perform many of its operations, such as input/output (Chapter 10) and process scheduling (Chapter 11). Other requirements for low-level support have been described in Chapters 2 and 3. The purpose of this chapter is to collect together all these requirements to provide

1. a complete specification for the low-level support and
2. guidelines for its implementation.

The program which implements this low-level support is called the *Kernel*.

Since the Kernel must execute on a multiprocessor system, it should be possible for it to be executed simultaneously on all processors. This means that the Kernel must really consist of two parts: one that is private to each processor, and the other shared by all processors. After we describe the Kernel, we shall identify the parts that are private to a processor and those that are shared by all processors.

Modes of Operation

While executing a user program, a job process can call the operating system for a service (e.g. to read text from a device). When the service is completed, the job process returns to the program from where the call originated. Thus, a job process may execute either a user program or part of the operating system, at different times. To protect the operating system from a malfunctioning user program, the parts of memory where the operating system and a user program reside are separately identified: the operating system resides in what is called the *system address space* and a user program resides in a *user address space*. We assume that the underlying architecture prevents any reference being made to the system address space while a processor is executing in a user address space.

When a processor is executing in a user address space, we say it is in *user mode*, and when executing in the system address space, it is in *system mode*. The *current state* of a processor is characterized by a set of registers whose values describe the current address space and the location of the instruction being executed. To avoid frequent saving and restoring of these registers when the processor switches from one address space to another, we assume each processor has two sets of these registers, one describing the system address space and the other a user address space. Thus, the current state of a processor is uniquely determined by its mode. A processor can be switched from a user address space to the system address space, or vice versa, by changing its mode appropriately.

When a process is to be executed on a processor, we need information about the processor state from which the execution should commence. This is provided in what we call a *frame*. When execution of a process is to be suspended, the current processor state must be saved in the process frame so that execution of the process can be resumed later. Each job process has two associated frames, one for the system address space and the other for a user address space, and a mode that determines its current state. When a processor is switched from a job process, both of its frames are saved, and when the processor is switched to another job process, both of its frames are restored. A system process (e.g. JobInitiator, JobManager) executes only in the system address space, so it requires a single frame. (In Chapter 11, two identical frames were supplied when a system process was scheduled for execution).

Entry to the Kernel

The first task performed by the Kernel is to initialize its data structures and to start execution of the scheduler processes of the operating system. From this point on, the Kernel is executed only when some particular service is to be performed. Broadly, the following services are provided by the Kernel:

1. A call from a user program to the operating system involves a switch from the user address space to the system address space: this can only be done with the help of the Kernel.
2. The Kernel provides several operations for use by the operating

system, which invokes them in the same way it invokes other procedures or functions: this is possible because both the Kernel and the operating system reside in the same (system) address space and use the same stack.

To implement many of these services, the Kernel needs to recognize *signals*, conventionally known as *interrupts*, raised by the hardware. These signals are of three kinds:

1. To execute a process for a specified time period, the Kernel sets a timer and executes the process until it receives a signal indicating that the time allotted to the process is over.
2. If an executing user program malfunctions, the processor raises an error signal. The Kernel then terminates the execution of the program and transfers control to the error handler (in Chapter 11, we saw that the error handler for all program faults is the procedure Depart).
3. To perform an input/output operation, the Kernel initiates the operation and then delays the executing process. On receiving the signal that the operation has been completed, the Kernel executes the appropriate device handler which continues the process that initiated the input/output operation.

When a processor is interrupted, it may be executing either in user mode or in system mode. On receiving the interrupt, the processor switches to system mode and starts executing the corresponding service routine (defined in the Kernel). When it is completed, the processor reverts to the mode it was in before it was interrupted, and resumes the interrupted execution.

At different times, the Kernel must switch the processor from one address space to another— this is known as *context switching*. The simplest case of context switching occurs when the processor is switched from the user address space of an executing process to the system address space of the same process, or vice versa. This can be implemented by merely changing the processor mode (and correspondingly the process mode). But when the processor is to be switched from one executing process to another, the current processor state must first be saved in the frame(s) of the executing process and a new processor state must be loaded from the frame(s) of the process to be executed. Context switching is implemented in a procedure, SwitchContext:

```
procedure SwitchContext;
    begin
        if "Time-slice over" or "Suspended" then
```

```
  begin
     "Save state of executing process";
     "Restore state of scheduler process"
  end
  else
     if "Process is to be executed" then
     begin
        "Save state of scheduler process";
        "Restore state of process to be executed"
     end;
     "Execute process"
  end SwitchContext;
```

Operating System Calls from a User

All calls to the operating system from user programs are routed through
the Kernel. When a user program is compiled, the compiler recognizes
calls to the operating system and converts each of them to a particular trap
instruction. When this trap instruction is executed in the user program, the
processor generates an interrupt that invokes the Kernel procedure,
OSCall. This procedure extracts the value parameters passed with the call,
and then makes an explicit call to the respective operating system
procedure or function with these parameters. On return, any result
parameters are stored in the user data space and control is returned to the
user program. Before returning to the user program, the procedure
SwitchContext is called: this procedure returns control to the user program
provided the job process has not exhausted its time-slice, otherwise it
switches the processor to the scheduler process.

A type, OSCallKind, enumerates the operating system procedures and
functions available to a user.

```
  type
     OSCallKind = (EnterCall, DepartCall, ...);

  procedure OSCall(Which:OSCallKind);
     begin
        "Change process mode to System mode";
        "Extract parameter values passed with the OS call";
        "Call the operating system procedure or function";
        "Store result parameters in the user data space";
        "Change process mode to User mode";
        SwitchContext
     end OSCall;
```

Kernel Calls from the Operating System

To the operating system, the Kernel appears as a library of procedures—in fact, as a pure class:

```
var
  Kernel: pure class;

    procedure Run("Process Number"; "Process Descriptor";
                "Time Allotted");

    procedure Suspend;

    procedure ProgramCall("Entry Point"; "Parameter Block");

    procedure ProgramReturn("Parameter Block"; "User Error");

    function Procld return "Process Number";

    function IsBlocked("Process Number") return "If Blocked";

    function WaitingForIO("Process Number") return "If IOWait";

    function Time return "Real-Time";

    function GetError return "Kind of Error";

    procedure LockGate("Gate");

    procedure UnlockGate("Gate");

    procedure LockLatch("Latch");

    procedure UnlockLatch("Latch");

    procedure HookProcess("Hook");

    procedure UnHookProcess("Hook");

    procedure DiskRead("Drive"; "Cylinder"; "Sector";
                "Memory Address"; "Size";
                var "Status");

    procedure DiskWrite("Drive"; "Cylinder"; "Sector";
                "Memory Address"; "Size";
                var "Status");

    procedure Read("Device Kind"; "Device Number";
                "Memory Address"; "Size";
                var "Status"; var "Count");
```

```
procedure Write("Device Kind"; "Device Number";
               "Memory Address"; "Size";
               var "Status"; var "Count");

procedure SetTTY("Terminal operation");

function TTYActive("Terminal Number") return Boolean;

end Kernel;
```

Calls from the operating system to the Kernel appear as simple procedure calls, e.g.

```
Kernel.Run(...);
```

EXECUTION OF PROCESSES AND PROGRAMS

In Chapter 11, we described different levels of process scheduling. The Kernel performs the lowest level scheduling, that of executing a process on a processor. This is implemented in the Kernel procedure, Run. It requires four parameters: (a) the system-wide unique number of the process to be executed, (b) the addresses of the user frame and the operating system frame describing the current states of the process to be executed, and (c) the time-slice allotted to the process for this execution.

```
const
   ProcessMax = 100;

type
   ProcIndex = 1 .. ProcessMax;

procedure Run(Proc:ProcIndex; UserFrameAdr,OSFrameAdr:Address;
             TimeAllotted:integer);
```

The procedure Run is invoked by the processor scheduler. Its function is to execute the process Proc (whose user and system frames have the addresses UserFrameAdr and OSFrameAdr) for a time period of TimeAllotted units.

An executing process will be interrupted after its time-slice is over. Sometimes, it may have to be suspended even before this: there are two such situations. The first is when a process gets blocked before entering a monitor or when it executes a **delay** statement (this is elaborated in the next section). The second is when the process executes the Suspend operation. In either case, the next process to be executed will be the processor scheduler.

An important feature of the operating system is that it allows a job process to call a user program: such program calls can be nested. The Kernel provides primitives to implement a call to a program and the corresponding return.

```
type
    ErrorKind = (NoError, MemoryError, DivideError, StackError,
                 ControlCsignal);

procedure ProgramCall(EntryPoint,ParBlockAdr:Address);

procedure ProgramReturn(ParBlockAdr:Address;
                        UserError:ErrorKind);
```

Here, ErrorKind is a type which enumerates the possible errors due to program malfunctions: the significance of these errors will be discussed later.

Before we proceed to describe in detail how the procedures Run, Suspend, ProgramCall and ProgramReturn are implemented, we shall first discuss the run-time representation for processes.

Process Representation

A process state is characterized by two kinds of attributes. The first category contains:

1. its run-status: whether it is currently runnable on a processor, if it is blocked in a queue, or if it is waiting for the completion of an input/output operation,
2. its mode: whether it is currently executing in a user address space or in the system address space,
3. its error-status: whether the last program executed by the process was terminated due to an error condition, and if so, the cause of the error, and
4. if the process is currently blocked in a queue, a link to the next process in the queue (a single link is sufficient because a process can be blocked only in a single queue, at any time).

This information, for all processes, is collected together in a single low-level monitor, Proclnf. (We have already used low-level monitors in Chapter 11. Their implementation will be described in this chapter.)

The second category describes the context for the process—where its instruction and data segments reside and what values the processor registers had when it was last executed on the processor. The context information of a process needs to be saved when the process calls a program and restored on return from the called program. Thus, context information must be preserved for each nested program call made by a process. This is done in the operating system, using the Kernel class type, Frame, which provides the run-time representation for a frame.

We shall first describe the low-level monitor ProcInf and then the class type Frame.

```
type export
    StatusKind = (Runnable, Blocked, IOWait);
    ModeKind = (User, System);
    ProcRange = 0 .. ProcessMax;

var
    ProcInf: monitor*;

    var
        Status: array [ProcIndex] of StatusKind;
        Mode: array [ProcIndex] of ModeKind;
        ErrorValue: array [ProcIndex] of ErrorKind;
        Link: array [ProcIndex] of ProcRange;

    procedure export SetStatus(Proc:ProcIndex; Kind:StatusKind);
        begin
            Status[Proc] := Kind
        end SetStatus;

    function export GetStatus(Proc:ProcIndex) return StatusKind;
        begin
            return Status[Proc]
        end GetStatus;

    procedure export SetMode(ModeVal:ModeKind);
        begin
            Mode[ProcId] := ModeVal
        end SetMode;

    function export GetMode return ModeKind;
        begin
            return Mode[ProcId]
        end GetMode;

    procedure export SetErrorVal(ErrVal:ErrorKind);
        begin
            ErrorValue[ProcId] := ErrVal
        end SetErrorVal;
```

```
function export GetErrorVal return ErrorKind;
  begin
    return ErrorValue[ProcId]
  end GetErrorVal;

procedure export SetLink(Proc:ProcIndex; LinkVal:ProcRange);
  begin
    Link[Proc] := LinkVal
  end SetLink;

procedure export GetLink(Proc:ProcIndex) return ProcRange;
  begin
    return Link[Proc]
  end GetLink;

begin {ProcInf}
  for I in 1 to ProcessMax do
  begin
    Status[I] := Runnable; Mode[I] := System;
    ErrorValue[I] := NoError; Link[I] := 0
  end
end ProcInf;
```

A frame contains the base addresses and sizes of the instruction and data segments, PSeg and DSeg, the value of the instruction pointer and the values of other registers. The class, Frame, provides a procedure to set PSeg and DSeg for the user address space, two procedures to save and restore the processor context, and a procedure to set the instruction pointer to an entry address.

```
type
  Frame = class;

    var
      ContextInf:
        record
          PSeg, DSeg: Seg;
          InstrPtr, StackPtr: Address;
          Regs: array [1 .. RegMax] of Register
        end ContextInf;

    procedure export SetUserSegs(ProgSeg,DataSeg:Seg);
      begin
        with ContextInf do
        begin
          PSeg := ProgSeg; DSeg := DataSeg
        end
      end SetUserSegs;
```

```
procedure export SaveContext(Mode:ModeKind);
  begin
    case Mode of
      User: "Save previous user context in ContextInf";
      System: "Save previous system context in ContextInf"
    end
  end SaveContext;

procedure export RestoreContext;
  begin
    case ProcInf.GetMode of
      User: "Restore user context from ContextInf";
      System: "Restore system context from ContextInf"
    end
  end RestoreContext;

procedure export SetEntry(EntryPoint:Address);
  begin
    ContextInf.InstrPtr := EntryPoint
  end SetEntry;

end Frame;
```

Of the procedures defined in Frame, only SetUserSegs is called by the operating system. The other procedures are used within the Kernel to save and restore the process state. The procedures SaveContext and RestoreContext are called only from the procedure SwitchContext. To restore a user context, the context information can be loaded straightway into user segment registers but restoration of the operating system context should be delayed until the actual context switch takes place in SwitchContext. In an actual implementation, the procedures SaveContext, RestoreContext and SwitchContext may have to be programmed using machine-dependent features.

The operating system passes two frame addresses as parameters to the Kernel procedure, Run. These frames must be used to restore the state of the process to be executed. For programming convenience, we use a simple form of type conversion: we define a pointer type, FramePtr, bound to the type Frame, and specify the type of the parameters as FramePtr, instead of Address (assuming pointers have the same run-time representation as the type Address, the rules of run-time parameter passing are not violated by this type conversion).

```
type
  FramePtr = pointer Frame;

procedure Run(Proc:ProcIndex; UserFrameAdr, OSFrameAdr:FramePtr;
              TimeAllotted:integer);
```

Executing Processes

To execute a process for a specified amount of time, we need a facility to accurately measure the time duration for which it is executed. The architecture provides two devices (cf. Chapter 3): (a) a system clock whose value provides the 'real-time', and (b) an interval timer on each processor which interrupts the processor after a specified time period. The interval timer can be set by the procedure SetTimer, which is used only by the Kernel. This procedure deposits a specified value in the interval counter register:

```
procedure SetTimer(Interval:integer);
   begin
      "Store Interval in the interval counter register"
   end SetTimer;
```

The interval counter is decremented (by the hardware) once for each clock 'tick'. When its value becomes zero, the timer interrupts the processor and the Kernel procedure TimerSignal (explained later) is invoked.

To execute a process on a processor, the following sequence of operations is performed:

1. the processor is first switched from the scheduler process to the scheduled process;
2. the scheduled process is then executed on the processor for the duration of time specified;
3. finally, the processor is switched from the scheduled process to the scheduler process.

To switch the processor to a scheduled process, the scheduler process calls the Kernel procedure Run:

```
var
   UserFramePtr, OSFramePtr: FramePtr;
   CurrentProc: ProcIndex;
   RunProcess: Boolean;

procedure Run(Proc:ProcIndex; UserFrameAdr,OSFrameAdr:FramePtr;
             TimeAllotted:integer);
   begin
      UserFramePtr := UserFrameAdr;
      OSFramePtr := OSFrameAdr;
      CurrentProc := Proc;
      SetTimer(TimeAllotted);
      RunProcess := true;
      SwitchContext
   end Run;
```

This procedure stores the frame pointers for the user and system address spaces of the scheduled process in the variables, UserFramePtr and OSFramePtr, and the process identifier, Proc, in a variable, CurrentProc. It sets the interval timer to the time allotted to the process and the Boolean variable RunProcess to **true**, and then invokes SwitchContext. (The SwitchContext procedure first saves the scheduler state, and then restores the frames of the process, Proc, so that its execution can be started.)

When a process has exhausted the time it was allotted, i.e. when the interval counter decreases to zero, the interval timer interrupts the processor and this causes the timer service routine, TimerSignal, to be invoked.

```
var
    TimeSliceOver, InterruptMode: Boolean;

procedure TimerSignal {invoked by interrupt};
    begin
        TimeSliceOver := true;
        InterruptMode := true;
        SwitchContext
    end TimerSignal;
```

This routine sets a Boolean variable TimeSliceOver to **true** and invokes SwitchContext so that the executing process may be pre-empted. If the process is currently executing in the operating system or in the Kernel (which is always true of an operating system process), it is not pre-empted even if it has used up its time-slice. But, if the process is currently executing in a user program, the SwitchContext procedure pre-empts the process. This it does by saving the sate of CurrentProc and then resuming the execution of the scheduler process. In the TimerSignal routine and, in fact, in all interrupt service routines, a Boolean variable InterruptMode is set to **true** before calling SwitchContext so that it can take special action for returning from an interrupt.

There are two other situations when execution of a process must be pre-empted. One is when the executing process gets blocked on monitor entry or by executing a **delay** statement; this will be explained in the next section. The other is when the Kernel procedure Suspend is explicitly called by an executing operating system process. This procedure sets the Boolean variable Suspended to **true** and invokes SwitchContext, which, once again, saves the state of the executing process and resumes execution of the scheduler process.

```
var
    Suspended: Boolean;
```

```
procedure Suspend;
  begin
    Suspended := true;
    SwitchContext
  end Suspend;
```

Program Calls

The procedure ProgramCall is called by the operating system procedure, Enter. It stores the parameter block supplied with the program call in the data segment of the current user frame, sets the entry address for the instruction segment of this frame and initializes the error state for the process. It sets a Boolean variable SwitchProgram to **true** so that when SwitchContext is called again, the processor state corresponding to user address space is restored from the new user frame of the job process.

```
var
  SwitchProgram: Boolean;

procedure ProgramCall(EntryPoint,ParBlockAdr:Address);
  begin
    "Extract parameters from ParBlockAdr and
      store them in user data space";
    UserFramePtr.SetEntry(EntryPoint);
    ProcInf.SetErrorVal(NoError);
    SwitchProgram := true
  end ProgramCall;
```

The complementary procedure, ProgramReturn, stores result parameters and error information in the user data segment. This procedure is called by the operating system procedure, Depart. It sets SwitchProgram to **true** so that when SwitchContext is called again, the processor state is restored to that of the caller program.

```
procedure ProgramReturn(ParBlockAdr:Address; UserError:ErrorKind);
  begin
    "Extract result parameters from ParBlockAdr
      and store them in user data space";
    "Store UserError in user data space";
    ProcInf.SetErrorVal(NoError);
    SwitchProgram := true
  end ProgramReturn;
```

Note that no context switching is done in the procedures ProgramCall and ProgramReturn. They merely return to the calling procedures, Enter and Depart, respectively.

Pre-emption of Program Execution

Malfunctions occurring during the execution of a program are intercepted by the Kernel. They are characterized by the type, ErrorKind.

```
type
    ErrorKind = (NoError, MemoryError, DivideError, StackError,
        ControlCsignal);
```

Of these, MemoryError, DivideError and StackError are serviced in a similar way—they record the error value for the process (in ProcInf), and call the operating system procedure Depart, which is the error-handler for program faults. We give here the service routine for MemoryError—those for DivideError and StackError are programmed similarly.

```
procedure SignalMemoryError {invoked by interrupt};
    begin
        ProcInf.SetMode(System);
        ProcInf.SetErrorVal(MemoryError);
        Depart;
        ProcInf.SetMode(User);
        InterruptMode := true;
        SwitchContext
    end SignalMemoryError;
```

ControlCsignal occurs when a Control-C character is typed on a terminal to terminate execution of the current program. Three cases must be considered. In the first case, the terminal is the controlling terminal for the currently executing process and the process is executing in User mode. This is recognized by the terminal monitor (described in the section on input/output programming) which sets a Boolean variable Preempted to **true** and then calls SwitchContext. The SwitchContext procedure stores the ControlCsignal with ProcInf and calls the operating system procedure Depart so that control is transferred to the caller program.

```
var
    Preempted: Boolean;

procedure SwitchContext;
    begin
        .
        if Preempted then
        begin
            Preempted := false;
            ProcInf.SetMode(System);
            ProcInf.SetErrorVal(ControlCsignal);
            Depart;
```

```
        ProcInf.SetMode(User);
        "Switch to caller program"
      end;
        .
        .
      end SwitchContext;
```

The second case is when the terminal is the controlling terminal for the currently executing process but the process is executing in System mode. The third case is when a process other than the one controlled by the terminal was executing on the processor. As we shall see in the section on input/output programming, in both these cases, the ControlCsignal is stored so that execution of the program can be terminated later: when the process returns to user mode (in the second case) or when it is next scheduled for execution (in the third case).

The Kernel has an array, Terminals, of terminal monitors, one for each terminal. Each terminal monitor has a Boolean function, ControlCpending, which returns the value **true** if ControlCsignal for that terminal is still awaiting action. The function, GetControlDev, returns the identification of the controlling terminal of an executing process. The second case is handled by modifying the procedure OSCall, and the third case by modifying the procedure Run.

```
      procedure OSCall(Which:OSCallKind);
        begin
          ProcInf.SetMode(System);
          "Extract value parameters passed with the OS call";
          "Call the respective OS procedure or function";
          "Store result parameters in user data space";
          if Terminals[GetControlDev].ControlCpending then
          begin
            ProcInf.SetErrorVal(ControlCsignal);
            Depart
          end;
          ProcInf.SetMode(User);
          InterruptMode := true;
          SwitchContext
        end OSCall;

      procedure Run(Proc:ProcIndex; UserFrameAdr,OSFrameAdr:FramePtr;
                    TimeAllotted:integer);
        begin
          UserFramePtr := UserFrameAdr;
          OSFramePtr := OSFrameAdr;
          CurrentProc := Proc;
          SetTimer(TimeAllotted);
          RunProcess := true;
          if ProcInf.GetMode = User then
```

```
      if Terminals[GetControlDev].ControlCpending then
      begin
        ProcInf.SetErrorVal(ControlCsignal);
        ProcInf.SetMode(System);
        "Store the value DepartCall on system stack";
        OSFramePtr.SetEntry("Address of procedure OSCall")
      end;
    SwitchContext
  end Run;
```

Context Switching

The code for the procedure SwitchContext can now be given. This procedure makes use of the Boolean variables Suspended, TimeSliceOver, RunProcess, SwitchProgram, Preempted and InterruptMode. If Suspended has the value **true**, the state of the currently executing process is saved, and the processor is switched to the scheduler process. If TimeSliceOver has the value **true**, two cases are considered: if the processor is in System mode, which can happen either because the current process is executing in System mode or because an interrupt is being serviced, execution is allowed to continue but, if the processor is in User mode, it is switched to the scheduler process after saving the state of the executing process. If RunProcess has the value **true**, the state of the scheduler process is saved in a variable, SchedulerFrame, and the processor state is restored from the user and system frames of the currently executing process. If SwitchProgram or Preempted have the value **true**, the processor state corresponding to the user address space is restored to the user frame of the currently executing process. In all cases, if InterruptMode has the value **true**, a special action is performed.

```
      var
        SchedulerFrame: Frame;

      procedure SwitchContext;
      begin
        if Suspended then
        begin
          Suspended := false;
          if "Job Process"
            then UserFramePtr.SaveContext(User);
          OSFramePtr.SaveContext(System);
          SchedulerFrame.RestoreContext
        end
        else
          if TimeSliceOver and
            (ProcInf.GetMode = User) then
```

```
                    begin
                      TimeSliceOver := false;
                      UserFramePtr.SaveContext(User);
                      SchedulerFrame.RestoreContext
                    end
                    else
                      if RunProcess then
                      begin
                        RunProcess := false;
                        SchedulerFrame.SaveContext(System);
                        if "Job Process"
                          then UserFramePtr.RestoreContext;
                        OSFramePtr.RestoreContext
                      end
                      else
                        if SwitchProgram or Preempted then
                        begin
                          if Preempted then
                          begin
                            Preempted := false;
                            ProcInf.SetMode(System);
                            ProcInf.SetErrorVal(ControlCsignal);
                            Depart;
                            ProcInf.SetMode(User)
                          end;
                          SwitchProgram := false;
                          UserFramePtr.RestoreContext
                        end;
                  if InterruptMode then
                  begin
                    InterruptMode := false;
                    "Return from interrupt and execute process"
                  end
                  else "Execute process"
                end SwitchContext;
```

Miscellaneous

The following functions are provided for use by the operating system.

The function, ProcId, returns the identification of the currently executing process:

```
        function ProcId return ProcIndex;
          begin
            return CurrentProc
          end ProcId;
```

This and CPUId, another function, which returns the identification of the executing processor, are assumed to be implicitly available in all modules of the operating system.

The functions, IsBlocked and WaitingForIO, test if a process is currently blocked in a queue, or waiting for the completion of an input/output operation, respectively.

```
function IsBlocked(Proc:ProcIndex) return Boolean;
  begin
    return (ProcInf.GetStatus(Proc) = Blocked)
  end IsBlocked;

function WaitingForIO(Proc:ProcIndex) return Boolean;
  begin
    return (ProcInf.GetStatus(Proc) = IOWait)
  end WaitingForIO;
```

The function, Time, returns the current value of the real-time clock:

```
function Time return integer;
  begin
    return "current value of clock register"
  end Time;
```

The function, GetError, returns the cause of termination for the program last executed by the calling process.

```
function GetError return ErrorKind;
  begin
    return ProcInf.GetErrorVal
  end GetError;
```

PROCESS SYNCHRONIZATION

Implementation of a monitor must guarantee that processes that access the monitor mutually exclude each other in time. This is done by blocking a requesting process if the monitor is already in use by some other process, and by unblocking one of the blocked processes when the process leaves the monitor. As we have seen in Chapter 11, an unblocked process cannot be executed on a processor until it is once again scheduled by the operating system. For some monitors, this delay in process execution is undesirable. In such cases, it is necessary to make the process 'busy-wait' until the monitor is released by the current user. Such monitors must be specially recognized: we call them *low-level* monitors, and use an asterisk (⋆) after the keyword **monitor** to identify them. In contrast, the conventional monitors that can block processes are called *high-level* monitors. We shall first describe the implementation of high-level monitors and then that of low-level monitors. In fact, we shall implement each high-level monitor using a low-level monitor.

High-Level Monitors

With each high-level monitor variable used in a CCNPascal program, the compiler allocates space for an instance of a Kernel defined type, MonitorGate. This is a low-level monitor which defines two procedures, Lock and Unlock. It has a Boolean variable, Open, which has the value **true** when the high-level monitor is not currently being used by any process. It also has two variables, MonQHead and MonQTail, which represent the head and tail of a queue of processes waiting to use the high-level monitor.

```
var
  Open: Boolean;
  MonQHead, MonQTail: ProcRange;
```

If Open has the value **false**, some process is currently executing within the high-level monitor. So, if any other process requests entry to the monitor when Open is **false**, it is blocked on the monitor queue. This is implemented in the procedure Lock.

```
procedure export Lock;
  begin
    if Open
      then Open := false
      else
      begin
        "Enter the executing process in the monitor queue";
        "Block the executing process"
      end
  end Lock;
```

Before a process executing in a high-level monitor leaves the monitor, it checks if any other process is waiting to enter the monitor and, if so, allows the process at the head of the monitor queue to enter the monitor. This is implemented in the procedure Unlock.

```
procedure export Unlock;
  begin
    if MonQHead = 0
      then Open := true
      else
```

```
    begin
      "Remove the process, Proc, from
       the head of the monitor queue";
      "Unblock the process Proc"
    end
  end UnLock;
```

Two local procedures, EnterMonQ and RemoveMonQ, are provided to enter
and remove a process from the monitor queue. Another procedure,
NewMonQHead, is provided to put a given process at the head of the
monitor queue: this will be used later in the implementation of the **delay**
and **continue** operations on **queue** variables. The complete description of
MonitorGate can now be given.

```
    type
      MonitorGate = monitor*
                        import
                            var : ProcInf, Suspended
                        end;

    var
      Open: Boolean;
      MonQHead, MonQTail: ProcRange;

    procedure EnterMonQ(Proc:ProcIndex);
      begin
        if MonQHead = 0
          then MonQHead := Proc
          else ProcInf.SetLink(MonQTail, Proc);
        MonQTail := Proc;
        ProcInf.SetLink(MonQTail, 0)
      end EnterMonQ;

    procedure RemoveMonQ(var Proc:ProcIndex);
      begin
        Proc := MonQHead;
        MonQHead := ProcInf.GetLink(MonQHead)
      end RemoveMonQ;

    procedure export Lock;
      begin
        if Open
          then Open := false
          else
          begin
            EnterMonQ(ProcId);
            ProcInf.SetStatus(ProcId, Blocked);
            Suspended := true
          end
      end Lock;
```

```
procedure export UnLock;
  var
    Proc: ProcIndex;
  begin
    if MonQHead = 0
      then Open := true
    else
    begin
      RemoveMonQ(Proc);
      ProcInf.SetStatus(Proc, Runnable)
    end
  end UnLock;

procedure export NewMonQHead(Proc:ProcIndex);
  begin
    ProcInf.SetLink(Proc, MonQHead);
    if MonQHead = 0
      then MonQTail := Proc;
    MonQHead := Proc
  end NewMonQHead;

begin
  Open := false; MonQHead := 0; MonQTail := 0
end MonitorGate;
```

A subtle issue must be considered in the implementation of processes and monitors. A process has some initialization code (implicitly inserted by the compiler) which is used to initialize its global variables (e.g., classes, monitors, pure classes). The shared variables (i.e., monitors and pure classes) declared by a process should not be used by other processes until they are initialized. To guarantee this, the Open flag of a monitor gate is initialized to **false** (as shown above). The compiler inserts a call to UnLock at the end of the initialization code of the high-level monitor (but no call to Lock is inserted at the beginning of the initialization code).

Queues

Within a monitor, there may be instructions to delay an executing process on a **queue** variable, or to continue a process that was previously delayed. When a **continue** operation is performed, the process that is to be resumed is put at the head of the monitor queue (with its status remaining Blocked). The executing process continues to execute the monitor code. When it leaves the monitor (by invoking the procedure UnLock on the monitor gate), it changes the status of the process waiting at the head of the monitor queue to Runnable.

A CCNPascal **queue** variable is represented as an instance of the class

type, ProcessHook. It provides two procedures, DelayProcess and ContinueProcess, corresponding to the **delay** and **continue** operations of
CCNPascal.

```
type
  ProcessHook = class
                  import
                    var : ProcInf, Suspended
                  end;

  var
    HookInUse: Boolean;
    HookedProc: ProcIndex;

  procedure export DelayProcess(Gate:MonitorGate);
  begin
    if not HookInUse then
    begin
      HookInUse := true;
      HookedProc := ProcId;
      ProcInf.SetStatus(HookedProc, Blocked);
      Gate.UnLock;
      Suspended := true
    end
  end DelayProcess;

  procedure export ContinueProcess(Gate:MonitorGate);
  begin
    if HookInUse then
    begin
      HookInUse := false;
      Gate.NewMonQHead(HookedProc)
    end
  end ContinueProcess;

  begin
    HookInUse := false
  end ProcessHook;
```

Low-level Monitors

We have used low-level monitors (in Chapter 11, as well as in this chapter)
as a means of guaranteeing mutual exclusion and synchronization, not by
blocking a calling process when the monitor is busy, but by forcing its host
processor to busy-wait until the monitor is released by some other
processor. In the previous section, low-level monitors were also used in the
implementation of high-level monitors. We shall now describe the
implementation of low-level monitors.

Instead of MonitorGate, we use a different abstraction, Latch, for the implementation of low-level monitors.

```
type
    Latch = class;
        procedure Lock;
        procedure UnLock;
    end Latch;
```

When a processor (to be precise, a process executing on the processor) requests entry to a low-level monitor by making a call to the procedure Lock, a test is made to see if some other processor is already executing the monitor code: if so, the requesting processor is made to loop until that processor relinquishes control. If no processor is currently executing the monitor code, the requesting processor is allowed to enter the monitor. When a processor executing the monitor code relinquishes control, by making a call to the procedure UnLock, one of the processors waiting (i.e. looping) to execute the monitor is allowed to do so.

At the outset, it appears that the procedure Lock can be implemented by using a Boolean variable to record if the monitor is currently in use by some processor, and by testing the Boolean variable before allowing a processor to execute the monitor code. But there is the danger that two or more processors simultaneously test the Boolean variable, find the monitor free, and simultaneously start executing the monitor code. This problem can be resolved if the underlying architecture provides an indivisible 'test and set' instruction. Equivalently, it is sufficient if the architecture provides indivisible 'read–modify' memory cycles— which is what we assume about the underlying architecture (cf. Chapter 3). But, then, a Boolean variable cannot serve the purpose. Instead, we use an integer variable WaitCount in which we maintain the negative of the number of waiting processes.

We should also ensure that no processor is kept waiting indefinitely to enter a low-level monitor. For this, we require an array of Boolean variables which are allocated in shared memory. Each elememt of the array is used record the status (waiting or otherwise) of a particular processor. We also need to identify, for each looping processor, the latch on which it is looping: we do this by using the address of the variable WaitCount as the identification of the latch. With this background, the class, Latch, can be programmed.

```
var
    WaitingCPU: array [1 .. CPUMax] of Boolean;
    LatchId: array [1 .. CPUMax] of Address;
    {both arrays allocated in shared memory}
    {each element of waitingCPU initialized to false}
```

```
type
  Latch = class
            import
               var : WaitingCPU, LatchId
            end;

    var
      WaitCount: integer;

    procedure export Lock;
      begin
        WaitCount := WaitCount − 1 {indivisible operation};
        if WaitCount < 0 then
        begin
          WaitingCPU[CPUId] := true;
          LatchId[CPUId] := varadr(WaitCount);
          while WaitingCPU[CPUId]
            do {nothing};
        end
      end Lock;

    procedure export UnLock;
      var
        J: 1 .. CPUMax;
      begin
        if WaitCount < 0 then
        begin
          J := CPUId;
          for I in 1 to CPUMax do
          begin
            J := (J mod CPUMax) + 1;
            if WaitingCPU[J]
                and (LatchId[J] = varadr(WaitCount)) then
            begin
              WaitingCPU[J] := false;
              exit
            end
          end
        end;
        WaitCount := WaitCount + 1 {indivisible operation}
      end UnLock;

    begin {Latch}
      WaitCount := 1
    end Latch;
```

Here, CPUId is a function which returns the identification (an integer between 1 and CPUMax) of the executing processor. Fairness in scheduling is guaranteed by a round-robin strategy.

As in a high-level monitor, **queue** variables and the **delay** and **continue** operations can also be used in a low-level monitor. But, when used in a low-level monitor, they must be implemented differently. The procedures DelayProcess and ContinueProcess implementing the **delay** and **continue** operations in a low-level monitor must take a variable L of type Latch as a parameter instead of a MonitorGate. The code for DelayProcess is the same except that it should now use L.Unlock instead of Gate.Lock. The procedure ContinueProcess should set HookInUse to **false** and should do no more (note that there is no monitor queue stored with a low-level monitor). A **delay** operation used in a low-level monitor should be implemented as a call to DelayProcess and immediately followed by a call to L.Lock, i.e., the latch must be acquired anew before the process can continue.

Routing Calls to Synchronization Operations

The procedure Lock of type MonitorGate sets the Boolean variable Suspended to **true** but it does not call the procedure SwitchContext. In fact, SwitchContext should not be called from any low-level monitor for, otherwise, the executing processor will be switched away from the low-level monitor but without releasing its latch: as a result, no other processor will ever be able to enter the low-level monitor, and this is a deadlock situation. For uniformity, we also avoid calling SwitchContext from the type ProcessHook and, instead, in its procedure DelayProcess, we set Suspended to **true**. As part of the Kernel pure class, we shall now define procedures which route calls to these synchronization operations and which also call SwitchContext where necessary.

```
var
  Kernel: pure class
          import
              procedure : SwitchContext
          end;

      ...
    procedure export LockGate(Gate:MonitorGate);
      begin
        Gate.Lock;
        SwitchContext
      end LockGate;

    procedure export UnlockGate(Gate:MonitorGate);
      begin
        Gate.Unlock
      end UnlockGate;

    procedure export LockLatch(L:Latch);
      begin
        L.Lock
      end LockLatch;
```

```
procedure export UnlockLatch(L:Latch);
  begin
    L.Unlock;
    if InterruptMode
      then SwitchContext
  end UnlockLatch;

procedure export HookProcess(Hook:ProcessHook;
                                     Gate:MonitorGate);
  begin
    Hook.DelayProcess(Gate);
    SwitchContext
  end HookProcess;

procedure export UnhookProcess(Hook:ProcessHook;
                                     Gate:MonitorGate);
  begin
    Hook.ContinueProcess(Gate)
  end UnhookProcess;
  ...
end Kernel;
```

An exported procedure of a low-level monitor may be designated as an interrupt service routine (this feature is not provided for high-level abstractions, namely, **class, monitor, pure class** or **process**). We use this feature in all device monitors, which happen to be low-level monitors, described in the next section. It is necessary to call SwitchContext at the end of each device interrupt service routine but, as we have mentioned already, SwitchContext should not be called from a low-level monitor before releasing its latch. To avoid this problem, we programmed the UnlockLatch procedure of the Kernel pure class (see above) so that it first unlocks the latch and, if InterruptMode has the value **true**, also calls SwitchContext.

INPUT/OUTPUT PROGRAMMING

The machine configuration underlying our operating system supports four kinds of devices: disk drives, card readers, line printers and terminals. A disk is a shared device. The card reader, line printer and terminal are assigned devices. Controlling access to assigned devices by multiple users is done by the operating system (cf. Chapter 10). In the Kernel, we assume that for each assigned device there can be at most one user at any time. Access to a disk is controlled within the Kernel by queuing and scheduling requests. We shall first describe the device handlers and then the common interface to the rest of the operating system.

Disk Device

In Chapter 2, we described one version of the elevator algorithm for efficient scheduling of disk accesses where the disk scheduler was programmed as a monitor. To provide fast access to the disk, and to increase disk utilization, we shall use a slightly different version in the Kernel. This version differs from the earlier one in two ways:

1. DiskMonitor is programmed here as a low-level monitor, which ensures that a requesting process is not blocked because another request is being registered.
2. The procedure Release of DiskMonitor is implicitly invoked by an interrupt from the disk controller after the completion of each disk transfer, and this guarantees that the next disk transfer, if one is pending, is initiated soon after the completion of the earlier request.

Instead of exporting the procedure Request, two procedures Read and Write are exported: these make use of the local procedure Request.

```
type
    IOStatus = (Done, OffLine, TransferErr, EndOfFile):

type
    DiskMonitor(DriveNum: integer) = monitor*
                                import
                                    var : InterruptMode;
                                    procedure : DiskTransfer
                                end;

    type
        TransferType = (DiskRead, DiskWrite);

    var
        DiskQ: array [1 .. ProcessMax] of
                    record
                        TransferKind: TransferType;
                        CylinderNum, SectorNum, {disk address}
                        DataSize, {size of data to be read}
                        MemoryAdr: integer;
                        DiskStatus: IOStatus;
                        Q: queue
                    end DiskQ;
        Up, {gives direction of disk-head movement}
        Busy, {true only if an I/O is in progress}
        Selected: Boolean; {true if the next user has
                                already been selected}
        HeadPosition: integer; {Current disk-head position}
        CurrentUser, {I/O of this user in progress}
        NextUser: ProcIndex; {next user to be served}
```

```
procedure InitTransfer(Proc:ProcIndex);
  begin
    with DiskQ[Proc] do
    begin
      DiskTransfer(DriveNum, TransferKind,
                         CylinderNum, SectorNum,
                         DataSize, MemoryAdr);
      HeadPosition := CylinderNum
    end;
    CurrentUser := Proc;
    Selected := false
  end InitTransfer;

procedure SelectNextUser;
  procedure FindNextUser;
    begin
      "search pending requests in the direction of
        current head movement and select process NextUser
        whose request is closest to current HeadPosition";
      Selected := "true if such NextUser was found and
                         false otherwise"
    end FindNextUser;
  begin {SelectNextUser}
    FindNextUser;
    if not Selected then
    begin
      Up := not Up;
      FindNextUser
    end
  end SelectNextUser;

procedure Request(Kind:TransferType;
                     CylNum,SectNum,Size,MemAdr:integer;
                     var Status:IOStatus);
  begin
    with DiskQ[ProcId] do
    begin
      TransferKind := Kind;
      CylinderNum := CylNum;
      SectorNum := SectNum;
      DataSize := Size; MemoryAdr := MemAdr;
      if not Busy then
      begin
        Busy := true;
        InitTransfer(ProcId)
      end;
      SelectNextUser;
      delay(Q);
      Status := DiskStatus
    end
  end Request;
```

```
procedure export Read(CylNum,SectNum,Size,MemAdr:integer;
                          var Status:IOStatus);
  begin
    Request(DiskRead, CylNum, SectNum, Size, MemAdr, Status)
  end Read;

procedure export Write(CylNum,SectNum,Size,MemAdr:integer;
                          var Status:IOStatus);
  begin
    Request(DiskWrite, CylNum, SectNum, Size, MemAdr, Status)
  end Write;

procedure export Release {invoked by interrupt};
  begin
    with DiskQ[CurrentUser] do
    begin
      DiskStatus := "Status of the disk operation
                          as obtained from disk status register";
      continue(Q)
    end;
    if not Selected
      then SelectNextUser;
    if Selected
      then InitTransfer(NextUser)
      else Busy := false;
    InterruptMode := true
  end Release;

begin {DiskMonitor}
  Up := true; Busy := false; Selected := false;
  CurrentUser := 0; NextUser := 0
end DiskMonitor;
```

The procedure, DiskTransfer, initiates data transfer between the disk and main memory. Completion of this operation is signalled by an interrupt which is serviced by procedure Release of DiskMonitor.

It is possible that a process initiates a disk operation while it is executing on a different processor from the one to which the disk is connected. In such cases, the inter-process interrupt (IPI) mechanism of the underlying architecture (see Chapter 3) is used to initiate the disk operation. A similar method is used for other devices.

We need a separate disk monitor to control operations on each of the DriveMax disk units; we organize them in an array of type DiskMonitor:

```
var
  Disks: array [1 .. DriveMax] of DiskMonitor;
```

Card Reader

The card reader monitor has a procedure, ReadCard, which is called by a user to read a card, and a procedure, ReadDone, which is implicitly invoked by the card reader controller (by an interrupt) after the completion of a read operation.

```
type
  CardReader(DevNum: integer) = monitor*
                                import
                                    var : InterruptMode
                                end;

    var
      ReadStatus: IOStatus:
      Q: queue;

    procedure export ReadCard(MemAdr:integer;
                              var Status:IOStatus);
        begin
          "Initiate operation to read from device number DevNum
           to memory locations starting at MemAdr";
          delay(Q);
          Status := ReadStatus
        end ReadCard;

    procedure export ReadDone {invoked by interrupt};
        begin
          ReadStatus := "Status of card-read operation as
                             obtained from card reader status register";
          continue(Q);
          InterruptMode := true
        end ReadDone;

    end CardReader;

var
  CRs: array [1 .. CRMax] of CardReader;
```

Line Printer

The line printer monitor is very similar. It has a procedure, PrintLine, which is called by a user to print a line, and a procedure, PrintDone, which is implicitly invoked by the line printer controller (by an interrupt) after the completion of a print operation.

```
type
    LinePrinter(DevNum: integer) = monitor*
                                    import
                                        var : InterruptMode
                                    end;

    var
        PrintStatus: IOStatus:
        Q: queue;

    procedure export PrintLine(MemAdr:integer; var Status:IOStatus);
        begin
            "Initiate operation to print on device number DevNum
            from memory locations starting at MemAdr";
            delay(Q);
            Status := PrintStatus
        end PrintLine;

    procedure export PrintDone {invoked by interrupt};
        begin
            PrintStatus := "Status of print-line operation as
                                obtained from the line printer status register";
            continue(Q);
            InterruptMode := true
        end PrintDone;

    end LinePrinter;

var
    LPs: array [1 .. LPMax] of LinePrinter;
```

Terminals

For the Kernel, a terminal is a pair of devices: a keyboard and a display.
Input from a keyboard is read even when no read operation has been
requested on the terminal. Output to a display, however, is done only on
explicit request. Several options are available for a terminal—these are
characterized by a type, TTYOp (cf. Chapter 10).

```
type
    TTYOp = (Echo, NoEcho, Format, NoFormat, ContrlDev,
            NotContrlDev);
```

If the Echo option is requested, each character typed on the keyboard is
immediately displayed before it is buffered in a line; the NoEcho option
suppresses echoing. If the Format option is requested, the characters
Control-O, Control-R and Rub-Out (or Delete) have special significance.

A Control-O inactivates the display (echoing is unaffected) and another Control-O reactivates the display. A Control-R has the effect of displaying the contents of the current keyboard line buffer. A Rub-Out character deletes the last character in the keyboard line buffer. If a terminal is the controlling terminal for a job process, and if a Control-C character is typed on the keyboard while a program is executing, the program is abruptly terminated and a return is forced.

It is necessary to maintain a mapping of processes and their controlling terminals. A procedure SetControlDev assigns a given terminal as the controlling terminal for the executing process. A function GetControlDev can be used to get the controlling terminal number of the executing process.

```
type
    TerminalRange = 0 .. TerminalMax;
var
    ControlTTYs: array [ProcIndex] of TerminalRange;
    {allocated in shared memory}

procedure SetControlDev(TTYNum:TerminalRange);
    begin
        ControlTTYs[ProcId] := TTYNum
    end SetControlDev;

function GetControlDev return TerminalRange;
    begin
        return ControlTTYs[ProcId]
    end GetControlDev;
```

An instance of the (low-level) monitor type, Terminal, is used to control both the keyboard and the display of a terminal.

```
type
    Terminal = monitor*
                    import
                        var : Preempted, InterruptMode;
                        function : GetControlDev
                    end;

        const
            LineLength = 200;
            CR = 15B; LF = 12B;

        type export
            CharSet = set of char;

        var
            TTYId: TerminalRange;
            ToBeDisplayed, ToBeEchoed, ToBeFormatted, WritePending,
```

```
        ControlCoption, ControlCchar, ControlRchar: Boolean;
        KBDBuf, TTYBuf: string(LineLength);
        KBDPtr, TTYPtr: 0 .. LineLength;
        ReadSize, WriteSize: integer;
        KBDQ, TTYQ: queue;
        KBDStatus: IOStatus;
        KBDChar: char;
        EndChars: CharSet;

    procedure export Read(MemAdr:Address; Size:integer;
                            var Status:IOStatus; var Count:integer);
      begin
        ReadSize := Size;
        if KBDPtr < ReadSize
          then delay(KBDQ);
        "Move characters from KBDBuf to MemAdr";
        Count := KBDPtr; KBDPtr := 0;
        Status := KBDStatus; KBDStatus := Done;
        ReadSize := 0
      end Read;

    procedure export ReadDone {invoked by interrupt};
      begin
        KBDChar := "Character obtained from keyboard buffer";
        if (KBDChar = ControlC) and ControlCoption then
          if (GetControlDev = TTYId)
               and "previous processor mode is User"
            then Preempted := true
          else ControlCchar := true
        else
          if KBDChar = ControlZ
            then KBDStatus := EndOfFile
          else
            if (KBDChar in CharSet[ControlO, ControlR, RubOut])
                            and ToBeFormatted then
              case KBDChar of
                ControlO: ToBeDisplayed := not ToBeDisplayed;
                ControlR:
                  begin
                    ControlRchar := true;
                    if not WritePending
                      then "enable interrupt for output on TTYId"
                  end;
                RubOut:
                  if KBDPtr > 1
                    then KBDPtr := KBDPtr - 1
              end
            else
            begin
              if ToBeEchoed and not WritePending
                then "display KBDChar on TTYId";
```

```
            KBDPtr := KBDPtr + 1;
            KBDBuf[KBDPtr] := KBDChar
          end;
      if (KBDPtr = ReadSize) or (KBDChar in EndChars)
          or (KBDStatus = EndOfFile) or ControlCchar
        then continue(KBDQ);
      InterruptMode := true
    end ReadDone;


  procedure export Write(MemAdr:Address; Size:integer);
    begin
      if ToBeDisplayed then
      begin
        "Extract characters to be output from MemAdr
          and store them in TTYBuf";
        TTYPtr := 0;
        WriteSize := Size;
        WritePending := true;
        "Enable interrupt for output on TTYId";
        delay(TTYQ)
      end
    end Write;


  procedure export WriteDone {invoked by interrupt};
    begin
      if WritePending
        then
        if (TTYPtr < WriteSize) and ToBeDisplayed then
        begin
          TTYPtr := TTYPtr + 1;
          "Display TTYBuf[TTYPtr] on TTYId"
        end
        else
        begin
          WritePending := false; continue(TTYQ)
        end
      else
        if ControlRchar then
        begin
          TTYBuf[1] := chr(CR);
          TTYBuf[2] := chr(LF);
          for I in 1 to KBDPtr
            do TTYBuf[I + 2] := KBDBuf[I];
          WriteSize := KBDPtr + 2;
          ControlRchar := false;
          "Enable interrupt for output on TTYId"
        end
        else "Disable interrupt for output on TTYId";
      InterruptMode := true
    end WriteDone;
```

```
    procedure export SetEndChars(Chars:CharSet);
      begin
        EndChars := Chars
      end SetEndChars;

    procedure export SetTTYOp(Op:TTYOp);
      begin
        case Op of
          Echo: ToBeEchoed := true;
          NoEcho: ToBeEchoed := false;
          Format: ToBeFormatted := true;
          NoFormat: ToBeFormatted := false;
          ContrlDev: ControlCoption := true;
          NotContrlDev: ControlCoption := false
        end
      end SetTTYOp;

    function export ControlCpending return Boolean;
      var
        Status: Boolean;
      begin
        Status := ControlCchar;
        ControlCchar := false;
        return Status
      end ControlCpending;

    procedure export SetTTYNum(TTYNum:TerminalRange);
      begin
        TTYId := TTYNum
      end SetTTYNum;

    function export InputPending return Boolean;
      begin
        return (KBDPtr > 0)
      end InputPending;

  begin
    ToBeDisplayed := true;
    ToBeEchoed := true;
    ToBeFormatted := true;
    WritePending := false;
    ControlCoption := true;
    ControlCchar := false;
    ControlRchar := false;
    KBDStatus := Done;
    EndChars := CharSet[chr(CR), chr(LF)];
    BufPtr := 0; ReadSize := 0; WriteSize := 0
  end Terminal;

var
  Terminals: array [1 .. TerminalMax] of Terminal;
```

Routing Calls to Input/Output Operations

The part of the Kernel pure class that routes calls to input/output operations
is given below.

```
var
  Kernel: pure class
            import
                var : Disks, CRs, LPs, Terminals
            end;

    type export
      DevKind = (DiskDev, CRDev, LPDev, TTYDev);

    procedure export DiskRead(Drive,Cylinder,Sector:integer;
                              MemAdr:Address; Size:integer;
                              var Status:IOStatus);
      begin
        Disks[Drive].Read(Cylinder, Sector, Size, MemAdr, Status);
      end DiskRead;

    procedure export DiskWrite(Drive,Cylinder,Sector:integer;
                               MemAdr:Address; Size:integer;
                               var Status:IOStatus);
      begin
        Disks[Drive].Write(Cylinder, Sector, Size, MemAdr, Status);
      end DiskWrite;

    procedure export Read(Kind:DevKind; DevNum:integer;
                          MemAdr:Address; Size:integer;
                          var Status:IOStatus; var Count:integer);
      begin
        case Kind of
          CRDev: CRs[DevNum].ReadCard(MemAdr, Status);
          TTYDev: Terminals[DevNum].Read(MemAdr, Size, Status,
                                         Count);
        end;
      end Read;

    procedure export Write(Kind:DevKind; DevNum:integer;
                           MemAdr:Address; Size:integer;
                           var Status:IOStatus;
                           var Count:integer);
      begin
        case Kind of
          LPDev: LPs[DevNum].PrintLine(MemAdr, Status);
          TTYDev: Terminals[DevNum].Write(MemAdr, Size)
        end;
      end Write;
```

```
procedure export SetTTY(TTYNum:integer; Op:TTYOp);
begin
    Terminals[TTYNum].SetTTYOp(Op)
end SetTTY;

function export TTYActive(TTYNum:integer) return Boolean;
begin
    return Terminals[TTYNum].InputPending
end TTYActive;

end Kernel;
```

Miscellaneous

CCNPascal provides a function **varadr** to compute the absolute address of a variable; this is used, for example, when calling the device monitors. It is implemented in the Kernel as the function GetVarAdr:

```
function GetVarAdr(Adr:Address) return integer;
begin
    "Compute absolute address using the appropriate data segment"
end GetVarAdr;
```

DISCUSSION

To implement the Kernel in a multiprocessor environment, it is necessary to identify the parts of the Kernel that must be shared by different processors and those that must exist separately for each processor. Data for all monitor variables declared in the Kernel must be allocated in the shared memory. Additionally, the arrays WaitingCPU and LatchId, which are used in the implementation of processor exclusion, as also the array ControlTTYs, must be allocated in the shared memory. A separate copy of the variables CurrentProc, UserFramePtr, OSFramePtr and SchedulerFrame must be allocated for each processor. Similarly, the Boolean variables Suspended, TimeSliceOver, SwitchProgram and RunProcess must be allocated for each processor, and they must all be initialized to the value **false**.

With regard to the code for timer and error interrupts, it is desirable to have a separate service routine for each processor and store it in its local memory (this ensures fast execution of interrupt service routines). Similarly, for each device, a separate interrupt service routine may be used for each processor to which the device is connected. The rest of the Kernel code is re-entrant and can be shared by all processors. However, to improve performance, it may be preferable to store the Kernel code separately in the local memory of each processor.

We have considered only some of the errors that can be signalled by a malfunctioning program or processor. In an actual implementation, it is usually necessary to recognize other kinds of errors (e.g. power failure) and service them appropriately.

EXERCISES

1. Some parts of the Kernel program (e.g., the procedures SwitchContext and OSCall) cannot be programmed in CCNPascal as they require use of machine-dependent features. Taking any particular machine, code these procedures in a low-level language. If possible, assume you have a multiprocessor configuration.

2. High-level monitors have been implemented using the operations of low-level monitors, and the implementation of low-level monitors has been described separately. If the system has a single processor, are low-level monitors still required? Code the program components MonitorGate and ProcessHook for a single processor system.

3. Assume the operating is required to provide an operation, TimeWait, which can be used by any user program to suspend its execution for a specified number of time units. How can this operation be implemented and what additional Kernel operation(s) will be required? Will these Kernel Operations suffice for implementing another operating system operation, WaitUntil, which allows a user program to wait until a specified time of the day?

4. Design a version of DiskMonitor to use the operations provided by a real disk controller. For this disk, how would the parameters of the disk space allocator (Chapter 7) need to be set?

THE KERNEL PROGRAM

```
{***          ***}
{*** Kernel   ***}
{*** –Outline ***}
```

var
  Kernel: **pure class**;

    procedure Run("Process Number"; "Process Descriptor";
           "Time Allotted");

    procedure Suspend;

    procedure ProgramCall("Entry Point"; "Parameter Block");

    procedure ProgramReturn("Parameter Block"; "User Error");

    function ProcId **return** "Process Number";

    function IsBlocked("Process Number") **return** "If Blocked";

    function WaitingForIO("Process Number") **return** "If IOWait";

    function Time **return** "Real-Time";

    function GetError **return** "Kind of Error";

    procedure LockGate("Gate");

    procedure UnlockGate("Gate");

    procedure LockLatch("Latch");

    procedure UnlockLatch("Latch");

    procedure HookProcess("Hook");

    procedure UnHookProcess("Hook");

    procedure DiskRead("Drive"; "Cylinder"; "Sector";
          "Memory Address"; "Size";
          var "Status");

    procedure DiskWrite("Drive"; "Cylinder"; "Sector";
          "Memory Address"; "Size";
          var "Status");

```
procedure Read("Device Kind"; "Device Number";
               "Memory Address"; "Size";
               var "Status"; var "Count");

procedure Write("Device Kind"; "Device Number";
                "Memory Address"; "Size";
                var "Status"; var "Count");

procedure SetTTY("Terminal operation");

function TTYActive("Terminal Number") return Boolean;

end Kernel;


{***                      ***}
{***      Kernel          ***}
{*** –Implementation ***}
```

```
const export
  ProcessMax = 100;
type export
  ProcIndex = 1 .. ProcessMax;
var
  CurrentProc: ProcIndex;


type
  ProcRange = 0 .. ProcessMax;
  StatusKind = (Runnable, Blocked, IOWait);
  ModeKind = (User, System);
  ErrorKind = (NoError, MemoryError, DivideError, StackError,
               ControlCsignal);

var
  ProcInf: monitor*;

    var
      Status: array [ProcIndex] of StatusKind;
      Mode: array [ProcIndex] of ModeKind;
      ErrorValue: array [ProcIndex] of ErrorKind;
      Link: array [ProcIndex] of ProcRange;

    procedure export SetStatus(Proc:ProcIndex; Kind:StatusKind);
      begin
        Status[Proc] := Kind
      end SetStatus;

    function export GetStatus(Proc:ProcIndex) return StatusKind;
      begin
        return Status[Proc]
      end GetStatus;
```

```
procedure export SetMode(ModeVal:ModeKind);
  begin
    Mode[CurrentProc] := ModeVal
  end SetMode;

function export GetMode return ModeKind;
  begin
    return Mode[CurrentProc]
  end GetMode;

procedure export SetErrorVal(ErrVal:ErrorKind);
  begin
    ErrorValue[CurrentProc] := ErrVal
  end SetErrorVal;

function export GetErrorVal return ErrorKind;
  begin
    return ErrorValue[CurrentProc]
  end GetErrorVal;

procedure export SetLink(Proc:ProcIndex; LinkVal:ProcRange);
  begin
    Link[Proc] := LinkVal
  end SetLink;

procedure export GetLink(Proc:ProcIndex) return ProcRange;
  begin
    return Link[Proc]
  end GetLink;

begin {ProcInf}
  for I in 1 to ProcessMax do
  begin
    Status[I] := Runnable;
    Mode[I] := System;
    ErrorValue[I] := NoError;
    Link[I] := 0
  end
end ProcInf;

type
  Frame = class;

    var
      ContextInf:
        record
          PSeg, DSeg: Seg;
          InstrPtr, StackPtr: Address;
          Regs: array [1 .. RegMax] of Register
        end ContextInf;
```

```
procedure export SetUserSegs(ProgSeg,DataSeg:Seg);
  begin
    with ContextInf do
    begin
      PSeg := ProgSeg; DSeg := DataSeg
    end
  end SetUserSegs;

procedure export SaveContext(Mode:ModeKind);
  begin
    case Mode of
      User: "Save previous user context in ContextInf";
      System: "Save previous system context in ContextInf"
    end
  end SaveContext;

procedure export RestoreContext;
  begin
    case ProcInf.GetMode of
      User: "Restore user context from ContextInf";
      System: "Restore system context from ContextInf"
    end
  end RestoreContext;

procedure export SetEntry(EntryPoint:Address);
  begin
    ContextInf.InstrPtr := EntryPoint
  end SetEntry;

end Frame;

type
  FramePtr = pointer Frame;

var
  UserFramePtr, OSFramePtr: FramePtr;
  SchedulerFrame: Frame;
  Suspended, TimeSliceOver, RunProcess, SwitchProgram, Preempted,
  InterruptMode: Boolean;

procedure SwitchContext;
  begin
    if Suspended then
    begin
      Suspended := false;
      if "Job Process"
        then UserFramePtr ↑ .SaveContext(User);
      OSFramePtr ↑ .SaveContext(System);
      SchedulerFrame.RestoreContext
    end
    else
```

```
            if TimeSliceOver and
               (ProcInf.GetMode = User) then
            begin
              TimeSliceOver := false;
              UserFramePtr ↑ .SaveContext(User);
              SchedulerFrame.RestoreContext
            end
            else
              if RunProcess then
              begin
                RunProcess := false;
                SchedulerFrame.SaveContext(System);
                if "Job Process"
                   then UserFramePtr ↑ .RestoreContext;
                OSFramePtr ↑ .RestoreContext
              end
              else
                if SwitchProgram or Preempted then
                begin
                  if Preempted then
                  begin
                    Preempted := false;
                    ProcInf.SetMode(System);
                    ProcInf.SetErrorVal(ControlCsignal);
                    Depart;
                    ProcInf.SetMode(User)
                  end;
                  SwitchProgram := false;
                  UserFramePtr ↑ .RestoreContext
                end;
        if InterruptMode then
        begin
          InterruptMode := false;
          "Return from interrupt and execute process"
        end
        else "Execute process"
      end SwitchContext;

    procedure TimerSignal {invoked by interrupt};
      begin
        TimeSliceOver := true;
        InterruptMode := true;
        SwitchContext
      end TimerSignal;

    procedure SignalMemoryError {invoked by interrupt};
      begin
        ProcInf.SetMode(System);
        ProcInf.SetErrorVal(MemoryError);
        Depart;
        ProcInf.SetMode(User);
```

```
      InterruptMode := true;
      SwitchContext
   end SignalMemoryError;

type
   MonitorGate = monitor*
                    import
                       var : ProcInf, Suspended
                    end;

   var
      Open: Boolean,
      MonQHead, MonQTail: ProcRange;

   procedure EnterMonQ(Proc:ProcIndex);
      begin
         if MonQHead = 0
            then MonQHead := Proc
            else ProcInf.SetLink(MonQTail, Proc);
         MonQTail := Proc;
         ProcInf.SetLink(MonQTail, 0)
      end EnterMonQ;

   procedure RemoveMonQ(var Proc:ProcIndex);
      begin
         Proc := MonQHead;
         MonQHead := ProcInf.GetLink(MonQHead)
      end RemoveMonQ;

   procedure export Lock;
      begin
         if Open
            then Open := false
            else
            begin
               EnterMonQ(CurrentProc);
               ProcInf.SetStatus(CurrentProc, Blocked);
               Suspended := true
            end
      end Lock;

   procedure export UnLock;
      var
         Proc: ProcIndex;
      begin
         if MonQHead = 0
            then Open := true
            else
            begin
               RemoveMonQ(Proc);
```

```
            ProcInf.SetStatus(Proc, Runnable)
        end
    end UnLock;

    procedure export NewMonQHead(Proc:ProcIndex);
        begin
            ProcInf.SetLink(Proc, MonQHead);
            if MonQHead = 0
                then MonQTail := Proc;
            MonQHead := Proc
        end NewMonQHead;

    begin
        Open := false; MonQHead := 0; MonQTail := 0
    end MonitorGate;

type
    ProcessHook = class
                    import
                        var : ProcInf, Suspended
                    end;

    var
        HookInUse: Boolean;
        HookedProc: ProcIndex;

    procedure export DelayProcess(Gate:MonitorGate);
        begin
            if not HookInUse then
            begin
                HookInUse := true;
                HookedProc := CurrentProc;
                ProcInf.SetStatus(HookedProc, Blocked);
                Gate.UnLock;
                Suspended := true
            end
        end DelayProcess;

    procedure export ContinueProcess(Gate:MonitorGate);
        begin
            if HookInUse then
            begin
                HookInUse := false;
                Gate.NewMonQHead(HookedProc)
            end
        end ContinueProcess;

    begin
        HookInUse := false
    end ProcessHook;
```

```
var
  WaitingCPU: array [1 .. CPUMax] of Boolean;
  LatchId: array [1 .. CPUMax] of Address;
  {both arrays allocated in shared memory}
  {each element of WaitingCPU initialized to false}

type
  Latch = class
              import
                 var : WaitingCPU, LatchId
              end;

  var
    WaitCount: integer;

  procedure export Lock;
    begin
      WaitCount := WaitCount – 1 {indivisible operation};
      if WaitCount < 0 then
      begin
        WaitingCPU[CPUId] := true;
        LatchId[CPUId] := varadr(WaitCount);
        while WaitingCPU[CPUId]
            do {nothing};
      end
    end Lock;

  procedure export UnLock;
    var
      J: 1 .. CPUMax;
    begin
      if WaitCount < 0 then
      begin
        J := CPUId;
        for I in 1 to CPUMax do
        begin
          J := (J mod CPUMax) + 1;
          if WaitingCPU[J]
              and (LatchId[J] = varadr(WaitCount)) then
          begin
            WaitingCPU[J] := false;
            exit
          end
        end
      end;
      WaitCount := WaitCount + 1 {indivisible operation}
    end UnLock;

  begin
    WaitCount := 1
  end Latch;
```

```
type
  IOStatus = (Done, OffLine, TransferErr, EndOfFile);

type
  DiskMonitor(DriveNum: integer) = monitor*
                                    import
                                        var : InterruptMode;
                                        procedure : DiskTransfer
                                    end;

  type
    TransferType = (DiskRead, DiskWrite);

  var
    DiskQ: array [1 .. ProcessMax] of
                record
                    TransferKind: TransferType;
                    CylinderNum, SectorNum, {disk address}
                    DataSize, {size of data to be read}
                    MemoryAdr: integer;
                    DiskStatus: IOStatus;
                    Q: queue
                end DiskQ;
    Up, {gives direction of disk-head movement}
    Busy, {true only if an I/O is in progress}
    Selected: Boolean; {true if the next user has
                          already been selected}
    HeadPosition: integer; {Current disk-head position}
    CurrentUser, {I/O of this user in progress}
    NextUser: ProcIndex; {next user to be served}


  procedure InitTransfer(Proc:ProcIndex);
    begin
      with DiskQ[Proc] do
      begin
        DiskTransfer(DriveNum, TransferKind,
                        CylinderNum, SectorNum,
                        DataSize, MemoryAdr);
        HeadPosition := CylinderNum
      end;
      CurrentUser := Proc;
      Selected := false
    end InitTransfer;


  procedure SelectNextUser;
    procedure FindNextUser;
      begin
          "Search pending requests in the direction of
          current head movement and select process NextUser
          whose request is closest to current HeadPosition";
```

```
      Selected := "true if such NextUser was found and
                   false otherwise"
    end FindNextUser;
  begin {SelectNextUser}
    FindNextUser;
    if not Selected then
    begin
      Up := not Up;
      FindNextUser
    end
  end SelectNextUser;


procedure Request(Kind:TransferType;
                  CylNum,SectNum,Size,MemAdr:integer;
                  var Status:IOStatus);
  begin
    with DiskQ[CurrentProc] do
    begin
      TransferKind := Kind;
      CylinderNum := CylNum;
      SectorNum := SectNum;
      DataSize := Size;
      MemoryAdr := MemAdr;
      if not Busy then
      begin
        Busy := true;
        InitTransfer(CurrentProc)
      end;
      SelectNextUser;
      delay(Q);
      Status := DiskStatus
    end
  end Request;


procedure export Read(CylNum,SectNum,Size,MemAdr:integer;
                  var Status:IOStatus);
  begin
    Request(DiskRead, CylNum, SectNum, Size, MemAdr, Status)
  end Read;


procedure export Write(CylNum,SectNum,Size,MemAdr:integer;
                  var Status:IOStatus);
  begin
    Request(DiskWrite, CylNum, SectNum, Size, MemAdr, Status)
  end Write;


procedure export Release {invoked by interrupt};
  begin
    with DiskQ[CurrentUser] do
    begin
      DiskStatus := "Status of the disk operation
                     as obtained from disk status register";
```

```
                continue(Q)
              end;
              if not Selected
                then SelectNextUser;
              if Selected
                then InitTransfer(NextUser)
              else Busy := false;
              InterruptMode := true
            end Release;

         begin {DiskMonitor}
            Up := true; Busy := false; Selected := false;
            CurrentUser := 0; NextUser := 0
         end DiskMonitor;

type
   CardReader(DevNum: integer) = monitor*
                                   import
                                     var : InterruptMode
                                   end;

   var
      ReadStatus: IOStatus:
      Q: queue;

   procedure export ReadCard(MemAdr:integer;
                               var Status:IOStatus);
      begin
        "Initiate operation to read from device number DevNum
         to memory locations starting at MemAdr";
        delay(Q);
        Status := ReadStatus
      end ReadCard;

   procedure export ReadDone {invoked by interrupt};
      begin
        ReadStatus := "Status of card-read operation as
                        obtained from card reader status register";
        continue(Q);
        InterruptMode := true
      end ReadDone;

  end CardReader;

type
   LinePrinter(DevNum: integer) = monitor*
                                   import
                                     var : InterruptMode
                                   end;

   var
      PrintStatus: IOStatus:
      Q: queue;
```

```
procedure export PrintLine(MemAdr:integer; var Status:IOStatus);
  begin
    "Initiate operation to print on device number DevNum
     from memory locations starting at MemAdr";
    delay(Q);
    Status := PrintStatus
  end PrintLine;

procedure export PrintDone {invoked by interrupt};
  begin
    PrintStatus := "Status of print-line operation
                       as obtained from the
                       line printer status register";
    continue(Q);
    InterruptMode := true
  end PrintDone;

end LinePrinter;

type
  TTYOp = (Echo, NoEcho, Format, NoFormat, ContrlDev,
            NotContrlDev);
  TerminalRange = 0 .. TerminalMax;

var
  ControlTTYs: array [ProcIndex] of TerminalRange;
  {allocated in shared memory}

procedure SetControlDev(TTYNum:TerminalRange);
  begin
    ControlTTYs[CurrentProc] := TTYNum
  end SetControlDev;

function GetControlDev return TerminalRange;
  begin
    return ControlTTYs[CurrentProc]
  end GetControlDev;

type
  Terminal = monitor*
                import
                  var : Preempted, InterruptMode;
                  function : GetControlDev
                end;

  const
    LineLength = 200;
    CR = 15B; LF = 12B;
```

```
type export
  CharSet = set of char;

var
  TTYId: TerminalRange;
  ToBeDisplayed, ToBeEchoed, ToBeFormatted, WritePending,
  ControlCoption, ControlCchar, ControlRchar: Boolean;
  KBDBuf, TTYBuf: string(LineLength);
  KBDPtr, TTYPtr: 0 .. LineLength;
  ReadSize, WriteSize: integer;
  KBDQ, TTYQ: queue;
  KBDStatus: IOStatus;
  KBDChar: char;
  EndChars: CharSet;


procedure export Read(MemAdr:Address; Size:integer;
                      var Status:IOStatus; var Count:integer);
  begin
    ReadSize := Size;
    if KBDPtr < ReadSize
      then delay(KBDQ);
    "Move characters from KBDBuf to MemAdr";
    Count := KBDPtr; KBDPtr := 0;
    Status := KBDStatus; KBDStatus := Done;
    ReadSize := 0
  end Read;


procedure export ReadDone {invoked by interrupt};
  begin
    KBDChar := "Character obtained from keyboard buffer";
    if (KBDChar = ControlC) and ControlCoption then
      if (GetControlDev = TTYId)
          and "Previous processor mode is User"
        then Preempted := true
      else ControlCchar := true
    else
      if KBDChar = ControlZ
        then KBDStatus := EndOfFile
      else
        if (KBDChar in CharSet[ControlO, ControlR, RubOut])
                      and ToBeFormatted then
          case KBDChar of
            ControlO: ToBeDisplayed := not ToBeDisplayed;
            ControlR:
              begin
                ControlRchar := true;
                if not WritePending
```

```
                          then "Enable interrupt for output on TTYId"
                    end;
                  RubOut:
                    if KBDPtr > 1
                      then KBDPtr := KBDPtr - 1
              end
            else
            begin
              if ToBeEchoed and not WritePending
                then "Display KBDChar on TTYId";
              KBDPtr := KBDPtr + 1;
              KBDBuf[KBDPtr] := KBDChar
            end;
          if (KBDPtr = ReadSize) or (KBDChar in EndChars)
              or (KBDStatus = EndOfFile) or ControlCchar
            then continue(KBDQ);
          InterruptMode := true
        end ReadDone;

  procedure export Write(MemAdr:Address; Size:integer);
    begin
      if ToBeDisplayed then
      begin
        "Extract characters to be output from MemAdr
         and store them in TTYBuf";
        TTYPtr := 0;
        WriteSize := Size;
        WritePending := true;
        "Enable interrupt for output on TTYId";
        delay(TTYQ)
      end
    end Write;

  procedure export WriteDone {invoked by interrupt};
    begin
      if WritePending then
        if (TTYPtr < WriteSize) and ToBeDisplayed then
        begin
          TTYPtr := TTYPtr + 1;
          "Display TTYBuf[TTYPtr] on TTYId"
        end
        else
        begin
          WritePending := false; continue(TTYQ)
        end
      else
        if ControlRchar then
        begin
          TTYBuf[1] := chr(CR);
          TTYBuf[2] := chr(LF);
          for I in 1 to KBDPtr
```

```
            do TTYBuf[I + 2] := KBDBuf[I];
          WriteSize := KBDPtr + 2;
          ControlRchar := false;
          "Enable interrupt for output on TTYId"
        end
        else "Disable interrupt for output on TTYId";
      InterruptMode := true
    end WriteDone;

procedure export SetEndChars(Chars:CharSet);
    begin
      EndChars := Chars
    end SetEndChars;

procedure export SetTTYOp(Op:TTYOp);
    begin
      case Op of
        Echo: ToBeEchoed := true;
        NoEcho: ToBeEchoed := false;
        Format: ToBeFormatted := true;
        NoFormat: ToBeFormatted := false;
        ContrlDev: ControlCoption := true;
        NotContrlDev: ControlCoption := false
      end
    end SetTTYOp;

function export ControlCpending return Boolean;
    var
      Status: Boolean;
    begin
      Status := ControlCchar;
      ControlCchar := false;
      return Status
    end ControlCpending;

procedure export SetTTYNum(TTYNum:TerminalRange);
    begin
      TTYId := TTYNum
    end SetTTYNum;

function export InputPending return Boolean;
    begin
      return (KBDPtr > 0)
    end InputPending;

begin {Terminal}
  ToBeDisplayed := true;
  ToBeEchoed := true;
  ToBeFormatted := true;
  WritePending := false;
  ControlCoption := true;
```

```
            ControlCchar := false;
            ControlRchar := false;
            KBDStatus := Done;
            EndChars := CharSet[chr(CR), chr(LF)];
            BufPtr := 0; ReadSize := 0; WriteSize := 0
        end Terminal;

var
    Kernel: pure class
            import
                var : ProcInf, CurrentProc,
                        UserFramePtr, OSFramePtr, SchedulerFrame,
                        RunProcess, Suspended, SwitchProgram,
                        InterruptMode;
                    procedure : SetTimer, SwitchContext
                end;

    type export
        DevKind = (DiskDev, CRDev, LPDev, TTYDev);

    var
        Disks: array [1 .. DriveMax] of DiskMonitor;
        CRs: array [1 .. CRMax] of CardReader;
        LPs: array [1 .. LPMax] of LinePrinter;
        Terminals: array [1 .. TerminalMax] of Terminal;

    procedure export Run(Proc:ProcIndex;
                            UserFrameAdr,OSFrameAdr:FramePtr;
                            TimeAllotted:integer);
        begin
            UserFramePtr := UserFrameAdr;
            OSFramePtr := OSFrameAdr;
            CurrentProc := Proc;
            SetTimer(TimeAllotted);
            RunProcess := true;
            if ProcInf.GetMode = User then
                if Terminals[GetControlDev].ControlCpending then
                begin
                    ProcInf.SetErrorVal(ControlCsignal);
                    ProcInf.SetMode(System);
                    "Store the value DepartCall on system stack";
                    OSFramePtr ↑ .SetEntry("Address of procedure OSCall")
                end;
            SwitchContext
        end Run;

    procedure export Suspend;
        begin
            Suspended := true;
            SwitchContext
        end Suspend;
```

```
procedure export ProgramCall(EntryPoint,ParBlockAdr:Address);
   begin
      "Extract parameters from ParBlockAdr and
       store them in user data space";
      UserFramePtr ↑ .SetEntry(EntryPoint);
      ProcInf.SetErrorVal(NoError);
      SwitchProgram := true
   end ProgramCall;


procedure export ProgramReturn(ParBlockAdr:Address;
                                     UserError:ErrorKind);
   begin
      "Extract result parameters from ParBlockAdr
       and store them in user data space";
      "Store UserError in user data space";
      ProcInf.SetErrorVal(NoError);
      SwitchProgram := true
   end ProgramReturn;

function export ProcId return ProcIndex;
   begin
      return CurrentProc
   end ProcId;


function export IsBlocked(Proc:ProcIndex) return Boolean;
   begin
      return (ProcInf.GetStatus(Proc) = Blocked)
   end IsBlocked;


function export WaitingForIO(Proc:ProcIndex) return Boolean;
   begin
      return (ProcInf.GetStatus(Proc) = IOWait)
   end WaitingForIO;


function export Time return integer;
   begin
      return "current value of clock register"
   end Time;


function export GetError return ErrorKind;
   begin
      return ProcInf.GetErrorVal
   end GetError;


function GetVarAdr(Adr:Address) return integer;
   begin
      "Compute absolute address using the appropriate data
       segment"
   end GetVarAdr;
```

```
procedure export LockGate(Gate:MonitorGate);
  begin
    Gate.Lock;
    SwitchContext
  end LockGate;

procedure export UnlockGate(Gate:MonitorGate);
  begin
    Gate.Unlock
  end UnlockGate;

procedure export LockLatch(L:Latch);
  begin
    L.Lock
  end LockLatch;

procedure export UnlockLatch(L:Latch);
  begin
    L.Unlock;
    if InterruptMode
      then SwitchContext
  end UnlockLatch;

procedure export HookProcess(Hook:ProcessHook;
                            Gate:MonitorGate);
  begin
    Hook.DelayProcess(Gate);
    SwitchContext
  end HookProcess;

procedure export UnhookProcess(Hook:ProcessHook;
                              Gate:MonitorGate);
  begin
    Hook.ContinueProcess(Gate)
  end UnhookProcess;

procedure export DiskRead(Drive,Cylinder,Sector:integer;
                         MemAdr:Address; Size:integer;
                         var Status:IOStatus);
  begin
    Disks[Drive].Read(Cylinder, Sector, Size, MemAdr, Status);
  end DiskRead;

procedure export DiskWrite(Drive,Cylinder,Sector:integer;
                          MemAdr:Address; Size:integer;
                          var Status:IOStatus);
  begin
    Disks[Drive].Write(Cylinder, Sector, Size, MemAdr, Status);
  end DiskWrite;
```

```
procedure export Read(Kind:DevKind; DevNum:integer;
                      MemAdr:Address; Size:integer;
                      var Status:IOStatus; var Count:integer);
  begin
    case Kind of
      CRDev: CRs[DevNum].ReadCard(MemAdr, Status);
      TTYDev: Terminals[DevNum].Read(MemAdr, Size, Status,
                                                      Count);
    end;
  end Read;

procedure export Write(Kind:DevKind; DevNum:integer;
                       MemAdr:Address; Size:integer;
                       var Status:IOStatus; var Count:integer);
  begin
    case Kind of
      LPDev: LPs[DevNum].PrintLine(MemAdr, Status);
      TTYDev: Terminals[DevNum].Write(MemAdr, Size)
    end;
  end Write;

procedure export SetTTY(TTYNum:integer; Op:TTYOp);
  begin
    Terminals[TTYNum].SetTTYOp(Op)
  end SetTTY;

function export TTYActive(TTYNum:integer) return Boolean;
  begin
    return Terminals[TTYNum].InputPending
  end TTYActive;

type
  OSCallKind = (EnterCall, DepartCall, ...);

procedure OSCall(Which:OSCallKind) {invoked by interrupt};
  begin
    ProcInf.SetMode(System);
    "Extract value parameters passed with the OS call";
    "Call the respective OS procedure or function";
    "Store result parameters in user data space";
    if Terminals[GetControlDev].ControlCpending then
    begin
      ProcInf.SetErrorVal(ControlCsignal);
      Depart
    end;
    ProcInf.SetMode(User); InterruptMode := true;
    SwitchContext
  end OSCall;

end Kernel;
```

13 REVIEW AND CONCLUSIONS

Review of the Operating System

At the end of any project, it is usually an instructive exercise to go back to the original premises on which the project was based, to look again at the requirements that were to be met, and to take a somewhat dispassionate view of the achievements. Projects which have received funds from an agency, or from a company, will often be reviewed to see how effectively the funds have been used and how far the original aims of the project have been met. And, if a project results in a usable product, the review continues through the life of the product. In this last case, there is no time at which the project can really be said to be complete: even exhausted members of the project team will have ideas about how things could have been done, or how they should be done the next time around, and users of the product will have almost unending suggestions about how the product could be altered to meet new, perhaps unanticipated, requirements. Let us therefore go back to the requirements we started with in Chapter 4 and evaluate what we have accomplished.

First, our requirements were fairly general and we have been liberal in their interpretation. The most important concern was to design an operating system *structure* which could be adapted to various needs. The reader who is dissatisfied with some component of this structure now has the means to replace it with one of his own design. For example, we described two different basic memory allocators to illustrate how either of them could be used without requiring changes in the design of the rest of the system. There is no reason why a third allocator could not be designed, to replace both of these. With only minor alterations, it would also be possible to have different allocators for main memory and disk space. Replacing some other components, such as the file system, would be a more demanding task. But, even in such cases, it is not difficult to change parts of the file system without altering the whole structure.

Several indispensable components of the operating system have been left in skeleton form. For example, only a general structure has been prescribed for the Job Initiator, and little has been said about the Operator process. Adding form and detail to such components is a relatively straightforward exercise, as most of the operations necessary for their functioning have been provided in data structures like the Program Table and the Job Table. The considerations that would apply to the design of two important procedures in the Job Manager, ChooseSwapIn and ChooseSwapOut, have been described but their designs would depend on the system—on the amount of main memory available, on the speed of access to the disk, and on the maximum number of jobs to be executed.

What of the operating system structure itself? How easily can this be changed? The alert reader will have noticed many points at which minor structural changes can be made. But it was not our intention that this structure be amenable to major change. The purpose of this book is to illustrate how both the structure and the detail of a large operating system can be designed in a manageable way. This exercise should have equipped the reader with the means, and the confidence, to design his or her own operating system; so it would seem a better idea to design a new structure than to alter this one substantially. In a new design, the reader should of course be able to use any components of the existing structure that can be adapted to new needs.

Finally, many readers will never need either to design or to alter an operating system, but may still wish to understand how it 'works'. Commercial operating systems are not amenable to inspection and it is usually only the most devoted of system programmers who will be able to wend their ways through documentation and code to understand their structure. For such readers, the operating system in this book should serve as an illustration and a guide.

The Programming Language

It should now be clear to the reader that CCNPascal has many similarities with both Pascal and Concurrent Pascal, and also that it has some important differences. The last fact is only of significance because of where the differences lie. The more important of the new features can be briefly described as:

1. The use of *pure classes*, which serve to encapsulate sets of re-entrant procedures.
2. The ability to treat errors, and to return errors from procedure calls.
3. The use of parameterized types; we have restricted use of this feature to size parameterization because that is its most important use, and because there appear to be disproportionate difficulties in implementing more complex forms of parameterization (as in the 'generics' of Ada (Ichbiah *et al.*, 1980))
4. At a lower level of detail, there are changes from Concurrent Pascal in the mechanism for program calls, and in the **continue** operation used on queue variables (in CCNPascal, the **continue** operation need not be the last to be performed in a monitor procedure, and more than one waiting process may be 'continued' by a single process).

Several other languages have been used for writing operating system programs: some have simply served as high-level languages, and others have been specially designed to support particular methodologies. The better known of these are BCPL (Richards, 1969), Bliss (Wulf *et al.*, 1971), Sue (Clark and Horning, 1972), Concurrent Pascal (Brinch Hansen, 1975), Modula (Wirth, 1977), C (Kernighan and Richie, 1978), and Mesa (Geschke *et al.*, 1978), each of which has had a distinctive effect on operating systems programmed in that language. We can make some general comments on the approaches embodied in these languages.

BCPL and C, which are closely related languages (C originated from BCPL), can be said to share an objective with Bliss in that they are all basic notations which do not claim to suggest how operating systems should be constructed—they are each, more or less, machine-independent and methodology-independent. Many different kinds of operating system structures can be programmed in such languages, with each structure being represented as collections of procedures and data structures. In their original forms, they did not have features for describing any particular abstractions necessary for programming operating systems so a different, informal, notation had to be used to describe the structure of each operating system. Programmer-defined concurrent programming abstractions cannot be checked at compile- time, and the compiler checks only for a lower-level of syntactic and semantic consistency. The freedom that this permits has allowed a lot of experimentation with operating system structures, but the integrity of each structure has to be enforced by programmer discipline.

Sue, Mesa, Concurrent Pascal and Modula have well-defined structuring concepts and these languages can be used to build a wide, but certainly restricted, class of operating systems. The restrictions vary in their severity but all these languages have taken account of progress in programming methodology to make choices about the kind of program structures that can be designed. This means that the structure of an operating system programmed in one of these languages is apparent from the language constructs used—there is less reliance on informal conventions and there are many more compile-time checks. But each of these (and similar) languages faces a problem introduced by its level of description. When this level is high (as, for example, in Concurrent Pascal), important but lower-level features of the computer system cannot be accessed or manipulated by programs. The need for a Kernel in our operating system is one illustration of this, as our Kernel performs functions that cannot be programmed entirely in CCNPascal.

In contrast to this, Modula provides features to allow most of the typical lower-level operations of a system to be programmed in that language. But this has its consequences too, as Modula is a language specially designed for programming real-time or dedicated operating systems where there are no user programs: it is not a language well-suited for programming general purpose operating systems. Mesa, which by this reckoning would be a high-level notation, addresses this problem by providing 'loopholes' in the language. A loophole is a means of escaping from the strict syntactic and semantic checks of the language, so it is a potentially unsafe feature as it allows relatively uncontrolled access to machine features. However, the use of loopholes is made explicit in the language so any programmer studying the statements of a Mesa program can immediately see where an unusual operation is being performed. We have also made some use of loopholes in this operating system: for example, by the use of the functions **varadr** and **varsize**.

The programming language Ada is a synthesis of many of the features of languages we have mentioned in this section. Its main purpose is for the programming of 'embedded' systems, where the computer system forms part of some larger system. In that respect, its requirements are closer to Modula than to Concurrent Pascal and there are features in Ada to allow access to almost any machine feature. It is too early to comment on the success with which operating systems can be constructed in Ada, but this would at any rate seem to depend very heavily on how efficiently the Ada concept of a 'task' (which is like a process) can be implemented. Indeed, there is some controversy over the degree to which a complex language like Ada can be efficiently implemented at all, and about whether the diversity and richness of its features are a burden or an asset.

Operating System Structure

The operating system has been built in two main levels: the Kernel level, and the main operating system. We have used this hierarchy to embed in the Kernel all the support needed for the concurrent features of the language. But the Kernel also provides abstractions for input and output, and functions to perform other actions that cannot be programmed in the language. Within the main operating system, different components are structured in hierarchical fashion but there are no clear levels across the entire operating system. This is in contrast to some operating systems which are built as hierarchies of 'virtual machines', where each virtual machine constitutes a level. Such operating systems are often described as being simpler to understand and more reliable in practice. We have not had need for such a structure because we have used the rules of the language to ensure the integrity of the program; moreover, the use of a rigid hierarchy usually results in a loss of efficiency.

We can describe our operating system as having *functional hierarchies*: each major component in the system is built as a hierarchy of smaller components. The decomposition into smaller components has been done to simplify the design (as in the file system), or to increase concurrency within the operating system, or both. Notice that though the operating system has few processes of its own, each call for service by a user program results in a job process executing part of the operating system program. In fact, the only operating system processes required are those that perform functions (such as swapping and scheduling) that must be done independently of requests from individual job processes. A user program will thus bear much of the overhead that results from its calls to the operating system. As an alternative to this, it is possible to have 'service' processes which perform operations within the operating system in response to calls from a job process. Our experience, and that of many others, has been that the use of many processes leads to loss of speed (due to the large amount of context-swapping that is needed), at least with the present generation of computer systems. We have therefore attempted to keep the number of processes to a minimum.

Building and Testing the Operating System

As each component of the operating system is designed and programmed, it becomes necessary to test it in the environment in which it will eventually execute. So we must start with testing the Kernel on the 'bare' machine, then test the lower-level components which make use of the Kernel, and then add the higher-level components. Many of the components can first be tested as *sequential* programs if they are classes, or if they are monitors (i.e., by assuming they are being called by only one process). This allows many trivial errors to be removed before the testing begins on the actual system. In fact, it is a good idea to test as much of the system as possible in this way because the next level of testing is much harder to perform.

The most difficult part is to test the concurrent portions of the operating system. It is here that the use of language features for concurrency have their advantage because these features guarantee disciplined access to resources and safe communication between processes. But to ensure this, we must first informally verify the correct execution of the Kernel operations that support concurrency. This difficult task can be made easier if the operations are first programmed and verified in a high-level language and then, where required, systematically translated into low-level notation. Even after this, the operations must finally be tested on the system. On a multiprocessor system, testing mutual exclusion operations requires test programs to be executing on each processor. This is difficult to perform, but it is a necessary step if severe problems are to be avoided later in the testing.

An ideal, and almost irreplaceable, piece of support software is a symbolic debugging system that can be interfaced with the output of the compiler to trace, monitor and execute a program in steps. Such systems are common at the user level, but they need careful alteration to be of use for testing an operating system, especially on a multiprocessor. If a symbolic debugger is capable of printing values of program variables, it will also occupy a great deal of memory space to store tables of symbolic names of variables and procedures. This means that only small sections of the operating system can be tested in this way. Use of a symbolic debugger must be complemented by writing test programs which exercise operating system components.

An attractive possibility is to use what is now called a 'programming environment', which provides tools for program version management, syntax-directed editing, incremental compilation and monitoring. Such environments have been developed for small languages and systems and considerable effort is being directed to designing new environments for large-scale software development, for example for the Ada programming language.

Practical Results

This book has been based on the design of a real operating system for a multiprocessor, so the experience of that exercise may be useful to designers of similar systems. The CCN operating system was designed and built for a system with three 16-bit processors, each with some local memory and sharing a larger common memory through a switch. Major peripherals were connected by a switch to pairs of processors, while other peripherals were connected to single processors.

The operating system was designed in relatively independent parts: the Kernel was programmed and tested while the other components of the operating system were being designed. Apart from simple tests, the Kernel was really tested only when components of the operating system were ready for testing. Despite this, few program errors of any kind were discovered during the testing phases. Errors were usually found to be due to one of a few causes.

1. The commonest error was caused by the inadvertent omission of the word **var** from reference parameters of procedures! Initially, these errors were unexpected and were difficult to trace. Later, it became standard practice to check all parameter lists whenever any error was discovered. (The current version of the language does not allow assignment to value parameters!)

2. A series of inexplicable errors was traced to errors in support routines, e.g. one provided for the **delay** operation. Fortunately, these appeared early on in the testing so a thorough check at that stage eliminated what would have been extremely difficult to isolate at a later stage. Needless to say, the particular routine had neither been first coded in high-level notation nor verified.

There were, of course, other errors in both the Kernel and the operating system. But it was amazing how few these were. There were probably not more than 20–30 errors discovered in the whole system, and the first few of these were found fairly quickly. The later errors were considerably more troublesome—their effects were sometimes difficult to repeat or were the causes of other errors. More careful programming, more thorough checking and a variety of other measures might have helped to avoid these errors, but it seems likely that some errors would have escaped most checks.

We have not included here the series of hardware errors that made program testing difficult and, at times, impossible. We shall draw a veil over this, merely saying that it would be prudent to build a complex system over reliable hardware!

Summary

The traditional description for an operating system is in the form of user's manuals, flow charts, and descriptions of table structures and routines. More recently, the organizational details of a few operating systems have been presented: the now classic T.H.E. operating system structure is presented in Dijkstra (1968), the Multics operating system has been described in Organick (1972), and an account of Hydra, which is the kernel for a capability-based multiprocessor operating system, appears in Wulf, Levin and Harbison (1981).

It is comparatively rare to find even segments of an operating system program in published form. A fairly detailed description of the RC4000 operating system developed by Regnecentralen is available in Brinch Hansen (1973) but the system itself was programmed in assembly language. The first description of an entire operating system, OS6, was given in the form of program text and a commentary by Stoy and Strachey (1972). OS6 was a single user operating system for the Modular 1 computer; it was written in BCPL and extensively used the notion of 'streams' to handle all input and output. It has proved to be long lived and versions of the system upto OS13 have recently been heard of!

The next operating system to be described in the same detail was SOLO, the operating system written in Concurrent Pascal to be run on a PDP 11/45 (papers on SOLO and Concurrent Pascal can be found in *Software Practice and Experience*, Vol. 6, (2), 1976; and in Brinch Hansen (1977)). This saw the introduction of monitors, classes and processes into a real operating system. As its name suggests, SOLO was a single user system and it has since been implemented on many other systems.

Independently of such developments, the study of operating system techniques gave rise to new ways of organizing operating systems, and better methods for resource management. So, while this book follows the path laid by Stoy and Strachey, and by Brinch Hansen, we have felt there is need for the techniques used in our design to be placed in the framework of techniques currently used in the construction of operating systems. We must in any case do this by way of acknowledgement, since many of our techniques have been borrowed or adapted from those of others, but we do so also to illustrate that many practical techniques are amenable to systematic description. Techniques pass from folklore into subjects of critical scrutiny when they are presented in precise but easily understandable form. In making such an exposition, however, the temptation to 'idealize' a technique must be tempered by the need to understand the practical considerations that govern its use.

In one respect, we have been remiss in the design of this operating system. There are several formal methods of specifying programs that we have not used while developing the design. It would, for example, have been extremely valuable to have developed invariants alongside the development of a program so that the code and informal reasoning about its correctness could appear together. Unfortunately, this would have added so considerably to the size of the book that it would have become necessary to omit large parts of the description. And if that had been done, the book would no longer serve its purpose of describing a complete operating system.

The study of the physical sciences has a well-established tradition in which experiments are used to verify hypotheses drawn from a body of theory. Can this framework be extended to the discipline of computer science? In some cases, experiments in computer science can clearly be used to verify theory: for example, performance studies of different search methods can be expected to give results that approximate to theoretical predictions. But there are areas, such as the study of programming, where more qualitative measures must be used and where experiments serve to provide paradigms for theory and models for practice. It is in this sense that we visualized this book as a description of an experiment. And since this experiment is concerned with methodology, there seemed no better way to understand it than to participate in the exercise of its development.

BIBLIOGRAPHY

Brinch Hansen P, 1973, *Operating System Principles*, Prentice-Hall, Englewood Cliffs.

Brinch Hansen P, 1975, The Programming Language Concurrent Pascal, *IEEE Trans. on Softw. Engg.*, **1**(2), 199–207.

Brinch Hansen P, 1976a, The Solo Operating System: A Concurrent Pascal Program, *Softw. P & E*, **6**, 141–149.

Brinch Hansen P, 1976b, Processes, Monitors and Classes, *Softw. P & E*, **6**, 165–200.

Brinch Hansen P, 1977, *The Architecture of Concurrent Programs*, Prentice-Hall, Englewood Cliffs.

Burroughs Corporation, 1973, *B7700 Information Processing Systems: Reference Manual*, Burroughs Corporation, Detroit.

Clark BL, Horning JJ, 1972, Experience with a New System Programming Language for the IBM System/360, *Proc. CIPS*.

Courtois PJ, Heymans F, Parnas DL, 1971, Concurrent Control with 'Readers' and 'Writers', *Comm. ACM*, **14**(10), 667–668.

Denning PJ, 1967, Effects of Scheduling on File Memory Operations, *Proc. AFIPS SJCC*, **31**, Thompson Book Co., pp.9–21.

Dennis JB, Van Horn EC, 1966, Programming Semantics for Multiprogrammed Computations, *Comm. ACM*, **9**(3), 143–155.

Digital Equipment Corporation, 1977, *DEC System 10 Technical Summary*, Digital Equipment Corporation, Maynard.

Dijkstra EW, 1968, The Structure of the T.H.E. Multiprogramming System, *Comm. ACM*, **11**(5), 341–346.

England DM, 1974, Capability Concept Mechanisms and Structure in System 250, *Proc. Int. Workshop on Protection in Op. Sys.*, IRIA, pp.63–82.

Fuller SH, Harbison SP, 1978, *The C.mmp Multiprocessor*, Tech. Report, Department of Computer Science, Carnegie-Mellon University.

Geschke GM, Morris JH Jr., Satterthwaite, 1977, Early Experience with Mesa, *Comm. ACM*, **20**(8), 540–553.

465

Hoare CAR, 1972, Notes on Data Structuring, in *Structured Programming*, *A.P.I.C.* Studies in Data Processing, **8**, Academic Press, London.

Hoare CAR, Perrott RH (Eds), 1972, *Operating Systems Techniques*, Academic Press, London.

Hoare CAR, 1974, Monitors: an Operating System Structuring Concept, *Comm. ACM*, **17**(10), 549–557.

Hondek ME, Soltis FG, Hoffman RL, 1981, IBM System/38 Support for Capability Based Addressing, *Proc. 8th Ann. Symp. on Comp. Arch.*, *SIGARCH Comp. Arch. News*, **9**(3), 341–348.

Honeywell Inc. and Cii Honeywell Bull, 1980, *Reference Manual for the Ada Programming Language*, United States Department of Defense.

Intel, 1981, Intel 432 GDP Architecture Reference Manual, Intel Corporation.

Jones AK, Chansler RJ Jr., Durham I, Schwans K, Vegdahl SR, 1979, StarOS: A Multiprocessor Operating System for the Support of Task Forces, *Proc. 7th Symp. on Op. Sys. Princ.*

Katsuki D, *et al.*, 1978, Pluribus—An Operational Fault-Tolerant Multiprocessor, *Proc. IEEE*, **66** (10), 1146–1159.

Kernighan BW, Ritchie DM, 1978, *The C Programming Language*, Prentice-Hall, Englewood Cliffs.

Knuth DE, 1968, *The Art of Computer Programming*, Vol. 1: *Fundamental Algorithms*, Addison-Wesley.

Lampson BW, 1981, Atomic Transactions, in *Distributed Systems—Architecture and Applications*, Lampson BW (Ed.), *Lecture Notes in Comp. Sc.*, **105**, Springer-Verlag.

Liskov BH, Snyder A, Atkinson RR, Schaffert C, 1977, Abstraction Mechanisms in CLU, *Comm. ACM*, **20**(8), 564–576.

McKeag RM, Hoare CAR, 1972, A Survey of Store Management Techniques, in *Operating Systems Techniques*, Hoare CAR, Perrott RH (Eds), Academic Press, London, pp.117–151.

Newell A, Robertson G, 1975, Some Issues in Programming Multi-Mini-Processors, *Beh. Res. Methods and Instr.*, **7**(2), 75–86.

Organick EI, 1972, *The Multics System: An Examination of its Structure*, MIT Press, Cambridge, Mass.

Ousterhout JK, Scelza DA, Sindhu PS, 1979, Medusa: An Experiment in Distributed Operating System Structure, *Proc. 7th Symp. on Op. Sys. Princ.*

Parmelee RP, Peterson TI, Tilman CC, Hatfield DJ, 1972, Virtual Storage and Virtual Machine Concepts, *IBM Syst. J.*, **11**(2), 99–130.

Randell B, 1969, A Note on Storage Fragmentation and Program Segmentation, *Comm. ACM*, **12**(7), 365–369, 372.

Richards M, 1969, *The BCPL Reference Manual*, Tech. Mem. 69/1, Computer Laboratory, University of Cambridge.

Ritchie DM, Thompson K, 1974, The UNIX Time-Sharing System, *Comm. ACM*, **17**(7), 365–375.

Stoy J, Strachey C, 1972a, *The Text of OSPub*, Tech. Mem. PRG-9 (c), (t), Programming Research Group, Oxford University Computing Laboratory, July.

Stoy J, Strachey C, 1972b, An Experimental Operating System for a Small Computer, *Computer J.*, **15**(2).

Sturgis HE, Mitchell JG, Israel J, 1980, Issues in the Design and Use of a Distributed File System, *Op. Sys. Rev.*, **14**(3), 55–69.

Swan RJ, Fuller SH, Siewiorek DP, 1977, Cm*—A Modular Multi-Microprocessor, *Proc. Nat. Comp. Conf.*, Dallas.

Welsh J, McKeag M, 1980, *Structured System Programming*, Prentice-Hall, London.

Wilkes MV, Needham RM, 1979, *The Cambridge CAP Computer and its Operating System*, North-Holland, Amsterdam.

Wirth N, 1971, The Programming Language Pascal, *Acta Inf.*, **1**, 35–63.

Wirth N, 1977a, Modula: a Language for Modular Multiprogramming, *Softw.P & E*, **7**(1), 3–35.

Wirth N, 1977b, The Use of Modula, *Softw. P & E*, **7**(1), 37–65.

Wirth N, 1977c, Design and Implementation of Modula, *Softw. P & E*, **7**(1), 67–84.

Wong CK, 1980, On Some Discrete Optimization Problems in Mass Storage Systems, *Proc. 9th Symp. Math. Found. of Comp. Sc.*, Rydzna, Poland, 1980, *Lecture Notes in Comp. Sc.*, **88**, 75–93, Springer-Verlog.

Wulf WA, Russell DB, Habermann AN, 1971, Bliss: A Language for Systems Programming, *Comm. ACM*, **14**(12), 780–790.

Wulf WA, London RL, Shaw M, 1976, An Introduction to the Construction and Verification of Alphard Programs, *IEEE Trans. on Softw. Engg.*, **2**(4), 253–264.

Wulf WA, Levin R, Harbison SP, 1981, *C.mmp/Hydra: An Experimental Computer System*, McGraw-Hill, New York.

Bibliography on the CCN Project

(*In chronological order*)

Joseph M, Ramani S, 1976, Computer Systems Based on Minicomputers, *South East Asia Regional Computer Conf.*, North-Holland, pp.449–463.

Joseph M, Prasad VR, 1978, More on Nested Monitor Calls, *Op. Sys. Rev.*, **12**,(2).

Prasad VR, 1978, *Report on the Concurrent Programming Language CCNPascal*, NCSDCT Tech. Report 28, October.

Joseph M, 1979, Towards More General Implementation Languages for Operating Systems, *Operating Systems—Theory and Practice*, Lanciaux D (Ed.), North-Holland.

Joseph M, Prasad VR, Narayana KT, Ramakrishnan IV, Desai S, 1979, Language and Structure in an Operating System, *Operating Systems—Theory and Practice*, (Ed.) D.Lanciaux, North-Holland.

Prasad KVS, Natarajan N, Sinha MK, 1979, Physical and Logical Abstractions in a Kernel, *Operating Systems – Theory and Practice*, Lanciaux D (Ed.), North-Holland.

Narayana KT, Prasad VR, Joseph M, 1979, Some Aspects of Concurrent Programming in CCNPascal, *Softw. P & E*, **9**, 749–770.

Natarajan N, Sinha MK, 1979, Language Issues in the Implementation of a Kernel, *Softw. P & E*, **9**, 771–778.

Prasad VR, 1980, Variable Number of Parameters in Typed Languages, *Softw. P & E*, **10**, 507–517.

INDEX

PROGRAM COMPONENT INDEX